MODERN HUMANITIES RESEARCH ASSOCIATION

TUDOR & STUART TRANSLATIONS

VOLUME 11

General Editors
ANDREW HADFIELD
NEIL RHODES

MARGARET TYLER

MIRROR OF PRINCELY DEEDS AND KNIGHTHOOD

MARGARET TYLER

MIRROR OF PRINCELY DEEDS AND KNIGHTHOOD

Edited by

Joyce Boro

MODERN HUMANITIES RESEARCH ASSOCIATION
2014

Published by
The Modern Humanities Research Association,
1 Carlton House Terrace
London SW1Y 5AF

© The Modern Humanities Research Association, 2014

Joyce Boro has asserted her right under the Copyright, Designs and Patents Act 1988 to be identified as the author of this work.

Parts of this work may be reproduced as permitted under legal provisions for fair dealing (or fair use) for the purposes of research, private study, criticism, or review, or when a relevant collective licensing agreement is in place. All other production requires the written permission of the copyright holder who may be contacted at rights@mhra.org.uk

First published 2014

ISBN 978-1-907-322-16-7 (hbk)
ISBN 978-1-78188-115-6 (pbk)

Copies may be ordered from www.tudor.mhra.org.uk

MHRA TUDOR AND STUART TRANSLATIONS

GENERAL EDITORS

Andrew Hadfield (University of Sussex)
Neil Rhodes (University of St Andrews)

ASSOCIATE EDITORS

Guyda Armstrong (University of Manchester)
Fred Schurink (University of Northumbria)
Louise Wilson (University of St Andrews)

ADVISORY BOARD

Warren Boutcher (Queen Mary, University of London); Colin Burrow (All Souls College, Oxford); A. E. B. Coldiron (Florida State University); José María Pérez Fernández (University of Granada); Robert S. Miola (Loyola College, Maryland); Alessandra Petrina (University of Padua); Anne Lake Prescott (Barnard College, Columbia University); Quentin Skinner (Queen Mary, London); Alan Stewart (Columbia University)

For details of published and forthcoming volumes please visit our website:

www.tudor.mhra.org.uk

TABLE OF CONTENTS

General Editors' Foreword viii
Acknowledgements ix
Introduction 1
Further Reading 37
Bibliographical Descriptions 38
Editorial Policy 43
MIRROR OF PRINCELY DEEDS AND KNIGHTHOOD 45
Textual Notes 239
Glossary 250
Neologisms 265
Bibliography 266
Index of Characters 272
Index to Introduction and Notes.. 276

GENERAL EDITORS' FOREWORD

The aim of the *MHRA Tudor & Stuart Translations* is to create a representative library of works translated into English during the early modern period for the use of scholars, students and the wider public. The series will include both substantial single works and selections of texts from major authors, with the emphasis being on the works that were most familiar to early modern readers. The texts themselves will be newly edited with substantial introductions, notes, and glossaries, and will be published both in print and online.

The series aims to restore to view a major part of English Renaissance literature which has become relatively inaccessible and to present these texts as literary works in their own right. For that reason it will follow the same principle of modernisation adopted by other scholarly editions of canonical literature from the period. The series will have a similar scope to that of the original *Tudor Translations* published early in the last century, and while the great majority of the works presented will be from the sixteenth century, like the original series it will not be rigidly bound by the end-date of 1603. There will, however, be a very different range of texts with new and substantial scholarly apparatus.

The *MHRA Tudor & Stuart Translations* will extend our understanding of the English Renaissance through its representation of the process of cultural transmission from the classical to the early modern world and the process of cultural exchange within the early modern world.

Andrew Hadfield
Neil Rhodes

ACKNOWLEDGEMENTS

About four years ago, at a conference on Tudor Translation in Newcastle upon Tyne, Neil Rhodes and Andrew Hadfield told me about a new and exciting series of English translations that they were editing for the MHRA. Towards the end of the conference, we discussed the possibility of my editing Margaret Tyler's *Mirror of Princely Deeds and Knighthood* for the series. I don't think I understood just how large and all encompassing the project would be, but once I began working on Tyler's romance, I was hooked. The road was not always easy, and I incurred many debts along the way. It is my greatest pleasure to be able to acknowledge them here. I would first like to thank Neil and Andrew for all of their patient guidance and for providing my edition with such a wonderful home in this fantastic series. Thanks must also be extended to the friends and colleagues who read and commented on parts of my manuscript, helpfully discussed the project with me, and encouraged me to keep on going when I thought I was going to drown in variants and linguistic minutiae: José María Pérez Fernández, Helen Cooper, Jean Brink, Tiffany Werth, Brenda Hosington, Anne Coldiron, Valerie Wayne, Louise Wilson, Barbara Fuchs, Marina Brownlee, Jennifer Drouin, Alexandra Gillespie, Kimberley Coles, Michael Sinatra, Gail Scott, Jane Malcolm, Lianne Moyes, Robbie Schwartzwald, Heike Harting, and my fellow members of the Shakespeare Performance and Research Team. Daniel Eisenberg's edition of *Espejo de príncipes y caballeros* was indispensible to my work. I am very appreciative of the financial support provided by the Social Sciences and Humanities Research Council of Canada (SSHRC), the Henry E. Huntington Library, and the Folger Shakespeare Library. I would also like to acknowledge the valuable assistance given by the staff at the Huntington and the Folger libraries, as well as my research assistants at the Université de Montréal. As always, my parents and my brother have provided me with much support. This project has also benefitted greatly from Rose's and Sam's laughter, energy, curiosity, and love; their incessant questioning ('but why . . . ?') has furnished me with productive research and writing methodologies. My greatest thanks are reserved for Julie, whose love, reassurance, and general amazingness make anything and everything possible.

INTRODUCTION

'THOU HAVE HERE, GENTLE READER, THE HISTORY': MARGARET TYLER'S *MIRROR OF PRINCELY DEEDS AND KNIGHTHOOD*

When Margaret Tyler's *Mirror of Princely Deeds and Knighthood* was printed in 1578, decades had elapsed since the publication of a new chivalric romance in England. Earlier compositions such as *Guy of Warwick* and *Bevis of Hampton* continued to be reprinted, adapted, and read throughout the sixteenth century, but only a handful of new chivalric romances appeared after the 1520s: for example, *Arthur of Little Britain* had its first publication *c.* 1560, although it was written at least 30 years earlier, and *Sir Lamwell* appeared in *c.* 1548–60. Romance was not an unappreciated genre at the time. Far from it! Women and men from across the social spectrum voraciously consumed medieval romance in manuscript and print, and in dramatic, verse, and prose adaptations. Rather than herald the death of romance, the early modern period epitomizes a vibrant era in which romance flourished and was reinvented and transformed repeatedly. Yet, while chivalric romance continued to be read, it was no longer at the pinnacle of its success. It was generally recognized as a medieval genre, viewed by many as old-fashioned and allied with Catholicism. Furthermore, its readership was increasingly shared with new types of prose fiction, such as the sentimental and humanist romances and the Italianate novella.

Mirror revitalizes the chivalric romance, initiating a new appreciation for the genre. Drawing on the enduring love for the romance, *Mirror* reconfigures the style and contents of its source text, recasting it for a specifically sixteenth-century, English audience. Medieval and Renaissance chivalric romance share similar plot elements, character types, tropes, and literary memes.[1] For example, recalling its medieval predecessors, *Mirror* is a genealogical romance, which narrates the adventures of Trebatio and his descendants as they travel across a vast geographical expanse from Asia through North Africa to Eastern and Western Europe, in search of love, honour, and military victory. The romance is replete with magical islands and objects, enchanters, beautiful ladies, Amazons, powerful kings and emperors, and noble knights who fight magnificent battles with rival knights, giants, lions, and dragons. These wonderful adventures are balanced by moralizing passages on the fickleness of fortune, the workings of Providence, the transitory nature of beauty, and the importance of embracing virtue and eschewing vice. Differentiation between medieval and early modern chivalric romance exists largely in the realm of prose style, character development, narrative subjectivity, a post-Reformation, Protestant perspective, and the crafting of a self-conscious authorial stance, all of which characterize *Mirror*. Some of these traits originate in *Mirror*'s Spanish source, but Tyler is equally responsible for modernizing and anglicizing the romance, adapting it to the cultural and aesthetic sensibilities of her era. As Anne Coldiron reminds us, every translation is '[a]lways already different' and 'manifests a nonliteral but literary and aesthetic version of Mary Louise Pratt's "contact zones"'.[2] As a reflection of English culture and modes of expression, *Mirror* is more than an English language rendering of a Spanish narrative: it is an English romance, rather than the English translation of a foreign text. This skilled national transposition is impressively effected through only slight changes to the Spanish romance. *Mirror* is a fairly direct translation of *Espejo*; however, the consistency of the alterations has a monumental effect. Running counter to Mary Ellen Lamb's gendered taxonomy of translations, *Mirror* is not a typically female, 'exceedingly literal [. . . .] line-by-line

---

[1] Cf. Helen Cooper, *The English Romance in Time: Transforming Motifs from Geoffrey of Monmouth to the Death of Shakespeare*.
[2] Anne E. B. Coldiron, *English Printing, Verse Translation, and the Battle of the Sexes, 1476–1557*, p. 5.

transliteration', rather, like the translations of her male contemporaries, it is 'magnificent and occasionally quirky' and revelatory of 'individuality of expression'.[3] As will be discussed below, Tyler diminishes battle descriptions; includes supplementary classical and literary allusions; refashions letters so that they adhere to the dictaminal mode of epistolary composition; adds rhetorical and poetic tropes and devices as well as particularly English expressions; renders the narrative more vivid and immediate through discursive shifts; corrects flawed geographical references; contributes an abundance of first person narrative commentary and addresses to the audience; and complicates *Mirror*'s metafictional textual heritage, forging a complex, multi-layered narrative that provides a solid defence of female romance authorship.[4]

Amongst literary critics *Mirror*'s preface and dedication have garnered attention disproportionate to the romance since they articulate a justification of women's authorship and provide a rare glimpse of female authorial self-perception.[5] In her startling preface, the first of many signals of the subtle yet transformative ways in which this romance looks distinctly English and early modern, Tyler disingenuously dismisses her text as an 'idle conceit [. . . .] devised to beguile time'. Yet, despite her assessment, *Mirror* represents a significant moment in the romance genre's evolution. *Mirror* is the first romance written by an Englishwoman and the first romance translated in its entirety directly from Spanish. Moreover, Tyler's seminal work marks the appearance of Spanish chivalric romance in England, setting the stage for the translation of a host of other texts in the genre, as will be surveyed below.

'THEIR SPANISH DELIGHT TURNED TO AN ENGLISH PASTIME': FROM *ESPEJO* TO *MIRROR*

Mirror translates the first book of *Espejo de príncipes y cavalleros* by Diego Ortúñez de Calahorra, which was written prior to 1554 and first printed in 1555. Ortúñez hailed from Nájera, near Logroño, in the northern Spanish province of La Rioja.[6] Other than his birthplace, Ortúñez's biography is sparse. Comments in *Espejo* on the changing literary scene alongside Ortúñez's archaic language and the tone of his prologue lead Daniel Eisenberg to conclude that he was likely a mature man at the time of the romance's composition.[7]

Multiple reprints, continuations, translations, and adaptations swiftly followed the publication of *Espejo*. Divided into three books, *Espejo* underwent six editions (1555, 1562, 1579, 1580, 1583, 1617). Pedro de la Sierra Infanzón's sentimental and somewhat melancholic sequel

---

[3] Mary Ellen Lamb, 'The Cooke Sisters: Attitudes toward Learned Women', p. 124. The different quality of the translation may be attributed to the genre in which Tyler was writing, which did not require the same degree of accuracy as religious translations.

[4] These alterations reflect contemporary taste, and many characterize new Renaissance romance forms such as the humanist and sentimental romances and the Italianate novella. For a description of these types of romance, see Joyce Boro, 'All for Love: Lord Berners and the Enduring, Evolving Romance', pp. 87–102.

[5] See the discussions of the prefatory material in E. D. Mackerness, 'Margaret Tyler: An Elizabethan Feminist', pp. 112–13; Stefania Arcara, 'Margaret Tyler's *The Mirrour of Knighthood*', n.p.; Catherine Gallagher, 'A History of the Precedent: Rhetorics of Legitimation in Women's Writing', pp. 309–27. The preface is the only excerpt from her work provided in Moira Ferguson, ed., *First Feminists: British Women Writers, 1578–1799*, pp. 51–52; Betty Travitsky, *The Paradise of Women: Writings by Englishwomen of the Renaissance*, pp. 114–15, pp. 144–46; Randal Martin, *Women Writers in Renaissance England*, pp. 15–24. The romance is studied by Tina Krontiris, *Oppositional Voices: Women as Writers and Translators of Literature in the English Renaissance*, pp. 44–62; Helen Hackett, *Women and Romance Fiction in the English Renaissance*, pp. 55–75; Lorna Hutson, *Male Friendship and Fictions of Women in Sixteenth-Century England*, pp. 91–98. Deborah Uman and Belén Bistué, 'Translation as Collaborative Authorship: Margaret Tyler's *The Mirrour of Princely Deedes and Knighthood*', pp. 298–323.

[6] Daniel Eisenberg, *An Edition of a Sixteenth-Century Romance of Chivalry: Diego Ortúñez de Calahora's Espejo de Principes y Cavalleros [El Caballero del Febo]*, pp. xxxvii–xxxviii.

[7] Eisenberg, *An Edition*, p. xxxvi.

INTRODUCTION

appeared in 1581.[8] A four-part continuation by Marcos Martínez (1587) amplifies the role of the female knight errant, which originated with Claridiana in Ortúñez's romance. Part five was written anonymously after 1589; the sole extant manuscript is held at the Biblioteca Nacional de España in Madrid (MSS/13137). In addition to these sequels, *Espejo*'s influence can be detected in many literary works, including texts by Calderón and Cervantes.[9] Indeed, *Don Quijote* is replete with allusions to *Espejo*'s plot and style. *Espejo*'s popularity extended beyond the Iberian Peninsula, with translations into Italian (1601), French (1617, 1740, 1780), and German (1781–83). As these numerous textual productions suggest, *Espejo* was much beloved by European readers. Indeed, in Spain, most chivalric romances written in the 1530s and later were not even reprinted (*Rogel de Grecia* is the exception), and only *Florisel de Niquea* had a seventeenth-century edition (in 1636). Similarly, while romance serialization was common, very few romances were continued in the latter half of the sixteenth-century. In contrast, *Espejo* inspired four sequels by as many different authors. Its 'influence [...] upon later romances of chivalry would no doubt have been greater if there had been more of them'; however, by 1555, the genre was on the decline, with very few chivalric romances appearing in the second half of the sixteenth century.[10]

Tyler's romance was as popular as its Spanish counterpart. The first edition of *Mirror* was licensed in 1578, and Thomas East printed it shortly thereafter.[11] The second and third editions appeared in 1580(?) and 1599(?), also under the imprimatur of East. *Mirror*'s success doubtless inspired the translation and publication of all four Spanish volumes, which were partitioned into nine English books. Books 2 through 6 were translated by R. P. (Robert Parry or Parke), the first five issuing from East's press, while Edward Allde printed the last for Cuthbert Burby. Books 2 (1585, 1599) and 3 (1586?, 1598, 1599?) correspond to the second and third part of the first book of *Espejo*. De la Sierra's continuation was translated as Books 4 and 5 (1583, 1585, and 1598), and Book 6 is a translation of the first part of Martínez's sequel (1598). Books 7 and 8 of the series, equivalent to Books 2 and 3 of Martínez's *Espejo*, were translated by L. A. and printed by Thomas Creede for Burby in 1598 and 1599. The final instalment of Martínez's romance, Book 9 of *Mirror*, sometimes attributed to R. P., was also printed for Burby, probably by Simon Stafford, in 1601.

Mirror initiated a craze for Spanish chivalric romance.[12] Indeed, following its publication 'romances reclaim an important position in the literary marketplace'.[13] In addition to all of *Espejo*'s sequels, *Mirror* was followed by translations of the romance cycles of *Amadís de Gaula* and *Palmerin*, and of the two independent chivalric romances *Belianís de Grecia* and *Florando de Inglaterra*. The Spanish *Amadís* cycle consists of twelve books, which narrate the adventures of the eponymous hero and his progeny. The success of Rodríguez de Montalvo's Books 1–4 of *Amadís* (1508) inspired eight continuations by different authors, which met with the acclaim of

---

[8] This and all subsequent dates in parentheses indicate the year of the first printed edition.

[9] Eisenberg, *An Edition*, pp. lxviii–lxxi; A. Valbuena Briones, 'La influencia de un libro de caballerías en *El castillo de Lindabridis*', pp. 373–83.

[10] Eisenberg, *An Edition*, p. lxvi. Sieber discusses some social and cultural shifts that rendered the genre somewhat incongruous with readers' interests, see Harry Sieber, 'The Romance of Chivalry in Spain: From Rodríguez de Montalvo to Cervantes', pp. 213–18.

[11] Unlike Joseph de Perott, who conjectures that publication occurred in 1579 or 1580, I follow the *STC* in ascribing the date 1578 to the first edition. Joseph de Perott, 'The Mirrour of Knighthood', pp. 397–402.

[12] Cf. Krontiris, *Oppositional Voices*, p. 45; Helen Hackett, '"Yet Tell Me Some Such Fiction": Lady Mary Wroth's Urania and the "Femininity" of Romance', p. 44. On the love for Spanish chivalric romance in England see also, John J. O'Connor, *Amadis de Gaule and Its Influence on Elizabethan Literature*, p. 3. Earlier studies of Anglo-Spanish romance do not discuss *Mirror*. See Martin Hume, *Spanish Influence on English Literature*, esp. 115–21; John Garrett Underhill, *Spanish Literature in the England of the Tudors*; Mary Patchell, *The Palmerin Romances in Elizabethan Prose Fiction*; Henry Thomas dismisses it as 'a vast compendium of chivalresque nonsense' in *Spanish and Portuguese Romances of Chivalry: The Revival of the Romance of Chivalry in the Spanish Peninsula, and its Extension and Influence Abroad*, p. 120. His disparaging plot summary extends from p. 120 to p. 127.

[13] Joshua Phillips, *English Fictions of Communal Identity, 1485–1603*, p. 144, cf. 122–23.

contemporary readers: the Spanish *Amadís* cycle boasts a total of 59 editions. Anthony Munday's five-part English translation of *Amadís* (1590?, 1595, 1598, 1618) was based on an intermediary French translation by Nicolas de Herberay. In his use of the French text, Munday followed the precedent of the earlier fragmentary Englishings of the romance: in 1571, Charles Steward translated a small portion of Book 1; and the rhetorical manual *The Treasurie of Amadis of Fraunce* consists of selections from Herberay's work (1572). Munday is additionally responsible for introducing the *Palmerin* cycle to English readers, again via French intermediaries. The Spanish cycle begins with the anonymous *Palmerin d'Oliva* (1511) and *Primaleon* (1512), and continues with Francisco de Moraes's *Palmerin of England* (1547–48). Like *Amadís* and *Mirror*, the *Palmerin* cycle is genealogical: Palmerin d'Oliva's adventures are followed by those of his sons, Primaleon and Palmendos, and his grandson, Palmerin of England. Munday's *Palmerin d'Oliva* appeared in two parts (1588, 1597). Its sequel, *Primaleon*, was likewise subdivided and renamed after the romance's heroes: *Palmendos* (1589) was followed by the three books of *Primaleon of Greece* (1595, 1596, 1619) and the three books of *Palmerin of England* (Books 1 and 2, 1596; Book 3 1602). As with his other Spanish romance compositions, Munday used a French version of *Florando de Inglaterra* (1545) to execute his translation of *Palladine of England* (1588). Besides translating Books 7–8 of *Mirror*, L. A. is also credited with the English rendering of Jerónimo Fernández's *Belianís de Grecia* (1545). His *The Honour of Chivalrie* (1598), based on an Italian intermediary translation, is the only Spanish romance translation to have inspired an original English continuation: John Shirley's second and third parts of *Don Bellianis of Greece* appeared in 1683. This practice of translating Spanish literature via French or Italian intermediaries was common. In fact, Tyler was the first to translate an entire romance directly from Spanish, and thus the first to access an Iberian text without intermediating interferences from other linguistic-literary systems.[14]

The numerous contemporaneous references to *Mirror* further indicate its popularity, although the uses to which the allusions are put are varied and contradictory. Attesting to *Mirror*'s initial fashionableness, Euphues recalls *Mirror*'s enchanters in John Lyly's *Euphues and his England* (1580).[15] Rosicleer is the vehicle for praise in *Philaster* and *Antonio and Mellida*, but his name elicits mockery in *Wit in a Constable*.[16] *The Gamester* evokes Donzel del Febo's heroism, but associations with him are condemnatory in *The Little French Lawyer* and *The Scornful Lady*.[17] The exemplary qualities of the romance and its heroes are recalled in *The Malcontent*, *Hudibras*, and *Honoria and Mammon*, yet ridiculed in *The Bird in a Cage* and *The Knight of the Burning Pestle*.[18] In Dekker's *Satiromastix*, Tucca asks Sir Quintilian, 'Dost love her, my finest and first part of the Mirror of Knighthood?', amusingly metamorphosing the title into a term of endearment, and Ben Jonson includes it amongst the books absent from Beaufort's ideal library.[19] Claridiana's name becomes synonymous with 'beloved', as in *Albertus Wallenstein* and *The Alchemist*.[20]

---

[14] John Bourchier, Lord Berners used a Spanish version of *Cárcel de amor* for the final section of his translation, but the majority of his *Castell of Love* is based on both Spanish and French versions. Joyce Boro, '"this rude laboure": Lord Berners's Translation Methods and Prose Style in *Castell of Love*', pp. 1–23.

[15] John Lyly, *Euphues: The Anatomy of Wit; Euphues and his England*, p. 428.

[16] See John Beaumont and John Fletcher, *Philaster*, 5.4.350; Anthony Marston, *Antonio and Mellida*, 2.1.37–38. In the first edition of Marston's play, Rosicleer's name is mangled by the printing house and he becomes *Don Bessiclers* (Thomas, *Spanish and Portuguese Romances of Chivalry*, p. 270). Henry Glapthorne, *Wit in a Constable*, 4.1.126.

[17] James Shirley, *The Gamester*, 3.2.52–53; John Marston and John Fletcher, *The Little French Lawyer*, 2.3.299–300; John Beaumont and John Fletcher, *The Scornful Lady*, 3.1.122.

[18] John Marston, *The Malcontent*, 5.3.15–19; Samuel Butler, *Hudibras*, Canto 1.15–120; James Shirley, *Honoria and Mammon*, 2.1.83–84; *The Bird in a Cage*, 3.2.22–24; Francis Beaumont, *Knight of the Burning Pestle*, 2.2.

[19] Thomas Dekker, *Satiromastix*, 3.1.108–09; Ben Johnson, *The New Inn*, 1.6.123–28.

[20] Henry Glapthorne, *Albertus Wallenstein*, 3.2.49; Ben Jonson, *The Alchemist*, 1.1.175. The most famous of *Mirror*'s heroines is Lindabrides, from part 2 and 3 of the romance, see Thomas, *Spanish and Portuguese Romances of Chivalry*, pp. 272–74.

INTRODUCTION

The romance is also involved in discussions of the value and dangers of romance reading, a topic that will be considered in detail below. Francis Meres includes Tyler's translation in a list of romances he deems 'hurtfull to youth', since, in William Vaughan's words, it is 'prodigious, idle, and time-wasting'.[21] Echoing Robert Burton's concerns that 'silly Gentlewomen' would be 'incensed by reading amorous toys', such as *Mirror*, Thomas Overbury and Philip Massinger invoke *Mirror* to articulate the dangers of female romance reading.[22] Overbury famously sketches the character of the chambermaid who 'is so carried away with the *Mirrour of Knighthood*, she is many times resolv'd to runne out of her selfe, and become a lady errant'.[23] For her part, Calypso in Massinger's *The Guardian* (1633) finds the romance's verisimilitude equally persuasive and captivating.[24] The association of *Mirror* with female, working-class readers illustrated by Overbury's chambermaid and Calypso is perpetuated in *Eastward Hoe*, with Gertrude's unfavourable comparison of her beloved to the Knight of the Sun, and in Lodowick Barrey's *Ram Alley*, in which Mistress Taffeta asks whether married life will entail having her maid read aloud romances such as 'Donzel del Phoebo'.[25] Indeed, 'as the century turned the Iberian romances were increasingly regarded less as dangerous than as old fashioned, ridiculous and *déclassé*' (Hackett, p. 65), but they continued to be read, which is amply supported by these numerous allusions. The linked parodic treatment of Spanish romance and women, to be further considered below, is not an accurate reflection of their readership, but rather, it is a cultural construction resulting from their progressive decline in status, 'exaggerated for rhetorical and satirical purposes' (Hackett, p. 67).

Mirror may have initiated the trend in Spanish chivalric romance translation, but prior to its publication, Spain was already an increasingly popular textual origin: between 1518 and 1578, sixty-two texts, approximately one text per year, were translated from Spanish.[26] Moreover, Spanish romance had already achieved a modicum of popularity in England with the sentimental romances: Juan de Flores's *Grisel y Mirabella* (*c*.1495) and Diego de San Pedro's *Arnalte y Lucenda* (1491) and *Cárcel de amor* (1492). The sentimental romance is a sub-genre of the Medieval Spanish romance, generally distinguished from the exploit-driven chivalric romance by its focus on emotion rather action; its interest in rhetoric, epistolarity, and narrative experimentation; and its participation in the woman debate. *Grisel* was twice translated into English, only a fragment is preserved of the first translation (1527–1535), and the second forms part of a quadrilingual French, Spanish, Italian, and English edition (1556). Adaptations include the prose romance, *A Paire of Turtle Doves, or, The Tragicall History of Bellora and Fidelio* (1606), and the dramas, *Swetnam, The Woman-Hater* (1620) and John Fletcher's *Women Pleased* (1647). Following John Clerc's translation of *Arnalte* (1543), Claudius Hollyband's retranslation was issued in a bilingual English-Italian edition (1575). It was later adapted by Leonard Lawrence (1639) and Thomas Sydserf (1660). Lord Berners translated *Cárcel de amor* in the late 1520s (1548?). Thus, while chivalric romances were not pouring from the presses alongside *Mirror*, the text participates in a tradition of Iberian romance translation and publication and can be credited with initiating the late sixteenth-century vogue for Spanish tales of chivalry.

---

[21] Francis Meres, *Palladis Tamia. Wits and Treasury being the Second Part of Wits Commonwealth*, pp. 268[r-v]; William Vaughan, *The Golden Fleece*, p. 11.
[22] Robert Burton, *The Anatomy of Melancholy*, 1.2.3.15, 2.2.4.1, 3.2.2.4.
[23] Thomas Overbury, *New and Choise Characters, of Seuerall Authors*, p. ¶4[v].
[24] Philip Massinger, *The Guardian*, 1.1.472–77.
[25] George Chapman, Ben Jonson, and John Marston, *Eastward Hoe*, 5.1.32–34; Lodowick Barrey, *Ram Alley*, 3.1.233.
[26] *Anglo-Spanish Literary Relations* (database).

'INSTRUCTED [...] IN THE TRUE AND PERFECT LAW OF GOD': A CATHOLIC TRANSLATOR? A CATHOLIC TRANSLATION?

Speculation regarding Tyler's religion abounds. Her association with Thomas Howard and her knowledge of Spanish arouse suspicion of Catholicism in many scholars, such as Randall Martin, Tina Krontiris, Moira Ferguson, and Deborah Uman and Belén Bistué. Archival work by Louise Schleiner reveals evidence that simultaneously advances and negates the possibility of Tyler's Catholicism. The few known details of Tyler's biography merit a re-examination through the lens of a nuanced understanding of the significance of Spanish language acquisition, *Mirror*'s textual history, and the religious perspective articulated in the romance. While Tyler had established affiliations with several Catholics and Catholic allies, including Howard, East, and her probable husband, John Tyler, her romance expresses a deep suspicion of the marvellous that is consonant with the Protestant poetics conveyed in anti-Papist texts and in the romances of her Reformed contemporaries, such as Sidney, Spenser, and Wroth. However, notwithstanding the typically post-Reformation handling of the marvellous, the romance's presentation of Saracens betrays a residual Spanish Catholic conception of religious and cultural otherness.

Mirror is Tyler's only known work. At the time of its composition, Tyler was an older woman. She notes her 'years' twice in her preface, and in the dedication to Thomas Howard, she explains that she translated the romance 'the rather to acquaint myself with mine old reading', suggesting a lengthy readerly career. Her age is further suggested by the archaisms she employs, such as 'lien' for 'lain' (10.55), 'ware' for 'aware' (14.86), 'stake' for 'stuck' (30.34), and 'rust' for 'rest' (50.68). Her date of birth is unknown, but she composed her will in June 1595, and died later that year.[27] She married John Tyler, with whom she had two children: a son named Robert, and a daughter, whose married name was Ross. 'This John Tyler', a scribe in the Howard household in the 1560s, 'would be a likely husband for the translator, both of them middle-level literate employees of the Duke in the early 1560s' (Schleiner, p. 6). Other than his professional position, little is known with certainty about John Tyler. The name is not common, but still, a small handful of records for different John Tylers have been located (Schleiner, p. 6). Tyler's family life may have inspired some additions to the romance. For instance, she emphasizes the emotional aspects of childbirth (12.15–20, 28–30) and the maternal relationship of Briana to Rosicleer (14.87–91), and she includes comments on a wife's love for her husband (25.141–42), parent-child relationships (44.404), and women in labour (47.32).

Tyler ended her life in Castle Camps, a village near Audley End, where her patron, Thomas Howard, later Earl of Suffolk, resided.[28] She had worked as a professional waiting woman in the household of Howard's parents, Thomas Howard, Duke of Norfolk and his second wife Margaret Audley Howard, *c.* 1558 to 1564. The Duke of Norfolk was executed in 1572 for his plan to marry Mary Queen of Scots, his support of the Scottish Queen's accession to the English throne, and his support of the later rebellion of the northern earls. Tyler's continued loyalty to the Duke in *Mirror*'s dedication, written six years after his death, has fuelled speculation regarding her faith. Whereas Margaret Audley Howard, whom Tyler served, was a confirmed Protestant, the Howards were known Catholic allies. Even while Margaret Audley Howard was Duchess, the household 'would have been different in spirit from those of fervent Protestants', conjectures Louise Schleiner: 'It must have had some of the tone and habits of pre-reformation religious practice', and 'a crypto-Catholic waiting woman might well have felt comfortable there'

---

[27] Biographical information is based on the archival work of Louise Schleiner, 'Margaret Tyler, Translator and Waiting Woman', pp. 1–9.
[28] Building on Tyler's suspect relationship with the disgraced Howards, Moira Ferguson raises the possibility that Margaret Tyler was a pseudonym for Margaret Tyrrell, a woman also linked to the Howards and a member of the prominent Catholic Tyrell family. See Moira Ferguson, *First Feminists: British Women Writers, 1578–1799*, pp. 51–52.

(pp. 4–5). Donna Hamilton ascribes great importance to Tyler's dedication to Howard, observing that 'Tyler initiated a series of [Spanish] romance publications dedicated to people in England of or close to the Catholic party'.[29] Certainly, Thomas Shelton's *Don Quixote* was dedicated to Thomas Howard's son, Theophilus Howard, and Anthony Munday dedicated romances to the Earl of Oxford (*Zelauto, Palmerin d'Oliva*), the Earl of Essex (*Palladine of England*), Philip Herbert, Earl of Montgomery (*Amadis*), Henry de Vere (*Primaleon*), and the recusant Ralph Marshall (*Gerileon of England*). The translators' and dedicatees' links to the English Catholic minority definitely recall the heterogeneous religious landscape of post-Reformation England and set them apart from native, Protestant romance compositions. Because of its dedication, Hamilton situates *Mirror* within a Catholic, Spanish romance tradition that runs counter to the Protestant romance poetics more famously crafted by writers such as Sidney, Spenser, and Wroth, but, as will be investigated below, Tyler's approach to the marvellous is entirely consonant with the values expressed in native English romances composed even by inveterate Reformed writers.

Religion, however, is not the only possible explanation for Tyler's continued devotion to the Howards through the 1570s. Following her engagement with the Howards, Tyler served Anne Bacon Woodhouse and Anne Gresham Bacon, respectively sister and wife to Nathaniel Bacon of Stiffkey, moving from Bacon Woodhouse's household to Gresham Bacon's around 1573–78. Nathaniel Bacon was a fervent Protestant and an avid hunter of recusants (Schleiner, pp. 3–4). His home seems an unlikely shelter for a Catholic; although it is conceivable that, if Tyler were a Catholic, she managed to keep her religious beliefs secret during her period of employment. 'The Woodhouses and Greshams had business dealings with the Duke of Norfolk and, as country gentry, would have paid him at least yearly social calls' (Schleiner, p. 3). Tyler is likely to have gained her employment with them due to her previous service for the Howards, which may have instilled in her a debt of gratitude that persisted following Howard's disgrace and execution; as *Mirror*'s narrator declares: 'it is natural in man to prefer those of whom they receive benefits' (16.100).

Tyler's knowledge of Spanish is equally unpersuasive evidence of Catholicism. Spain was certainly an especially dangerous textual origin since the Renaissance represents an era of heightened Anglo-Spanish tension. As a Catholic super-power, Spain posed significant political and ideological threats to England. English racial bigotry effected the perception of Spaniards, who were feared not only for their Catholicism, but also for their supposed Moorish or Jewish heritage. Essential to the national imagination and to the self-construction of Englishness was a differentiation from Catholic continental Europe and a perception of England as a strong, unique Protestant nation. Yet, paradoxically, despite the abundance of documented hostility towards Spain, steadily increasing numbers sought to learn the language, and readers enjoyed Spanish literature, as evidenced, for example, by the numerous references to *Mirror* in contemporaneous texts.

Krontiris deems Tyler's knowledge of Spanish to be exceptionally 'amazing', asserting that Spanish was 'rarely studied even by educated men of her time'.[30] Martin likewise notes 'the unusual addition of Spanish' to her education, attributing it to a peculiar Howard 'family tradition', possibly 'related to the Howard family's Catholic connections'.[31] Yet, Schleiner astutely separates language and religious affiliation, observing that Spanish 'was a useful commercial language for families in international trade even on a small scale, and clever merchants' daughters were sometimes taught it'. She continues: 'Such would have been the education of the servant-waiting women — i.e. those not of gentry rank — who entertained

---

[29] Donna B. Hamilton, *Anthony Munday and the Catholics, 1560–1633*, p. 80.
[30] Krontiris 'Breaking Barriers of Genre and Gender: Margaret Tyler's Translation of *The Mirrour of Knighthood*', p. 19.
[31] Martin, *Women Writers*, p. 16.

ladies with "reading" to them, probably spot translating, out of French and Spanish romances' (Schleiner, p. 4). French was the only vernacular formally taught in medieval England and it remained the most popular second language in the Renaissance, but interest in Italian was strong, and Spanish increasingly grew in importance as the sixteenth-century century progressed.[32] Not only was the mastery of a foreign language a mark of erudite refinement, but for merchants, diplomats, scholars, and avid, curious readers, Italian, French, and Spanish were becoming ever more essential. Accordingly, Spanish manuals, grammars, dictionaries, dialogue books, *vulgaria*, translations, and polyglot works proliferated. Spanish texts circulated in England, forming important parts of libraries. Writers such as Raphael Holinshed, William Harrison, John Florio, and Harvey note the abundance and wide social range of female and male Spanish language-learners.[33] Their comments are neither purely theoretical nor anecdotal, nor do they apply solely to the Catholic segment of the population. By the later decades of the sixteenth century a range of English people, including devoted Protestants such as Harvey, William Cecil, John Fletcher, and Queen Elizabeth, could read or speak Spanish. Moreover, several of the scholars who contributed to the spread of Spanish in England, including Antonio del Corro, were Spanish Protestant exiles, with very little sympathy for Catholic agendas. Knowledge of Spanish was certainly not an outward sign of closeted Catholicism.

More persuasive evidence of Tyler's Catholicism may be derived from the documentary sources used to compile her biography. Schleiner posits that Tyler's will 'quite accords with practices of will writing sometimes used by recusants', in which business acquaintances and movables are not specified (p. 5). Likewise, she conjectures that Tyler's final residence in Castle Camps may be explained by her religious affiliation: 'If she were a recusant on the move, the restraining act of 1592 would have forced her home, or to some place she could decide to call home and stick to, which in light of the patronage of Thomas Howard of Walden would be the neighbourhood of Audley End' (Schleiner, p. 5). Moreover, in 1588–89, a 'Margaret Tiler' is fined for recusancy in Benacre, Suffolk. There is no definite proof that this woman is our translator, but it seems likely since her probable husband, John Tyler, was a recusant with connections to the Catholic judge, Sir Anthony Brown, who lived five miles from Benacre and who is known to have helped co-religionists.

The publication history of *Mirror* is also suggestive of Tyler's Catholicism. Desirous to capitalize on the success of *Mirror*, Thomas East entered *Mirror*'s as yet un-translated sequel in the Stationers' Register in order to prevent other publishers from acquiring the rights to the volume. Registering a book prior to its composition was unusual and so the master and warden of the Stationers' Company stipulated that the volume was 'soe to be printed, condiconally notwithstandinge that when the same is translated yt be brought to them to be perused, and yf any thinge be amisse therein to be amended'.[34] Whereas Jeremy L. Smith situates East's peremptory registration of *Mirror*'s sequel within a narrative of fiscal opportunism, Hamilton deems it analogous to the circumstances surrounding the publication of several of Munday's romances, including *Palmerin of England* and *Amadis*, which also specify the possible necessity of future corrections and inspections by the authorities. Hamilton concludes that the romances 'of Tyler and Munday, were regarded suspiciously for religious and political reasons'.[35]

---

[32] On Spanish language learning, see Joyce Boro, 'Multilingualism, Romance, and Language Pedagogy: Or, Why Were So Many Sentimental Romances Printed as Polyglot Texts?', pp. 18–38; cf. Kenneth Charlton, *Education in Renaissance England*, pp. 227–52; R. Simonini, *Italian Scholarship in Renaissance England*, p. 12; Jason Lawrence, *'Who the Devil Taught Thee So Much Italian?': Italian Language Learning and Literary Imitation in Early Modern England*, pp. 1–61.

[33] Raphael Holinshed, *Chronicles*, f. 83v, col 2; William Harrison, *The Description of England*, p. 228; John Florio, *Florio his Firste Fruites*, pp. 51[r–v]; Gabriel Harvey, manuscript annotation in Antonio del Corro, *The Spanish Grammer* (London, 1590) Huntington Library, HEH 53880, A1v.

[34] Edward Arber, *A Transcript of the Registers of the Company of Stationers of London, 1554–1640 A.D*, II.414.

[35] Hamilton, *Anthony Munday*, pp. 80–81.

INTRODUCTION

H. S. Bennett likewise records the abnormality of the entry for *Mirror*'s sequel, observing that '[t]ranslations, particularly those of Spanish works, were hedged about with conditions'.[36]

East is best characterized as a trade printer, financially motivated and mostly printing books for other publishers, stationers, or booksellers; *Mirror* and its sequels are amongst the minority of books that East both published and printed. As a lengthy work, controversially written by a woman, in an era when new chivalric romances were sparse, *Mirror* was an expensive, risky venture. East published other romances, such as *Le Morte d'Arthur* (1585), John Lyly's *Euphues* (1579) and *Euphues and his England* (1580), together with *Mirror*'s sequels; he also entered *Oliver of Castile, Bevis of Hampton, The Four Sons of Aymon* in the Stationers' Register in March 1581–82, but *Mirror* was his 'trailblazer' romance.[37]

East's rationale for the publication of *Mirror* may best be understood in relation to his personal and professional connections within the Catholic community, including his collaboration with the Catholic musician William Byrd, and his link to Edmund East, a renowned recusant and probable relative, as well as to other notable recusants, agitators, and conspirators.[38] East printed and distributed many of Byrd's texts that would have appealed to Catholics, such as music for illegal Catholic masses, *Psalmes, Sonnets & Songs*, and hidden, and secret editions of masses. In the later part of his career East printed, published, or sold several politically charged works, many with his professional successor, Thomas Snodham, including John Dowland's *Second Book of Songs* (1600), George Ker's *A Discoverie of the Conspiracie of Scottish Papists* (1603), John Hayward's *An Answer to the First Part of a Certaine Conference* (1603), John Savile's *King James His Entertainment at Theobalds* (1603), and *J. H.'s Work for Chimny-sweepers: Or A Warning for Tabacconists* (1602). Despite East's regular contact with recusants and treasonous political activists, his biographer cautions: 'In the virtual absence of evidence to the contrary from parish records, recusant rolls, or litigation papers, it must be considered that East was not, at least in any overt way, a religious dissenter or a Catholic recusant'.[39] However, his activities reveal definite Catholic sympathies in the years just after *Mirror*'s publication and they may explain his willingness to undertake the precarious venture of printing *Mirror*. Were East and Tyler linked through their respective connections within the Catholic community? Did East print *Mirror* because he and Tyler shared religious beliefs?

Turning to the romance itself, *Mirror* reveals many of the inconsistencies that evoke a Protestant sensibility.[40] However, the treatment of Catholic customs in the romance indicates a general sense of acceptance, which intimates that Tyler was unlikely to have been a zealous Protestant. For example, allusions to the *novena* and to the specifically Catholic practice of rising and hearing mass are omitted (54.3–4), but Tyler also adds Catholic references: Briana is likened to 'an anchoress' (11.4) and a 'holy vowess' (12.10), and her fasting is described (11.44, 53–54; 56.22). Fasting may have a place in the Reformed Church, but it is a ritual most commonly associated with Catholicism. More fruitful, however, is a comparison of the treatment of the marvellous in *Espejo* and *Mirror*. The repeated occlusion of the marvellous in *Mirror* unveils a post-Reformation, typically Protestant conceptualisation of romance, suggesting Tyler's profound discomfort with what Tiffany Werth has called 'the supernatural marvelous, an aspect of romance that purportedly aroused and engaged readerly memory through a mode that appeared uncomfortably sympathetic to Catholic habits of faith' (p. 33). Werth argues that romance authors such as Sidney, Spenser, Shakespeare, and Wroth 'write texts that take seriously the Protestant indictments against an imaginative genre and by so doing reveal how profoundly religious attacks affected the ways these authors thought about romance, provoking

---

[36] H. S. Bennett, *English Books and Readers, 1558–1603*, p. 62.
[37] Thomas Plomer, 'Thomas East, Printer', pp. 298–310.
[38] Jeremy L. Smith, *Thomas East and Music Publishing in Renaissance England*, p. 204.
[39] Smith, *Thomas East*, p. 96.
[40] Cf. John Harington's translation of *Orlando Furioso*.

a battle over its recuperation as well as its interpretation' (p. 5). Tyler's re-visioning of the marvellous points to a similar attempt to negotiate and reconcile public fascination, fear, and condemnation of romance. As a point of comparison, Munday does not systematically alter or reduce the marvellous in his romances.

Despite the appropriation of romance by Protestant writers, anti-Catholic sentiment fed into denunciations of the genre. Rooted in Italian, French, Spanish, or medieval English forms, romances were suspect because of their associations with Catholicism and, hence, depravity. This link enabled the activation of religious and moral polemic against romance, which led to the perception of romance reading as a comprehensive social and religious predicament; it was believed that the papist, monastic fictions could corrupt those who perused them. Supernatural marvels or 'fabulous devices' were closely allied with both romance and Catholicism in the Reformed imagination. Papists were accused of being engaged in 'conjurations, magicall artes, false miracles, lying wonders, deceivable signes, malitious devises'.[41] Employing similar discourse, Edward Dering condemns romances as 'idolatrous superstition' and 'spiritual enchauntmentes [. . .] which Satan had made, Hell had printed, and were warranted unto sale under the Popes priviledge'.[42] Romance's supernatural components, combined with its medieval and continental heritage, led the genre to be closely identified with Catholics in post-Reformation England. This highly popular 'literary form [. . .] had come to represent a crisis in faith' (Werth, p. 33).

In *Mirror*, the term 'marvel' (Spanish: *maravilla, maravillar*) and its derivatives are almost always omitted or replaced by other terms such as 'noble' (1.46), 'disquiet' (23.20), 'troubled' (20.114, 44.179), 'muse(d)'/'musing' (19.151; 28.72; 32.322), 'rejoicing' (21.9), 'praising' (28.106), 'wondered' (29.38; 31.23; 37.69), 'delight(ed)' (30.53; 37.95; 44.9), 'very glad' (30.112–13), 'abashed' (30.134; 31.31; 40.217; 44.244; 53.21), 'dismayed' (32.312), 'great' (32.323), 'dares' (33.86), 'amazed' (44.537; 45.147; 54.84), and 'strange' (51.94). At times, other sensory expressions replace 'marvel', such as 'had enough to occupy their eyes' (20.26–27), 'stood looking upon' (24.44), and 'attentively listening' (31.61). 'Marvel' is omitted at least fifty more times. Not only is 'marvel' omitted, but semantically related terms such as 'strange', 'amaze', 'magic', 'magical arts' and their derivatives are also often excluded from or altered in the translation. The sword that Lirgandeo gives Donzel del Febo is depicted as a wonderful work of art, but it is not 'maziço' (20, I.163.13–14 [magical]).[43] Likewise, the portrayals of Artimodoro's magical work in creating Rosicleer's armour and their tent are substituted by an account of human, non-magical work: the armour was 'framed so cunningly as for workmanship, cost, and secret virtue' (31.128–29, I.272.16–20), and the tent 'could never have been wrought but by an exquisite seamster' (32.165, II.19.19–21).

Espejo emphasizes the heroes' superhuman powers and compares them to divine beings, while Tyler routinely excludes such emphasis. For example, in *Espejo* characters repeatedly think that Donzel del Febo has descended from heaven (I.142.27–28; I.130.10–13) and they express disbelief in his humanity (I.121.16–17; I.135.5–7). *Mirror*'s characters are amazed by the hero and laud him as exemplary, but he remains human (18.10–20; I.136.16–18). This type of alteration does not only affect the portrayal of Donzel del Febo: Florion describes Africano as being 'unparagonized for manhood' (22.83), while in the Spanish they did not consider him to be human (I.183.24–25); in *Espejo*, Florion is a divine young gentleman (I.146.23) who divinely kills Brandafileo (I.146.24). Tyler similarly omits the following details: Rosicleer's suspicion that Artimodoro's island is a terrestrial paradise (I.269.14–15); Zoilo's compliments to Claridiana that her beauty exceeds all human reason and understanding (II.219.23–24); and the king's amazement at Brandizel's superhuman defeat of the giant (II.238.15–16). One of the few

---

[41] *A Reply with the Occasion Thereof*, Ar4, qtd. in Werth, *Fabulous Dark Cloister*, p. 173.
[42] Edward Dering, *A Briefe & Necessary Instruction*, A2ᵛ.
[43] All references to *Espejo* are to Eisenberg, *Espejo de príncipes y cavalleros*. The text is cited according to volume, page, and line number.

references of this type that is preserved serves to highlight the fallacy of non-Christian belief: Radamira, a Saracen, ascertains that Donzel del Febo is 'more than manlike' and possessed with 'some divine blood in him which she thought to have descended from some of her false gods' (20.153).

Giants compose part of the romance marvellous, but they are not subject to the same treatment of occlusion as other marvels. More than a dozen villainous giants stomp their way through *Mirror*'s imaginative landscape. Staunchly opposed to the Christian heroes, these colossal foes embody a threatening reminder of the uncivilized: they refuse to adhere to legal and social norms as they attack the innocent and engage in acts of trickery and vengeance. Yet, not all giants are equally execrable. Genesis depicted the unnatural, sinfulness of giants (6.1–4), yet the Aristotelian theory — that a giant is created when the quantity of matter exceeds the dimensions of the form — accounted for both magnificent and repugnant giants.[44] Aristotle posits that correspondence of form and matter result in an admirably large, beautiful man, while inconsistency leads to monstrosity. Indeed, the figure of the giant is epistemologically dichotomous, linked to both guarding and blocking and 'fertility and terror'.[45] Discussing the revised *Arcadia*, which, like *Mirror*, 'banishes monsters [while] giants rove', Werth suggests: 'This may be because although larger in scale, giants remain human'.[46] Under the right conditions they could be assimilated into Christian society, as in the romances *Ralph the Collier* and *Fierabras*, or in the historical, nationalistic English appropriation of Gog and Magog.[47]

The giant's duality is epitomized in *Espejo*, where, in addition to the repulsive, we encounter three heroic quasi-giants: Donzel del Febo, Trebatio, and Briana. *Mirror* alters and omits many references to the heroes' size, thereby distancing these heroic, large characters from the evil giants typical of romance. Trebatio is still 'called the Great Trebatio because he was eight foot in height and very strong timbered' (1.32–33), but several references to his dimensions are omitted (for example, I.54.28; I.59.13; II.190.9–13; II.202.36–203.1). Donzel del Febo's size is handled very carefully: although he is taller than his father, he is not a giant. He is so 'well featured' and 'proportion[ed]' that 'the bigness of his body' is the exemplary standard of beauty for all Greek and Assyrian artists (18.59–66). Similarly, Briana is as exquisite as Helen and she 'excell[ed] the other gentlewomen in height a span' (6.27). Briana and Donzel del Febo demonstrate that big is beautiful. While giants may be quasi-human and potentially allied to Christianity and to social, legal and civic stability, *Mirror* distinguishes between giants and heroes, firmly estranging the giants from the heroic realm and prioritizing their monstrosity. The preservation of nefarious giganticness and the reformulation of Trebatio, Donzel del Febo, and Briana are entirely in keeping with the Protestant poetics that governs the treatment of the marvellous in *Mirror* and other contemporaneous romances, such as the revised *Arcadia* and *The Faerie Queene*.

Running counter to her handling of the marvellous elsewhere in the romance, in Chapter 44, which recounts the Knight of the Sun's rescue of Trebatio from Lindaraza's island, Tyler adds 'marvel' and other semantically related terms and she supplements the narrative with marvellous elements. Readers knew that Trebatio was captive in Lindaraza's castle, but the extent of its powers is not articulated until the wondrous Chapter 44. In this chapter, descriptions of marvellous voyages, buildings, paths, landscapes, combats, and 'deeds of arms' are preserved. Some elements, such as the fountain, are added, while the importance of other marvels, including the marble stone, is accentuated.

The intensity of the island's marvels in Chapter 44 is also heightened comparatively since the fantastical is diminished at the castle's first description in Chapter 9. Chapter 9 explains how

---

[44] Suzanne Conklin Akbari, *Idols in the East: European Representations of Islam and the Orient, 1100–1450*, p. 173.
[45] Anne Lake Prescott, *Imagining Rabelais in Renaissance England*, pp. 16, 31.
[46] Werth, *Fabulous Dark Cloister*, p. 173, n. 5. Cf. Victor I. Scherb, 'Assimilating Giants: The Appropriation of Gog and Magog in Medieval and Early Modern England', pp. 59–84.
[47] Scherb, 'Assimilating Giants', p. 84; Prescott, *Imagining Rabelais*, p. 18.

Trebatio's altered state arises from the island's 'secret virtue' rather than its enchantment (9.97; I.78.1–2).⁴⁸ In *Mirror*, Lindaraza's voice no longer seems to reach the heavens (I.77.12–13), and her hair does not resemble skeins of gold (I.77.17). Furthermore, while *Mirror* admits that Trebatio 'was so estranged from himself' and that he was 'deprived of his understanding', *Espejo* specifies the marvellous nature of Trebatio's imprisonment, which deprives him of his reason and his memory of his former life (9.74; 9.145, I.75.16–19; I.81.27–29). The Spanish romance returns to emphasize his forgetting and his self-estrangement on three occasions, but these passages are altered in *Mirror* so that the extremity of Trebatio's predicament cannot be fully grasped (I.76.3–4; I.78.7–9). Notwithstanding the less wondrous description of Lindaraza and her castle, *Mirror*'s narrator teases her readers with the promise of future marvels: 'the secret virtue of the place [...] shall be recited hereafter' (9.97). Similarly prefiguring Chapter 44, Lindaraza is presented as an 'enchantress' rather than a 'donzella' (lady, 9.96, I.77.19). By postponing the description of the wonders until later in the text, when the extent and potency of the magic is revealed, we are surprised and relieved to discover that Trebatio has been absent against his will.

As a result, the island is configured as a unique locus of marvel and fantasy, which works to justify Trebatio's lengthy, problematic absence from his political and familial obligations, and to reinforce the dichotomy of the island's sensual ruler, Lindaraza, and Trebatio's first love, the chaste Briana. Many characters are saddened and perplexed by Trebatio's mysterious, unexplained absence. However, once the excessively marvellous nature of the island is revealed, *Mirror*'s readers understand Trebatio's behaviour, prefiguring his subsequent joyous and forgiving acceptance by his family and subjects. Trebatio is neither a negligent husband nor a corrupt ruler, as many fearfully suspected; he has been held captive by potent magical forces, and so he is not to blame for his disappearance. Lindaraza, the enchantress/seductress who detains Trebatio, lies at the root of the island's marvels. Her overt sexuality is intertwined with the marvellous, which heightens her opposition to Briana, whose residence in a monastery accurately reflects her purity and modesty. Whereas Briana demonstrates the productive, generative force of female sexuality, Lindaraza is the fantastical object of 'a masculine wish-fulfilment fantasy'.⁴⁹ By presenting her island as a unique locus of magic, the dangerous immorality of unbridled sexuality is restricted and prevented from contaminating the rest of the romance universe. Indeed, this marginalization of female sexuality reflects early modern anxieties about romance and it contributes to Tyler's paratextual authorizing strategies, as will be discussed below. Interestingly, by restricting the marvellous to the island, the opposition of island and monastery is reinforced. This stresses the monastery's association with chastity rather than marvels, which negates the Protestant polemic that links the romance marvellous to the corruption inherent in monastic, Catholic enclosures. The Protestant poetics governing Tyler's handling of the marvellous is thereby problematized due to the lingering dichotomy of Briana and Lindaraza that was established in *Espejo*.

The treatment of Saracens in *Mirror* likewise betrays a residual, non-native, Spanish conception of racial and cultural difference. The portrayal of Saracens in English romance, to be investigated below, is illustrative of Edward Said's conceptualization of Orientalism, which predicates difference at the root of the construction of European superiority. In contrast, stemming from the extensive Spanish co-habitation of Spaniards and Moors, their cultural relationship is characterized by proximity and intimacy; there is a shared material culture rather than a dominating hierarchical binary.⁵⁰ Despite the Reconquest and 'other sporadic disturbances and

---

⁴⁸ The expression 'secret virtue' is also used to describe the marvellous armour in Chapter 31: 'the excellency whereof in the imagery and workmanship cannot be declared' replaces 'sus estrañas y maravillosas labores, no ay lengua humana que lo pudiesse contar, ansí como tampoco pudo ser hecho por humanas manos' (31.73–74, II.75.24–26).
⁴⁹ Hackett, *Women and Romance*, p. 59.
⁵⁰ Cf. Barbara Fuchs, *Exotic Nation: Maurophilia and the Construction of Early Modern Spain*, pp. 74–76.

persecutions', there was 'astonishing tolerance' between the cultures. Contact was 'constant, and normal',[51] 'proximate or intimate' (Fuchs, p. 7), so that by the sixteenth century the nature of the interaction renders differentiation impossible. Islamic influences on literature persisted in the Siglo de Oro, resulting in a widespread tradition of literary Maurophilia. 'It would seem contradictory that the figure of the Moor should be praised, decked in the richest garments, and given brightly-shining weapons of war exactly at the moment when the Moor of flesh and blood was forbidden his own cultural identity', but this is indeed the reality.[52] Barbara Fuchs argues that 1492 is an unstable dividing line, since after the Reconquest, Spain 'retained and even celebrated the culture of al-Andalus' (Fuchs, p. 1). While the literature of Maurophilia contains exoticizing elements, Fuchs demonstrates how in sixteenth-century Spain, the exotic is paradoxically quotidian. Furthermore, Maurophilia is prevalent in the *romancero morisco*, a genre recalled by *Mirror*'s treatment of Saracens, that 'suggests the possibility of a highly enjoyable, idealizing identification that is very different from the staging of otherness in European representations of an Islamic East outside the Spanish context' (Fuchs, p. 75).

In her study of Anthony Munday and Catholicism, Hamilton contends that the invocation of an alternate worldview is typical of English translations of Spanish chivalric romances. She attributes an intentionalist, destructive agenda to Munday's oeuvre, positing that through his extensive programme of 'gathering, translating, reporting, collaborating, and revising, Munday repeatedly put back into print materials that Protestant versions of English or British identity had eliminated and were continuing to invalidate'. She writes that as '[c]ultural work of the first order, these acts involved feeding, even aggressively contaminating, English ideological and historiographical discourses with materials from Catholic, European and pre-Henrician traditions'.[53] Hostility is absent from *Mirror*; instead the Spanish ideology of comfortable otherness that permeates *Espejo* quietly lingers, even though such culturally ingrained assumptions are dichotomous to the ideology of cultural hegemony and segregation that defined anti-Catholic, anti-Spanish England.

Investigating the role of divinity in epic poetry, Tobias Gregory asserts that 'the distinction between true and false religion [. . .] between godly and infidel weaves a red thread though the heterogeneous body of Renaissance heroic poetry';[54] this is equally true of chivalric romance. *Mirror*'s narrator strongly identifies herself as Christian, all the while presupposing a Christian readership and distinguishing Christians from Saracens. A reference to 'Christians' is replaced with 'we', forging a relationship of complicity between narrator and readers based on their shared religious heritage (19.215). Added first person plural pronouns function likewise, intensifying the spiritual link, especially when coupled with the dismissal of pagan 'learning [which is] not worth a rush' (19.218). Further emphasizing her Christian morals and piety, Tyler adds references to the Christian God (39.181; 42.104) and 'Christendom' (40.248), and omits allusions to sex (9.135–37) and incest (39.151).

Yet, despite the strength of the Christian perspective, the romance evinces a degree of comfort with Saracens and their world that is unusual for English romance; rather, it is indebted to the Spanish tradition. Drawing important distinctions between the treatment of Muslims and Saracens in romance, Siobhan Bly Calkin posits that anxiety about 'going Saracen' is produced when Saracens are presented as resembling actual Muslims and a realistic Islamic world is presented. Like *Mirror*, *Bevis, Guy*, and Munday's *Zelauto* present a Muslim world operating independently of the Christian West, but whereas *Bevis, Guy*, and *Zelauto* express anxiety prior to dismissing all possibility of assimilation, no sense of apprehension is articulated in *Mirror*. Similarly to Donzel del Febo, Brandizel, and Clavergudo, Bevis inhabits a Muslim world from

---

[51] Luce López-Baralt, *Islam in Spanish Literature*, pp. 30–31.
[52] López-Baralt, pp, 209–10. For the critical history of Maurophilia, see pp. 209–15.
[53] Hamilton, *Anthony Munday*, pp. xviii–xix.
[54] Tobias Gregory, *From Many Gods to One*, p. 13.

infancy. Yet, Bevis 'has moments when he appears to affirm a Saracen identity for himself only subsequently to reject such a possibility', thereby symbolically curbing the prospect of more wide-scale Christian incorporation.[55] *Guy* evokes a complex Muslim political scene, but '[b]ecause Saracen-Christian interactions never move beyond war, however, the slight evocations of historical Islam in *Guy* promote no anxiety about proximity' (Bly Calkin, p. 54). *Zelauto* exhibits awareness of religious difference and, through the hero's adventures in Persia, anxiety about the impact of Islam on Christians.[56] In contrast, the actualization of a self-contained Islamic world fails to produce concern in *Mirror*; instead, it reveals the heroes' familiarity and ease with Christian and Muslim co-habitation, suggesting a perspective dichotomous to that usually expressed in English romance. This presentation of effortless co-existence recalls the historical circumstances of pre-*Reconquista* Spain and the Spanish literature of Maurophilia.

Zoilo and Florion likewise emerge from and reflect this Spanish tradition, rather than the typically hegemonic English treatment of Saracens. Zoilo is a noble, heroic Saracen who is redeemed through his virtue, his alliances with Christian knights, and, especially, his predestined future conversion. He may be from Tartaria, but he originates 'in that part which bordereth upon Christendom' (40.248), thereby symbolically invoking his affinity to Christianity. Like Bevis, Zoilo synechdochially represents his community; his conversion is a microcosmic figuration of his society's conversion, epitomizing the desired assimilation of Islam into Christianity.[57] While Moorish conversion remained the norm in early modern Spanish literature, a pervasive counter-tradition extends from underground *aljamiado* literature to mainstream romances that narrate the adventures of great Saracen heroes who shun conversion, including the eponymous Abindarráez and Rodrigo Díaz de Vivar of *El poema de mío Cid*, and *Mirror*'s Florion.[58] Prince Florion, the heroic Saracen, is descended from a long line of Persian kings, but he counts Donzel del Febo, Brandizel, and Clavergudo amongst his closest friends, and his first adventure consists of defending Babylon from Africano, 'the stoutest pagan in all the heathen country' (17.109). Florion's community shares his animosity towards Africano and his love for the Christian heroes. Lirgandeo's prophecy that one from 'among the Christians' will save Babylon is heartily welcomed by the population (16.55). Florion's story presents 'Pagansie' not as something to be 'renounced' and forgotten, but as a potentially acceptable form of religious observance for heroic characters.

English romance cannot permanently accommodate heroic Saracens: conversion is mandatory. The distinctions between the monstrous and heroic Saracen operating within Florion's narrative are typical of English romance: romances present 'attractive, European-looking Saracens side by side with dark-skinned, grotesque Saracens having the bodies of giants and the bodily features of animals' (Akbari, p. 156). Loathsome Saracens must be destroyed or converted, but they typically resist Christianity and must be exterminated. The darkness of their skin or other forms of 'monstrosity' are markers of extreme alterity, whereas white skin 'suggests that the spiritual transformation of conversion would simply be the completion of a transformation that is already evident on the level of the flesh' (Akbari, p. 157). Bly Calkin observes that the only characters 'who desire a Saracen identity despite having the option to convert are Saracen giants' (p. 51). Spanish heroic Saracens, like Florion, do not exhibit the same imperative towards conversion.

Heroic Saracens in English romance are astonishing for the degree to which they resemble their Christian counterparts. The cross-cultural shared values of knighthood present knighthood

---

[55] Siobhain Bly Calkin, *Saracens and the Making of English Identity: The Auchinleck Manuscript*, p. 51.
[56] Benedict S, Robinson, *Islam and Early Modern English Literature: The Politics of Romance from Spenser to Milton*, p. 29.
[57] Cf. Akbari, *Idols in the East*, pp. 157–58.
[58] In *aljamiado* literature, sixteenth-century crypto-Muslim 'authors were engaged in religious proselytism, and they give witness to their collective disgrace and misfortune for a readership within their own persecuted community' (López-Baralt, p. 219).

as a universal, unconstructed phenomenon and develop the perception of a chivalric social class that transcends geographic and cultural borders. In Middle English romance, the sameness amongst knights, irrespective of their backgrounds, responds to anxieties regarding the difficulty of differentiating between the French and English in the centuries following the Norman Conquest and the concomitant discordances of loyalty that ensued, especially leading up to and during the Hundred Years' War. As a result, no matter how precise the similarities between Christian and Saracen knights, religious identification is a reliable marker of difference in allegiance: adherence to Islam marks the knight as enemy (Bly Calkin, p. 44). In these instances, '[w]hen Saracens closely resemble their Christian opponents, conversion becomes both possible and desirable' (Bly Calkin, p. 39). Conversion is ubiquitous in English romance. As Geraldine Heng has observed, 'Converging upon Christian centres from an Islamic "Orient" that stretches from the West, to the South, to the East, in an encompassing sweep of cardinal points that designate the horizons of the world, Saracens in romance are none the less neatly managed and contained by the military and conversionist strengths of triumphal Christianity'.[59] Saracens 'were shown to be eminently vanquishable' and they 'were only too ready to consort with the Christian enemy, turn renegade and convert to Christianity' (Heng, p. 259). This ideology endures in early modern texts: 'The early modern romances that feature Saracens encode, to varying degrees, a crusading impulse, a pressure for conquest or assimilation that often provides closure for the text'.[60] Yet, whereas conversion plays a part in Zoilo's biography, the English imperative of conversion does not govern *Mirror*, as illustrated by Florion's narrative, because the romance originates in a different politico-religious culture.

This consideration of Saracens and Spanish *moriscos* may appear to have unnecessarily distanced us from the consideration of Tyler's and *Mirror*'s religious outlook, but it is formative to an understanding of their cultural values. The fact is that until more biographical documentation is discovered, Tyler's religion will remain matter for speculation. The available facts point to the likelihood of her Catholicism, but too much of the evidence is potentially unreliable, and thus prevents any definitive conclusions. Hamilton conjectures that Tyler, parallel to Munday, wrote potentially subversive Catholic romances, yet a close reading of *Mirror* reveals the opposite. *Mirror*'s portrayal of the Saracen world does indeed articulate a conception of alterity that is opposed to the vision typical of English romance. However, this exceptional worldview originates in *Espejo* and lingers residually in *Mirror*; it enables *Mirror* to recall and to signify difference, but it cannot be used to ascribe a politico-religious agenda nor an affiliation to Tyler. In contrast, alterations to *Espejo*'s marvels are sustained and consistent. Tyler's treatment of the marvellous is consistent with Protestant scepticism and distrust of the fantastic which is apparent in anti-Catholic polemic and in the romances of her Protestant contemporaries. This romance cannot be definitely assigned to either camp; it reflects that hybrid sensibility that is typical of so many texts in Reformation England. So, to return to the questions posed at the outset of this section: Was Tyler a Catholic translator? Probably. Is *Mirror* a Catholic translation? Definitely not.

'VERY WISE [...] AND AS THE TIMES AFFORDED, VERY WELL LEARNED': TYLER'S EDUCATION

In a revealing addition, Tyler praises Olivia as 'very wise [...] and as the times afforded, very well learned' (34.55), a description equally applicable to Tyler herself. Like Tyler's religion, her educational background is shrouded in mystery. Krontiris plausibly conjectures that '[s]ervice in aristocratic households [...] became an opportunity for learning', providing Tyler with access

---

[59] Geraldine Heng, 'Jews, Saracens, "Black Men," Tartars: England in a World of Racial Difference', p. 260.
[60] Robinson, *Islam and Early Modern English Literature*, p. 38.

to a wide range of vernacular and classical texts (p. 27). We do not know where or how she was educated, but her proficiency in Spanish combined with her extensive knowledge of classical, literary, and Biblical sources, oratory, and rhetoric show her to be 'as the times afforded, very well learned' indeed.

Exhibiting the scope of her reading, Tyler adds references to classical authors, characters, locations, and objects including: Mansolus's tomb (9.77), Ulysses (9.91; 44.328), Xerxes's armies (22.37), the Trojan horse (23.99), the cedars of Libanus (23.90), the sibyls (25.60), Mars (31.73), Cupid (32.30), Romulus (39.121), Virgil (39.148), Agathocles King of Sicily (39.144), Jupiter Ammon (39.154), Sophonisba (40.134), Hector (43.133), the island of Paros (44.61), the harts of Crete (44.45), the sons of Titan (44.245), Jupiter (44.246), Argos (44.329), Lucius Tarquinius Superbus (39.136), and the Roman consuls, Aulus Atilius Serranus and Lucius Quinctius Cincinnatus (39.130). The romance tradition is summoned with references to Gawain (32.112), Roncesvalles (19.189), and Rogel de Grecia (19.222). English drama is equally invoked (34.54–55; 36.131–32). Added scriptural allusions include the Sodomites (28.79) and Jephthah (39.155). Such references imbue the text with a greater scope of reference and they demonstrate the wide extent of Tyler's knowledge.

Classical allusions are occasionally altered or corrected. Tyler changes Marco Tulo to Cicero (39.128); she situates Vulcan's forge in Lemnos (24.15); Macón is corrected to Mars (24.120), and Pirgotiles to Praxiteles (44.179). Discussing 'Servius Tullius [who] was son to a bondwoman', she adds 'as his name importeth', exhibiting a working knowledge of Latin (39.137). She omits the link of Pluto to the Furies, rendering the allusion more accurate (I.206.1; 24.119); the Furies were occasionally linked to Pluto because they were all situated in the underworld and because of confusion between Pluto and Zeus Chthonios and between the Eumenides and the Furies (Zeus Chthonios was the Eumenides' father.)

In several instances, Tyler enlarges the extant allusion, manifesting her intellectual engagement with her source. For example, the passage, 'And as the learned well know, Achilles hath his Pallas in Homer, and Aeneas his Venus in Virgil, goddesses assistant unto men in their dangerous conflicts — Homer and Virgil meaning no other thing than the care of God towards his' (15.14), exhibits a familiarity with the classical stories as well as their source texts. Hutson argues that by personifying the deities Tyler emphasizes female agency, which reflects her authorial self-presentation in the dedication to the romance, as 'assistant unto men in their dangerous conflicts', as will be considered below.[61] The addition moreover demonstrates her involvement with the material, as she attempts to reconcile classical narrative to Christian doctrine. A similar concern is apparent in the added allusion to Phaeton and Phoebus (17.144–47).

Since the excision of classical allusions is atypical of Tyler's methodology, the rare instances of omission merit investigation. The absences of Cupid (33.113; 44.7), African Hannibal (38.120), Samson (38.121–22), and Caesar (40.134–35) are puzzling and no logical explanation can be conjectured. The two elisions of Diana, however, especially when considered in conjunction with the substitutions of Minerva for Diana, seem intentional; they reduce Diana's associations with the moon and emphasize her hunterly skills, thereby firmly linking the goddess to Claridiana. After replacing a personification of the moon as Diana (I.258.2) with a simple reference to the moon (30.119), a comparison of Diana to the moon and to Princess Olivia is excised (I.258.3). *Espejo* compares Olivia's and Diana's beauty, emphasizing their extreme attractiveness by likening them to the moon's brightness as compared to less luminous stars (II.23.7–11); by removing Diana from the laudatory comparison, her link to the moon is expunged while praise for Olivia's luminous beauty remains (32.225).

As Diana's connection to the moon is diminished, her link to the hunt is increased. Tyler corrects Ortúñez's erroneous association of Minerva with hunting: Diana is the goddess of the hunt, whereas Minerva is the goddess of wisdom, poetry, and weaving. Accordingly, references

---

[61] Hutson, *Usurer's Daughter*, pp. 92–93.

to Minerva as a 'lady huntress' are replaced with allusions to Diana. Upon first meeting Claridiana, Zoilo compares her to Diana rather than Minerva, because of her beauty and her 'lady huntress['s . . .] attire' (45.42). Claridiana's response accordingly maintains her resemblance to Diana rather than to Minerva (45.48). Not only are these allusions to Diana more accurate than those in *Espejo*, but also the comparison of Claridiana to Diana underscores their link to the hunt. The nexus of Claridiana, Diana, and hunting is further accentuated in Claridiana's autobiographical revelations: she discloses that she has practised the sport since childhood and that her mother is named Diana. Furthermore, since Claridiana's mother is the queen of the Amazons, a race of warrior women renowned for their prowess in hunting and war, hunting is further invoked through her genealogy. In early modern English writing, Diana was not commonly recognized as the leader of the Amazons; however, Diana and the Amazons are often linked because of their nebulous connection to lesbian sexuality.[62] Here, positioning Diana at the helm of the Amazons echoes the connection of the goddess Diana to hunting, and the prominence of hunting concomitantly serves to neutralize the feminist, separatist Amazonian ideology since Claridiana's entourage is comprised of equal numbers of male and female knights and 'there is no distinction between the function of the Amazons and that of the Christian knights'.[63]

Diana's strength as a huntress is transferred to Claridiana, who is configured as heir to her prowess. The genealogical alliance of Diana and Claridiana coupled with their shared proficiency is, of course, strengthened by Claridiana's name. The prefix *clari-* is derived from the Latin verb *clarare*, which signifies to make bright, clear or visible, or to make illustrious or famous. Claridiana is thus a bright, famed Diana. Although Diana's affinity to the moon is diminished in *Mirror*, Claridiana's name recalls Diana's associations with the moon's luminance and her renown as a celebrated goddess. This more subtle invocation of Diana's lunar attributes does not detract from her physical prowess, which remains foregrounded in her representation and, thus, dominates the portrayal of Claridiana. This presentation also accords more closely with Queen Elizabeth's metaphorical likeness to Diana, which draws on her virginity, strength, and luminous beauty (the latter, of course, is more thoroughly emphasized through her association with Cynthia, Diana's lunar aspect), which may partially explain Tyler's careful sorting out of allusions.

Alongside her extensive reading, Tyler's knowledge of oratory and rhetoric are also suggestive of a high level of education. Slight alterations made to the epistles exchanged by Rosicleer, Olivia, and Briana ensure that they conform to proper dictaminal format. The *ars dictaminis* is the branch of rhetoric devoted to the systemization and instruction of letter writing. It was the dominant epistolary technique throughout the Western European Middle Ages and it continued to influence letter writing in the early modern period through Latin and vernacular epistolary manuals and through instruction in formal educational institutions including grammar schools and the Inns of Court and Chancery.[64] Based on the Ciceronian oration, the dictaminal letter is divided into five parts: *salutatio*, the formal greeting; *captatio benevolentiae* or *exordium proverbium*, the securing of good will; *narratio*, the statement of facts; *petitio*, the request for action; and *conclusio*, the formal leave taking. Accordingly, a *salutatio* and *conclusio* are added to Olivia's letter to Rosicleer in Ch 40 and to Rosicleer's letter to Briana in Chapter 41. At the start of Africano's letter to the sultan, the phrase 'send greeting unto thee' replaces 'a ti' (to you,

---

[62] Jennifer Drouin, 'Diana's Band: Safe Spaces, Publics, and Early Modern Lesbianism', *Queer Renaissance Historiography*, pp. 85–110.
[63] Joan Curbet, 'Repressing the Amazon: Cross-Dressing and Militarism in Edmund Spenser's *The Faerie Queene*', p. 166. Curbet offers a comparison of the Amazons in *Mirror* with those in *The Faerie Queene*.
[64] See James J. Murphy, *Rhetoric in the Middle Ages: A History of Rhetorical Theory from Saint Augustine to the Renaissance*.

I.181.26), enabling the sentence to function as a proper salutation (22.43). Also, an English superscription adorns Rosicleer's letter to Olivia.

Like the epistolary transformations, the additions of rhetorical tropes and devices establish Tyler's erudition, but they also bear witness to her literary sophistication as they enrich, enliven, and anglicize her text, as will be further discussed in the next section. As Deborah Uman and Belén Bistué declare: 'While not strictly word for word, Tyler's careful translation of the Spanish text suggests that she is in control of the small variations in syntax and vocabulary that bring the text closer to her English audience'.[65] She adds, and this list is far from exhaustive, alliteration (5.21; 9.108; 9.123; 23.166; 26.10; 41.75; 51.82), similes (15.95–96; 23.59; 32.211; 34.27; 35.46; 41.75; 44.30; 51.83), synecdoche (24.181), anaphora (21.104), allegory or extended metaphor (33.282–86; 34.163–67; 39.98–109), *exclamatio* (32.230–31; 36.32–33; 38.25; 39.32; 44.466–67), rhyme (39.232), *adhortatio* (47.187), apostrophe (32.226–31; 40.129–30), comparison (30.30; 31.24–25), *diacope* (32.48; 40.137), litotes (23.52; 46.68; 52.87), hyperbole (31.128–29), personification (7.31; 21.41; 31.50; 32.275–86; 34.163–67), *conduplicatio* (32.145; 40.137), and *syncrisis* (49.37), polyptoton (34.147–48), antanaclasis (36.177), and irony (29.79–80). She also embellishes her prose with a variety of *erotema* or rhetorical questions (29.111–12; 31.114–17; 42.50–52; 44.496–97; 50.14–16), such as *anacoenosis* (18.60–61; 23.174–76; 24.87–89), *psyma* (21.90–93; 21.103–12) *epiplexis* (20.83; 21.103–10; 51.52–56; 52.42; 55.44–45), *dianoea* (40.93–103), and *anthypophora* (39.215–16; 42.44–47; 44.267–68). Countering this tendency to add interrogative phrases, questions are also occasionally transformed into declarative statements (9.61–62; 11.5–6; 23.175–77; 40.93–94; 45.123–24; 52.43–45), *exclamatio* (18.12), or *aganactesis* (44.354). An abundance of metaphors is added (7.50; 8.46; 10.46; 11.16; 11.46; 18.17; 18.20; 19.198–200; 21.113; 25.14–16; 25.38–89; 26.4–5; 27.29–30; 29.5; 30.174; 31.107–08; 32.273; 32.342–43; 34.8; 34.56; 35.31; 36.99–100; 39.104–09; 39.171–74), some of which form figurative clusters of theatre imagery (34.54–55; 36.131–32; 44.395), educational imagery (36.182–84; 52.101) imagery of the elements, specifically wind and fire (19.198; 21.113; 25.14; 32.273; 35.31), imagery of flowering or flourishing (26.4–5; 31.107–08; 32.41; 39.59) imagery of consuming food or drink (29.5; 32.342; 36.99–100; 41.75–77), medical language (11.16; 19.142–43; 34.59–60; 36.99–100; 39.97; 39.100; 50.21), legal language (7.50; 20.85–86; 32.274–85), and nautical language (15.86; 16.77–79; 30.116). Whether or not Tyler received any formal education, her rhetorical proficiency, her knowledge of classical, literary, and biblical sources, and her deeply attuned literary sensibility, demonstrate the erudition and sophistication of her writing, which is astonishing for a woman of her era and social class.

'DONE INTO ENGLISH FOR THY PROFIT AND DELIGHT': TRANSLATION METHODOLOGY

Mirror is a cautious and meticulous translation of *Espejo*. Since the variants between the two Spanish editions that predate *Mirror* — 1555 and 1562 — are slight, and since, rather than proceed lexeme by lexeme, Tyler tends to work at the unit of the phrase or sentence, it is difficult to positively identify Tyler's source. However, in Chapter 39, a line is omitted from the 1555 edition, creating an incomprehensible text. Tyler omits the flawed sentence in its entirety, which suggests that she was working from that first edition (II.109.4–10).

Tyler's work is accurate and impressive. Mistranslations are few, and are indicated in the textual notes. As she translates she condenses the text by omitting doublets, adjectives, descriptive phrases, and repetitions. In most instances, each more succinct English sentence has its Spanish counterpart. By the end of *Mirror*, Tyler takes more liberties with her source, habitually replacing sequences of sentences or whole paragraphs with single English sentences,

---
[65] Uman and Bistué, 'Translation as Collaborative', pp. 298–323.

all of which accurately summarize her source. Because her *modus operandi* is to reduce and summarize rather than to omit whole scale, her translation remains faithful to her source text: the plot is preserved intact, but the verbal expansiveness of her source is replaced by a crisper, smoother text. Tyler's translation methodology is also characterized by tendencies to increase stylistic variety through changes to the narrative mode and the addition of poetic language, and to anglicize the romance, all of which will be considered below. Anglicization through the post-Reformation portrayal of the marvellous and the addition of various rhetorical devices and tropes has already been discussed, but anglicization is likewise a crucial element of Tyler's translation methodology. She makes her text appear more like a native English romance though an increased emphasis on the themes of friendship and jealousy, a more positive depiction of the English Prince Edward, the addition of English expressions and proverbs, references to English fauna and flora and customs, omissions of the importance of marriage for the sole female heir, and corrected allusions to English geography.

This sentence from the beginning of *Mirror* illustrates Tyler's habitual methodology of condensation:

> His virtue, by the report of such as knew him, was so rare that it was generally thought none of his predecessors to have had advantage over him, but rather he was of greater force then any one of them all for many men were witnesses of his mighty strokes. (1.29–32)

And *Espejo*:

> Y era tanta su bondad, que no pensavan los que conoscían averle tenido ventaja ninguno de sus antepassados. Antes dezían aver seído de mayores fuerças que ninguno dellos, porque le vieron muchas vezes hender y partir por medio un cavallero armado. (I.28.3–8)

Both passages explain that Trebatio is deemed to be of equal greatness to his illustrious ancestors. His standing is then qualified, as the text explains that those who have seen Trebatio perform chivalric deeds would rank him more highly than his predecessors. The essential points are there, but slight differences between the two accounts exist. Tyler classifies his virtue as 'so rare' and she replaces the gory detail of cleaving knights in two with the more neutral 'mighty strokes'.

Blood, gore, battle scenes, and descriptions of the knights' armour are invariably abridged. An illustrative example occurs in Chapter 44, in which Tyler halves the description of the Knight of the Sun's fight with the serpent on Lindaraza's island: 197 English words convey approximately 400 words in *Espejo*. But notwithstanding the reduction of the text, the essential details are preserved. *Espejo* evocatively begins:

> E la espantosa serpiente, como se vio suelta, dando grandes y temerosos silvos començó de subir por las gradas arriba con la boca abierta, que fácilmente cupiera un hombre por ella. E mostrava unos grandes y muy agudos colmillos; que según parescía de fiera y cruel, qualquier buen cavallero huviera pavor de verla. (II.180.4–10)

while *Mirror* simply asserts: 'The monstrous dragon beneath was ready to receive him' (44.100–01). It continues:

> But the nephew of Alicante lightly esteemed all this and rather took courage in this that there was something worthy his pains behind when the castle was kept by such ugly porters. (44.101–02)

The sentence preserves the vital facts from *Espejo*:

> Mas el nieto de Alicante, que contra sí vio venir la fiera bestia, no sólo no recibió temor por ello, mas el coraçón se le alegró, paresciéndole que alguna grande cosa se le ofrescía en aquel castillo, pues por tales porteros era guardada. (II.180.10–15)

The euphemistic appellation of the Knight of the Sun is retained, although he becomes a nephew rather than a grandchild, as is the sense of his increased courage and his augmented valuation of his endeavours when he observes the type of porters guarding the castle. However, there are significant omissions, such as the approach of the fierce dragon and the mention of fear. As in the previous sentence, Tyler excises details regarding the dragon.

Espejo then relates:

> Y sacando la espada, como la serpiente llegasse a él, la boca abierta por le coger entre sus duros y agudos colmillos, le dio un tal golpe por encima de la cabeça que bien pensó avérgela hecho dos partes. Mas assí surtió la espada para arriba como si fuera de madera, sin que entrasse cosa alguna en la cabeça de la serpiente, aunque con la demasiada fuerça del terrible golpe fue algo desatinada, y no pudo hazer la presa que quería. Mas luego tornó a endereçarse, y fue otra vez por coger al Cavallero del Febo. (II.180.15–25)

Tyler again retains key information — the drawing of his sword, an unproductive blow, the serpent's reaction — thereby allowing the narrative to progress faithfully, but she persists in condensing the text:

> And drawing out his sword, he struck at the serpent a blow on the top of the head, but it did him no more harm than if it had lighted upon a smith's anvil, but it a little benumbed his senses and beguiled him of his fore-hoped grip. (44.103–05)

Her tendency to abridge is curtailed in the next sentence with the assertion, 'This little harm which he had done to the serpent did much amaze him, and the better to save himself from the serpent, he got under the pillar', which renders the Spanish almost exactly: 'Y él, muy espantado del poco daño que le avía hecho, por defenderse della se puso debaxo de la columna' (II.180.26–28). The only difference resides in the substitution of 'to save himself' for the more heroic 'to defend himself'.

Equally typical of Tyler's translation methodology is her propensity to vary and improve upon the style of her text through changes to the narrative mode and the addition of poetic language. Alterations from direct to indirect speech, or vice versa, also often herald welcome shifts in style and tone, directing the reader's attention to a specific aspect of the narrative. For instance, the increased use of direct and interjectory speech renders *Mirror* more gripping. Written in the present tense, direct speech is the most mimetic narrative mode. The lack of narrative mediation provides the illusion of immediacy, providing readers with direct access to the characters. The stylistic advantages of direct speech are equally visible in *Mirror*: frequently inserted in the midst of lengthy passages of narrative description, direct speech varies the rhythm. The additions of direct speech and alterations from indirect to direct discourse range from short added interjections, such as 'Stay!' (19.379), 'Yea' (20.111), 'Alarm!' (23.16), 'Marry', (26.24; 36.159; 37.98; 38.98; 39.170; 45.102; 45.106; 52.9) 'Amain!' (41.7) 'Peccavi!' (42.153), and 'Yea, assuredly', (44.472), to alterations of complete sentences, paragraphs, and even entire dialogues.

At the end of Lirgandeo's prophetic advice to Florion, the text switches from indirect to direct discourse as the wise man predicts: '"With these," sayeth he, "you shall return to Babylon, for these are the nurses of your good hap"' (16.73–74, I.120.23–25). By altering the final line of Lirgandeo's speech, Tyler emphasizes it, lending weight to the final portion of the prophecy, and thereby stressing the importance of the Knight of the Sun and Clavergudo in Florion's good fortune. Similarly, in the climactic moment when Trebatio takes off his helmet, revealing his identity to Clandestria, *Espejo* has a lengthy description of the event (II.274.10–21), which Tyler replaces with a short dialogue (49.92–98). In a few words the conversation expresses the revelation and surprise as effectively as the description of the events, if not more so. Direct speech may also be used to increase a character's significance. Telio's voice emerges as he speaks directly to Rosicleer and becomes a named character in the romance. Upon his request to serve Rosicleer, the text reflects his transformation from 'a younger brother of Liverba's called Telio' to 'Telio', a named, actualized character in his own right (30.20). The Spanish relates Telio's question indirectly (I.253.18–21).[66]

Transformations of direct into indirect speech are equally effective in terms of style and narrative structure. Unlike in *Espejo*, in *Mirror* the old man begins to recount Princess Arguirosa's history as indirect speech: 'he told him in few words that [. . .]' (47.50). When his story converges with the present situation and his own involvement in the story, the narrative mode shifts and *Mirror* faithfully returns to the direct speech used throughout the discursive unit in the Spanish text: '"I am kinsman," sayeth he, "to the princess [. . .]"' (47.65). Emphasis is thus duly placed on the crucial section of the man's story. Similarly, by transforming the beginning of one of Rosicleer's speeches from direct to indirect speech, discursive variety is utilized to alert readers to Rosicleer's key point. The narrator explains how Rosicleer offered thanks to the old man, before letting Rosicleer's voice emerge. Rosicleer's thanks are a formal necessity of politesse; they are not significant in terms of characterization or plot development. The most significant information is Rosicleer's offer to fight Rolando and his denial of all knowledge of the new knight, although he is that new knight. The importance of these declarations is highlighted through the discursive shift.[67]

Tyler also provides stylistic variety by adorning her text with poetic language. Often she only alters her text slightly, but the effect is striking, as in the following two examples. The statement 'The hour clock hath smitten thrice since they entered the lists' (21.117–18) replaces the prosaic assertion that three and a half hours had already passed since they began the battle (I.173.2–3). Rather than simply identifying the amount of elapsed time, Tyler adds auditory imagery and renders a passive sentence active. Likewise, *Mirror* recounts 'that the enemy whom they purposed to find abroad came to seek them at their own doors' (22.23–24) rather than 'en su tierra' [on their land] (I.180.15–17). By substituting 'doors' for 'land', the enemy threat becomes more personal: beating down the front doors of their homes is more intimidating than an enemy force arriving somewhere in the country. In the next example, Tyler adds a series of evocative poetic devices. She translates 'Porque ansí es, que quando alguna cosa es forçado que se le ha de seguir al hombre próspera, qualquier adversidad o impedimento que le venga suele ser camino para llegar a ella' (I.218.11–15) as 'For so it is that when anything is forced by the stars as to succeed prosperously unto a man, albeit mountains of adversity impugn and assail him, yet can they never expunge his good fortune, but in the end he recovereth his quiet rest maugre the malice of misadventure' (26.9–10). Her additions include allusions to the stars and fortune, the metaphor and personification of 'mountains of adversity', the descriptions of 'quiet rest' and 'malice of misadventure', and the personification and alliteration in the latter phrase. The changes draw links between the hero and his relationship to the natural and supernatural worlds, emphasising their interconnectedness and their respective agency in the outcome, while the alliteration creates two opposed linguistic and thematic nexuses of recovery / rest and malice / misadventure. By writing 'to see the liquid sea so soon converted to solid earth' (31.38–39), Tyler opposes the material states of liquid and solid and refers to a transformative process, while her source recounts simply that where he saw that there was sea he now saw this island (I.267.12–14). In the next example, by describing the princess's tears and adding the adjective 'tender', the emotional intensity is heightened. Tyler's 'it might wring some tears from so tender a princess, yet in process of time would as well dry them up, his valour making amends for his sudden departure' (27.91–92) translates 'su partida causasse alguna pena a la princessa, quél haría

---

[66] Other instances of added direct speech occur in Chapters 4.34–36; 5.95; 9.54; 14.72–73; 17.73–74; 17.133–34; 20.111; 21.137; 23.62; 23.198; 28.72; 30.23; 30.27–29; 32.189; 33.86; 36.158; 38.48–49; 40.60–61; 42.19; 42.153; 50.80; 51.97; 52.52–53; 54.9–10; 55.55–56; 55.71–72; 56.15–16.
[67] For some additional examples of the shift to indirect speech, see Chapters 20.13; 23.129; 29.55; 33.57–59; 40.182; 45.142–43; 46.41; 47.50–51.

después tales cosas por donde viniessse a lo tener por bien, y a ser muy contenta en quél huviesse dexado aquella vida que tenía' (I.234.6–9). The series of oppositions — wet and dry, 'process of time' and 'sudden departure', her tenderness and his valour, his action and her being acted upon — economically evokes a dynamic, psychologically passionate situation.

Friendship was of great interest to writers in England and on the Continent, although the theme did not attract Ortúñez to the same extent as it did Tyler. Reflecting the importance of amity in early modern thought, additions and alterations advance friendship as an important theme in the romance, helping to lend the text a more contemporaneous feel. Fortune is described as 'friendly' rather than 'próspera' [prosperous] (1.10, I.26.9; 4.47, I.41.21; I.127.7). Briana (11.18–19), Olivia (39.208), Fidelia (39.186), and Florinaldes (52.99–103) worry about their reputation amongst their friends. Romantic love and friendship are compared or equated by Clarinea (46.99, II.236.16), Olivia (40.110–11), and Claridiana (45.54–55). Gratitude for mercy, care, or salvation is replaced with thankfulness for friendship by Calinda (31.5–6; I.264.9), Artimodoro (31.77, I.269.2), Rosicleer (43.166–67, II.169.3–4; II.167.11), the Knight of the Sun (26.110, I.225.8), and the King of Polonia (46.126, II.238.7). Sadness results from being estranged from friends for Rosicleer, Telio, and the narrator (30.33–34, 168–71). Additions or alterations stress the intensity of the friendships between Donzel del Febo and Brandizel (34.98–99), Zoilo and Rosicleer (40.250), and Fidelia and Olivia (39.208, II.110.19). Bargandel, Liriamandro, and Zoilo's friendship with Rosicleer is emphasized (32; 34; 45). The adjective 'friendly' is used to describe the Sultan's 'countenance' (18.36), Florion's 'manner' of reclaiming his land (25.51, I.215.26), Balides's and Claridiana's hospitality (28.106; II.219.5), Rosicleer's 'embrace' (37.13) and his acquaintance with Donzel del Febo (47.13). Family members (48.86, II.264.10), many onlookers (29.32, I.245.10), a principal man (52.118, II.304.1–2), those people (20.167, I.164.4) and the king and all the mighty princes and knights (34.56, II.43.19–20) all become 'friends'. News of the tournament in Great Britain is spread through 'friends' letters' (30.90), and Rosicleer mentions 'counsel of friends' (38.127) in his letter to Olivia.

Friendship's underside, jealousy, also accrues in importance in *Mirror*. The emotional sin rears its head when 'los otros' (the others, I.148.20) succumb to 'gran embidia' (great envy, I.148.20) of Donzel del Febo. By expanding upon this suggestion of jealousy in *Espejo*, intrigue and emotional complexity come to characterize Donzel and Clavergudo's relationship. Clavergudo 'wish[es]' Donzel's victory 'to himself', and his jealous desire to rival his friend in greatness inspires Clavergudo's actions (19.185). Florinaldes's jealousy of Donzel is transformed into friendship, further revealing the affinity of the two themes (54). Rosicleer's triumphs likewise arouse jealousy in his friends: Bargandel and Liriamandro were 'in some jealousy of the knight' (34.97). These additions expand upon and nuance the notion of amity, invoking its treacherous retroversion: jealousy can rapidly corrode alliances, transforming friends into enemies.

The alternate political, nationalist visions manifested in *Espejo* and *Mirror*, previously discussed in relation to the presentation of the Saracens, are also revealed through anglicizing alterations made to the portrayal of Prince Edward. Shortly after we encounter 'the great Trebatio', Prince Edward of Great Britain is introduced: 'This young knight — strong, and valiant' is also 'greatly enamoured on the Princess Briana' (2.30–31). Parental consent attained, Edward sets off to Hungary to aid Briana's father in his war against Trebatio and to claim his bride. The opposition of Edward to Trebatio, who is clearly identified as the romance's hero, should caution readers from sympathizing too greatly with Edward. However, since Edward is 'young [. . .] strong and valiant', our initial impression is positive. By likening him to the great champion Paris, his heroic status is increased. Since Paris won Helen, the allusion implies that Edward will likewise attain success in his pursuit of Briana. Moreover, his Englishness renders him more sympathetic to an English audience than an eastern European emperor. When Trebatio falls in love with Briana, seeking to marry her despite her betrothal to Edward and her father's enmity, the English reader becomes disoriented because, first, our hero Trebatio's desires are dishonourable and, second, he becomes Edward's enemy. The disorientation is arguably greater for English readers: not only are they more inclined than readers of other nationalities to accept the Prince of Great Britain as a rival hero to Trebatio, but in *Espejo* Edward is first introduced as 'orgulloso' (proud, I.33.2), a detail omitted by Tyler.

It is once Trebatio and Edward meet that *Mirror* begins to cast doubt on Edward's character, admitting that he was 'given to somewhat less modesty in his talk then behoved such a prince' (5.63–64). She twice mediates the character defect 'sobervio' (haughty, 5.63; 5.77, I.46.2, 23–24), replacing it with the more ambiguous adjective 'stout', which can mean 'proud', but also denotes 'fierce, brave, resolute' and strong.[68] His make-up is only tarnished immediately prior to the fatal battle when it is revealed that his bravery is due to 'immeasurable pride' (5.77). But as his moral flaw is revealed, it is qualified; the depiction of him as peerless is retained: 'Howbeit for this and other faults, he was a very valiant and strong knight, such a one as neither in Great Britain, neither in the Kingdom of Hungary, was thought to have his peer' (5.64–66). Whereas an excess of pride is not befitting a romance hero, its attribution to Edward is overdue and comes with too many qualifications to entirely alter the English perception of Edward as heroic and worthy of Princess Briana. Furthermore, his proud behaviour in this situation is entirely appropriate since he must defend himself and his knights from Trebatio and his men who have ignobly ambushed them. Dramatic irony is used to warn readers of Edward's demise: the journey to Hungary 'seemed long unto him as being ignorant of the sour sauce and woeful wedding which was in providing' (5.20–21); he 'not well foreseeing his own fall', fights Trebatio; and he is plagued by 'adverse fortune and unhappy destinies' (5.73–74; 5.80). The foreshadowings of Edward's death, just like the tardy mentions of his pride, are too little too late; they cannot dislodge the earlier evocation of his heroic status. As a result we lament Edward's death, and a sense of horror is invoked through Trebatio's dishonourable treatment of the English knights as he massacres them, fleeces their bodies of the weaponry and documents he may need, callously tosses them into an unmarked communal grave, and 'covered them with earth in such sort that there was never memory of them' (5.116). Trebatio's gruesome actions in this shocking scene definitively assert his superiority over the British contingent and confirm that Edward is not *Mirror's* hero. Expectations are reversed and English readers are forced to shift sympathies and follow the adventures of Trebatio, the romance's real hero. Notwithstanding Tyler's attempts at anglicization, *Mirror's* roots are not English.

In contrast, the inclusion of characteristically English expressions naturalizes the text, somewhat obscuring its Spanish roots. For instance, 'no se queriendo detener con ellos en palabras' (I.65.19–20) becomes 'without either good-even or good-morrow' (8.45); 'sin le hablar palabra' (I.124.14–15) is 'without "God speed you"' (17.22–23); 'I would suffer a thousand deaths' (20.97) replaces a simple mortal wish (I.158.8–9); 'el qual no podrá sufrirte más sin te dar la muerte' (I.195.22–23) is changed to 'But I will curtail thy copy with this currish answer' (23.166–67); 'ink and paper' and 'it' are expanded to 'pen, ink, and paper', and the expression also comprises an addition (39.223, II:112:1; 42.162; 42.164, II:150:6, 8). The following expressions are added: 'to make up a full mess of disport' (9.9), 'won his spurs' (24.13), 'and at his first good-morrow' (26.47) and 'for other good-morrow' (43.86), 'hue and cry' (28.12), 'hurly burly' (38.54), 'Why how now' (36.13), 'it was no boot' (38.25), 'the rod of due correction' (47.196), 'But if I may meddle in school points' (52.101).

A similar effect is created through the addition of proverbs and apothegms. Some such examples are: 'well may the body lawfully enter where the heart is harboured' (6.31–32); 'more haste by half than good speed' (19.91; H197);[69] 'and with bag and baggage to march homewards' (13.10); 'let him win her and wear her, for be he what he may be' (21.96–97; W731); 'lest by overslipping the opportunity we too late repent our too much daintiness' (25.15–16; recalls G17, M875, R32, R80, R77); 'But thy ignorance makes thee leap beyond thy lash (33.91); 'abandoned

---

[68] 'stout', *OED* A.I.1.a, b and 3.a, II.6.a.
[69] Citations refer to M. P. Tilley, *A Dictionary of Proverbs in England in the Sixteenth and Seventeenth Centuries*.

themselves to wind and weather' (28.74; recalls W220, W414, W446, which link wind and weather); 'no kith nor kin' (41.61; K117); and 'one nail driveth out another' (39.198; N17).

Added references to typically English fauna and flora and to English customs similarly anglicize the romance. For example, a light bird (I.66.18) is rendered more specifically as a 'swallow' (8.60); woodland animals large and small (II.76.2–3) become the 'little beaverette and the small cony [. . .] beside the light squirrel climbing the tall oak' (44.41–42); A 'hazel wand' (44.202) replaces a thin stick (II.189.16). The swallow, beaver, cony, squirrel, and oak and hazel trees may exist outside of England, but since they are all well known to English readers they help readers visualize a familiar, native landscape. Tyler makes reference to the 'chamber of presence' (34.193), 'groom-porter' (51.10), 'Lords and Barons' (32.45, II.10.25–26), a 'muffler' (46.142), and she adds the passage in which Rosicleer's device and posy are described (33.8–10). *Letras* or posies are typical of both Spanish and English romance, but the addition of this romance device helps to make *Mirror* adhere to the generic expectations of English readers in which such mottos were frequently described. The Spanish-Arabic architectural style 'a la morisca' (I.269.20), which could alienate English readers due to its unfamiliarity, is replaced by statement of firm complicity, referring to the 'craft of masonry in our days' (31.66).

Further anglicizing the romance, Tyler omits both of King Oliverio's reassurances to Princess Olivia that he will not arrange her marriage without her consent. Notwithstanding this commitment to his daughter, he vocalizes commonly held worries about an unmarried queen's ability to successfully rule and defend the kingdom alone. These concerns regarding female leadership were much debated throughout Elizabeth's reign. Because women were deemed intellectually and physically inferior to men and thus incapable of engaging in political strategizing or warfare, it was generally believed that a queen could only rule with the assistance of a strong consort. As David Atkinson observes, 'Whereas romance and consent could play a role in the formation of nuptial bonds for many couples, for a princess and heir to the throne, forging viable political connections trumped consent'.[70] Acting counter to expectation, Elizabeth's control over her marital status resulted in large-scale national anxiety: marriage and the production of an heir were deemed necessary for political stability and the continuance of the Tudor line. Elizabeth clearly understood the political aspects of marriage, as demonstrated by her successive negotiations with continental suitors. However, by the late 1570s, the time of *Mirror*'s composition, Elizabeth was already in her 40s and the prospect of birthing an heir was slim. She had already begun to inspire a cult of virginity as well as accusations of irresponsibility and selfishness for creating a succession problem, thereby leaving England open to invasion or civil war after her death. This controversy is likely to have informed Tyler's omission of the question of a princess's consent in marriage.

The romance heroes traverse a large geographical expanse from England across Europe and into Asia and Northern Africa. Many place names are altered in *Mirror*, either in an attempt to make them more familiar to English readers, to correct flaws in her source, or to increase the text's realism, recalling the treatment of English geography discussed above. In *Mirror*, 'El mar Tirreno' becomes the Mediterranean, also referred to as the Middle Earth Sea (22.15, I.180.1; 44.17, II.172.13) or the Mediteraneum (44.7, II.172.13). The Tyrrhenian Sea is the part of the Mediterranean just off the west coast of Italy, enclosed by the islands of Corsica, Sardinia, and Sicily. While it is the more accurate name for the body of water described in the romance, the Mediterranean is a more commonly used name for the sea. The better-known Mediterranean likewise stands in for 'Ponte Euxino', the Graeco-Roman name for the Black Sea (16.71, I.120.20). The alteration of the fictional 'el mar Oceano' [the Ocean Sea] to 'ocean' (26.113, I.225.13–14; 44.7, II.172.11–12) or 'wide West Seas' (26.114–15; I.225.17), a name common for the Atlantic, increases the text's realism. Two more references are made to the West Ocean, one is a straightforward addition and the second renders an allusion to 'el mar' [the sea] more specific

---

[70] 'Marriage under Compulsion in English Renaissance Drama', p. 486; see also, Lawrence Stone, *The Crisis of the Aristocracy 1558–1641*, pp. 594–612.

INTRODUCTION

(44.5, II.172.16). Through a slight omission *Mirror* corrects the assertion that Rosicleer can see the African island of Mauritius from the Tyrrhenian Sea (II.173.10). In the same passage the reference to 'las Españas' (II.173.11–12) is explicated as 'Spain, Portugal' (44.17). Before describing the Knight of the Sun's circumnavigation of the Italian peninsula, Tyler develops the setting: 'Although by shore on the right hand he left Africa, Carthage, and Tures', again intensifying the verisimilitude (44.19–20). *Espejo* asserts that as the Knight of the Sun passes Mount Etna he could also see the ruins of Carthage (II.173.28). Tyler alters Carthage to the 'ruinous relics of old Syracuse' since it is impossible to simultaneously view Mount Etna and Carthage: Carthage is across the sea to the west of Sicily whereas Mount Etna is on the island's east coast; Syracuse, however, is also located on the eastern coast island of Sicily, approximately 75 kms south of Mount Etna. Ortúñez accidentally declares that Prince Edward was missed in Hungary rather than in his native England, which Tyler remedies (30.195, I.262.27). Zoilo twice declares that he is from Great Tartary, adjoining Europe (37.26–27, II.75.26–27; 44.246–47, II.222.8–9) but of the two Tartaries the smaller one (modern Crimea) was closer to Europe, and the larger Tartary extended across most of central Asia. By omitting 'aquella mayor' [the greater] as a qualification of Tartary, Tyler remedies yet another error.

When the heroes arrive in England, Tyler corrects geographical errors and also renders the setting more precise. *Espejo* repeatedly situates the English court in London, rather than Westminster. Tyler either omits 'London' (32.326–27; 34.3; 36.3; 36.165) or alters it to 'court' (35.101; 36.146; 39.4; 40.224). She specifies that after travelling through Germany the port that Rosicleer encounters is Picardy (30.46), clarifies that the lists are in Great Britain (31.139), the jousts are in London (30.97), and that Zoilo landed 'on the English shore, then coming out of Duchland' (40.249). She also exclaims upon the great value of London: 'and would have bought out the giant's presence if he might for more than London is worth' (32.116). Additional references to 'the villages near to London' (32.37) and 'the Thames' (40.80) likewise augment the realism, situate the narrative firmly in England, and render it more English. The romance is further anglicized and grounded in the country through additions such as: 'able to make English of every word' (31.110), and the patriotic 'that never England more flourished of knights, nor never nation was like to England' (32.41).

'A MATTER MORE MANLIKE THAN BECOMMETH MY SEX': GENDER AND ROMANCE

Despite Tyler's linguistic proficiency and her command of such a wide range of scholarly material, she demeans her intellectual abilities in *Mirror*'s prologue. This is unsurprising considering her gender, the genre in which she was writing, and the cultural status of translation. Perceived as allied with Catholic, medieval, and continental immorality, romance was subject to harsh criticism by contemporary moralists, as examined above. It was considered to be dangerous reading material, and deemed as especially perilous for women, who were thought to be lacking the necessary intellect to avoid its precarious snares. Many of the prolific warnings against romance configure the literary form as specifically and decisively female. Yet, despite the feminization of romance, women did not write texts in the genre. Tyler was the first woman to write a romance in English, which explains her extensive justification of her actions in *Mirror*'s prologue. Rather than dwell on attacks such as Vives', which counsel women to avoid romance, Tyler harnesses the feminization of romance and uses it to her advantage. Her argument is enhanced and supported by the gendering of translation as feminine and inferior to original compositions. As John Florio famously declared, 'all translations are reputed femalls' because they are 'defective'.[71]

---

[71] *The essayes or morall, politike and millitarie discourses of Lo: Michaell de Montaigne*, A2ʳ. See Lamb, 'The Cooke Sisters', pp. 115–17, for an analysis of Florio's language. Cf. Lori Chamberlain, 'Gender and the Metaphorics of Translation', p. 59.

In contrast to the more active, masculine domain of authorship, the relative passivity of translation, coupled with its secondary, derivative status rendered the activity acceptable for women. 'Yet the permission to translate did not also carry with it a licence to cross the boundaries of gender and subject matter' (Krontiris, p. 17). Thus, like many contemporary female translators, Tyler employs the modesty topos, hides behind the persuasive influence of 'others', who urge her to write, and invokes the authority of a male patron.[72] Devising a highly sophisticated strategy of self-authorization, Tyler employs the negative assumptions about female intellect, the frivolity of romance, and the perceived inferiority of translation in order to articulate a highly prescient manifesto for female romance authorship. Unfortunately, her romance is 'an isolated and idiosyncratic case' (Hackett, p. 62): her cause was not taken up until more than forty years later by Mary Wroth, whose *The Countess of Montgomery's Urania* was published in 1621.

The romance genre was feminized through a variety of textual and paratexual strategies including prefatory dedications and narratorial asides to female readers, the popularity of female eponymous characters, and moral attacks and satires of female readers of the genre. Following on from this generic presentation, romance reading was configured as a sexualized male experience whereby men could spy on a private female sphere. Yet while these factors gender the genre as feminine, they do not necessarily point to an audience comprised exclusively, or even preponderantly, of women. Running counter to their conventional feminization, the authoring and reading of romance were primarily masculine activities. Scholars of the romance and of female reading practices have identified this association of genre and gender as a potent literary convention serving to validate male authorship at the expense of a largely imagined female readership.[73] Indeed, scholars such as Lori Humphrey Newcomb and Lorna Hutson demonstrate that for male romance writers and readers the trope of the feminized romance was central to homosocial strategies of literary advancement. Despite the professed aversion to the romance, its publication history, its regular presence in library inventories, the evidence of its manuscript circulation, and the abundance of romances adapted into dramatic form, suggest its continued appeal to a readership of both sexes.

However much men dominated the reading and writing of romance, it is important to recognize that women *did* read romances, and that they did not necessarily read them for the eroticized experiences imagined by their male contemporaries. Many scholars have convincingly argued for the possibility of subversive female reading practices, in which romance was read 'against the grain'.[74] Romances often narrate the adventures of female protagonists fighting seemingly insurmountable obstacles in order to achieve emotional fulfilment. Such accounts may have presented modes of behaviour that were in stark opposition to that of the ideal woman — stationary, domestic, chaste, silent, and obedient — which women were consistently encouraged to emulate. In fact, given the consistent aspersions cast on the morality of women who read romance, Lynette McGrath characterizes the very activity of reading them as rebellious.[75] Yet regardless of who read romances or why, it is incontestable that the genre was gendered as feminine and that it offered a recognizable imaginative space of female agency.

---

[72] Many female translators, such as Anne Cooke-Bacon, Elizabeth I, Anne Locke, and Mary Sidney, equally sought refuge in dedications to respectable women. Suzanne Trill, 'Sixteenth-Century Women's Writing: Mary Sidney's *Psalmes* and the "Femininity" of Translation', p. 145. Cf. Krontiris, *Oppositional Voices*, p. 21; Lamb, 'The Cooke Sisters', pp. 117–18.

[73] Newcomb, *Reading Popular Romance*, pp. 37–47, 104–17, Hackett, *Women and Romance*, pp. 4–19; Juliet Fleming, 'The Ladies' Man and The Age of Elizabeth', pp. 158–81; Hutson, *Usurer's Daughter*, pp. 87–114, Derek B. Alwes, 'Robert Greene's Duelling Dedications', pp. 373–95.

[74] Lamb, *Gender and Authorship in the Sidney Circle*, pp. 111–12; Krontiris, *Oppositional Voices*, pp. 26–28; Alwes, 'Robert Greene's', pp. 390–94; cf. Janice A. Radway, *Reading the Romance: Women, Patriarchy, and Popular Literature*.

[75] Lynette McGrath, *Subjectivity and Women's Poetry in Early Modern England: 'Why on the ridge should she desire to go?'*, pp. 116–17.

INTRODUCTION

While romance held the potential imaginative space for female agency, other genres afforded early modern English women a safer locus for self-expression. Female writers took refuge in genres deemed acceptable for them, such as translation, epitaphs, letters, and private devotional meditations. Spiritual writings were the most common, because women were permitted to break their silence without tarnishing their honour in order to show and promote religious devotion.[76] Women were supposed to be humble, discreet, pious, and modest; 'asserting their own intellectual competence in any secular and in most religious spheres [. . .] was to risk the charge, perhaps even by their own consciences, of being foolish, indiscrete, vain, and even irreligious, all attributes of "loose" women'.[77] Education and intellectual ability needed to be downplayed and excused. But 'whereas modern critics have suggested that the genres in which sixteenth-century women wrote [. . .] meant that they were "relegated to the margins of discourse", the contemporary writers [. . .] clearly saw their involvement in these areas as being of central social importance'.[78] Indeed, as Margaret Hannay argues, subversion and the articulation of personal and political opinions were central to female translation methodologies (Hannay, p. 4). The belief that the translator literally conveys the opinions and ideas presented in the original text, rather than vocalizing a new, personal perspective, is a major factor contributing to the feminization of translation and its perception as an appropriate activity for women. But obfuscation of the self is not a defining quality of translation. 'It was, then, the point the translator wished to make, or the meditation he or she wished to offer regarding a particular issue on a given occasion, from a particular place, by means of a translation, which prevailed over any desire to offer a textually accurate version of a noted author's work'.[79] Like the romance, which, despite its feminization, was predominantly written and read by men, translation may have been gendered female, but it was primarily a masculine activity of scholarship, and literary, political, and intellectual display (Boutcher). Indeed, translation was highly valued, even central to early modern culture and knowledge formation.[80] Tyler's authorial stance of diffidence is particularly effective because it combines the translator's and the female author's tendency towards self-deprecation, all the while encompassing the underlying belief in the significance of her voice and the value of her composition. Despite Tyler's modest claims of innocence, *Mirror* articulates her viewpoint firmly.

Tyler's concern for her reputation extends throughout the prologue, and is especially visible in her apologetic stance. Male authors and translators often adopt similar stances, 'but for women, whose right and ability to write and publish was open to serious question, it was an absolute necessity to safeguard their personal reputation from any suggestion of immodesty and pride'.[81] Female writers thus accompany their texts 'often with apologetic prefaces' with 'stories of being 'pressed' to do so [write or print] by male relations' (Martin, p. 5). Tyler accordingly employs a modesty *topos* and equivocates: 'The invention, disposition, trimming, and what else in this story is wholly another man's, my part none therein but the translation, as it were' (To reader.31–33). She is just the mouthpiece for another's ideas and is not even accountable for the

---

[76] Hannay, 'Introduction', pp. 4–5. Cf. Valerie Wayne, 'Some Sad Sentence: Vives' *Instruction of a Christian Woman*', pp. 26–27. On the predominance of religious translations amongst women's oeuvre, see Patricia Gartenberg and Nena Thames Whittemore, 'A Checklist of English Women in Print, 1475–1640', pp. 1–3, in *Renaissance Cultural Crossroads*.
[77] Lamb, 'The Cooke Sisters', p. 115.
[78] Trill, 'Sixteenth-Century Women's', pp. 146–47. On women and these genres, see Lamb, 'The Cooke Sisters', pp. 117–24.
[79] Warren Boutcher, 'The Renaissance', in *The Oxford Guide to Literature in English Translation*.
[80] See Brenda M. Hosington, 'The "Renaissance Cultural Crossroads" Catalogue: A Witness to the Importance of Translation in Early Modern Britain', pp. 251–69. Cf. F. O. Matthiesson's oft cited comment, 'A study of Elizabethan translations is a study of the means by which the Renaissance came to England', which opens his seminal work, 'Translation, an Elizabethan Art', p. 3.
[81] Jane Farnsworth, 'Margaret Tyler, Dedication, *The Mirrour of Princely Deeds and Knighthood* (1578)', p. 333.

text selection, claiming that 'so was this piece of work put upon me by others' (To reader.44–45), although she concedes that she did have the power to refuse.

In the romance, Princess Olivia echoes Tyler's rhetorical technique of professing inferiority in order to claim authority. Both women vocalize false modesty, which is rapidly subverted by their actions. In a poignant addition to the text, the princess affirms that determining the tournament's winner 'is more than hard, because it pertaineth to judgement in deeds of arms, whereunto my sex is not sufficiently abled' (34.150–52). Olivia feigns inability to judge male prowess, but then swiftly proceeds to execute judgement on the knights, awarding the honours to Rosicleer. Her behaviour recalls the custom that so scandalized Vives: 'They tell me that in certain places it is the custom for girls of noble birth to be avid spectators at tournaments of arms and to pass judgment on the bravery of the combatants [. . .]' (p. 73). Like Tyler, Olivia invokes the modesty *topos* as a shield to protect her from scorn and condemnation while she ventures into the masculine chivalric realm.

Despite her capitulation to the persuasion to write, she admits that *Mirror*'s content is 'unseemly for a woman to deal in' since its 'chief matter [. . .] is of exploits of wars', which is 'a matter more manlike then becommeth my sex' (To reader.4–5, 16). There is an implied recognition here of Vives' widely-accepted admonition that 'a young woman cannot easily be of chaste mind if her thoughts are occupied with the sword and sinewy muscles and virile strength'. Chastity is, in his estimation, 'defenseless, unwarlike, and weak' (p. 73). But Tyler neutralizes this question of acceptable subject matter by sidestepping it; instead, she shifts the focus by raising the stakes, opening up the possibility of women actually engaging in 'manlike' activity, which she does not condone. Weighed against Claridiana's knightly 'attempt[s]' and her 'bold' 'intermeddl[ing] in arms' and against what 'the ancient Amazons did', Tyler's own decision 'yet to report of arms is not so odious' (To reader.25–26). Whereas *Espejo*'s title page advertised the great chivalric deeds and very strange loves of the beautiful and excellent princess Claridiana, *Mirror*'s invokes Briana. Tyler introduces Claridiana cautiously, delaying the Amazon's entry into the romance until Tyler is able to mediate the scandalous nature of her behaviour with a comparativist explanation that enables Tyler to preserve the alignment of the masculine and the martial and to avoid the issue of women writing about war.[82] This is a highly effective auxiliary justification of female authorship, since for a woman, wielding a pen is more acceptable than a sword. But, in fact, like Claridiana, Tyler encroaches on the masculine domain.[83] However, her transgression is more covert: she presents herself as a helpless, innocent non-combatant, a drummer or a bugler, which adheres to the acceptable image of women encouraging men to achieve greatness and sharing the glory of their victory. Her secondary status is further playfully affirmed through a series of metaphorical references to herself as an injured or castrated male: a soldier with 'privy maims', a man without a plough, and an archer without a bow (To reader.19).

Additionally, the focus on the 'manlike' martial themes serves to detract attention from the romance's much more controversial and pervasive amatory and sexual content.[84] From Briana's quasi-rape by Trebatio through exclamations of lust and desire by lovesick characters to the erotic pleasures of Lindaraza's bed and her female attendants with 'breasts bare and white as snow', sexual instances, imagery, and emotion infuse the text. Harry Sieber classifies *Espejo*'s 'love motif' as 'titillating ornamentation', and it certainly persists in *Mirror*.[85] The romance's

---

[82] Since Tyler was not able to advertise female knight errantry on her title page, I have decided to put an Amazon on the cover of this edition.
[83] Cf. Uman and Bistué, who observe that Claridiana, like Diana and Lindaraza, echo Tyler's paratextual representation of an alternative to women's helplessness, 'Translation as Collaborative', pp. 318–19.
[84] Cf. Krontiris, *Oppositional Voices*, p. 48.
[85] Sieber, 'The Romance of Chivalry', p. 211. Sieber compares the consummation of Trebatio and Briana's relationship to Perión and Elsinea's, and the Knight of the Sun and Claridiana's union to Amadís and Oriana's, in order to highlight the heightened eroticism of *Espejo*.

eroticism is wisely ignored in Tyler's prefatory material: a woman writing of war could be justified, especially when compared to the possibility of a woman waging war, but her chastity would definitely be tarnished if she were to pen a text of a sexual nature.[86]

Since the opening of the romance situates the narrative within the framework of the more valued, didactic chronicle genre, the text is advertised as being of greater importance than a simple romance narrative of love and sexual adventure.[87] Yet, Tyler uses the prologue framework to undercut this possible accretion in value. Her 'author's purpose appeareth to be' didactic, aiming 'to animate thereby and to set on fire the lusty courages of young gentlemen to the advancement of their line by ensuing such like steps', an objective accepted for history and often claimed for romance (To reader.6–7). But Tyler distances *Mirror* from didactic potentialities as she prevaricates: 'Whither a true story of him indeed or a feigned fable, I wot not' (To reader.2–3). Notwithstanding *Espejo*'s historicity and didacticism, Tyler stresses that *Mirror* is not educational: she invokes the twinned Horatian concepts of 'profit and delight', but emphasizes the romance's status as a 'delight', a 'pastime', a 'sport', 'a merry jest' (To reader.77, 78, 81, 87). Further trivialising her romance according to convention and readers' expectations, she demeans it as 'woman's work' (To reader.16). This is reinforced through Tyler's language that is saturated with domestic imagery drawn from biblical parables which reflect the habitual activities of an honourable, pious woman (Matthew 5:15, 25:14–30).[88] In addition, by referring to her text as 'labour', 'travail', 'increase', and 'delivery' she invokes the act of childbirth thereby feminizing the trope of authorship as parenthood (To reader.42, 44, 57, 92; Dedication 25; To reader.38; Dedication 9; To reader.15).[89] *Mirror* is simply a pleasurable text, written by a simple woman.

By presenting her text as a trifle 'rather devised to beguile time', Tyler counters the traditionally accepted practices of genre and gender, according to which men are permitted to write romances and women may acceptably write devotional texts (To reader.84). Because the binary paradoxically suggests the valuation of romance over religion, she not only derogates her text, but she provides a corrective to the dichotomy by accentuating the seriousness of theology. Given the complexity of religious discussions and their affinity to controversy, her alleged inability to tackle the material seems accurate. She opposes the 'controversy' and potential for 'offence' in 'divinity' to her own poor 'judgement' (To reader.73–76). Her argument gestures towards the absurdity of the convention that prevents women from writing light-hearted romances, while entrusting them with potent theological concerns. The trifling, feminized nature of romance thus combines with the translator's and female author's humility in a powerful, logical neutralization of Tyler's controversial authorial status.

Grounding her argument on the prevalence of romances written by men for women, Tyler logically develops a theory of authorship. She controversially asserts that if romances are presented to women, then women can read and analyse romances. Then, moving one scandalous step further, she extrapolates that romance reading should license romance writing:

> And if men may, and do, bestow such of their travails upon gentlewomen, then may we women read such of their works as they dedicate unto us. And if we may read them, why not farther wade in them to the search of a truth? And then much more, why not deal by translation in such arguments? [. . . .] my persuasion hath been thus: that it is all one for a woman to pen a story as for a man to address his story to a woman [. . .] (To reader.59–73)

---

[86] On the sexuality of the Iberian romances and Tyler's 'possibly [. . .] purposeful manoeuvre' to emphasize the martial over the sexual, see Hackett, pp. 55–75, esp. p. 60. Arcara argues that Tyler repeatedly alludes to her age in order to present herself as an asexual being.

[87] The romance's quasi-historical status will be carefully explored in the following section.

[88] Cf. Jane Farnsworth, 'Margaret Tyler', p. 333.

[89] Uman and Bistué discuss these metaphors in terms of Tyler's subversion of fixed gender roles, p. 309. Cf. Wendy Wall, *The Imprint of Gender: Authorship and Publication in the English Renaissance*, p. 181.

The patronage relationship harbours an indemnificatory hierarchy of subservience between author and patron since the author relies upon the patron's reputation, class, or wealth to facilitate the production and favourable reception of their text.[90] Yet, Tyler concentrates on the intellectual paradigm in which the author's creative forces imbue him with agency and the dedicatee passively accepts the author's text. According to her logic, women are only elevated above their acceptable, receptive, inert role within textual production once they relinquish the position of dedicatee and come to inhabit an authorial role. The 'argument steps boldly beyond the surviving rhetorical subservience [. . .] by attacking the patriarchal idealisation of women as the muses or patronesses of men's art who merely inspire or, worse, passively receive men's dedications of works they are not allowed to read'.[91] While the latter seems bizarrely improbable, it is an accurate reflection of literary practice, as evidenced, for example, by the numerous romances dedicated to women coupled with the equally abundant prohibitions against female romance reading. Romances would not be repeatedly dedicated to women, nor would there be a need to continually prohibit women from reading romances if a large, avid female readership did not exist. Indeed, the paradigm is so idiosyncratic, that merely noting the very oddity of the situation is argumentatively adequate, enabling Tyler's discussion to progress rapidly from female reading to writing.

Her writerly act may be unprecedented, yet the 'rhetoric of normalization' diffuses the threatening nature of her achievement (Gallagher, p. 310). By claiming that there is '[n]othing strange or untoward in her behavior, Tyler explains [that] she is merely joining a legitimate and accepted enterprise', to which she is 'traditionally entitled', and which is, according to Catherine Gallagher, a diachronic, prevalent, and effective justificatory strategy (p. 309). The passage also invokes a fluid relationship between author and reader in which both have equal intellectual rights of ownership over the arguments presented in the text: as the reader 'wade[s]' into a text and discovers its 'truth[s]' she appropriates them, and they become hers to 'deal in'. Exclusive possession of truth is unfeasible; rather, a book's argument is shared between the author who gives it linguistic articulation and the reader who uncovers it. It is 'all one'. 'Everyone therefore has a precedent for dealing in the arguments of a book: the precedent of the writer' (Gallagher, p. 312).

Tyler's gender may represent the most overt socio-cultural threat, but as Uman and Bistué argue, '[b]y recontextualizing the romance and highlighting its Englishness and interest in the plight of women, Tyler makes historical and societal similarities detectable and creates a new set of meanings that can be associated with the tale' (p. 318). They demonstrate how Tyler uses Briana's narrative to investigate questions of marital and political succession and legitimacy that parallel the issues surrounding female authorship investigated in her preface. Through sexual metaphors, Tyler likens translation to prostitution, presenting the female translator as a sexualized commodity who finds it 'convenient to lay forth [her] talent for increase'. For Tyler as for Briana, 'there appeared likewise little liberty in [their] first yielding'. Krontiris identifies three additional key areas in which *Mirror* counters accepted cultural belief and practice, none of which are even alluded to in the preface: marriage and social class, sexual double standards, and violence against women.[92] The love stories of Briana and Trebatio and of Olivia and Rosicleer explore the tensions between love and both gender and class and the problematic nature of the commodification of women. Their relationships highlight the incompatibility of love and materially advantageous unions and affirm the primacy of an amorous connection over the imperative to marry within one's social class. Duchess Elisandra and Trebatio's circumstances decry the injustice and disparity inherent in attitudes towards men and women in sexual matters,

---

[90] Cf. Arthur Marotti, *Manuscript, Print, and the English Renaissance Lyric*; Wall, *Imprint of Gender*.
[91] Douglas Robinson, 'Theorising Translation in a Woman's Voice', p. 161.
[92] While these were not the problems explicitly targeted by polemicists, they are aspects of the romance that counter cultural norms.

such as fidelity. And, violence against women, presented as physical, emotional, and fiscal, is widespread and repeatedly denounced.

Supporting these ideological subversions, Krontiris notes an absence of language of subordination of women, very few stereotypical presentations of women, and a paucity of belittling descriptions of women, all of which is in keeping with tendencies already observed in Tyler's translation methodology.[93] Indeed, Tyler's proto-feminist inclinations additionally govern several of the alterations that she makes to her Spanish source. A stereotypical comment on female loquacity and the description of the Knight of the Sun's misogynistic invective against the power of women's beauty are omitted from *Espejo* (I.96.10–15; II.199.8–13). Tyler neglects to blame 'una muger mala' [a bad woman] for Hannibal's 'passions' (40.104, II.118.9). In her description of Socrates' parentage, she alters the focus from his father to his mother: *Espejo* says he was born to a 'cantero' (stonemason), whereas *Mirror* recognizes his mother, a midwife (39.125, II.102.7).

'WHENCE ALSO THIS, HIS CHRONICLE, BORROWETH THIS TITLE': METAFICTION AND AUTHORIAL SELF-JUSTIFICATION

Just as Tyler's proto-feminist ideology transcends the prologue, influencing her translation of the romance, so does her discomfort with the association of romance and history. As examined above, the prologue overturns 'the author's' claims to didacticism and historicity by stressing *Mirror*'s entertainment value. Tyler persists in subverting the romance's alleged factuality by complicating the metafictional predilections of *Espejo* in her translation. Adding to *Espejo*'s multiple Greek and fictional authors, *Mirror*'s narrator invokes multiple auxiliary sources of authority, such as chronicles, artistic monuments, fictional authors, and her own personal observations. However, rather than endow the text with added weight, this plethora of quasi-historical sources coupled with the omniscient, self-reflexive, omnipresent narrator fragment textual authority. Building on the metatextual aspects of her source as well as the metafictional tendencies of the medieval English romance — which frequently contains references to the storytelling narrator, allusions to other romances, appeals to the audience to listen, 'go little book' formulae, and *questions d'amour* — Tyler crafts a sophisticated narrative that recalls Chaucer's works and resembles new short fiction, such as *The Adventures of Master F. J.* and the English translations of Spanish sentimental romances, such as *Cárcel*, *Arnalte*, and *Grisel*. More importantly, however, this narrative fragmentation subverts the authority of the chronicle itself. But rather than leave her readers with a textual void, with a source-less and author-less text, Tyler fills the expanse with her narrator, who is presented as wise, authoritative, and trustworthy: 'she claims authority even as she undermines the foundation of authority'(Uman and Bistué, p. 309). As previously observed, several changes that Tyler makes to the text — including comments about being a wife and mother, Venus and Athena's providential role, the importance of Christianity, her self-presentation as analogous to several female characters, the valuation of female agency, etc. — reflect her personal opinions and situation, which suggests Tyler's identification with her narrator. In fact, Hutson posits that the expressions of female agency present in, and added to, *Espejo* reflect authorial perspective, stressing 'the formal analogy which she permits to be inferred between the agency of women in the romance of lineage which she translates, and her own service in translating' (p. 96). In addition to the invocation of Venus and Athena as paralleling Tyler's responsibility of 'assistant to men in their dangerous conflicts', discussed above, Hutson further explains how Tyler 'makes the preservation of [Trebatio's] lineage by Briana and Clandestria analogous to her own act of writing, which she sees as contributing to the transmission of ancestral *virtus*'(p. 92). Authorial and narrative voice

---

[93] Krontiris, *Oppositional Voices*, pp. 52–62, esp. p. 61.

flow into each other and intermingle, rendering separation impossible. 'Because she is the only "translator" in the English version, the English reader can easily hear the "I" of the fictional translator that appears in the first and last lines of the text as Tyler's voice'(Uman and Bistué, p. 303). Tyler's approach to authority corresponds to her profound connection to her narrator; her efforts to valorize her narrator's voice are ultimately the continuation of the arguments advanced in the prologue in support of female authorship. By claiming authority for her narrator, Tyler affirms it for herself.

The romance's title suggests the text's didacticism and exemplary value. The terms *espejo* and *mirror* are based on the medieval uses of the Latin term *speculum*, which denoted a wide, almost encyclopaedic, textual reflection and description of a specific subject area. Texts of the *mirror, glass, or speculum* genre usually tackled spiritual (*The Mirror of the World, The Mirror or Glass of the Sinful Soul*), political (*A Mirror for Magistrates, Mirror for Princes*), or scientific (*Speculum alchimiae, Speculum astronomiae*) material. The rare instances when the nomenclature was applied to a fictional composition reveal an interest in emphasizing the narrative's didactic potentialities. For example, Munday's *Palmerin d'Oliva* is subtitled, *The mirrour of nobilitie, mappe of honor, anotamie [sic] of rare fortunes, heroycall president of Loue: Wonder for chiualrie, and most accomplished knight in all perfections*, perhaps inspired by Tyler's text. Robert Greene invokes a *christall mirror of feminine perfection* in the subtitle of *Penelope's Web*, thereby employing the *mirror* genre to denote the compendiousness and instructional worth of his story collection. Analogously, the subtitles of *Mervine* and *Montelyon* (in its post-1661 editions) hail the eponymous heroes' fathers as mirrors for princes, stressing the exemplary values of the knights' lives. Tyler's *Mirror* is unique as the only romance that includes the term *mirror* (or related terms such as *glass* or *speculum*) within its formal title.

Analogously, *Espejo*'s title differs from most other Spanish chivalric romances, which are usually named after their protagonists. Like *Mirror*, *Espejo* recalls the generic horizon of expectation of the *speculum* tradition, but it also more specifically invokes the recently-published, popular, tripartite educational series *Espejo de caballerías* (1525 [part 1], 1527 [part 2], and 1547 [part 3]). Moreover, the title page of the first edition of *Espejo* distinguishes it from previous and contemporary chivalric romances: 'Other romances of chivalry [. . .] have on their title pages a woodcut or engraving of the protagonists, often on horseback in a chivalric scene. It can be no accident that the title of *Espejo de principes* is set within a "compartment border"' (Eisenberg, p. xliv). The title page visually echoes Ortúñez's prologue in which he stresses the exemplary value of his romance and its affinity to history; *Espejo* is replete with 'fontenzicas de philosophía' (I.20.23), but the sweetness of the story makes the moral medicine, which Tyler denies, easier to swallow and digest.

Indeed, in both *Espejo* and *Mirror*, the chronicle genre works cooperatively with the *speculum* in order to defend the romance narrative. Notwithstanding Tyler's refusal to claim *Mirror*'s resemblance to history, by positing that her text is 'no[t] yet altogether fruitless, if example may serve, as being historical', the chronicle is invoked. The exemplary value of history was widely accepted by Tyler's contemporaries and, unlike romance, history was deemed to be important, didactic reading material; for example, after a lengthy diatribe against romance in which he severely circumscribes women's reading, Vives concedes that history is acceptable because of its educational value. As explored above, Tyler equivocates regarding *Mirror*'s affinity to the chronicle because of the contradictory demands of her multifaceted argument. In her prologue, emphasizing the romance's entertainment value rather than its didacticism proves the most effective mode of defending female romance authorship; but the valorization of the romance genre itself relies upon its kinship with the chronicle. Moreover, its title and the very structure of the romance — its open-endedness — emphasizes its affinity to the chronicle; like the chronicle, any ending is arbitrary because the story is always in the process of actualization and continuation.[94] By

---

[94] On the dilatory structure of romance, see Patricia Parker, *Inescapable Romance: Studies in the Poetics of a Mode*.

suggesting this redemptive connection to history, even though it is also negated, Tyler foreshadows her romance, in which she subverts attempts to self-authorize through the chronicle.

Emulating a chronicle, the romance begins by situating the narrative at a precise historical moment in Emperor Constantine's reign, imbuing the text with realism. Of all the emperors who succeeded Constantine

> none seemed to have raised his own name or to have made it so famous as the great and mighty Emperor Trebatio, whose worthy deeds, with the valiant acts of the knights of his time, I will report here, according as Artimodoro the Grecian hath left them written in the great volumes of his Chronicle. The story sayeth thus: that if at any time, Fortune, being always uncertain and variable [. . .]

From the outset, readers are directed beyond the imaginary universe of the romance to a source text: a chronicle written by an ancient Greek named Artimodoro will provide the author with information about the hero and his contemporaries. The English renders *Espejo* almost exactly verbatim. As in *Mirror*, *Espejo*'s narrator explains that he wishes to recount Trebacio's heroic deeds according to the report made by Artimodoro in his chronicle. He then states that what follows is what is written in the chronicle: 'según que Artimidoro el griego en los grandes volúmines de sus corónicas lo dexó escripto, el qual dize ansí: Quando [. . .] fortuna [. . .]' (I.26.2–7). He clearly equates the continuation of the narrative with the content of Artimodoro's chronicle. However, by altering the sentence division and replacing 'el qual' [the which] with 'the story', *Mirror* creates grammatical and textual space between Artimodoro's chronicle and 'the story'. Whereas *Espejo* self-presents as a Spanish translation of a Latin rendering of a Greek-authored chronicle, *Mirror* 'extends this game' (Uman and Bistué, p. 306) and creates a more complex textual situation as it differentiates romance from chronicle.

Yet, Artimodoro's presence adds a supplementary narrative stratum to both texts because Artimodoro is a character in the romance. Furthermore, Artimodoro's relation of the circumstances surrounding his authorial activity introduces another fictional author. Artimodoro promises to be Rosicleer's chronicler and reassures the knight that Lirgandeo will chronicle Donzel del Febo's deeds (31.82–85). Lirgandeo is a character in *Mirror*, and as can be inferred from Artimodoro's speech, the supposed author of the extensive narrative sections that recount Donzel del Febo's exploits. By ascribing narrative agency to Artimodoro and Lirgandeo, fictional characters become the source for a significant portion of the text. This meta-fictional description of the text's creation collapses authorial stability; imaginary characters have written their own text.

Despite the introduction of a fictional author, Chapter 1 continues its historical localization of Trebatio. His lineage is impressive and includes Alicante, Molosso, Pyrrhus, and Achilles. Trebatio and Alicante are imaginary characters, but Molossus is the son of Pyrrhus (aka Neoptolemus), who founded a dynasty in Epirus, in northwest Greece, and in Greek mythology, Achilles is the greatest Greek warrior in the Trojan War (Eisenberg, p. 26). Thus, not only are Greek chronicles invoked as sources for the story, but Trebatio can boast of great classical heroes and historical figures amongst his ancestry. Continued allusions to Greek mythology strengthen the romance's connection to the ancient world, but they remain within the imaginary realm of mythology. Africano uses Vulcan's armour (24.84), and the heroes and heroines repeatedly are compared to their classical counterparts for their strength and beauty: Briana is likened to Helen; Claridiana to Diana; and Bargandel, Liriamandro, and Zoilo are likened to Hector, Paris, and Troilus. Trebatio's connection to the Greeks differs since his genealogy encompasses both historical and mythological figures, but it is typical of the mingling of the factual and imaginary that defines the narrative universe of the romance.

The line between history and fiction continues to blur as *Mirror*'s sources multiply. Towards the end of Chapter 1, the narrator relates:

> [Trebatio's] historians say that he was the crown of the Greeks and the clear mirror of all the princes and knights of the world. Whence also this, his chronicle, borroweth this title, especially having therein to remember the marvellous deeds of the Knight of the Sun with Rosicleer, both sons unto Trebatio [. . .] (I.36–39)

This text is not a feigned story; we are not reading a romance about Trebatio and his sons, but 'his chronicle'. Moreover, Trebatio is elevated above the fictional by classifying him as a 'mirror' of princes and knights. This passage introduces two sources: the author of 'this, his chronicle' and 'Trebatio's historians'. Neither source is privileged. The historians' information temporally precedes 'this, his chronicle', but the comprehensiveness of their account is unknown. Also, their medium is unknown: 'the historians *say*' (emphasis added) could refer to either an oral or written communicative mode. As the chronicle's narrator borrows the historians' assessment of Trebatio for her title, she intertwines chronicle and biography in a reflexive relationship: Trebatio's deeds make him the *mirror of princes and knights* and so he is the eponymous hero of *the mirror of princely deeds and knighthood*. The difference between the English and Spanish romances is slight, but substantial (2.36–37, I.28.16–29). *Espejo* explains that his chronicle is worthy of renown without linking Trebatio's reputation and the chronicle's title. The difference between the English and Spanish texts stems from Tyler's translation of 'por donde dignamente esta su corónica mereció gozar de tal renombre' as 'borroweth this title'. In fact, this may indeed be a mistranslation of 'renombre' (renown) rather than an alteration since she later renders the semantically and lexically similar term 'nombrado' (renown) as 'mighty' (1.6) and as 'name' (18.27). But whatever the explanation for the alteration, *Mirror*'s disruption of *Espejo*'s metatextual authorizing tendencies is unaffected.

Indeed, *Mirror* persists in countering and undermining *Espejo*'s invocations of the chronicle's authority. *Mirror* narrates that 'some of the Grecians compiled this noble history' to inspire greatness in others who would read about the heroic deeds (1.47–48). The textual identity of 'this noble history' is uncertain. Its Greek authors may or may not be 'Trebatio's historians' alluded to previously: first, Trebatio's historians' account may have been orally transmitted; and, second, given the multiplication of sources, there is nothing compelling us to equate these two. For example, the chronicle that 'borroweth this title' recounted by *Mirror*'s narrator (as discussed above) and the 'Grecians' . . . noble history' certainly differ. Since the narrator describes the authors as 'some of the Grecians' and not as some of *us* Grecians, she clearly differentiates her authorial voice. This ambiguity is absent from *Espejo*, which declares that the Greeks compiled Trebatio's noble deeds into a dozen books and that the narrative which follows is the first of the twelve (I.30.6–11). A complex metafictional move is exercised here as the narrator/author-figure abdicates responsibility for the subsequent text. While Tyler's sources remain enigmatic, Ortúñez consistently invokes this authorial stance. His narrator repeatedly effaces himself and advances the Greek chroniclers as the authors. In *Espejo*, story and chronicle remain identical.

Recalling the start of Chapter 1, the second chapter also opens by positioning Trebatio's narrative at a precise temporal locus and by conjuring the chronicle's power of authorization. But, again, also echoing the first chapter, ambiguity characterizes *Mirror*'s recourse to history since the declaration introduces an additional fictional character, Emperor Helio III, into Trebatio's quasi-historical genealogy and potentially ushers in yet another source: 'an ancient Greek chronicle' (2.4). The equivalency of 'an ancient Greek chronicle' with 'this noble history' complied by 'some of the Grecians' or the witness of Trebatio's historians is indeterminate; however, this 'ancient Greek chronicle' is certainly distinct from 'the chronicle that borroweth this title'. The reference to this additional Greek source is unproblematic in *Espejo* because of its tendency to self-present as a Greek-authored chronicle, as noted above.

Mirror also plays with conceptions of historicity through representations of monuments commemorating the heroes. These descriptions recall authorizing strategies typically employed in chronicles as well as in romances such as *Le Morte D'Arthur*, which maps the Arthurian legend onto English geography. In *Mirror*, the quasi-real mementoes add supplementary levels to the narrative, extending the fragmentation and subversion of textual authority. The narrator describes 'great volumes', 'devices in verse', buildings, paintings, temples, and sculptures 'penned and portrayed' 'in such sort that you might pass by no part of all Greece where was not recited, sung, or painted the histories and noble deeds of these knights' (1.41–46). Crucially, these monuments are presented as authentic, rather than imaginary. Unlike *Espejo*'s narrator, who offers a description of the monuments' appearance, *Mirror*'s narrator situates herself in the same temporal plane as her readers, assuring them that their contemporaries have seen the memorial artefacts: 'in long time after, this monument [. . .] was found by our age in the pursuit of adventures in that country' (30.40–41).[95] The supposedly real existence of these commemorative objects muddles the romance's fictional status because they attest to the characters' existence in the non-imaginative realm inhabited by the romance's readers.

The subversion of the chronicle's univocal authority is furthered through the narrator's frequent revelations that she possesses supplementary, superior information about the events described. Through the addition of expressions such as 'I dare not say' (14.112), 'which I let pass' (9.11), 'And as I read' (11.7), 'I may forget to tell you' (30.168), and 'as I have heard' (39.158), the narrator gestures towards a world outside the text to which she has exclusive access.[96] Moreover, these statements differentiate the narrator's voice from those of the chroniclers, and they also undermine the chronicle's authority because they allude to other narratives, other material, other versions of events. They reveal that the chronicle is not the ultimate, reliable, comprehensive source. Indeed, the narrator presents her knowledge and her version of events as superior to that provided by the ancient chronicles. For example, when Briana falls in love with Rosicleer, Tyler makes the following addition to her source: '[. . .] she thought none merited to be a peer and match for her beauty, being (as my author sayeth), such in her own conceit as if no prince were worthy of it. *But the truth is* that the blind boy, shooting at random, had overreached his mark, as appeared in the second shot at the coming in of Rosicleer' (32.28–31; emphasis added). The narrator's source offers one explanation, but her version of events is more truthful and accurate.

The narrator can successfully compete with the chronicle's prestigious voice due to her wisdom, her connection to God, and her complicity with her readers. Her perspective is authorized through her repeated digressions, which present herself as a fount of wisdom, offering her readers moralizing commentary on topics as diverse as love, marriage, true knighthood, human frailty and failings, tyranny, vengeance, the superiority of Christianity, and the transitoriness of worldly things. Such discourse, some added by Tyler and some already present in *Espejo*, imbues the narrative voice with power. Her authority is intensified when considered alongside her supreme omniscience, as evidenced by her avowals of her proximity to God. In a series of additions to *Espejo*, the narrator claims knowledge of events that were 'provided by the divine majesty of God' (37.133–34). She alone is aware of when 'God so directed Rosicleer's hand' (37.135), and she is privy to what 'the Creator of all things minded to manifest' (15.3) and how 'he ordered the celestial influences and powers of the planets' (15.5).

Readers are inclined to accept the narrator's authority because she forges a solid relationship of complicity with them by routinely addressing them directly and by aligning herself with their values and perspective. This includes more than twenty short interjections, all added by Tyler, such as: 'as I say' (27.89), 'I deny not' (9.135), or 'I doubt not' (36.105–06).[97] She also engages with the readers' opinions at least fifteen times, implicating them in the text, with comments

---

[95] Cf. 'que por largos tiempos no se perdió la memoria de la libertad del valle' (I.254.9–10).
[96] Additional examples are in Chapters 10.6; 16.83; 16.94; 23.98; 30.164; 32.236; 32.237; 34.92; 44.265–66; 52.101; 55.8.
[97] See also Chapters 14.5; 14.52–53; 18.70; 19.15; 24.16; 34.46–47; 42.26; 44.16; 54.91.

such as 'And I will leave him to your several considerations' (30.169); 'Now with what courage fought he, think you (20.65–66); 'Tell me, I pray you, gentle readers' (43.153).[98] These are all English additions. The abundance of first person plural pronouns, added to those already extant in the Spanish, deepens the connection between reader and narrator. The narrator speaks of 'we', 'our age', and 'us'. The effect is to join reader and narrator, situating them in the same historical moment, attributing shared opinions and perspectives to them, and ultimately presenting the narrator as a trustworthy source, who is able to compete with the chronicle for supreme authority.

Through a series of additions, omissions, and alterations, Tyler creates a romance that evinces a profound mistrust of the chronicle's authority. Whereas in her preface she invokes the ubiquitous argument of romance's likeness to history in order to valorize the romance, she refuses to claim definitive kinship between *Mirror* and the chronicle. Her refusal stems from the argument's perceived incompatibility with the prologue's larger agenda of justifying female romance authorship. As the narrative progresses, an even deeper mistrust of the chronicle emerges. Rather than present chronicles as authoritative documents, *Mirror*'s narrator shows them to be partial, unreliable, and multiple. Indeed, Lirgandeo even explains that 'although things before done carry a greater burden of authority than that which we ourselves can testify', their authority is not proof of their superiority (24.129–30). *Espejo* is a metatexual, multi-layered text. Authored by Ortúñez, its narrator represents the text as a Greek chronicle partially composed by Artimodoro and Lirgandeo, two fictional authors who are active in the text; but despite any narrative playfulness, the chronicle's trustworthiness and supremacy is maintained. Tyler intensifies the metatextual status of the romance through the introduction of additional authorial voices and sources. While Tyler's preface and dedication unequivocally assert that *Mirror* is a Spanish romance that she translated, as the text progresses the narrator reveals that we are reading a conglomeration of multiple, incomplete chronicles of events that combine history, fiction, and mythology, which were written or orally recounted by different historians, some of whom are fictional characters operating within the text, and that the only reliable witness for the story is the narrator herself. This complex textual situation ultimately devalues the chronicle and concomitantly ascribes merit to the narrator's perspective. Because the narrator's and Tyler's voices are so close, the attribution of authority to the narrator is ultimately an act of self-valorization which continues Tyler's rational justification of female authorship so eloquently articulated in the prologue. Though this intricate metatextual play, Tyler demonstrates that women can successfully challenge masculine authorial traditions.

---

[98] See also Chapters 9.3; 17.149; 18.75–76; 21.75; 26.160; 32.103; 34.188–89; 34.209; 43.126; 43.196; 44.255; 49.5; 52.83–84; 55.4.

FURTHER READING

Coad, Kathryn, intro., *Margaret Tyler*, Early Modern Englishwoman: A Facsimile Library of Essential Works, vol. 8 (Aldershot: Scolar Press, 1997)

Eisenberg, Daniel, ed., *Espejo de príncipes y cavalleros: el cavallero del Febo*, by Diego Ortúñez de Calahorra (Madrid: Espasa-Calpe, 1975)

Hackett, Helen, *Women and Romance Fiction in the English Renaissance* (Cambridge: Cambridge University Press, 2000)

Hutson, Lorna, *The Usurer's Daughter: Male Friendship and Fictions of Women in Sixteenth-Century England* (London: Routledge, 1994)

Krontiris, Tina, 'Breaking Barriers of Genre and Gender: Margaret Tyler's Translation of *The Mirrour of Knighthood*', *English Language Review*, 18 (1988), 19–39

Schleiner, Louise, 'Margaret Tyler, Translator and Waiting Woman', *English Language Notes*, 29 (1992), 1–9

Uman, Deborah and Belén Bistué, 'Translation as Collaborative Authorship: Margaret Tyler's *The Mirrour of Princely Deedes and Knighthood*', *Comparative Literature Studies*, 44 (2007), 298–323

BIBLIOGRAPHICAL DESCRIPTIONS

1. Thomas East, [1578]. Complete copy: Huntington Library (HEH) 62809. Other copy: British Library (BL) C.56.d.15. (folio 124 is mutilated); *Short Title Catalogue* (*STC*) 18859.

Title page. [within a frame of four separate pieces, 104 × 163 mm: top piece, 71 × 10 mm, a floral and foliate motif; bottom piece, 71 × 10 mm, a floral and foliate motif; left-hand piece 15 × 163 mm, a floral and foliate motif; right-hand piece, 15 × 163 mm, a floral and foliate motif]

¶ *The Mirrour of Princely* | deedes and Knighthood: | Wherein is shewed the worthinesse of the | Knight of the Sunne, and his brother | Rosicleer, sonnes to the great Empe= | rour Trebetio: with the strange | loue of the beautifull and ex= | cellent Princesse Briana, | and the valiant actes of | other noble Prin= | ces | and Knightes. | Now newly translated out of Spanish | into our vulgar English | tongue, by M. T. | ¶ Imprinted at London | by Thomas East.

Collation. 4º. A^4, B-Z^8, 2A^4 [$5 (-A1, B5, G5, L5, O5, P5, S5, 2A3; C2 misigned C3) signed]. [4] pages, 1–15 pages, 9–179, [1] leaves (29 misnumbered 26, 75 misnumbered 73, 76 misnumbered 74, 123 misnumbered 116, 125 misnumbered 118, 135 misnumbered 134, 135 misnumbered 135, 138 misnumbered 137, 149 misnumbered 142, 151 misnumbered 142, 152 misnumbered 151, 167 misnumbered 168, 168 misnumbered 169, 170 misnumbered 169, 176 misnumbered 175), total of 398 pages.

Contents. Title page (A1r); Dedication to Thomas Howard (A2r–A2v); Dedication to the Reader (A3r–A4v); Text (B1r–2A3r); Table of contents (2A3v–2A4v).

Type. One size of black letter type, three sizes of roman, and two sizes of italics are used. The bulk of the text is written in a black letter font of 82 mm to 20 lines. Roman letters of approximately the same size are used for many proper names, chapter titles, salutations and signatures of epistles, parts of the title page, some running headers, and the dedication to Thomas Howard. A slightly larger roman font is used for a few words on the title page. A small roman font is used for some running headers, the marginal glosses, and the chapter title on B5v. The italic font is used for the first line of the title page, the title of the first dedication, and the running header through the text. A smaller italic font is used for Margaret Tyler's name on A2v and for some common names. A variety of fonts are used for the initial capital letters at the beginnings of chapters: some are roman capitals 1–2 lines deep, others are black letter capitals of 2 or 3 or 4 lines. All chapters, with only two exceptions, are introduced by these types of undecorated capital letters: 1. The initial T on A2r is a large decorated letter, 6 lines deep. A naked figure surrounded by leaves and flowers holds the white letter within a square frame. 2. The A which begins the text on B1r is 8 lines deep. The white letter is set against a crude foliate background, with a cup bearing a feline face between the descenders of the A.

Decoration. Decoration is minimal. In addition to the two large initial letters, a paragraph symbol is used to mark chapter titles. Part of the title page decorative frame is reused on the final leaf of the narrative (2A3r) forming a rectangle 24 × 20 mm. The printer's device on the title page depicts a king in a chariot lead by two horses, moving right to left, 38 × 28 mm.

BIBLIOGRAPHICAL DESCRIPTIONS

Copy-specific information: HEH 62809

Binding. The nineteenth-century binding, produced by Francis Bedford, is of brown leather. The fore-edges are gilt, and a triple blind rule adorns the front and rear covers. On the spine, in gilt letters, is the inscription: MIRROUR OF PRINCELY DEEDES | FIRST PART | LONDON | 1578. It is surrounded by additional gilt decoration. Three leaves are added by the binder at the front and the back of the volume. The front and rear pastedowns are burgundy marbled paper. Gilt dentelle decorates the edges of the inner front and rear covers. Huth's bookplate in gilt and black leather adorns the centre of the front pastedown.

Size. The copy measures 141 × 184 mm and the leaves are of the dimensions 130 × 179 mm. The maximum printed space, with catchwords, signature markings, and headers is 86 × 168 mm; without the catchwords, signatures, and headers the average printed space is 86 × 147 mm. A complete page contains 36 lines of type. Catchwords and signature markings, when they appear, are positioned on the 37th line.

Provenance. The earliest known owner of this volume was Henry Huth (1815–1878). The bookseller Bernard Quaritch purchased the copy at the Huth auction in 1916, as lot 5028 on the 32nd day of the auction.[99] The copy was 'collated by Williams at Quaritch' (HEH catalogue) and was then bought by the Huntington, also in 1916.

Watermarks. Watermarks of a goblet, an eagle, and a hand can be discerned but they cannot be identified with any of Briquet's marks.[100]

2. Thomas East, 1580(?). Complete copies: HEH 60627, Folger STC 18860. BL C.70.b.27 is lacking the title page and several leaves are imperfect. *STC 18860*.

Title page. [within a foliate frame, 105 × 160 mm] THE FIRST PART | *of the Mirror of Prince-* | *ly deedes and Knighthood:* | WHEREIN IS SHEW-| ED THE WORTHINESSE OF | the Knight of the Sunne, and his brother | Rosicleer, sonnes to the great Emperour | Trebatio, with the strange loue of | the beautifull Princesse Bri- | ana, & the valiant actes | of other noble Prin- | ces and Knights. | Now newly translated out of Spanish into | our vulgar English tongue, by M. T. | ¶ Imprinted at London by | Thomas East.

Collation. 4º. A⁴, B-Z⁸, 2A⁴ [$5 (-A1, B5, F5, G5, L5, O5, P5, S5, U5, Z5, 2A3, 2A4]. [4], 1–179 [1] (29 misnumbered 39, 30 misnumbered 40, 34 misnumbered 3, 73 misnumbered 93, 74 misnumbered 94, 79 misnumbered 99, 80 misnumbered 100, 133 misnumbered 125, 134 misnumbered 126, 135 misnumbered 134, 136 misnumbered 135, 151 misnumbered 149, 152 misnumbered 150, 153 misnumbered 155, 157 misnumbered 517, 158 misnumbered 558, 165 misnumbered 565), total of 368 pages.

Contents. Title page (A1r); Dedication to Thomas Howard (A2r–A2v); Dedication to the Reader (A3r–A4v); Text (B1r–2A3r); Table of contents (A3v–2A4v).

---

[99] *Catalogue of the famous library of printed books, illuminated manuscripts, autograph letters and engravings / collected by Henry Huth, and since maintained and augmented by his son, Alfred H. Huth ; the printed books and illuminated*, p. 1430.
[100] Charles-Moïse Briquet, *Les filigranes: Dictionnaire historique des marques du papier des leur apparition vers 1282 jusqu'en 1600, avec 39 figures dans le texte et 16,112 fac-similés de filigranes*.

Type. One size of black letter type, three sizes of roman, and two sizes of italics are used. The bulk of the text is written in a black letter font of 82mm to 20 lines. Roman letters of approximately the same size are used for many proper names, chapter titles, salutations and signatures of epistles, parts of the title page, some running headers and the dedication to Thomas Howard. A slightly larger roman font is used for a few words on the title page. A small roman font is used for some running headers. The italic font is used for the second and final lines of the title page, the title of the first dedication, and the running header through the text. A smaller italic font is used for Margaret Tyler's name on A2v. A variety of fonts are used for the initial capital letters at the beginnings of chapters: some are roman capitals 1–2 lines deep, others are black letter capitals of 2 or 3 or 4 lines. All chapters, with only two exceptions, are introduced by these types of undecorated capital letters: 1. The initial N on A2r is enclosed within a square frame, 6 lines deep. Two naked figures face each other holding a wreath and a foliate motif fills the bottom of the square; and the letter is in the centre. 2. The A which begins the text on B1r is 6 lines deep. The white letter is set against an illustrated background, which depicts a reclining nude holding out his hand to stroke an animal.

Decoration. The edition contains two decorated initial letters, as described above. A paragraph symbol is used to mark most chapter titles. Part of the title page border is reused to decorate three pages: on the title page, forming a rectangle 27 × 19 mm; at the top of A2r, forming a rectangle 76 × 7 mm; and at the bottom of 2A3r, forming a rectangle 54 × 19 mm.

Copy-specific information: HEH 60627

Binding. The binding is nearly identical to HEH 62809. Also dating to the nineteenth century, it is a brown leather binding, with gilt fore-edges, and a triple blind rule, except it was produced by Riviere and Sons. On the spine, in gilt letters, is the inscription: MIRROUR | OF | PRINCELY | DEEDES| FIRST PART | LONDON | 1579. It is surrounded by additional gilt decoration. Three leaves are added by the binder at the front and the back of the volume. The front and rear pastedowns are burgundy marbled paper. Gilt dentelle decorates the edges of the inner front and rear covers. Huth's bookplate in gilt and black leather adorns the centre of the front pastedown.

Size. The copy measures 136 × 171 mm and the leaves are of the dimensions 122 × 179 mm. The maximum printed space, with catchwords, signature markings, and headers is 87 × 164 mm; without the catchwords, signatures, and headers the average printed space is 87 × 150 mm. A complete page contains 36 lines of type. Catchwords and signature markings, when they appear, are positioned on the 37th line.

Provenance. The earliest known owner was Henry Huth (1815–1878). The bookseller Bernard Quaritch purchased the copy at the Huth auction in 1916 as lot 5030 on the 32nd day of the auction. It was bought by the Huntington in 1916 (Huth catalogue 1432–33). The same lot included the second part of the first book (*STC* 18862) and the second book (*STC* 18866).

Watermarks. Watermarks of a goblet, a star, a hand, and an eagle are distinguishable, but none can be identified according to Briquet.

Manuscript notations. On 15r 'gave' is crossed out and corrected to 'have'. I5r has a manicule.

BIBLIOGRAPHICAL DESCRIPTIONS

3. Thomas East, 1599. Complete copies: HEH 62814 and BL C.71.b.34., Bodleian Douce O 113 (1), Harvard Houghton Library STC 18861. Imperfect copy: Cambridge University Library Syn.7.57.22 (imp). *STC* 18861.

Title page. [within a foliate frame, 92 × 154 mm] THE FIRST PART | *of the Mirrour of Prince-* | *ly deedes and Knighthood*. | WHEREIN IS SHEW-| ED THE WORTHINESSE OF | the Knight of the Sunne, and his brother | Rosicleer, sonnes to the great Emperour | Trebatio, with the strange loue of | the beautifull Princesse Briana, | and the valiaunt actes of | other noble Princes and | Knights. | Now newly translated out of Spanish into | our vulgar English tongue, by M. T. | *Imprinted at London by* | Thomas Este.

Collation. 4º. A^4, B-Z^8, 2A^4 [$5 (-A1, B5, F5, G5, L5, S5, Y5, 2A3, 2A4]. [4], 1–179 [1] (73 misnumbered 93, 74 misnumbered 94), total of 368 pages.

Contents. Title page (A1r); Dedication to Thomas Howard (A2r–A2v); Dedication to the Reader (A3r–A4v); Text (B1r–2A3r); Table of contents (2A3v–-2A4v).

Type. One size of black letter type, three sizes of roman, and two sizes of italics are used. The bulk of the text is written in a black letter font of 82 mm to 20 lines. Roman letters of approximately the same size are used for many proper names, chapter titles, salutations and signatures of epistles, parts of the title page, some running headers and the dedication to Thomas Howard. A slightly larger roman font is used for a few words on the title page. A small roman font is used for some running headers and marginal glosses. The italic font is used for the second and final lines of the title page, the title of the first dedication, and the running header through the text. A smaller italic font is used for Margaret Tyler's name on A2v and some common names. A variety of fonts are used for the initial capital letters at the beginnings of chapters: some are roman capitals 1–2 lines deep, others are black letter capitals of 2 or 3 or 4 lines. All chapters, with only two exceptions, are introduced by these types of undecorated capital letters. The two decorated letters are the same as those used in the second edition.

Decoration. The edition contains two decorated initial letters, as described above. A paragraph symbol is used to mark most chapter titles. Part of the title page border is reused in three instances forming a typographer's ornament: on the title page, in a rectangular pattern 25 × 18 mm; at the top of A2r, forming a rectangle 74 × 6 mm; and at the bottom of 2A3r, forming a rectangle 51 × 19 mm.

Copy-specific information: HEH 62814

Binding. The binding is modern, of simple brown leather. A single blind rule is tooled into the front and rear covers. On the spine, in gilt letters, is the inscription: MIRROR OF | PRINCELY | DEEDES. One leaf was added by the binder at the front and the back of the volume. An additional leaf was added at the front of the text by an earlier binder. The front and rear pastedowns are plain cream paper. The ex libris of Huth (in white leather and gilt) and the Earl of Charlemont (white paper and black ink; a crest framed by two dragons on either side with a crown on top) are on the front pastedown.

Size. The copy measures 156 × 196 mm and the leaves are of the dimensions 138 × 188 mm. The maximum printed space, with catchwords, signature markings, and headers is 92 × 160 mm; without the catchwords, signatures, and headers the average printed space is 92 × 147 mm. A complete page contains 36 lines of type. Catchwords and signature markings, when they appear, are positioned on the 37th line.

Provenance.[101] The earliest known owner is the Irish statesman James Caulfeild, 1st Earl of Charlemont (1728–1799). Isaac Reed (1742–1807) purchased the book from Charlemont. When Reed's entire collection was auctioned in 1807, the book was sold, as lot 2661 to Huth (p. 114) on day 12 of the sale for 11 pounds and 10s and 6d. Reed had an extensive collection of romances including several Spanish translations: *Palmerin d'Oliva* 1588, *Palmerin of England* 1639, *Primaleon of Greece* 1619, *Arnalte y Lucenda* 1639, *Amadis*, and two parts of *Don Quijote* translated by Thomas Shelton.[102] The book was sold in the Huth auction of 1916 as lot 5029. The lot also included the second part of first book (*STC* 18863), the third part of the first book (*STC* 18864 or 18865), the sixth book (*STC* 18868), the seventh book (*STC* 18869), the eighth book (*STC* 18870), and the ninth book (*STC* 18871), all of which have Charlemont's bookplate.

Watermark. A watermark of part of a hand or a bird's wing can be discerned on some pages, but the inner margins are too cropped to identify the mark with any certainty.

---

[101] On the extra sheet at the start of the volume is the inscription: 'Ic. Reed 1773. Bo^t at Daventry. / 3 parts of the Mirrour of Knighthood the first translated by Margaret Tyler the latter by RP Q if Painter / They appear to have been published at different times but there is no date except to the second part viz. 1599'. Below is written in pencil 'hinges cracked' which must apply to the earlier binding. On the bottom of the page is a paste-in describing Petrarch's *Phisicke against Fortune* (pub. Richard Watkins 1579) which may have once followed the three parts of the *Mirrour* in an earlier binding.

[102] *Bibliotheca Reediana: A Catalogue of the Curious & Extensive Library of the late Isaac Reed, esq. of Staple Inn, deceased* [...]

EDITORIAL POLICY

This edition takes as its base text the first edition of Margaret Tyler's *Mirror of Princely Deeds and Knighthood*, which was printed by Thomas East in 1578 (*STC* 18859). This print has been collated with the second and third editions of the romance, which appeared in 1580(?) and 1599(?), also under the imprimatur of East (*STC* 18860 and 18861, respectively). Extant copies of these prints are listed in the 'Bibliographical Descriptions'. For this edition, I have used the copies of all three editions of *Mirror* which are preserved at the Henry E. Huntington Library. In addition to these texts, I have also had recourse to the STC microfilms, the EEBO facsimiles, and the facsimile prepared by Kathryn Coad for The Early Modern Englishwoman series.

Textual variants and emendations follow the text, using the years of publication as sigla. Punctuation, capitalization, and paragraph divisions are editorial. The text is presented in modernized spelling. Word forms which appear as headwords in *OED* are retained; orthographic variants of headwords are changed to the form of their headword in the *OED*. The third form singular of verbs ending in 'eth' is retained. Words and expressions that are included in the glossary are marked with the symbol °, and superscript numerals refer to the critical and linguistic notes to *Mirror*, which are presented as footnotes. These notes focus on *Mirror*'s relationship to its Spanish source, as well as provide explanations of difficult passages, and explications of historical and literary allusions.

MARGARET TYLER

MIRROR OF PRINCELY DEEDS AND KNIGHTHOOD (1578)

¶ The Mirror of Princely Deeds and Knighthood[1]
Wherein is showed the worthiness of the Knight of the Sun and his brother, Rosicleer, sons to the great Emperor Trebatio, with the strange love of the beautiful and excellent Princess Briana, and the valiant acts of other noble princes and knights.[2]
Now newly translated out of Spanish into our vulgar° English tongue by M. T.[3]
Printed at London by Thomas East.

---

[1] As discussed in the introduction, the titular designation 'mirror' situates the romance within the tradition of didactic *speculum* texts.
[2] Whereas *Espejo*'s title page advertised the great chivalric deeds and very strange loves of the beautiful and excellent princess Claridiana, *Mirror*'s invokes Briana. As indicated in the introduction, Tyler needed to introduce this woman warrior cautiously in order to develop her argument for the justification of female authorship of romance. By placing an image of an Amazon on the cover of this edition, I aim to return Claridiana to prominence.
[3] *Mirror* is a translation of *Espejo de príncipes y cavalleros* by Diego Ortúñez de Calahorra (1555).

To the Right Honourable, the Lord Thomas Howard.[4]

    Not being greatly forward of mine° own inclination, Right Honourable, but forced by the importunity of my friends to make some trial of myself in this exercise of translation, I have adventured upon a piece of work not indeed the most profitablest,° as entreating of arms, nor yet altogether fruitless, if example may serve, as being historical, but the while, either to be born withal for the delight or not to be refused for the strangeness.[5] Further, I mean not to make boast of my travail,° for the matter was offered not made choice of, as there appeared likewise little liberty in my first yielding. The earnestness of my friends persuaded me that it was convenient to lay forth my talent for increase° or to set my candle on a candlestick, and the consideration of my insufficiency drove me to think it better for my ease, either quite to bury my talent, thereby to avoid the breaking of thriftless debts, or rather to put my candle clean out than that it should bewray° every un-swept corner in my house. But, the opinion of my friends' judgement prevailed above mine° own reason. So upon hope to please them, I first undertook this labour. And I have gone through withal, the rather to acquaint myself with mine° old reading. Whereto, since the dispatch thereof I have made my friends privy,° and upon their good liking, with request thereto, I have passed my grant unto them for the publication, reserving to myself the order for the dedication so as I should think best: either for the defence of my work or for some particular merit towards me. And herein, I took no long leisure to find out a sufficient personage. For the manifold benefits received from your honourable parents, my good Lord and Lady, quickly eased me of that doubt and presented your honour unto my view, whom by good right I ought to love and honour in especial,° as being of them begotten at whose hands I have reaped special benefit.[6] The which benefit if I should not so gladly profess openly, as I willingly received being offered, I might well be challenged of unkindness. But, were I as able to make good my part, as I am not ignorant what may be required at my hands, I would hope not be found ungrateful. In the meantime, this my travail° I commend unto your lordship, beseeching the same so to accept thereof as a simple testimony of that good will which I bore to your parents while they lived, then being their servant, and now do owe unto their offspring after their decease for their demerits.° Under your honour's protection I shall less fear the assault of the envious. And of your honour's good acceptation,° I have some hope in the mildness of your lordship's nature, not doubting but that as your lordship hath given no small signification, in this your noble youth, of wisdom and courage to so many as know you, it being the only support of your ancestor's line, so the same likewise will maintain your ancestors' glory and the hope of your own virtues with affability and gentleness, which was the proper commendation of your parents. The Almighty increase this hope with the other virtues before named, to the good hope of your country's peace, your princess's safety, and your own honour, with the joy of your kindred and friends, whom not a few your parents' good deserving hath assured unto you, and of whose earnest prayers you shall not fail to further your well doing. Amongst them, though last in worthiness, yet with the foremost in well wishing and desire of well deserving, your honour shall find me,

Your honour's humbly, most assured,
Margaret Tyler.

---

[4] Thomas Howard, Earl of Suffolk (1561–1626), the elder son of Thomas Howard, fourth Duke of Norfolk (1538–1572) and his second wife, Lady Margaret Dudley (1540–1564).
[5] She is alluding to the widely-accepted Horatian dictum that literature should offer both profit and delight.
[6] Thomas Howard and Margaret Dudley. Tyler was a serving woman in their household *c.* 1558–1564.

M. T., to the Reader.

    Thou have here, gentle reader, the history of Trebatio, an emperor in Greece.[7] Whether a true story of him indeed or a feigned fable, I wot° not.[8] Neither did I greatly seek after it in the translation, but by me it is done into English for thy profit and delight. The chief matter therein contained is of exploits of wars, and the parties therein named are especially renowned for their magnanimity and courage. The author's purpose appeareth to be this: to animate thereby and to set on fire the lusty° courages of young gentlemen to the advancement of their line by ensuing such like steps.[9] The first tongue wherein it was penned was the Spanish, in which nation, by common report, the inheritance of all warlike commendation hath to this day rested. The whole discourse, in respect of the end, not unnecessary for the variety and continual shift of fresh matter very delightful in the speeches short and sweet, wise in sentence, and wary in the provision of contrary accidents. For I take the grace thereof to be rather in the reporter's device than in the truth of this report, as I would that I could so well impart with thee that delight which myself findeth in reading the Spanish, but seldom is the tale carried clean from another's mouth.

    Such delivery as I have made I hope thou will friendly accept, the rather for that it is a woman's work, though in a story profane and a matter more manlike then becommeth my sex.[10] But as for the manliness of the matter, thou know that it is not necessary for every trumpeter or drumslare° in the war to be a good fighter. They take wages only to incite others, though themselves have privy° maims° and are thereby recureless.° So, gentle reader, if my travail° in Englishing this author may bring thee to a liking of the virtues herein commended, and by example thereof in thy prince's and country's quarrel to hazard thy person and purchase good name, as for hope of well deserving myself that way, I neither bend myself thereto, nor yet fear the speech of people if I be found backward. I trust every man holds not the plough which would the ground were tilled, and it is no sin to talk of Robin Hood though you never shot in his bow.[11] Or, be it that the attempt were bold to intermeddle in arms, so as the ancient Amazons did, and in this story Claridiana doth, and in other stories not a few, yet to report of arms is not so odious, but that it may be borne withal, not only in you men which yourselves are fighters, but in us women, to whom the benefit in equal part appertaineth of your victories.[12] Either for that the matter is so commendable that it carrieth no discredit from the homeliness of the speaker, or for that is it so generally known that it fitteth every man to speak thereof, or for that it jumpeth with this common fear on all parts of war and invasion. The invention, disposition, trimming, and what else in this story is wholly another man's, my part none therein but the translation, as it were: only in giving entertainment to a stranger, before this time unacquainted with our country guise.[13] Marry,° the worst perhaps is this: that among so many strangers as daily come over, some more ancient and some but new set forth; some penning matters of great weight and sadness in divinity or other studies, the profession whereof more nearly beseemeth my years; other some discoursing of matters more easy and ordinary in common talk, wherein a

---

[7] Whereas Trebatio is a fictional character, the romance situates him within a lineage of historical emperors, thereby conflating the generic boundary between romance and chronicle.

    Marginal note: 'The commendation of the story'. Typed marginal glosses appear in all three editions of *Mirror*. These glosses will be provided in the notes to the text as they appear.

[8] Her avowals of ignorance and modesty recall tropes habitually found in prefaces to both translations and original works by both male and female authors in the early modern period, as surveyed in the introduction.

[9] The exemplary value of the genre is frequently cited in romances' prefatory material. See the introduction for further discussion of this point.

[10] War and chivalry were deemed unacceptable material for female authors. Tyler's justification of her work is especially necessary and groundbreaking since she is the first English woman to write a romance.

    Marginal note: 'That a woman may write of war'

[11] Robin Hood: a legendary outlaw, famed for his exceptional archery skills, appearing in numerous chronicles and ballads, such as *Robin Hood and the Monk* (*c.* 1450) and *A Gest of Robyn Hode* (*c.* 1475).

[12] Amazons: a race of women warriors in Greek mythology

[13] By personifying her text as a stranger, Tyler highlights its Spanish origins.

gentlewoman may honestly employ her travail.°¹⁴ I have notwithstanding made countenance only to this gentleman, whom neither his personage might sufficiently commend itself unto my sex, nor his behaviour being light and soldier-like, might in good order acquaint itself with my years.¹⁵

So then the question now ariseth of my choice, not of my labour, wherefore I preferred this story before matter of more importance. For answer whereto, gentle reader, the truth is that as the first motion to this kind of labour came not from myself, so was this piece of work put upon me by others, and they which first counselled me to fall to work took upon them also to be my taskmasters and overseers, lest I should be idle; and yet, because the refusal was in my power, I must stand to answer for my easy yielding and may not be unprovided of excuse.¹⁶ Wherein if I should allege for myself that matters of less worthiness by as aged years have been taken in hand, and that daily new devices are published in songs, sonnets, interludes, and other discourses, and yet are borne out without reproach only to please the humour of some men, I think I should make no good plea therein. For besides that I should find thereby so many known enemies as known men have been authors of such idle conceits,° yet would my other adversaries be never the rather quieted. For they would say that as well the one as the other were all naught, and though peradventure° I might pass unknown amongst a multitude and not be the only gaze or the odd party in my ill doing, yet because there is less merit of pardon if the fault be excused as common, I will not make that my defence which cannot help me and doth hinder other men. But my defence is by example of the best, amongst which many have dedicated their labours — some stories, some of war, some physic,° some law, some as concerning government, some divine matters — unto diverse ladies and gentlewomen. And if men may, and do, bestow such of their travails° upon gentlewomen, then may we women read such of their works as they dedicate unto us. And if we may read them, why not farther wade in them to the search of a truth? And then much more, why not deal by translation in such arguments, especially this kind of exercise being a matter of more heed than of deep invention or exquisite learning? And, they must needs leave this as confessed: that in their dedications they mind not only to borrow names of worthy personages, but the testimonies also for their further credit, which neither the one may demand° without ambition nor the other grant without over-lightness. If women be excluded from the view of such works as appear in their name, or if glory only be sought in our common inscriptions, it mattereth not whether the parties be men or women, whether alive or dead. But to return, whatsoever the truth is — whether that women may not at all discourse in learning for men lay in their claim to be sole possessioners° of knowledge, or whether they may in some manner that is by limitation or appointment in some kind of learning — my persuasion hath been thus: that it is all one for a woman to pen a story as for a man to address his story to a woman. But amongst all my ill-willers,° some I hope are not so straight° that they would enforce° me necessarily either not to write or to write of divinity.¹⁷ Whereas neither durst° I trust mine° own judgement sufficiently if matter of controversy were handled, nor yet could I find any book in the tongue which would not breed offence to some.¹⁸

But, I perceive some may be rather angry to see their Spanish delight turned to an English

---

¹⁴ The translation or composition of pious, religious texts was deemed appropriate for women.
    Marginal note: 'That a woman of your years may write in this argument'
¹⁵ These references to her age throughout the preface help to defend Tyler against potential accusations of immodesty, which were most frequently levelled against young, unmarried women.
¹⁶ Translation as a remedy against idleness is another common trope seen in numerous contemporaneous texts. See the introduction for a discussion of this topic.
¹⁷ Marginal note: 'That you may not write of divinity'
¹⁸ Despite the conventional generic association of women with religious texts, Tyler here alludes to the post-Reformation religious controversies, which she desires to avoid. By invoking the doctrinal disputes, Tyler also reminds her readers of her text's suspicious origins in Catholic Spain. The following paragraph serves to neutralize the potential threat of the romance's Spanishness by stressing its value and by invoking the language of play and jest.

pastime.[19] They could well allow the story in Spanish, but they may not afford it so cheap or they would have it proper to themselves. What natures such men be of, I list° not greatly dispute. But my meaning hath been to make other partners of my liking, as I doubt not, gentle reader. But if it shall please thee after serious matters to sport thyself with this Spaniard, that thou shall find in him the just reward of malice and cowardice, with the good speed of honesty and courage, being able to furnish thee with sufficient store of foreign example to both purposes.[20] And, as in such matters which have been rather devised to beguile time than to breed matter of sad learning, he hath ever borne away the prize which could season such delights with some profitable reading. So, shall thou have this stranger an honest man when need serveth, and at other times either a good companion to drive out a weary night or a merry jest at thy board.°

And thus much as concerning this present story that it is neither unseemly for a woman to deal in, neither greatly requiring a less staid age then mine is.[21] But of these two points, gentle reader, I thought to give thee warning, lest perhaps understanding of my name and years thou might be carried into a wrong suspect of my boldness and rashness from which I would gladly free myself by this plain excuse. And if I may deserve thy good favour by like labour, when the choice is mine° own, I will have a special regard of thy liking. So I wish thee well.

Thine to use,

M. T.

---

[19] Marginal note: 'That you meant to make a common benefit of your pains'
[20] Marginal note: 'The use and profit of this Spanish translation'
[21] Marginal note: 'The conclusion'

CHAPTER 1

The Mirror of Knighthood

After that the great Emperor Constantine had peopled the city of Constantinople with the race of the noble citizens of Rome and had re-edified the ancient buildings founded by Pansanias, King of the Parthes, among all the emperors which succeeded in that Empire of Greece, none seemed to have raised his own name or to have made it so famous as the great and mighty Emperor Trebatio, whose worthy deeds, with the valiant acts of the knights of his time, I will report here, according as Artimodoro the Grecian° hath left them written in the great volumes of his Chronicle.[22] The story sayeth thus:[23] that if at any time, Fortune, being always uncertain and variable, showed herself more friendly to the Greeks than to all men besides, and if ever the Grecians° were feared in all the world, it was in the time of Trebatio, the son of Alicante, which man, by right line descended from the noble and ancient blood of Molosso, the second son of strong Pyrrhus, and in the third descent from the great Achilles, which was slain in the wars at Troy.[24]

This Trebatio, in the twenty-fifth year of his age, reigned in Epirus, where the said Pyrrhus and his ancestors had been kings. He was strong, and valiant in arms, and endowed with so many graces that his fame in the time was spread over all the world, and that there was neither king nor emperor but he was glad to hold him for his friend. Now, it happened in his time, by the death of the Emperor Theodoro the state of the Empire to be void, for that Theodoro had no son, and the Empire was to be given by election. So that the electors, not finding any whom with so good reason they might choose for emperor as the Great Trebatio, as well for his great valour as for his descent from so noble a race, they, with the willing and joint assent of all the imperials,° named him unto the Empire and brought him with great honour to Constantinople, where if before for his great fame they had praised and honoured him, now much more they held him dear, having in some part seen and known him.

Because he was of conditions very noble, pleasant, loving to all, liberal, courteous, sufferable,° pitiful, and above all very desirous to entertain in his court valiant and worthy knights, whom he honoured above all the princes of the earth, so that his court flourished with princes and knights, as well subjects as strangers, which much magnified his great estate. And himself held continual exercise in arms with them as being like inclined to nothing [else]. His virtue, by the report of such as knew him, was so rare that it was generally thought none of his predecessors to have had advantage over him, but rather he was of greater force than any one of them all for many men were witnesses of his mighty strokes.[25] He was called the Great Trebatio because he was eight foot in height and very strong timbered, so that without proof of his manhood they might thereby make conjecture of his force. In his life, customs, and conditions he was always so affable and courteous that never might be noted in him one little fault.

---

[22] 'mighty' is a mistranslation of 'nombrado'
  Constantine the Great: Emperor Constantine I (280?–337), the first Christian Roman emperor
  Constantinople: now Istanbul, capital of the Byzantine Empire, named in honour of Constantine the Great
  Parthes: Parthians, people of the Parthian Empire in Ancient Persia
[23] In *Espejo*, what follows is Artimidoro's chronicle, as noted in the introduction.
[24] Trebatio and Alicante are fictional characters.
  Molossus: the son of Pyrrhus (aka Neoptolemus), and grandson of Achilles. Molossus founded a dynasty in Epirus, in north-west Greece (*Espejo*, I.26).
  Achilles: in Greek mythology, the son of King Peleus and the sea nymph, Thetis. He was the greatest Greek hero in the Trojan War.
  Trojan War: in Greek mythology, a legendary war between Greece and Troy precipitated by Paris abducting Helen from her husband Menelaus, King of Sparta
[25] The source refers to his ease at cleaving armed knights in half. Tyler typically reduces descriptions of blood, gore, violence, and all battles and wars. Further instances will not be noted, but are investigated in the introduction.

Wherefore, his historians say that he was the crown of the Greeks and the clear mirror of all the princes and knights of the world. Whence also this, his chronicle, borroweth this title, especially having therein to remember the marvellous deeds of the Knight of the Sun with Rosicleer, both sons unto Trebatio, since whose time all the adventures of the ancient and famous knights were clean forgotten, and since whose time neither Ulysses, of whom Homer speaketh, neither any other songs or sonnets, ballads or interludes, were heard in Greece, only with these two knights they were familiarly acquainted.[26] Of these they made great volumes, and with a thousand devices° in verse they sang of their love. They made no building nor painture° without some story of them and their memory therein declared, in such sort that you might pass by no part of all Greece where was not recited, sung, or painted the histories and noble deeds of these knights, as if no other thing but arms or love were fitting for them.[27] And because that in the time to come so noble things should not be put in oblivion, some of the Grecians compiled this noble history to the encouraging of all nations that shall either hear or read this history.[28]

CHAPTER 2

The King of Hungary, pretending a title to the Empire, setteth himself against the Emperor Trebatio

It appeareth by an ancient Greek chronicle that the Emperor Helio III, predecessor in the Empire of Trebatio, had two sons, the eldest of the which two, the father being deceased, was chosen emperor.[29] The other was married with a princess inheritrix° of the kingdom of Hungary, whereby he became lord and ruler of that kingdom. The first son, which was elected for emperor, departed without issue, for which cause the Grecians chose another, which was the predecessor of Theodoro.[30] This seeing, the second son of Helio, which then reigned in Hungary and judging that with most reason the empire was his, as grieved with the election he assembled his power against the Grecians, thinking to be lord over them by force. In the end, as he was not so mighty as they, so he was vanquished and slain before he might attain his purpose. Yet, from that time forth, all the kings which succeeded in Hungary pretended always that the right of the empire rested in them by way of inheritance, and there never failed wars and dissensions between the Hungarians and the Greeks upon this occasion.

In like manner, when the Great Trebatio was chosen for emperor, then reigning in Hungary the King Tiberio, a very strong man and of great courage, besides of more might than all his ancestors, for he held in his subjection beside the Kingdom of Hungary, many other provinces, as Holland, Zeeland, Flanders, Zweueland, Bavaria, Austrich, Almaine, Alba, Denmark,

---

[26] 'borroweth this title' replaces 'por donde dignamente esta su coronica meresció gozar de tal renombre' (for which it is fitting that this chronicle deserves to enjoy such renown). The alteration stems from the mistranslation of 'renombre' (renown). *Espejo* explains that their deeds are so great that they cause those of ancient and famous knights to be forgotten.

Ulysses (aka Odysseus), King of Ithaca: the hero of Homer's epic poem the *Odyssey*, which narrates Ulysses' ten-year return journey to Ithaca after the Trojan War

Homer (fl. 9th or 8th century BCE): author of the *Iliad* and the *Odyssey*

[27] 'noble' renders the term 'maravilloso' (marvellous). The excision of the marvellous and its related terms is an essential feature of Tyler's translation methodology. Further instances will not be noted, but are examined in the introduction.

[28] *Espejo* indicates that many Greeks compiled the chronicles, rendering them into twelve books, and that the first book is the text which follows.

[29] Emperor Helio III: a fictional character

[30] Theodoro: a fictional character

20   Marcomandia, Persia, and other regions, with the which he deemed himself one of the mightiest kings in the world.[31] This Tiberio, knowing the election of the Emperor Trebatio and being more attached with the desire of the empire than any of his predecessors were — as it was to be gotten by war — so he assembled by summons the greatest of estate throughout his land, and declaring unto them his will, he commanded to gather all the people they might for to invade Greece.

Besides this, to the end his power might yet be greater, he determined to marry his daughter unto such a one as would and could maintain his quarrel. This maiden was called Briana, the most beautiful princess that was to be found in all those parts, being by the only report of her excellency° sued° unto by many worthy princes, especially by Prince Edward, son of Oliverio,
30   King of Great Britain.[32] This young knight — strong, and valiant, and greatly enamoured on the Princess Briana through the great fame of her beauty — had before dispatched his ambassadors towards the king, her father, to request her for wife.[33] To the which, her father, because he had already undertaken the battle against the Emperor Trebatio, easily condescended upon condition that the prince should come into Hungary with 20,000 chosen men of war for to aid him in the pursuit of his claim against the emperor. This, when Prince Edward understood, he had so great desire to have the Princess Briana that, by and by, he granted his request. And so as speedily as he might, he gathered the people that the King Tiberio required of him.

And with the consent of his father, he departed from Great Britain toward Hungary, giving intelligence before unto the King Tiberio of his coming. The king, knowing the succours which
40   came unto him, appointed a day when all his host should meet together. And finding himself of so great power, in the meanwhile until the prince came, he resolved to make a road into Greece, sacking all the little towns he might before that the Emperor Trebatio should perceive it. Afterwards, if the Emperor Trebatio should come to succour his subjects then to join battle with him at such time as the Prince should approach, which thing he put in practice diligently.

For with that power which he had, he entered into Greece, foraging the country, taking little towns of no great force, burning and wasting so much as he might, to the intent that the people of other fenced cities, stricken with fear, might abandon themselves to flight and enfeeble their forces. Howbeit, King Tiberio had not passed in Greece thirty miles when the Emperor Trebatio, having knowledge of it, came against him with a host of knights so valiant that at the first alarm°
50   the Hungarian reculed,° and by the chase of his enemies was forced to retire home into the city of Belgrade, which is in Hungary.[34] There he fortified himself and manned the town, unwilling as yet to go unto the field until the Prince of Great Britain should arrive, by whose coming, their powers being joined, he thought he might give the battle unto the Emperor Trebatio. Albeit he carried about him a maim° incurable in his body, not by any stroke lent him by his enemy, but by the only conceit° of the emperor's virtue, for he had seen the emperor demean himself more worthily than any of those which came with him, and namely in a kinsman of his, a very strong knight, whom the emperor at one blow, as it were, divided in two pieces. This, as it might be,

---

[31] Zeeland: maritime province in south-western Netherlands
Zweueland: Switzerland
Austrich: Austria
Almaine: Germany
Alba: in *Espejo* it is Albia, the Latin name for the Elbe River.
Denmark: in *Espejo* this is Daunia, a district in Apulia, southern Italy.
Marcomandia: the Marcomanii were a Germanic tribe engaged in extended feuds with the Romans. To escape Roman aggression in 9 BCE, they migrated east to Bohemia, where they established a powerful confederation of tribes under King Maroboduus.
[32] Her name recalls Amadis's beloved, Oriana, in *Amadis of Gaul*.
[33] 'valiant' replaces 'proud', thereby altering the characterization of Edward. The increased sympathy for the British prince that results from this change of emphasis is invesitgated in the introduction.
[34] Belgrade: capital of modern Serbia. It was for many centuries part of Hungary.

made him keep his chamber, because he himself confessed the valour of the emperor to be above the report of men, notwithstanding he had heard sufficiently of the emperor's prowess.

But because these things are not mentioned, but to give beginning to this history we run them briefly over, not rehearsing the great deeds of arms that the emperor and his people did in besieging the city, because we have other matters more noble in hand, in comparison whereof these things were needless. The story hereof begins in the chapter following.

CHAPTER 3

The Emperor Trebatio, by the hearsay of her beauty, was surprised with the love of the Princess Briana

Certain days the Emperor Trebatio lay at the siege of Belgrade, hoping that the King Tiberio would come out to give them battle, for that he had great desire to be avenged of the great harms which he had received in Greece. But the king would in no wise° leave the town, still abiding the coming of Prince Edward and his army out of England. The Emperor, marvelling much at it, commanded a prisoner to be brought before him, whom he had taken in the former battle. Of him he demanded the cause why the King Tiberio held himself so close with so many good knights mewed° up in the city and why he came not out to give the battle, with promise of life and liberty if he told truth, otherwise the certainty of most cruel death. The prisoner, thus placed before the emperor, what with fear of death and hope of liberty, durst° not declare other than the truth. And therefore, thus made answer unto him:[35]

'Know you, mighty Emperor, that when the King of Hungary, my master, first took upon him the entry into Greece, he would not have done it, although he hath so mighty a host as is seen, but in hope that before he should be espied and met withal there should come to his help Prince Edward, son to the king of Great Britain, with 20,000 knights. This number was promised upon condition that the prince should have the king's daughter, the Princess Briana, to wife. Which princess, I believe, is the fairest maid in all the world, and by such fame the prince is become enamoured of her. So as we hear that he is already departed from Great Britain with the number appointed, and shall take landing very soon in this country. The King Tiberio abideth his coming, and is determined to give the onset as soon as their forces shall be united.'

This said the prisoner. But the emperor, minding to know more of the matter, demanded of him where the Princess Briana remained and of what age she might be. The prisoner answered him:

'My lord, she is with the Queen Augusta, her mother, in the Monastery of the River, which is near to Buda, a pleasant and delectable house, wherein none are lodged but nuns and the queen's gentlewomen.[36] The princess is of the age of fourteen years, and be you assured that so many as shall see her will judge her rather a goddess than a woman, so much her beauty doth excel all the gentlewomen of the world.[37] Now, so soon as the prince shall land, he will straightways take his journey towards the Monastery of the River, because it is so appointed by the king, her father. The king himself will not be there, because he will not be absent in such a busy time from the city'.

When the prisoner had thus said, the Emperor Trebatio commanded him to be set free without speaking other thing to his people. But with a sorrowful and troubled countenance he withdrew himself into a secret chamber of his imperial tent, where tossing in his conceit° diverse and

---

[35] Marginal note: 'Prisoner's oration'. The note is omitted from the 1599(?) edition.
[36] Monastery of the River: several monasteries have borne this name, but none in or near Buda
   Buda: a Hungarian town that combined with Pest to form modern Budapest
[37] She is fifteen in *Espejo*.

sundry fancies,° he endured a wilful imprisonment without any bail or mainprize.° Thus, that force, which neither by tilt, tourney, nor barriers, neither by spear nor sword, neither by malice of the enemy nor pride of the mighty might at any time be subdued, was now vanquished by the only hearsay of a gentlewoman's commendation. Nay, that valiant heart which he held forcible enough against all the world failed in his own defence against a delicate damsel whom he had never seen. What force is it that may repulse this evil, since that with such flattering closes° it overthroweth so many noble hearts and strong bodies?

But to return, the Emperor Trebatio so much burned in love with the Princess Briana, that already he hath forgotten the damage received in his country, his travel out of his country with a huge army, the consuming of his treasure for to wreak his anger on the King Tiberio. Only he devised upon this: how to give remedy unto his amorous passion. For as the fire was great which enflamed him, so was the remedy by all semblance far from him. Because that on the one part, he was hindered by the enmity between him and her father, so that he durst not require° her for wife; and on the other side, she was already promised to the prince of Great Britain, who had put himself on his journey for the attaining of her person, so that likewise the king could not take her from him to give unto his enemy. These things bred such grief unto the emperor as that he hoped for nothing, but to die.[38] And so turning and overturning in his thought a thousand sort of remedies without finding any which might satisfy him, he conveyed himself into his most secret tent and there remained three days, not suffering any of his people to have access unto him or speak with him, except some squires-servitors,° from whom likewise he would willingly have exempted himself, but that he would not die so desperately.° Those of the camp which saw the sudden change and alteration in the emperor, as they knew not the cause of it, so were they much abashed and careful° to know what it might be. Some imagined that the delay of the war and the coming of Prince Edward were the occasions of his trouble. And so hoping that he should well overcome that grief shortly, they left him to his rest until he had resolved upon the pursuit of this, which followeth in the next chapter.

CHAPTER 4

Prince Edward entereth into Belgrade; the Emperor bethinkth himself of his remedy

Four days after that the Emperor Trebatio was thus wounded with the love of the Princess Briana, Prince Edward, with 20,000 [men], entered into the city of Belgrade, where he was welcomed by the king, who had great desire to see him, for he thought not only to depart with that city, but also to add thereunto a great part of the Empire of Greece. So soon as this news were spread in the enemy's camp, the emperor was cast into greater melancholy, as by the shortness of time not being able to find an issue for his late device.° Only this he thought that for to assure his uncertain hope, if there might be any: he had none other way than to cut off Prince Edward's enterprise, and so by shortening his life, better and more easily to compass° the obtaining of the princess.

Upon this resolution he made to call into his tent twelve knights, the most valiant and worthiest of all his host, among whom one was Alceo, father of Rodomarte, Prince of Sardinia, of whom there is made great account in this history.[39] The second was Alpineo, Lord of the island Lemnos. The third was called Alfonte, Lord of the island Sicily. The fourth was called Alcino, King of Thrace. The fifth, Liberio, Lord of Nicroponte. The sixth, Boristhines, whose son was Rodopheo, Prince of Rhodes. The seventh, Dardante, Prince of Dalmatia. The eighth,

---

[38] In *Espejo*, he thought he would die. Tyler intensifies his despair and has him commit a mortal sin through the development of suicidal thoughts.

[39] Rodomarte appears in Ortúñez's part 2, Chapters 11, 39, and 38, and in part 3, Chapter 30.

Melides, Lord of Ithaca, where Ulysses reigned king. The ninth, Argante, Lord of Pathmos. The tenth, Arimont, Lord of the Islands Cyclades. The eleventh, Artdoro, Prince of Candia. The twelfth and last, Nicoleonte, Lord Warden of the straits where Corinth stood.[40] All knights of great account, young, and very strong for to undertake any enterprise, all subjects unto the emperor, and all well beloved of him because he was privy° unto their great virtues. Now when the emperor saw all these knights in presence, with some shamefastness,° which the weight of the matter caused, he revealed to them wholly his grief, giving them to understand withal that unless he had some help his life were spilled.° Among all the best which he had found, he reckoned specially upon one, which was that secretly they should avoid the camp and follow him.

The knights having great desire to serve him and esteeming themselves happy that he would communicate with them part of his mind, they freely offered unto him their persons for the accomplishing of that which he should command them. And they all agreed to depart with him in such order as he had devised. Then the emperor made to call before him the King of Bohemia, which was his uncle, a very wise and expert man in arms, to whom he declared that he had urgent occasion to be absent a while from his army, the circumstances whereof sayeth he:

'You shall further know at our return. In the meantime, I commend unto you the charge of the war. And for your greater credit with the people, I deliver unto your hands the imperial sceptre'.[41]

The king, marvelling at this that the emperor did, without more demanding of him whither° or whereabouts he would go, accepted the charge and promised therein to employ his travail.°

Well, the night approaching with the hour agreed upon, the emperor and the twelve knights, armed at all points with rich and costly armour and with Hungarian bases, secretly left the camp without being heard or known of their enemies. Wherein they travelled all night until the day appeared. Then they alighted to rest their horses and fed upon such victuals as they had brought with them. After taking again their horses, they posted° on their journey until they were in the midway between Buda and Belgrade, which way Prince Edward of force° must have passed when he should go to the Monastery of the River. There, in a thick wood somewhat aside out of the way, they put themselves, having provision and furniture° of all things necessary, where they remained very close until that Fortune, friendly to the emperor and enemy to the prince, gave the prince into the emperor's hands, which shall be showed in the chapter following.

CHAPTER 5

Prince Edward, riding towards the Monastery of the River, was by the Emperor Trebatio encountered and slain

When Prince Edward had once set footing in Belgrade, he had great desire to see the princess so that the third day after his coming he would needs depart towards the Monastery of the River. The King Tiberio, understanding his desire (albeit he himself might not accompany him), yet he set him on his way thitherward,° only to have his aid and assistance in the battle with four aged knights in his company, being best known by the queen and the princess. These should be in the prince's retinue and other twelve knights more which he had brought out of his country.

---

[40] The characters are fictional, but the places are real. Nicroponte is modern Euboea and Candia is modern Crete (*Espejo*, I.39).

   Espejo mistakenly omits the eleventh knight, naming Artdoro, Prince of Candia as the twelfth. Tyler numbers him the eleventh and invents the 'twelfth and last'.

[41] This is one of many places were Tyler transforms indirect to direct speech, imbuing her text with immediacy. Further instances will not be noted, but are reviewed in the introduction.

10   And by these the king sent letters to the queen and the Princess Briana, the contents whereof were that the prince might speedily be betrothed unto her. But more company would he not send, thereby to have the match kept secret until the war which he held with the emperor were finished. For this matter was hushed, no man almost being privy° unto it; yet the prisoner which bewrayed° it unto the emperor had understanding of it by means of the king's service. In this time, the queen and her daughter, having intelligence of the prince's coming, attended his coming in the monastery with preparation for his entertainment.

Prince Edward, departing from the king one night the most covertly that he might, went out of the city with his own twelve knights and four of the king's. With these he took his way a whole night and a day with all the haste he might to end the great desire he had to see the
20   beautiful princess. This way, albeit short, yet it seemed long unto him as being ignorant of the sour sauce and woeful wedding which was in providing.[42]

Oh marriage, the slender and weak foundation of worldly things! How is it not only regarded by men, but highly reverenced?[43] How seldom was it ever steadfast? And how many thousands hath it beguiled? I mean not the base and common people, but even kings and emperors. Oh, how many impediments be therein left to hinder us from enjoying it? Oh, what a common thing it is to die, and how many ever saw happy end in it? How joyful and pleasant was to Paris the desired match of Helen?[44] And how sorrowful and lamentable was the end, not only to him, but to his parents and brothers° and the greatest part of all Asia? For not only in Greece, but in all the out° islands thereabouts was bewept° his bitter bridal. With how great care and diligence
30   do men hasten on the causes of their care, occasions of their heaviness, means of their pains, and matter of their grief, and do not content themselves with the continual affliction wherein Fortune schooleth them? But by new means they invent new matters of danger which crosseth them. At every step they frame new causes, and as it were, forge unto themselves sharp spurs to prick forward this woeful life. Where they think to find pleasure and rest, there they find for their loss travail° and trouble for the death which they would fly° from. To escape either nipping colds or scalding heat, this only one remedy they have: to climb up unto the mountains, where yet the wind hath most force and the sun doth soonest parch. Above all this, hath not the insatiable covetousness of man broken through the sturdy waves of the sea and cut out new passages on the mountains? But why do we complain on Fortune? Do not we bend her arms to
40   fight with us? Do not we maintain her weapons, which peradventure° lighteth on our own necks? As for example, if Paris had not made a way through the deep waves of the Sea Aegean, which the gods had placed as a peaceable bound between Europe and Asia, and if he had not sought Greece — since Asia was large enough to have found a fair wife in, and so it may be, much more honest then Helen was — then the Achians had not transported themselves into Asia to destroy Troy.[45]

And turning again to our matter, Prince Edward might have sought him a wife in his own country or more near home, of whose beauty his own eyes might have been witnesses and not have sought her in a strange land by the only bruit° of a cunning tale, especially upon so hard and sore conditions as to bring his own person and people to the war. Whosoever comes to seek
50   pleasure and delight for his youth, let him take that he finds and think it not strange because that unkind Fortune hath used the like unto others.

The prince, then being on his way, two of the king's knights were dispatched before by some secret by-ways very well known unto them to advertise° the queen and princess of the

---

[42] The poetic language and alliteration are added by Tyler. This type of rhetorical embellishment is surveyed in the introduction.
[43] This is one of many cases where a declarative statement is transformed into a question. Further instances will be noted in the introduction.
[44] Paris stole Helen from her husband Menelaus, thereby precipitating the start of the Trojan War.
[45] Achians: Greeks

approaching of the prince. These two held on their way, not ascried° by the ambush. But so soon as the prince with his knights had entered in the thicket, they were presently discovered by the emperor, who was already armed with his rich armour and mounted upon a strong and light horse. The emperor, taking a great spear in his hand, very sharp and well steeled for the purpose, went alone aside out of the wood with a soft pace to encounter with the prince and his knights. And being come right before them, said unto them:

'Know you, knights, that this passage is forbidden you except you leave your shields and your names in them, for that a lady whom I honour and serve hath commanded me to do it, whose love I could not otherwise obtain'.

The Prince Edward was by nature very stout° and by inclination given to somewhat less modesty in his talk than behoved such a prince.[46] Howbeit for this and other faults, he was a very valiant and strong knight, such a one as neither in Great Britain, neither in the Kingdom of Hungary, was thought to have his peer. But as he understood the demand° of the knight, very wroth he answered him:

'By God, knight, if the King Tiberio were as certain of the victory against the Emperor Trebatio as I hope to chastise thy folly, then the Prince of England should not need to come from so far a country to give him help. Take thou quickly that part of the field as shall seem good unto thee, and with one only choice thou shall see how dear and bitter thy love hath been unto thee'.

As the prince had said this and had pronounced with his own mouth that cruel doom, not well foreseeing his own fall, he took a great spear from one of his knights and broached° his horse with the spurs to meet the emperor. This he did, not for that his knights would not have put themselves in the adventure before him, every man claiming to be first, but for that no reason sufficed him. For his stoutness° and his immeasurable pride made him to forget the force of his enemy, and yet his enemy stood before him so great and so big made that he seemed to be a giant.[47]

But this prince's adverse fortune and unhappy° destinies would him to be foremost, so that the mighty Trebatio knew it as well by the riches of his armour as by the talk which had passed between him and his knights. And being very glad to see him the first which he met, he said unto himself:

'Oh, that my spear were now greater and stronger and the head forged by Vulcan, that it might not stay° in the armour of this knight.[48] For that according as I see him great and strong, so I fear he will escape my hands and then my travail° shall be all in vain'.

Thus, as he said, they by and by did put both their spears in their rests, and giving either horse his bridle, they ran together with such fury that they made the earth to tremble. And yet, the lightness of their horses was such that it seemed the grass yielded not under their feet. The prince hit the emperor in the middest° of the shield, and piercing farther, left the head remaining in the fine and well-steeled armour, whereby, the staff, broken in many shivers,° made a great whistling in the air. But the emperor's stroke was much more fell,° for he levelled it with such force that it entered not only into the shield and strong armour of the prince, but passed through unto his amorous heart, all bedewed with blood a whole arm's length. Then the prince fell dead, executing the sentence which he had given in these words: 'that that love should be very dear and bitter'.

When his people saw him stretched upon the ground, there might no sorrow be compared unto theirs. And as raging mad they ran all together upon the emperor, thinking to put in

---

[46] *Espejo* explains that he is naturally inclined to 'sobervio' (haughtiness, pride). This is one of many alterations that positively affects the characterization of Edward. Of course, the adjective 'stout' can denote 'pride', but it also signifies 'brave' and 'fierce'. The implications of this modification are reviewed in the introduction.

[47] 'stoutness' again translates 'sobervia'

[48] Vulcan: Roman god of fire, and blacksmith for the Roman gods. In his forge, he produced thunderbolts as well as formidable tools and weapons.

practice their deadly anger upon his carcass.[49] Some with spears and other with swords struck him on all parts with great rage and haste, so that if his armour had not been very good, in short space they had hewed it in pieces. But that most valiant Greek, no less strong than any of his ancestors, bearing his fine and sharp sword, turned himself among them in such manner that he sheathed it in their bodies. The first whom he met, he cleaved unto the eyes. The second's arm he cut off by the elbow. And being sore wounded, he overthrew the third at another blow. Neither stayed he here, but in his rage he dealt blows and wounded many, which for fear, accounting him rather a devil of hell than a knight, put themselves to flight. Albeit, they might have recovered some courage in that they were many and chosen knights always against one knight only. But the reason was for that, at this time, the emperor's knights showed themselves out of the wood, so that indeed, by the great manhood of their lord, they found none left alive save two knights of the king which were known by their Hungarian bases.° Those, the emperor commanded to be kept carefully for the thing before touched.

This being done, the knights and other footmen which the emperor had brought with him to guide his carriage took all the dead bodies upon their horses without leaving anything which was theirs. And altogether they carried them into the thick of the wood, from whence they before came out. There, in the thickest thereof, they made a great pit into the which they threw the prince and the knights, save the English bases° and the king's letters which were needful for his purpose. They covered them with earth in such sort that there was never memory of them.

At the time that the prince was entered, the emperor, being of conditions pitiful, felt so great dolour in his heart that the tears issued abundantly from his eyes, ruing the loss of so great a prince slain out of his own country in the beauty of his age, when also yielding a great sigh which seemed to have come from the bottom of his heart, he said with a troubled and low voice in this wise:°

'Oh unhappy° and unfortunate prince, God knoweth how sorrowful and grievous thy death is to me, and how fain° I would have given remedy in some other manner to that I most desired! And although thou was mine° enemy and come in favour of the King Tiberio to take from me my land and high estate, yet would I not have been so cruel an enemy unto thee but the entire love of the Princess Briana drove me more thereto than mine° own enmity. Now I wish that by some other means I might have been relieved, and not to have bought my life by thy loss. But as love is tyrannous, so marvel not though he want° pity towards thee, which could not otherwise purchase it to himself. Pardon me therefore, oh mighty and worthy prince, and judge if thou were alive what thou would do if by my death thou might find remedy of thy love!'

The emperor's knights, which heard these words and saw the tears trickling down his manly cheeks, perceived well how much the death of the prince disquieted him.[50] And they said amongst themselves that by good right the emperor deserved the praise of the most noble and worthy prince of the world.

But having made an end, the emperor caused to be brought before him the two knights belonging unto Tiberio. These two were very fearful of the death, seeing the things which were already done, and especially when they knew him to be the Emperor Trebatio, whom they held as their mortal enemy. Now when they came before him, the emperor said to them:

'If you will do that which I command you and keep secret that which I tell you, I will not only pardon you the death which I have given to your fellows, but also I will bring you with me into mine° empire, where you shall be very well contented'.

The knights, better satisfied than they were because he promised them life, before not hoping but the death, with good will they yielded themselves to do all that he would withal, swearing into his imperial hands their faith and obeisance. Then said the emperor:

---

[49] In *Espejo* they are compared to rabid dogs.
[50] The adjective 'manly' renders the Spanish term 'severo' (severe).

'That which I would have you do is this: I have great desire to have the Princess Briana for wife, and this may not be done except I go in the name of Prince Edward to ensure° myself to her in the Monastery of the River. For the which, it is necessary that you two, being known of the queen and the princess, should go in my company and say that I am Prince Edward. Now, sirs, discover not my secret to any person until that you be licensed thereunto by me. And in so doing, you shall do naught either against your lord or kingdom, since in this bargain the princess loseth not and the king with all his subjects win perpetually, for that by this mean, the great wars and contentions begun, shall take end'.

After that the emperor had said these and other things whereby the knights understood his will, it grieved them not a whit° of this talk. But they were rather joyous, weighing the benefit which the king, the kingdom, the Princess Briana, and all his should reap thereby, and especially the princess by obtaining to husband the most noble and worthy prince of all Christendom, as well for his person as for his estate. And so, with good will, they submitted themselves to do him pleasure and what else he commanded them.

With this, the emperor and his knights took the letters which were directed to the queen and the princess. And with more hope to achieve their inquest,° they put on the English bases,° which made them seem Englishmen. Then, taking their way toward the Monastery of the River, in the way the king's knights told the emperor how two of their fellows were gone before to give notice unto the princess of Prince Edward's coming, and that therefore it were good to go well advised, for they should meet them by the way. The emperor allowed° their advice and charged his people until they approached near them not to disclose themselves, lest they retiring, their secrets might be laid open. Now Fortune jumped so even with the emperor as that all things succeeded on his side until the accomplishment of his desire, which shall be recited in the chapter following.

CHAPTER 6

The Emperor Trebatio was received at the monastery by the Archbishop of Belgrade, and there betrothed by the name of Prince Edward

The emperor with his knights departed from the wood where the unfortunate prince was slain and took their way towards the city of Buda, until they came within six miles of the monastery, where they saw afar the two other knights which had returned to bring the prince on his way. When their fellows had espied them, they told it to the emperor. Upon this, the emperor commanded his knights to keep together, lest they should be known. And so, they kept on till they met. The other two, seeing the English bases,° thought him to be the Prince of England with his knights. But the emperor's knights, as soon as these were within their reach, laid hold on their bridles and with courteous words stayed° them until the other two knights of the king's had talked with them. These two declared unto the other that which had happened between Prince Edward and the Emperor Trebatio, and in the end made plain the meaning of the emperor, both praying them to keep it secret and threatening them with death if they did otherwise. No doubt they wondered at that which chanced, but what the emperor would that they promised him and were nothing repentant of their exchange.

The emperor, being ascertained° of their faith, went with them towards the Monastery of the River. Whereunto being come, they found not° in the monastery but the queen, the princess, and other gentlewomen (being servitors° to attend upon them), and the Archbishop of Belgrade, which there tarried for to ensure° them. This archbishop received the emperor at the gate, and thinking him assuredly to be the Prince of England, conducted him with his knights where the queen and the princess were in the company of beautiful and discreet ladies, abiding his coming.

When they had saluted each other and that the emperor had taken a full view of the princess, he was greatly abashed to see her beauty, for he could not be persuaded that so great comeliness had been in Helen; although dearly bought by his ancestors, he judged it more heavenly or angelical than human or earthly. Besides, she was of a goodly stature, excelling the other gentlewomen in height a span.[51] The princess, when she saw the emperor before her, she judged him to be the goodliest knight that might be in the world, which his beautiful face and pleasant countenance showed especially.

30   When thus by the eyes each of them were indifferently° satisfied, the emperor would have kissed the hand of the Queen Augusta, but she with great good will embraced him. By and by, turning himself again towards the princess, he took her by the hand and said, in effect, thus much:

'The fame of your great beauty, excellent princess, hath in such sort passed through the world that the only report thereof hath forced the Prince of England to leave his natural kingdom and soil to come and serve you in this country and to behold with his own eyes that which his ears would scarcely believe. God hath made me so fortunate that I have obtained the good will of the king, your father, and of the queen, your mother, for to have you to wife. Only now I want the consent of your part, which the king by his letters prayeth you to give unto me. And I, for

40   the desire that I have to be yours, beseech you not deny it me, for with it I may account myself the happiest knight of all the world'.

And with these words, kissing the king's letters, he delivered it into her hands, which the princess, receiving with a grave and sober countenance and after taking it to the archbishop for to read, the meantime made answer softly, on this wise:°[52]

'I would to God, most worthy prince, that I were such a one as with reason might deserve some part of the pains which you have taken only to see me, or that I might in some little respect recompense the great pleasure you have done to me and to all this kingdom in coming to succour us with your great force and power, but since desert° doth want so much in me, I will accomplish that which the duty of obedience unto the king, my father, forceth me unto. For that I must

50   subject my will unto his commandment, yet I so consider of this your offer and request, as that from this time I will dare to compare with you in like happiness'.

While these words were in speaking, the archbishop began to read the king's letters, wherein only was contained his consent with the desire of dispatch: that presently upon the prince's coming they should be married. The archbishop, with both their consents, taking their hands, married them with all the ceremonies and words which the Church ordaineth. After this, the emperor embraced the fair princess, and with unspeakable gladness kissed her on the white and red cheeks. And from thence brought her into a gorgeous chamber, where they drove forth the rest of the day with very amorous and delectable talk, which so much the more set his love on fire as he proceeded farther in his pleasant dalliance. Albeit, ere° night the most puissant emperor

60   was not altogether quieted in his thought, for fear lest someone which knew the prince might have bewrayed° them. At length, being certain that none in the monastery had seen either the one or the other, but only the king's four knights and his own men, which kept that matter close enough.

When the hour of supper approached, he supped with some pleasure and so held on a great part of the night, till it was time to take his rest.[53] Then the emperor was led to one side of the monastery, wherein there was a rich and stately lodging where he lengthened the night with many fancies,° not having as yet reached into the very depth of his enterprise, albeit stilled a little with that which already had happened. The beautiful princess, after leave taken of the emperor, accompanied the queen, her mother, because until that the war was ended between

---

[51] The significance of her height is explored in the introduction.

[52] Tyler adds the explanation that she gave the letter to the archbishop to read, thereby implying that Briana is illiterate.

[53] The sexual allusion to 'the great pleasure and rejoicing' in which they spent the night is excised (*Espejo*, I.56.26–27).

290 the king, her father, and the emperor, she was desirous to keep herself unknown. And so the king, her father, and the queen, her mother, had commanded, lest if ought should happen amiss to the prince in those battles, the princess should have remained both a maiden and a widow. This device little availed, as shall be manifested in the sequel.°

CHAPTER 7

The Emperor Trebatio driveth in his conceit° the order how to consummate the marriage, which in the end, he bringeth to pass accordingly

The Emperor Trebatio remained three days in the Monastery of the River, not having [the] opportunity to talk with the princess alone because she was not willing to give consent to his desire until the war with the emperor should be finished.[54] This inconvenience troubled his thought and increased his melancholy as nothing more for that the term which the king had set for his return was already expired, and being afraid lest the king would send for him, whereby his fault should be discovered, without giving remedy to that which had been the original of his grief.[55] In such wise° he was tormented that he could neither sleep nor eat. And in his imagination, he did naught else but gaze on the princess, expecting time when he might allay the heat of his amorous passion. But whether it were Fortune or the will of God, it fell so out that there was begotten between them the fruit of their desire. For one morning walking in his chamber, he espied out of a window the princess alone, in her nightgown, going towards a fresh and pleasant garden butting upon° his lodging (the garden before he had not seen).[56] Into this garden entered none but the princess and her gentlewomen. As he saw so good and prosperous a time, the most joyful man that ever was, he went towards the pleasant garden, and finding no entry but by the chamber of the princess, the door whereof was shut, he took two of those spears which his knights had brought and rearing them up against the wall with the blunt end upwards, as he was very nimble he lifted himself upon them lightly, and easily slid down between them into the garden without being seen of any, especially not of the princess, who was unwitting° of such a leap.[57]

The princess was nigh° a fountain well set about with roses and jessamines,° combing and dressing of her yellow° hair. Now when she saw herself thus suddenly taken by the emperor, with a fearful start she rose from whence she was, and gently smiling as somewhat overtaken with shamefastness, she beshrewed° him in this sort:

'Assuredly, my lord, needs must the hurt be great which you have sustained by your leap and great is the injury which the garden hath received by your entry, because that in it none have come but either myself or my gentlewomen, for whose solace it was first plotted out'.

'For this cause God hath showed me such favour', answered the emperor, 'because I have lodged my heart in your excellent beauty, and well may the body lawfully enter where the heart is harboured. Let not, therefore, my entry, good madam, seem strange unto you since that

---

[54] Four lines are omitted from the Spanish text which reiterate Trebatio's inability to be alone with Briana (*Espejo*, I.58.11–14). This type of repetition is frequently excised by Tyler.

[55] The allusion to melancholy is added. Medical discourse in the period was still heavily indebted to humoural theory, as codified by the ancient Greek physicians Hippocrates and Galen. The theory posits that an abundance or lack of any of the four bodily fluids affects human character and behaviour. Thus, the four main temperaments — sanguine, choleric, phlegmatic, and melancholic — are due to excesses of blood, yellow bile, phlegm, and black bile, respectively. The melancholic temperament is thought of as dry and cold, which contradicts the subsequent description of Trebatio as hot, stemming from his passion for Briana.

[56] The gated, private garden is a symbol of Briana's chastity. As a result, the fact that no man has entered her garden is emphasized.

[57] The phallic image of the spears with 'the blunt end upwards' is added.

neither hour nor moment I may depart from you. And if this, my rudeness, hath procured you any pain, by the freedom which you have given me, my heart shall make excuse unto your beauty, under whose safe-conduct, without demand of leave, my body hath entered'.[58]

The good emperor, having thus said, embraced and kissed her. And not leaving any leisure of reply, made her to sit down by him near unto the well. This place was so hedged and compassed about with odoriferous roses and sweet smelling jessamines° that they might not be perceived by any. And the gentle murmur that the running water made upon the pebble stones, agreeing with the delicate lays° which diverse birds made upon the green boughs, increased so much the longing desire of the emperor, that casting how to win the favour of his lady, already his tongue failed to speak and his hearing to receive that which she spoke. She then all trembled, as knowing his purpose, and through fear greatly desired to have shunned that place. But the emperor caught her between his arms and, with such haste to end his suit, left her unfurnished of her answer.

At that time, as the burning beams of the sun began with his golden rays to look through the thick jessamines,° all the fortunate aspects intermeddling their forces, at that time, by the grace of the Almighty, were begotten these two noble children, the Knight of the Sun and Rosicleer, the beams of whose knightly deeds so shined through the world as that the worthy prowess of their predecessors were thereby eclipsed. This was the plaudit° of his passion, and the beautiful princess now became a wife somewhat against her will.[59] But when she saw no remedy to that which was past, she comforted herself in that he was her lawful husband and, therefore, she pardoned him his boldness in troubling her. These two lovers shortened the time with good agreement until the emperor at his departure took his leave of her to mount up the way he came and to return into his lodging. The princess remained alone in the garden until her gentlewomen came for her to dinner.

After this, yet the emperor sojourned there three days, at the end whereof, fearing the king's jealousy over his tarrying and the event of his sending for, he took his leave of the queen and the princess, not without the courtesy of many tears on each part, and especially of the princess, whom he left very doleful, albeit sadder would she have been if she had foreseen the long time of his absence.

CHAPTER 8

The Emperor Trebatio, pursuing those which had stolen his lady, left all his knights and took another way

The Emperor Trebatio, thus having departed from the Monastery of the River, became very sorrowful in his heart with the leaving of the Princess Briana, for that the fire which enflamed him after he had known her was greater than the affection which he bore to her before by the hearing of her beauty. And that which caused his most grief was that he knew not how either to return speedily unto her or to salve that sore which he had already chaffed. He thought in himself that if he made peace with the King Tiberio, letting him understand of the matter, the king

---

[58] The allegory is absent from *Espejo*.
[59] Briana's modesty and Trebatio's virility are both stressed in this scene. His rape of Briana is somewhat excused due to the providential nature of the conception of their twin boys coupled with their marital status, as Briana notes in the following sentence. Helen Hackett argues that in this scene 'male desire is implicitly figured as a power which begets the heroes of the future, and thereby as a force of destiny which both Trebatio and Briana are powerless to resist'(p. 58). The scene recalls other instances of supernatural rape in literature, including Uther Pendragon's quasi-rape of Igraine during which King Arthur was conceived, numerous Ovidian narratives of rape, as well as the Virgin Mary's submissive conception of Christ (Hackett, p. 58).

would not accept of it, either for the great enmity which was between them or for the bond wherein he was bound to the Prince of Great Britain. And therefore, it would be a thing neither reasonable nor agreeing with his honour in lieu of the prince's pains, which he had taken to come from his country accompanied with so great a number of knights to serve him, and, in regard of the death which he there received in his service, now to become a friend to his foe and to give his daughter before espoused to the prince unto the deadliest foe which the prince had. Debating these and other things in his mind, about the time that they had got over their heads the thick wood wherein they had been before, now to the end not to tire their horses, they lighted down, unbridled their horses, and turned them to grass. They themselves feeding on such victuals as they had brought with them, although the meat whereon the emperor's stomach tired was most of all sobs and sighs, as receiving no pleasure in the absence of the princess.

Now the night assailed them and having not in them to make resistance, they yielded their forces, everyone taking his rest where it liked them best. But the emperor somewhat apart from the rest, casting himself upon the green grass and staying° his back against a tree, he there remained more than two hours broad awake staring at the clearness of the air and the brightness of the stars, when his thoughts renewed and the amorous passion, if before not clean buried, now revived afresh by the solitariness of his conceit.° At length his cares, the weariness of his way, and the sweet noise of the pleasant leaves through the hissing of the wind brought him to a gentle slumber, wherein he had scarcely been a half hour but that his fancy° presented to him again his Lady Briana.[60]

He dreamed that she was taken by force of two giants, the most fierce and strong that ever he had seen in all his life, and that she seeing him cried for help, through the grief whereof he awaked very much affrighted.[61] And indeed, this dream proved no game unto him, for by and by he heard a great noise near unto him, and listening where it might be, he beheld a fair chariot drawn with four horses and in the top of it two great burning torches set in silver candlesticks, by the light whereof he saw a lady in the chariot clothed with rich and princely robes and resembling so much the Princess Briana that he verily believed it was she.[62] The gentlewoman, leaning on her elbow and casting down her countenance, passed on still sighing, as one enduring some great force and torment. The emperor, prying about to see who were the guides of the chariot, perceived that she was carried away by two strong and huge giants with great battle axes in their hands, being on foot at the fore-end° of the chariot. These two had so fell° and cruel looks that they would have daunted the courage of any man which should have beheld them.

But the emperor, assured in his thought that this was the princess, with great anger started up and not remembering to call any of his knights, with his sword he paced towards the giants, where without either good-even° or good-morrow,° he lent the first whom he approached unto such a stroke that the giant would have mortgaged his part in the lady to have made sufficient payment of that blow. For lifting up his battle axe to receive the blow, the sword cut it into the middest° of the helm, and from thence, gliding down upon his armour, hewed it into many pieces. Then the other giant, hastening to smite the emperor, laid at his head with main° force. But the emperor warded° it on his shield, in which the giant's battle axe stuck so fast that he might no more draw it out until the emperor struck him on the right arm that he made him forego his hold. The two giants thus being left weaponless, with much lightness, more than was

---

[60] 'fancy' refers to the Scholastic psychological notion of fantasy, which is both the 'Mental apprehension of an object of perception [and] the faculty by which this is performed' (*OED*, 'fantasy' 1.a.).

[61] On the significance of giants, see the introduction.

A lively debate surrounded the potentially visionary or predictive quality of dreams; here, Trebatio's dream questions the truth-value inherent in dreams and their potential link to supernatural forces. See Carole Levin, *Dreaming the English Renaissance: Politics and Desire in Court and Culture*.

[62] 'preciadas' (precious) becomes 'princely', emphasizing Briana's status.

likely for their bigness, leapt into the chariot, whereby the emperor had no time to bestow another blow on them. Then a dwarf, being in the one end of the chariot, lashed forth the horses so that they ran with such swiftness as if they had flown.

With this noise the knights awaked, and with their swords in their hands came to learn what it should be. In the end, much abashed to see their lord in such a heat, as they demanded of him what befell. He was so troubled in his heart, the princess thus being led away, that he made them no answer. But taking his horse, he commanded them to follow him. The emperor spurred his horse with such fury that he made him to run as fast as the swallow flyeth in the air. It could not be that the palfreys which drew the chariot were horses because his horse was one of the best and most precious in the world, and his lord, having desire to overtake the princess, made him gallop more than an indifferent° pace, but the other were sprites of the air and infernal furies, I think, forced by [the] art [of] magic both to fly° and run.[63] Yet the Emperor followed the chase without losing the sight of them, although it was all in vain. The knights which remained in the wood, being loath to be far behind their lord, went to catch their horses. But were it that naturally they feared the giants or that the wicked sprites had bewitched them, they all broke out of that place and strayed here and there so that the knights spent more than two hours ere° they might take them. By this the emperor was so far from his knights with the haste he made that they knew not what way to take. And indeed it was not possible for them to get within the sight of him, albeit they had held on the beaten way which they thought that the emperor had taken. They rode one way and the emperor belike° posted° another way, for they never met.

But the emperor pursued so long until, in the end, he came to the brink of the River Danube, there where it divideth itself into five arms.[64] At the shore whereof there was a goodly and tall ship, as the emperor might well see, being a bowshot° behind the giants.[65] In this they put the chariot and withal hoisted their sails, and through the middle arm sailed with good speed. This outraged the emperor so that with spurring he caused his horse to fall down dead under him.

Being thus left on foot, notwithstanding he despaired not, but held on to that place from whence the chariot was taken, where he carefully looked about him to see if peradventure,° on the one side or on the other, he might trace out a way to follow, so loath he was to lose the sight of it.[66] But as all this was devised by enchantment, so likewise it happened him to see a little ship sailing in the river with great swiftness in the which there sat an old man with a white beard, by his countenance seeming to be a very honest man. To him the emperor called with a loud voice, desiring him to take towards the shore. The old man, which had the same thing in charge, incontinently° steered towards him and asked what he would have.

'That which I would have', quoth° the emperor, 'is to be conveyed in thy ship to that other ship which rideth before us, for they have in it stolen from me the thing which I love best in all the world. This pains, if thou will take for me, I will so well content thee as thou shall think thy travail° well employed'.

'Assuredly', said the old man. 'I am content to do it because your courtesy induceth me to a greater hope of your merit'.

Saying this, he guided his ship so near the shore that the emperor leaped up into it. And being on the hatches, turning himself to the old man to give him thanks, the old man vanished away and the emperor never saw him after. The ship kept the same course that it began with and the emperor was much astonished at it, the rather for that he wist° no man else aboard to rule the ship. Not knowing what else to say or think of this great wonder, he then beseeched God so to

---

[63] 'I think' represents one of many instances of added first person narratorial commentary, as investigated in the introduction.

[64] The Danube is a river in Central Europe. Originating in Germany it passes through several countries including Hungary, as indicated here, and finally empties into the Black Sea.

[65] The 'bowshot' as a unit of measurement is unique to *Mirror*; *Espejo* speaks of a 'trecho' (stretch).

[66] His lack of despair is added.

direct his voyage that he might yet obtain his lady, for he verily deemed her to be Briana which was in the chariot. In this order, being still within sight of the former ship and not straying from the way which he had kept, the Emperor sailed three days and three nights in the river without any lack of sufficient food. By reason of this travail° and thought, the meat which he ate was no more than would suffice nature. In the fourth day by morning, the ship with the chariot was driven into the great and large sea called Pontus Euxinus, through the which he yet sailed within the view of the other until the forwarder° ship arrived in a fair and delectable island, where the chariot took landing.[67]

Half an hour after, the emperor's ship rushed on the shore with such force that the ship rent° in pieces, and with the violence of the rush threw the emperor upon the bank, flatlings° on his back, where after he had stretched himself, he began again to travel on foot that way which he guessed the chariot had gone.[68] In this way, strange things befell him, as shall appear in the chapter following.

CHAPTER 9

The adventures of the emperor in following the enchanted chariot

The emperor, being, as you heard, cast on land, he beheld well how the island was.[69] As it were, walled about with fair and fresh water, the fairest that ever he had seen. Then looking further into the land, he marked also how it was furnished with so many trees and of so diverse sorts that it was very strange in respect of their immeasurable height and greatness. Underneath these, the ground was beautified with sweet roses and other fragrant flowers, amongst the beds whereof there ran by channels a very clear and crystalline water, able to delight the most wearied senses and travailed° mind that might be. Besides these, to make up a full mess° of disport°, there was a sweet and pleasant song of birds, which seemed to rejoice in the bright and clear morning, besides a thousand other pastimes which I let pass, too long to make a tale of.

But yet, of all these the noble emperor took no care, for the thought of his lady detained from him. But only he beat all both known and unknown ways to find out that wherein the chariot had gone. At length he winded one, but an unused way, which by all likelihood was the same which he would have, in that the grass seemed new pressed down. This tract the noble emperor followed on foot, without that either the heaviness of his armour or the length of the way made him to rest any whit.° From the morning, a full half day the emperor had continued his journey, not meeting any person at whom he might ask news of that which he most desired.

But afterwards, leaving the thick and pleasant wood, he came into a fair green or meadow, full of roses, and other sweet herbs, and flowers of all colours without any other shade in all the meadow than those trees which served for an hedge unto it. The length of this meadow seemed three bowshot° unto the middest,° where was situated a goodly° castle, and in good proportion.[70] It was four-square,° having at each corner a tower and on every side one in the middest° of the side, all of them so high as if they should have edged with the clouds. This great castle was enclosed and shut in with a high and thick wall, the stones whereof and the towers did shine like crystal or the well-polished steel against the sunbeams. Round about the wall there was a deep moat, the water being so broad as a man might scarce cast a stone from the one side to the other.

---

[67] Pontus Euxinus: The Black Sea
[68] The realistic detail of his stretching is added.
[69] The apostrophe 'as you heard' and subsequent added interpolations to the audience develop a relationship of complicity between narrator and reader.
[70] By claiming that it is three bowshots to the middle, Tyler doubles the size of the castle; in *Espejo* it measures three 'trechos' from one side to the other.

Over the water there was a bridge, very large and well towered, so strong according to the depth of the water that it might have withstood a thousand men. Three towers it had in all: one in the entrance, another in the middle, and the third at the farthest end, each of them very high and great, and wrought with the same stone that the great castle was built with. The two outermost towers of the bridge, as well the entry as that towards the castle, were gated and barred° with doors and locks of fine-filed steel, being so sheen° that it served for a looking glass unto the passengers. The locks were so shut that unless they were opened on the inside, it was impossible to undo them.

The good emperor scanned upon all this, the like whereof he had not seen in all his life. And concluding fully that no such building might be made by man's hand, yet he marvelled that of an island so fair and delectable there was no more noise bruited,° especially standing, as it seemed to him, in a sea so sailable. He believed that the princess was within because there appeared to him no other building in all the island. And therefore, taking wide steps, he passed on towards the gate of steel, where finding it closed, he took a great hammer° hanging thereby and bounced° at the gate with such force upon the sounding steel that the fury of the rap was heard through all the towers and a great part of the island. For all this, none showed themselves to make him answer, although he had stood more than a whole hour calling and knocking.[71]

At length, with some trouble, he departed from thence to coast the water if perchance he might light upon any other way into the castle. When he had gone a turn about, at one part of the wall he happened upon a gentlewoman, which was in a little boat newly taking land at a little postern° door of iron. When the gentlewoman had taken footing on the land, she opened the gates, making show as if she would have entered, leaving the vessel in the water. The emperor strained his voice to call unto her that she should stay, but she, feigning as though she heard him not, made to the wicket where as she was to fasten the door. The emperor cried yet louder. Then she turned toward him, and as though she had but then espied him, she said unto him:

'What would you have, Sir knight?'[72]

The emperor prayed her to come nearer, for that he would only demand a certain thing of her. With this, she took her boat again and with a little oar rowed towards the land where the emperor was. When she came somewhat near the bank, there staying, she said unto him:

'What is it that you would have, Sir knight, in that you have called me so loud?'

'That which I would, fair gentlewoman', answered the emperor, 'is that you would ferry me over in your boat unto the castle, for that I have to-do with one of the giants which are within'.

'If you have to deal with them', said the gentlewoman, 'they be no people on whom you may win honour'.[73]

'That is true', said the emperor. 'I have no desire to trouble them, if they will do that which I require them'.

'Since it is so', said the gentlewoman, 'I will do your commandment, because you look like a knight worthy of this service'.

'I give you great thanks for your courtesy', answered the emperor.

And with this he entered the boat. And shoving with the rudder towards the castle, he got thither.°[74] The gentlewoman went in, leading the emperor with her, and closing the door after her, conducting him through a little court to another privy° door, which was not the common entry. She opened a wicket with a key which she had at her girdle° and brought him further into

---

[71] 'and knocking' is added by Tyler to make sense of the source because the emperor is described as knocking at the door rather than calling.

[72] This is one of many instances in which indirect speech is transformed into direct discourse. Further instances will not be noted, but are surveyed in the introduction.

[73] In the Spanish, the gentlewoman asks why he has business with the giants.

[74] 'And shoving . . . thither' is added.

a garden, the most delightsome that art might devise.[75] The emperor now took himself to be in a terrestrial paradise. And gazing a while thereon, without remembering the occasion of his thither° coming he was so estranged from himself.[76] Out of this garden, by another door, they came into a large court of the castle built with bright alabaster, the excellency whereof in the imagery and workmanship cannot be declared. For in comparison of this enchanted castle, either the sumptuous building of Mansolus's tomb, or the famous pyramids of Egypt, or the maze of Daedalus's making, found in Crete, may well be forgotten.[77]

And as the emperor mused on all this, the gentlewoman, knowing him to be distraught, caught him by the hand and brought him to a pair° of stairs, the steps whereof were all of jasper. By them he mounted with her into a chamber, four-square,° of the largeness of a stone's cast. In this, yet, she opened another door with three steps of silver plate out of the goldsmith's shop, through which she brought the emperor into a more stately chamber, four-square° as the other was and very rich, whereof the ceiling and roof were engraven° gold and embossed with many precious stones, sending forth such a light as it was marvellous.[78] The emperor took no keep of the riches of the place, but of the beauty of a number of fair gentlewomen whom he saw sitting richly apparelled in every part of the chamber. Among these one seemed to be the principal, stalled° in a seat higher than the other and passing them all so well in beauty as in rich apparel. She, as lady and mistress above them all, held in her hand a lute, whereon she played and sung together with such a harmony that it was no less dangerous unto the poor emperor than the alluring song of the mermaids should have been unto Ulysses's company.[79] She sung sweetly and she withal reached her warbling notes so high and so shrill that it much pleased the emperor. Her fair and golden hair hung down her back and covered both her shoulders.

And you must pardon the emperor if by this he was wholly possessed with her love and forgot his late° wife, the Princess Briana. The entertainment was great.[80] And yet, this change proceeded not through the beauty of the enchantress, for his own wife was much fairer, but rather by the secret virtue of the place, which was thereto devised according as shall be recited hereafter. By this time the emperor had clean lost the remembrance of his wife, his empire, country, and what else pertained to him, only rejoicing in the love of Lindaraza, for so this lady was called; this he esteemed for his principal hap° and good fortune.[81] When the emperor had stood stone still a while, this lady rose from her seat, and laying down her lute which she held in her hand, with her gentlewomen waiting on her and with a good grace she made towards the emperor to take him by the hand, saying unto him:

---

[75] Whereas Tyler stresses the artifice and ingenuity of its fabrication, *Espejo* praises the garden as the greatest that could be imagined.

[76] *Espejo* provides a more substantial explanation, stressing the emperor's enchantment, as invesitgated in the introduction.

[77] Mansolus's tomb: the Tomb of Mausolus was built 353–350 BCE at Halicarnassus for Mausolus, a Persian ruler, and Artemisia, his wife and sister. It is one of the Seven Wonders of the Ancient World.

The Egyptian pyramids: one of the Seven Wonders of the Ancient World. Built in the second and third millennia BCE, most serve as tombs for the Pharaohs and their wives.

maze of Daedalus: in Greek mythology, the Minotaur was kept in the maze or labyrinth, which Daedalus built for King Minos of Crete.

[78] This urban, mercantile reference to the goldsmith's shop is added by Tyler.

[79] In Greek mythology, the Sirens, creatures who were part bird and part woman, lured sailors to their destruction through the enticing sweetness of their songs. In the *Odyssey*, when Ulysses' ship approaches the Sirens, Ulysses orders his men to block their ears and he has them tie him to the mast of their ship so that he can hear their song without falling victim to its seductive powers.

[80] This addition makes no sense, unless 'entertainment' was erroneously altered from 'enchantment' during the process of textual transmission.

[81] Again, details of the enchantment are omitted.

Lindaraza's name is a combination of *linda* (beautiful) and *raza* (race or lineage). Her pride in her lineage is seen in her decision to name her daughter after herself and in the evocation of the 'great and noble race' that she engenders.

'You are welcome, most noble and worthy Emperor Trebatio, for whose coming I have long time wished'.

The emperor, glad of such a welcome and making not strange of his courtesy, albeit he could not find whereby she should know his name, he answered her:[82]

'Madam, my arrival cannot be but good since by it I may behold the prick and price° of all the beauty in the world, conspiring as it were in your excellency. And since you receive me with such favour, I beseech you tell me who you are, least by not knowing you I might foreslow° that duty which I owe unto your person'.

'This account', replied the lady, 'shall be made in better time. Now know you that I am all yours and there shall not be done by me or my gentlewomen other thing but to do you pleasure in my palace'.

The emperor was entrapped with her pleasant speech and knew not whether he were in heaven or in the earth, and willing to kiss her hand for the grace she showed him, she thought no scorn of a kiss on her cheek when it was proffered.[83] Then, she led him by the hand unto the place where her own throne was. There the emperor felt in himself a great contentment by the touching of her white and delicate hands, imagining with himself that he was transferred into a second heaven.

Some of the ladies helped to unarm him and others were not idle, either playing on their harps or singing and making such music as well eased the minds of the enamoured. Some brought rich robes to attire the emperor withal, other conserves and comfits very comfortable with delicate wine in great plates and cups of gold to refresh him as he had need, by reason of the travel he had taken on foot; although other meat liked him better, which was the sight of the fair Lindaraza and her company.[84] And she, no less enamoured with him, beheld him goodly.°[85] And with her knife in one hand and a napkin in the other, she herself carved unto him of those pleasant conserves. I do not think that the emperor refrained upon strangeness. But she, to quicken his stomach with many a pleasant device° and other amorous persuasions, made him eat a-good. And very sweet were those morsels unto him.

When this collation° was ended, with some solemnity, the fair Lindaraza lead him aside unto a great bay window opening upon that fresh and gladsome garden, through which the emperor with the gentlewomen had before passed.[86] There they both beguiled the time with pleasant speech and melody, which the ladies made in a fresh arbour upon the top of two trees, the laurel and the cypress, the tenor being maintained among them only by nightingales. I deny not but the savour also of the sweet smelling flowers refreshing their spirits did increase their appetites and gave hope of better joy to come.[87]

When it was time to sup, the tables being spread, they were served of exquisite dainties.°[88] Supper being done, the two estates° fell to their wonted° discourses. It was now night, and yet there needed neither torch nor candle: the brightness of the stones enchased in the walls made the chambers as light as the day. When it was time to sleep, the fair Princess Lindaraza brought the emperor to her own lodging, richly adorned with silk and gold, wherein was a rich and stately bed.[89] And there, unclothed by her gentlewomen, both of them went to bed. And remaining thus, both of them rejoiced of their loves to their contentations.°

As the emperor had thus lived wantonly many days, deprived of his understanding, saving

---

[82] 'and making not strange of his courtesy' replaces a declaration of his love for Lindaraza.
[83] Rather than describe the kiss, the source relates Lindaraza's entreaty that Trebatio give up arms. The abandonment of his chivalric duties is less explicitly attributed to Lindaraza in *Mirror*.
[84] Tyler omits the choice metaphor of Lindaraza's 'tasty conversation'.
[85] Details of the meal are omitted.
[86] In *Espejo*, the solemnity refers to the music.
[87] The Spanish allusion to sexual activity — fulfilling their amorous pleasure at night — is omitted.
[88] The ladies have no responsibilities during the meal, whereas in the source they set the tables and Lindaraza carves.
[89] Tyler specifies that he shares 'her own' chambers.

only in honouring her which was before him.⁹⁰ In the end, the beautiful Lindaraza was great with child and bore him a daughter of rare beauty called Lindaraza, by her mother's name, from whom issued a great and noble race, which because in [t]his place it shall be largely declared, I shall overpass now, briefly touching such occurrents° as I read of in the meantime.⁹¹

CHAPTER 10

The emperor's knights find not their lord, and the Hungarians miss the Prince of England

When the Emperor Trebatio was in his quest of the enchanted chariot, the story telleth that his knights might not come near him: some because they could not take their horses, and some because his horse ran so fast. For he overcame in half a day's journey the travel of eight days, as I think, for that he was carried both by his own desire and the devil's driving, otherwise it had been impossible to have endured so great pains.⁹² For this cause, I say although the knights rode so fast as they might, yet they could not come within the sight of him nor find which way he was gone. Yet with sorrow and grief, especially through the fear which they conceived by his meddling with the giants, they parted companies, every man taking a several° way to seek the emperor. And they agreed at the month's end to meet at one place.⁹³

The month came when as yet none of them had heard any news of him, although they sought him in diverse parts. They all marvelled, but not knowing what to say. In the end, they determined at some other time to meet and to enter into this quest again. For this time, they all together took towards the camp, which they left before the city of Belgrade, where they abode not long. But remembering themselves of their promise, they met at the place appointed and divided themselves accordingly. The four Hungarian knights, fearing to be descried by those which went to seek Prince Edward, the covertliest° which they might, they went toward the camp of the emperor and there remained sometime.⁹⁴ After they followed into Greece, where they tarried till the return of the emperor, according as shall be mentioned hereafter.

Now by this time, with no less care and diligence, Prince Edward was sought by many knights in all the kingdom, for that the king had given him no longer time to remain in the Monastery of the River than three days. There was, already told, twenty days when he came not. First, then he sent many of his knights to know the cause of his tarrying. These returned unto the king with answer that they neither found him in the minster° nor could hear tidings of him by the way.⁹⁵ Then the king dispatched other messengers to enquire after him and his knights in all the land, but they brought the like answer. Yet again he sent more than 1000, well prepared for war, with authority of search through all his kingdom that they might bring news of life or death, but all was one. Last of all, fearing lest peradventure° he had been taken prisoner by his enemies, he wrote unto the emperor's camp to know the truth, to the end he might ransom him, if so it were.⁹⁶ But not hearing any news, he then bewailed the loss of the prince and became very sorrowful; like as contrariwise° the imperials° bemoaned their emperor.

These things happened so in the neck° one of another that Tiberio's judgment failed to decide

---

⁹⁰ Details of his enchantment are again omitted.
⁹¹ Princess Lindaraza appears in Ortúñez's Part 3, Chapter 7.
⁹² The propulsive force of his desire is added.
⁹³ This sentence is added.
⁹⁴ In the source, they remain there 'siempre' (always); the alteration is sensible since their stay in the camp is temporary.
⁹⁵ Their great wonderment at not finding him is further described in *Espejo*.
⁹⁶ *Espejo* does not mention the ransom.

the truth, and he pitied him with no less grief than if he had been his own son, partly for his daughter's sake, who must needs be partner of her husband's misadventure, and partly for the prince's parents, who could not without some sorrow conceive of his missing. Albeit all this happened more by the misgiving of his own mind than by any certainty he found. You have heard particularly the care of the King Tiberio, now you must consider of the diligence of the King of Bohemia by the semblable.°

Another month had end and the knights votaries[97] sped them homewards to the camp of the emperor without any news of their lord, which no doubt much molested the whole host. But in especial° it afflicted the King of Bohemia to see them come without him. As they made declaration of the whole month's travail,° it little pleased the king. Only for the love he bore to the emperor and the want of his presence in a time so dangerous, he wept as sore for him as if he had seen his little child give up the ghost. The loss of the emperor thus published through the army; there was no one which sorrowed not inwardly, for he had the love of all his subjects. Albeit this was bootless, yet his love beguiled him; for the king yet charged more than 2000 knights with the search of the emperor in all places, as well by sea as by land.[98] But it naught availed, for the island of Lindaraza held him so sure that he could not be found. And if he had been found, yet he was so well guarded that the whole host had not been able to have delivered him from the enchanted castle.

While these things were in doing, the King of Bohemia himself set the remainder on work to assault the city with full purpose not to leave the siege till either he knew where the emperor was or had lain a half year longer. At the end whereof he would raise the siege and so depart into Greece again. In this time the Hungarians issued out of their city against the Grecians,° and there was between them many cruel and bloody skirmishes. The Greeks did nobly, as you may read in their several histories. At this time, because they are not of the substance of my matter, I will not name them, only I will recount unto you the particular truth of that which followeth.[99]

CHAPTER 11

The Princess Briana taketh great sorrow at the loss of Prince Edward

Great was the diligence which the King of Hungary commanded his knights to make in seeking the Prince Edward. And as great was his grief in not finding him by the consideration of the towardness° of the noble knight and the dole° of his parents, being their dear and only son. But greater must needs be and inexpressible the mortal dolour which the Princess Briana conceived when she once heard of the miss of Prince Edward. And as I read, at the three months' end when nothing was reported, for very anguish of heart, besides her often swoonings, after when she recovered out of that trance,° she seemed to them nearer the death than the prince her husband was, as they thought. For believing that he was dead, she would neither eat, drink, nor sleep, but became weak and feeble and wasted her days with sorrow. She laid apart all her princely robes and precious jewels and attired herself in coarse mourning weeds of a widow. She kept herself in a secret chamber, only with the comfort of her gentlewomen, and coming not forth one step, demeaned° rather the life of an anchoress or religious woman than of a princess.[100]

---

[97] knights votaries: those knights who had vowed to seek the emperor
[98] Tyler adds this reference to the amorous enchantment.
   There are more than a thousand knights in the source.
[99] 'truth' is added, emphasizing the veracity of the narrative.
[100] anchoress: religious recluse.
   The Catholic vocation of the anchoress is added. The treatment of Catholic practices is probed in the introduction.

The queen mother, then abiding at Buda, came often times to visit her, and in her company other great ladies, but they could not remove the dullness° of her melancholy.[101]

Ere° the princess had long led this solitary life, she felt herself quick° with child, whence she took some joy.[102] But yet fearing the disclosing of it unto her friends, whom she would not have partakers° of it for all Hungary before the solemnization of the marriage was openly performed. And being notwithstanding desirous in time to seek remedy thereunto, she concionated° her secret only with one of her gentlewomen named Clandestria, whom she best loved, and with whom she was best acquainted for the good counsel she often gave her.[103] She which was wise and discreet kissed her lady's hands for the honour she did unto her in revealing such a secret, only a little withstanding her intent of concealment at the first and persuading that it was no reason why she should not bewray° her childbearing unto the king, her father, and the queen, her mother:

'For that seeing it pleased God to give you a child by a lawful husband, it were not amiss if it were known abroad, be it son or daughter. And', sayeth she, 'moreover, if God give you a man-child,° Prince Edward thus perishing, as we know no other, this your child is lawful inheritor of Great Britain in the right of his father, the king now living having no issue male.[104] Wherefore me thinks you should do him wrong, seeing he hath lost his father, to deprive him also of his lawful succession'.[105]

The Princess answered:

'Persuade me not to this, good Clandestria, for though the child which shall be born of me should be lord of the whole world, I would not tell this secret to anybody but to thee. And if it shall please God that the Prince Edward shall see us once again, it shall suffice. Let him discover it when he sees time. If it fall out otherwise, my son may well bear the loss of Great Britain and it be but to accompany me in the loss of so worthy a husband'.

Clandestria would have entered further in this persuasion with the princess, but seeing it would not be, she gladly made offer of her service. Then said the princess:

'What do thou think is best to be done in this thing?'

'The best which I can advise you', said the gentlewoman, 'is that you, Madam, govern° the child so that it perish not in your womb. And when the time of your travail° shall be at hand, that you fain unto your gentlewomen a solemn fast and prayer forty days without to be seen or visited of your gentlewomen or any person saving me, whom you will have to wait on you only for your necessary repast.[106] The glass° which you shall set on it shall be this: that you will pray to God for Prince Edward, your husband.[107] The show will be credible enough by means of your life hitherto. This would I have you do, Madam. For this cause, take your lodging in one part of the house joining to the wood, being very good and solitary for this purpose. If you be delivered in this time, I will convey it to a sister of mine lately married and dwelling in the city of Buda. She bore a son about a month past and will nurse your child carefully'.[108]

This counsel liked well the princess because it was consonant to her desire. The princess, now

---

[101] Her emotions are pathologized by referring to her melancholy. On melancholy, see note 55 to Chapter 7.

[102] 'Quickening' refers to the 'stage of pregnancy when movements of the foetus have been felt' (*OED*, 'quick' 5.b.).

[103] The source evokes Clandestria's discretion rather than the love Briana feels for her.

Clandestria's name highlights her secrecy: 'clandestina' means clandestine or secret.

[104] By adding the clause 'in the right of his father', Tyler clarifies the laws of inheritance. This is essential for English readers because whereas in Britain matrilineal inheritance was possible, such is not the case in this society.

[105] This sentence is added, thereby emphasizing succession issues, which would have been of particular interest to English readers during Elizabeth's reign.

[106] The allusion to the Catholic practice of fasting is added.

During the final month of pregnancy, an upper-class woman would be confined to her bed in order to avoid premature delivery.

[107] The added metaphor of the 'glass' recalls the title of the romance.

[108] The practice of wet nursing was common for women of Briana's social class in the period.

expecting the time of her lying down,° told her gentlewomen that she had undertaken a devotion of fast and prayer.[109] And before she entered into this observance she said she would a little take her rest, eating and sleeping somewhat more than she was wont, which indeed she did to preserve that which was in her belly, albeit it was well coloured by her continual sadness.[110]

In this time, the queen, her mother, was brought to bed of a beautiful boy, which much gladded all the kingdom.[111] His name was Liriamandro, a noble prince much advancing the honour of the Hungarians, as shall be showed you in his history. But this childing° of the queen was very commodious for the princess, for that when the queen was brought to bed she could not visit her daughter at the monastery as she was accustomed.

CHAPTER 12

The Princess Briana was delivered of two sons; Clandestria christened them and causeth them to be nursed

The princess, as you have heard, lived somewhat contented after that she felt herself to be with child, but yet not so but that her colour much abated and impaired her beauty.[112] And so driving on her days until the approach of her travail,°, she now feigned to begin her voluntary fast of forty days, which she before had signified unto them. And withdrawing herself into a chamber provided for her, she forbade the entry to all except only Clandestria for her table. This they thought the princess had done upon mere devotion.

The same night after she was now professed a holy vowess,° Clandestria took the keys of the back gates belonging to her lodging, and opening a door into the wood she passed by the fields to Buda, standing but a mile off.[113] And entering into her sister's house, secretly declared the cause of her coming, desiring her to be as secret because the princess would in no wise° have it manifested. She willingly promised silence, and withal departed with her towards the monastery. Ere° it was long they came before the princess, whom they found sitting alone, not altogether void of dread as being unacquainted with those pangs and heartily wishing for their coming as without knowledge to be her own midwife. When she felt the fits of her travail,° she was somewhat comforted with their coming.[114] And Clandestria with her sister enforced° their diligence to do her service, giving themselves to prayer until it pleased God to manifest his works in this noble princess.[115]

She bore two sons, so strange and rare of beauty that the gentlewomen not a little wondered. And yet they were more moved to see the tokens which either of them brought severally° from their mother's womb. For they marked well how that the first born had upon his left side a little face figured, shining as bright as if it had been a little sun, and how that the other had in the middest,° between his breasts, a white rose fashioned of so perfect making that it seemed to be gathered from some arbour of roses.[116]

---

[109] The allusion to fasting is again added.
'Lying down' denotes the period of lying-in or confinement.
[110] In *Espejo*, her ladies greatly fear her death.
[111] To be 'brought to bed' signifies to give birth a child. It is also used to refer to the postpartum period of lying-in, as in the subsequent sentence.
[112] In *Espejo*, Briana lacks a capacity for pleasure.
[113] The Catholic vocation of 'holy vowess' is added.
[114] The reference to the pains of labour is added.
[115] In the source, her sadness is contrasted with the bright Phoebus-like deeds that her sons will later perform.
[116] The rose in the Spanish text is white and red, thus resembling the Tudor rose. It is interesting that Tyler omits this iconic royal symbol even though she was writing during a Tudor monarchy.
These strange birthmarks are indicative of their greatness and recall other romance heroes such as Havelok the Dane and Segramour from *Emaré*, each of whom bears a 'kynmerk' (king's mark).

Before they swaddled them, they laid the little boys between the princess's arms, comforting her with that that God had given her two so excellent children. The mother, full of pain with the travail° which she had sustained as well as she could, laying them to her breasts, kissed and embraced them with such love and pity that the tears trickled down from her fair eyes.[117] And with a low and soft voice, she said thus:

'Oh, my sons, I beseech the lord, who hath made you so exceedingly fair, to bless you also with good hap° that you may ease your mother of that sorrow wherein she remaineth as now plunged, and that you prove such as by your valours you may recover that which your mother to cover her fault hath made you lose'.

These and other words spoke the princess, weeping bitter tears until the nurse took the children from her bed to swaddle them in cloth bands and to give them her breast. Now lest peradventure° they should be heard to cry, Clandestria said to the princess that it were good her sister should return to her own house where she would bring up the young princes as carefully as if she were daily in her presence.

The princess, very loath to part with her children, bade her do [so] notwithstanding what she would with them; so that she baptised them ere° they went for fear they should perish in the way.

'Let it be so, Madam', said Clandestria, 'for you have said very well'.

The nurse then took water, and pouring it on their heads, she christened them in the name of God, with other formal words of baptism as she could best do. Clandestria, with a very good grace, gave names to the little boys: the first she named Cavaliero del Febo, for the figure that she saw in his left side near upon the heart; the younger she called Rosicleer, for the rose between his breasts.[118] Of this the princess took some joy, saying she had given them names as they deserved.

The nurse took leave of the princess, and with her husband which came on the way and which had not stayed far off, she got readily into Buda before broad light, where she fostered these noble babes as carefully as her own.[119]

Clandestria, after she had shut fast the doors, went up again to the princess, whom she found discomforted for her children. The gentlewoman pained herself to comfort her, and soberly spoke unto her in this sort:

'Oh Madam, how unthankful are you to God for the great grace he hath bestowed on you in giving you two sons of so excellent beauty, and that with so little peril of your person. I believe and hold for certain that God hath not left you such sons never to know their father, nor made you such a princess never more to see your husband. The works of God are wonderful and that which we think is set for our grief and disease° he turneth to our commodity. What know you, Madam, if God, willing to preserve your husband, hath by some adventure brought him where he shall escape the great dangers and perils of death in which he was hourly like to incur in the battle that the king your father hath against Trebatio? Good Madam, quiet yourself! God will bring him unto you at such time when you shall be least mindful of him. And if you can so ill brook° the absence of your sons, they are not hence but one mile thither.° May you send me when it pleaseth you to know of their welfare'.

---

[117] The addition 'as well as she could' evokes an awareness of the emotional process of childbirth. Tyler's maternal experiences seem to be informing her translation here.

This is not an allusion to breastfeeding. Mothers would not breastfeed immediately after delivery since it was widely believed that the ingestion of colostrum was dangerous for babies. Moreover, women were directed against breastfeeding in the postpartum period while they were experiencing lochia. Adhering to typical practice, the nurse will soon feed the infants.

[118] Febo is Spanish for Phoebus, the god of the sun; his name thus evokes his birthmark. He is later often referred to as the Gentleman or Knight of the Sun. Likewise, Rosicleer's name recalls the rose on his chest.

Several changes increase the pathos of the scene. Here 'great' joy is diminished to 'some', and in the following paragraph Tyler adds 'pained herself to comfort her, and soberly'.

[119] Tyler adds the clause explaining the husband's presence.

Thus, Clandestria discoursed with her lady the Princess Briana, still beating upon this one point: that she should rest herself upon God's providence. And in the end she so assuaged her grief that she after well endured the forty days penance.[120] In the end, being better at ease and feeling herself more pleasantly disposed withal, as fresh as if she had never abode° any childbed, took her lodging among her gentlewomen, who seeing her so well and somewhat more merry than before, were glad of that alteration for they loved her so heartily that they willingly would have given their lives to have redeemed her from that discontentment wherein she lived.[121]

CHAPTER 13

The King of Bohemia raised the siege and the King of Hungary returned the prince's knights into England

Many and hot bickerings there were between the emperor's people and the King of Hungary while the siege lasted against the city of Belgrade, but because the history hath more to entreat° of other especial° adventures it remembreth not every particular which happened in the skirmish. It sayeth in effect that as those of the city were many, so they were well provided of all furniture° that the Greeks might not enter into the city, albeit many of them had done marvellous deeds in arms. After one year was come and gone, the King of Bohemia (with all the principal of his host) thought it best to raise the siege then lying before the city and with bag and baggage to march homewards to Constantinople to the end to give out a new order for the finding of the emperor.[122]

So within two days they had all charge to pack and prepare themselves for their return, the soldiers not yet forgetting the loss of their lord, which they showed by their cheer. The King of Bohemia, the emperor's uncle, well perceiving it and knowing how the good emperor was wont to encourage and comfort them, he took some pain in it at that time. And being well settled in Constantinople, for the better pacifying of all tumults, the army as yet not dispersed, he took upon him the government of the empire in his nephew's name at the humble suit of all the imperials. After, he provided the best that he might for a new search of the emperor, swearing many good knights unto this enterprise.

Which likewise, the King of Hungary did send certain news into England. And to have some sufficient guide to conduct the army homewards at the end of two years — all which time he detained the soldiers upon hope to find their captain, no news being heard of him — the king embarked them homewards to Great Britain with gifts and presents unto the King of England and sufficient rewards plentifully bestowed upon the meinie,° over and above the due payment of their wages. This, the liberality of the king, profited him not a little in other matters of great importance, as you shall understand in this history.

The knights thus shipped ready to depart were near in number 20,000.[123] In few days they coasted France, and entering in the narrow seas with a good wind they landed in Great Britain, where soon their hanging countenances gave testimony to the heavy news they brought. Which thing so sore appalled the whole realm that of a long time after their coming there was not used any exercise in arms. And the queen died also, adding to this mishap a new corsie.° This queen left behind her a daughter of young years named Olivia, so renowned for her beauty that she

---

[120] By referring to her lying-in as forty days of penance, the religious symbolism of the time period is evoked. In the Bible, the number 40 is usually associated with periods of trial or punishment (see especially, Exodus 24.18; Deuteronomy 9.18, 25; Numbers 13.26, 14.34; Ezekiel 4.6, Matthew 4.2, and Acts 1.2).
[121] 'being better . . . any childbed' is added.
[122] Tyler omits the detail that the knights who went to look for the emperor returned with no success.
[123] *Espejo* has 30,000 men.

well won to be loved and served of the most loyal knight of all the world. She was brought up as being inheretrix° to the state with great care by the king her father.

CHAPTER 14

Clandestria deviseth with the Princess Briana how her sons might be brought up in her company

The Princess Briana lived no doubt better contented after her delivery of the two fair boys, which she thought had been Prince Edward's, and yet, as I say, very religiously as it had been in a cloister, for the reason so often alleged. Now yet somewhat there was which impaired this contentation,° which was the absence of her children. This she thought to repair again by bringing them up in her own lodging, and having broken° it unto her gentlewoman Clandestria whom she desired to find the means for it. Clandestria, after conference had with her mistress, one day said unto her that she had well foreseen the mean. The princess then urged her to utter it, which Clandestria delivered in this speech:

'Madam, that which I have thought in this matter is like that one day when I shall come from the city of Buda, you shall demand° of me what news is there. I will answer you among other things that a sister of mine hath two sons born both in one day, so excellently fair that all the lookers-on do not a little commend so goodly creatures. They are born, moreover, with notable tokens, which they bring from their mother's womb. You, Madam, hearing this, may say that you have great desire to see these strange children and may will me to procure the bringing of them into this monastery with their mother. And here, in your company, they may be brought up, for that in such children you may take some solace, thereby to forget part of that which sore annoyeth° you. In this manner neither your gentlewomen nor any other person shall understand our secret'.

Clandestria's counsel seemed so good unto the princess that embracing her many times she said unto her:

'My faithful and loyal Clandestria, when shall the day come wherein I shall be restored unto the first joy and estate which I was wont to hold, and in which I may reward the good service thou has done to me? Go thy way and put in effect that which thou have devised for mine° ease!'

'Madam', said Clandestria, 'if my service may in any wise° assuage your grief, which I so sore pity, I think it sufficiently rewarded considering the duty wherein I stand bound unto your highness. And assuredly, no less is the pleasure which I receive by the acceptation° of my service than that which you have by the fruition of it. But since my counsel liketh you so well, I will make no tarrying. Go you, Madam, to your gentlewomen and I will presently to the city'.

'Go in God's name', said the princess.

And so she took her to her gentlewomen, Clandestria being in her way towards the city.

When Clandestria had performed unto her sister that which the princess had commanded, not long after she came to the monastery. At such time as the princess was in the company of her gentlewomen, Clandestria entered into the chamber making her obeisance. The princess, espying her, said unto her merely:

'Welcome, my Clandestria! How is it with the queen my mother and the young Prince Liriamandro my brother?'

'They are all very well, Madam', said Clandestria.

'And the queen your mother commendeth herself unto you by me'.

'Well', said the princess, 'but what news have they in the city? Say they anything of Prince Edward?'

'Of the prince, surely, I heard nothing', answered Clandestria, 'but I have news, if it please you to hear them, me thinks the strangest that you have heard'.

'Tell us them', said the princess. 'If they be such as you speak of, we shall have pleasure to hear them'.¹²⁴

'Know you then, Madam', said Clandestria, 'that a sister of mine, which is married and dwelleth in the city of Buda hath two sons of the age of two years, both born at one hour in the top and pitch of all beauty so that their matches are not to be had. They have, besides, marks on their bodies such as those which have seen them cannot tell what to think of them. The first born of them hath on his left side the form of a face very beautiful and so bright that I dare liken it to the sun, which overshadoweth the earth.¹²⁵ And for this cause, the little boy is called El Donzel del Febo.¹²⁶ The other little boy hath between his breasts a rose growing in the flesh, so fresh of hue and so perfectly coloured that they which see him say he beareth the badge of his mother's bed, as if he had been born in an arbour. For this token, they name him Rosicleer. I tell you, Madam, so excellent is their beauty that the best painter in Hungary need no other example to draw out° the picture of beauty'.¹²⁷

The princess, making a show of great marvel, and as it were mistrusting the report because of the strangeness, answered:

'Truly, Clandestria, you have brought us matter of some marvel. But I fear me the nearness of kin between you maketh you to speak of affection more than knowledge. I would that by sight of them you would prove unto us that which you have spoken'.

With this, the princess's gentlewomen, hungry after novelties, importuned Clandestria to deal herein so that they all might enjoy the sight of those two so rare children. Clandestria, turning toward her lady, said:

'By my faith, if my lady the princess be so contented, I will go to my sister and cause her to come hither with her little ones'.

The gentlewomen then besought the princess that she would command them to be brought thither.° The princess, telling them that she did it more at their request then of her own good will, said to Clandestria:

'You were best do this which your fellows require you. My liking you have, for I myself would gladly be a witness of so great a marvel'.

Clandestria took her leave of them, hasting towards the city where her sister dwelled and declared her message for the bringing of the princes. Her sister's husband was a very good gentleman born, though very poor. He and his wife made them ready to come before the princess with the little princes, which by this time were of some growth, being two years old, having both goodly looks, standing as it were upon a just temperature° of gravity and pleasance.

When they were come to the palace, Clandestria first entered into the lodging of the princess, being as yet in the company of her gentlewomen.¹²⁸ There she led in by the hand the fair and gracious Rosicleer. So soon as he was seen of the gentlewomen, they believed him to be no less than an angel of heaven, and that wherein Clandestria had before instructed them, she had nothing deceived them. The princess, not having seen her children since her first blessing of them, and now seeing the height of Rosicleer with his beauty above her hope, she made such joy as might have well been discerned by her countenance. But her gentlewomen, more attentive of the beauty wherewith God had endowed the young Rosicleer, were not ware° of it. Clandestria made the little boy bow his knees to the princess, and whether it were nature, or the beauty of his mother, or both, so soon as he beheld his mother he left the other

---

¹²⁴ Briana speaks of 'news' in the plural, based on the Spanish in which the noun is plural.
¹²⁵ *Espejo* situates the birthmark in between his breasts.
  'overshadoweth' is a strange word choice since *Espejo* has 'illuminates' and the sun is known for its luminosity rather than its dark shadowiness.
¹²⁶ 'donzel' signifies a young noble gentleman, who had yet to achieve knighthood.
¹²⁷ As a grown man, Donzel del Febo's beauty equally may serve as an example for artists, see Chapter 18.63–66.
¹²⁸ The alteration of 'monastery' to 'palace' is odd, since all previous references are to the monastery.

gentlewomen.¹²⁹ The mother, taking the little boy in her arms, kissed him many times, shedding upon his fair cheeks great abundance of tears for the memory which the son gave her of his father, and for the great joy she had in having him so near unto her.

Not long after, there entered Clandestria's sister with her husband, leading by the hand the fairest among the most fair: Donzel del Febo. At the sight of him, the gentlewomen repented them of their former judgment as concerning Rosicleer, that there might not be his like in all the world. In the end, the question arising of comparison, to part the strife they agreed that as the one moved everyone to love him tenderly by his gracious behaviour, so the other by his modest gestures made them to fear him with reverence. The difference only but in this: that the one had more majesty, the other more mirth and delight in his countenance.

The princess, having Rosicleer in her arms, when she saw her other son before her upon his knees to kiss her hand, with gladness she raised him from the ground, and with Rosicleer in one arm, took him on the other, kissing him upon his cheeks. And indeed, rather obeying the love she bore unto her sons than regarding the fear she was wont to have for being discovered. Albeit, to say the truth, the princess was of the better hand; for all the good will she showed, her gentlewomen imagined to proceed of their beauty. And yet to take all suspect° away, she could very wisely moderate her passions.¹³⁰

Clandestria's sister, the supposed mother of those children, and her husband, by name Armaran, kissed the princess's hands, where she, in token of good liking, entertained them as her servants, from thenceforth to remain with her as their sister Clandestria did. On this wise° the princes were nourished in their mother's presence, without that any knew the right parentage whereof they came. And they so enticed the gentlewomen to the liking of them, that there passed not one hour without playing and dalliance with them.

This joy on the princess['s] part was unspeakable — I dare not say, able to countermand her foreconceived° grief. But the worst was, it was not durable.¹³¹ For Fortune, ever mutable, changed her copy° and became so contrary that the date of her ease being out, there succeeded disease and mishap, so that her death should not have been half so irksome as her life was dolorous. This shall you hear of in the next chapter.

CHAPTER 15

Donzel del Febo was lost by misadventure

Now the Creator of all things minded to manifest the worthy deeds of the valiant Donzel del Febo, which as yet lay hidden in the arms of the delicate gentlewoman, his foster mother. And therefore, in such sort, He ordered the celestial influences and powers of the planets that scarcely had the young gentleman fully reached unto three years of his age, when he was carried from the princely graces of his unknown mother, leaving her pensive and sad, into a large and main° sea, whence, being tossed with waves and almost weather beaten at length, he escaped.¹³² Such an argument God left us of his prowess to come, since in so tender age He enabled him to subdue the most raging element that is. And you, which read this history, may be brought by good reason to give credit to this my report, since you yourselves are witnesses of the evident presence of the Almighty in so certain a danger. And as the learned well know, Achilles hath his Pallas

---

¹²⁹ The maternal relationship is strengthened here. In *Espejo* her social status is emphasized and her motherhood remains unstated.
¹³⁰ Again, the reference to her passions, added by Tyler, pathologizes her emotions.
¹³¹ This sentence is added.
¹³² The Spanish 'leaving her full of extreme anguish and mortal pain' much more accurately conveys her emotional state than 'pensive and sad'.

in Homer, and Aeneas his Venus in Virgil, goddesses assistant unto men in their dangerous conflicts — Homer and Virgil meaning no other thing than the care of God towards His [own].[133] Why may not we believe (that if it so pleased God) that this infant had the secret direction of God's mighty hand in all his enterprises?

But mine° author, willing to entreat° somewhat of him, setteth it down thus. That in the end of a year, these two beautiful boys being brought up in the Monastery of the River with great pleasure of the princess and her gentlewomen, one day in the month of May, the comfort of the sun there enforcing them to come abroad and seek their solace under green boughs.[134] The princess and her gentlewomen, leaving their lodging, went into a large and fair orchard exceedingly well cast° in one part of the monastery. There they took up their seats at a well's mouth, overshadowed with trees, that the heat of the sun could not annoy them. And sporting with the little Rosicleer, who was somewhat more given to play than his brother Donzel del Febo, they so much delighted in Rosicleer that they took no heed of Donzel del Febo sitting not far off. The little one, being very young yet greatly discontent to see the small account they made of him, in a fume° rose from the place where he was set and by soft paces got from them without being espied by the gentlewomen, saving of his mother so-called, which loved him no less than her own self.

She, rising from the place where she was set, followed him and took him by the hand, laughing a good to see the choler wherein he was.[135] And walking among the trees so long with him that she came to a large and deep water running through a part of the great orchard, where hard by were great store of trees, and whither° the princess, because the place was very pleasant, often resorted with her gentlewomen to rejoice herself. When they were there, the little boy, seeing the water, was desirous to play with it. The nurse, though otherwise willing to have contented him, yet fearing the danger of the water, went farther to find some sure place whereby to come unto the water. And taking a little boat at the bank, which the gardener used in coming into the orchard, put herself in it and the child with her. The boy, leaning his breast upon the brim of the boat, troubled the water with his hands and took up some to wash his face.

A while after, the water being calm and plain, he looked in it again, and seeing his shadow there, he began to play with it and stroke it with his hands.[136] Now because it would not give place,° but did that which he did, waxing angry, he prayed his mother to give him a rod, which lay upon the land, to beat the babe withal. It was a good pastime for her to see the displeasure which he had conceived against his own shadow. And leaving him thus, she leapt upon the land to reach him the stick that he required. Being thus on land, either with the force she put to the side of the boat in advancing herself out of the boat, or else because it was the will of God that the little boy should then be pressed to try the hazard of his constellation, so it was that the boat, being untied, it shoved from the shore.[137] The nurse, not perceiving it before she turned again, then was it more than two yards from the land.[138] And not having whereby to take hold, it bore so swiftly down the stream in a little time, and so far off that she lost the sight of it.

---

[133] Pallas: Pallas Athena, Greek goddess of wisdom, civilization, and the arts
  Achilles: Greek hero in the Trojan War and a central character in Homer's *Iliad*
  Aeneas: mythical hero of Troy and Rome, he was the son of the goddess Venus. Virgil narrates his adventures in the *Aeneid*.
[134] The 'force' rather than the 'comfort' of the sun entreats them to seek the shade in *Espejo*, which is a much more logical reading.
[135] The humoural language is added by Tyler.
[136] This scene recalls the myth of Narcissus, who fell in love with his reflection in a pool of water. Although Donzel del Febo responds to himself with anger rather than love, the allusion foreshadows his impending misadventure.
[137] The addition of the boy's 'hazard[ing] of his constellation' accords with the significance attributed to the trope of the rudderless boat in romance. The un-captained boat reveals the workings of Fortune and Providence and the hero's or heroine's state of grace as the boat conveys the character to safety.
[138] The English unit of measurement (yard) replaces the Spanish 'strokes'.

When she saw the danger wherein the little child was, not having power to succour it, she rent° her garments, and tore her hair, and fell to the ground, making such moan that the princess and her gentlewomen, sitting about the well, heard it, and much abashed, rose from the place to know what the noise meant. When they saw the pitiful dealings of the nurse upon the ground, quickening their pace, they got near her. And demanding° the cause of her great lamentation, they found her so sorrowful that she could not speak to them; but rather, the more she was comforted by them, the more she outraged° in crying, as that they judged her to be distraught. So long lasted these her cries that the princess, disquieted, went towards her, leaving Rosicleer with one of her gentlewomen.

60 As the princess came towards her, the nurse knew her. And not having the boldness to show how it fell out, in respect of the grief the princess would take for the loss of her son, before the princess came at her, she ran and leapt into the water with full intent to drown herself, the which she had done had not her clothes borne her up. And the gardener, hearing the great outcries she made, waded in the water for her and brought her to land all wet and bloody with the blows she gave herself in the face. This caused such pity and compassion in the princess and all her gentlewomen that, all astonished, they abode only to see the nurse's demeanour. In the end, at the instance of the princess, she declared how Donzel del Febo was got from her, for the which they imparted with° her grief. And especially the princess, benumbed of all her senses, sunk to the ground with no more colour and breath then if she had been quite
70 dead.

The gardener, entering into another boat there, which he had to fish withal, pushed up the stream amain° with his oar to overtake the boat in which Donzel del Febo was carried. But all his travail° was lost, for either by divine promission° or by [the] art [of] magic made by a learned man, as shall be told you hereafter, the boat rode faster than the violence of the stream might drive it. And in short time it entered into the great sea, where it followed the mighty waves more than a hundred miles in a short space, so that neither the gardener nor who else followed them might in any wise° attain unto him or bring news of him.

When the princess was revived and remembered the chance° of Donzel del Febo, she poured out so many salt tears from her fair eyes that, like as out of fountains or springs the water
80 gusheth out abundantly, so from her face streamed down floods of water, issuing with sobs and sighs as would have broke her heart in a manner such as commonly the fall of the water maketh from the steep mountains.[139] But for that she would not be heard of her gentlewomen, she turned herself and went towards her lodging, where remaining alone with Clandestria, she gave a fresh onset to her former complaints on this sort:

'Oh, mighty and sovereign Lord, wherefore doth Thy highness suffer the Princess Briana to live this long, seeing she doth roll° on this life with such sorrow and care?[140] Oh, Lord, wherefore gave Thou me a husband in this world so valiant, seeing that so soon as I had lost the name of a maiden, Thou made me an unfortunate widow? Wherefore gave Thou me sons with so strange tokens at their birth, if with so sudden misfortune I shall lose the one of them? Why did I reach
90 to so great estate, in which I must live with sorrow? And why gave Thou me beauty not to enjoy it? Alas, poor woman that I am, I see that each thing enforceth° my pain, for Fortune, the mistress of mishap, despitefully throwing down those on whom she frowns, hath turned her back on me, which desire to live without the compass of her wheel![141] Ah, silly° woman! The longer I rub out° this life, the more my grief increaseth. When I seek to mollify my grief, then my care redoubleth, and one sorrow surceasing,° there succeedeth another, as one billow

---

[139] The added metaphorical language increases Briana's piteousness.
[140] The nautical imagery is new to *Mirror*.
[141] In visual art and literature, Fortune was often depicted with a great wheel, which she would turn according to her whims. With the wheel's rotations, the fortunes of those seated upon it would rise or fall depending on their position. The wheel was a potent reminder of the vagaries of Fortune and of the temporality of earthly things.

followeth on the other's neck in the main° sea.¹⁴² Oh, Thou Lord which has created me, take me out of this deceitful world, if by death only the intolerable misfortunes may take end, which daily await me!'¹⁴³

These and other words spoke the Princess Briana, much aggrieving therewith her gentlewoman Clandestria, who a little altering the course of her answer from the platform of the other's complaint, drove with the princess unto these conclusions: first, that there was hope enough to recover her losses. The reasons which lead her thereunto were these:

'Albeit', sayeth she, 'God's works be unsearchable, yet thus bold may we be with them, not meddling with the causes to compare the evils together. And then surely the whole course of worldly things sufficiently teach us that God createth not such excellent personages but for excellent purposes, and not as in dumb shows upon a stage, where the players only present themselves and pass away.¹⁴⁴ Again', sayeth she, 'you are altogether uncertain of their death. And why not in so doubtful a case should hope be as ready as care. Or perhaps you think as soon happens the worse as the better, yet the ancient proverb is that "he which naught hopeth for, ought to despair naught," for hope and misgiving are in the same subject.¹⁴⁵ Therefore', sayeth she, 'you may well hope'.

The second was that she should comfort herself in the beautiful Rosicleer, who was then in her keeping, for sayeth she:

'He alone sufficeth to countervail all the harms which have chanced you. For I dare warrant, if God preserve him, that you may name yourself mother of the best knight in the world'.

With these and many other goodly counsels, Clandestria daily laboured the princess to give over her grief. But for all this, if God with his mighty hand had not held her up, it had gone wrong with her, for He provided her of comfort by a man very wise and well learned in [the] art [of] magic of whom shall be made mention in this history. By him, God permitted that the prison of the emperor with other appurtenances should be discovered, foreseeing by the signs, planets, and other natural operations, that which seemeth impossible unto us. Thus, the truth is that this wise man — knowing the great sorrow and care wherein the princess lived, and well perceiving that unless she had more succour at his hands than she had erst° by other, because of that which befell hereafter it should be impossible to maintain her life — determined in himself to comfort her.

And so one day as she sat alone, very sorrowful weeping with great abundance of tears, near unto the well where her two sons were begotten, he appeared to her in the shape of a nymph in the clear and crystalline water, with the hair loose and shedding° upon the greatest part of the body, and with a face so beautiful that the princess abashed° to see her, and in some fear for that she had not seen the like before, would have fled from thence.¹⁴⁶ But the nymph called unto her, saying:

'If thou knew, noble princess, who I am and how well I know thy great thoughts and passions, thou would not fly° from me, but rather stay and talk with me. Now, because the time affords me no leisure to tarry with thee and to discourse at large all the loyalty I bear unto thee and the desire I have to serve thee, in a word I pray thee take good courage unto thee to overcome the great adversities which may come, and ere° it be long are like to come unto thee, so that thou shall be left altogether comfortless.¹⁴⁷ I give thee yet to understand that Prince Edward is not

---

¹⁴² This added image of the billow in the sea recalls Donzel del Febo, who is lost at sea, and it links the workings of Fortune to the romance trope of the protagonist cast to sea in a rudderless boat.

¹⁴³ Here she anticipates future misfortune, whereas in *Espejo* she laments past sadness.

¹⁴⁴ The theatrical imagery is added.

¹⁴⁵ Proverbial; cf. Tilley D216, N319, N320

¹⁴⁶ In *Espejo*, 'abashed to see her' is 'amazed to see *him*' (emphasis added). The use of the feminine pronoun in *Mirror* reflects the princess's point of view; she sees a female nymph rather than a male sage.

Wells or fountains are often the locations of supernatural encounters in romance, as in *Ywain and Gawain*, *Melusine*, *Floris and Blanchefleur*, and *Orlando Furioso*.

¹⁴⁷ God's agency is discussed in *Espejo*.

Again, the English anticipates future sorrow, unlike the Spanish, which harks back to past misfortune.

now living, and that in the time wherein thy despair shall be highest, thou shall obtain thy husband again, as safe and sound as he departed from thee. And he shall acknowledge thy children, and shall joy in their virtues, that the joy which thou shall have hereafter shall surmount the pain wherein thou remain at this present. Assure thyself therefore, that as all shall come to pass which I have foretold thee, so were it good to keep it in memory, thereby to strengthen thy courage, the better to resist the malice of thy adversary Fortune, whose wheel as it is round and in continual motion. So persuade thyself when it is at the lowest must needs turn again upwards and restore thee thy damages. Farewell, and hope no more to speak with me until all be accomplished which I have said'.

In this sort,° preparing the princess to the conflict with her adversity, the fair nymph vanished away, diving down into the depth of the well. And the princess, devising° upon this saying was, as it were, beside herself, not fully knowing whether she had heard those words or dreamed them. For as she understood of the one part, that Prince Edward was dead, and of the other, that she should once again see her husband, she was so confused in her thought that she knew not what to judge, and said to herself that peradventure° she had mistaken the nymph.

In the end, resting upon the hope which she had made promise of, she was somewhat comforted, not doubting the accomplishment. Yet, she remained in the monastery, not willing to go out of her lodging, and clothed always in black mourning apparel, and delighting in nothing so much as in little Rosicleer. Rosicleer, as he increased in years so he exceeded also in beauty, goodliness of body, and excellent qualities, that a man might well prognosticate thereby of his valiancy.°[148] But, because the history shall more specially talk of him, I leave him for this time to his nurse, there to be instructed till he shall be called forth to greater matters.[149] Now it is time to go to the succour of Donzel del Febo his brother, who is all this time upon the river.

CHAPTER 16

The pedigree of the valiant Prince Florion and other matters as touching him

By the most ancient and true records of the Assyrians, it appeareth that in that time when Theodoro, predecessor of the great Emperor Trebatio, ruled in the Empire of Greece, there governed among the Persians the mighty Orixerges, King of Persia and Sultan° of Babylon, for his great power among the Pagans° much renowned and feared.[150] This man, after he had lived in great prosperity, died, leaving behind him three sons: the eldest, King of Persia; the second, Sultan° of Babylon; the third, lord of the Crimson Island, which is in the Red Sea, whence also it taketh the name because all the land is dyed with the colour.[151] This third brother from his youth was very studious and given above all to astrology and other unknown sciences. In these, he became so exquisite° that scarce in his time might any be compared unto him. The greatest part of his life time he dwelt in that island, choosing that place as most convenient for his study.

The eldest of the three brothers, being King of Persia, died about forty years after this distribution of their inheritance, having for heir a son of his twenty years old called Florion, a

---

[148] Rather than see these qualities as a sign of his 'valiancy', *Espejo* predicts that he will be amongst the greatest knights in the world.

[149] The Spanish source refers to the company of his mother rather than the instruction of his nurse.

[150] Assyrians: people of Assyria, a kingdom of northern Mesopotamia that became the centre of one of the great empires of the ancient Middle East. It was located in what is now northern Iraq and south-eastern Turkey.

  Orixerges: a corruption of Artaxerxes, the name of various Persian kings (*Espejo*, I.116)
  Pagan: a term used to refer to any non-Christian

[151] The alteration of 'rubia' (blond) to 'Crimson' is logical, given the description of the island as all red.
  This is anachronistic since Assyria and Babylon are pre-Christian cities, and while Persia existed at the time in which the romance is set, it was not a great empire as it was in the pre-Christian era and as it is portrayed here.

valiant and strong knight, big made, and of a goodly stature.[152] This Florion, being a young man but of a great courage, putting in his room° a viceroy for his kingdom, wandered as a knight errant through the world to seek adventures, where he did great and noble deeds of arms.[153] At the end of three years, after this his absence from his country, he struck° over towards the court of the Sultan° of Babylon, his uncle, where he remained sometimes very well welcomed and beloved of the Sultan,° for he was a good knight. The Sultan° had a little son and a marvellous fair daughter, whose name was called Balisea. Of her, Florion became enamoured, and requiring° her to wife of her father, she was granted him, and the marriage celebrated between them with great solemnity of feasts and triumphs.

While he was thus within doors sporting, there was worse news abroad, for a mighty Pagan called Africano, the bravest and boldest knight that ever was in all the coasts of Africa, had transported over into Asia, and by his great force, in few days, subdued the whole country of Media and two other kingdoms adjacent, belonging to two great Pagan princes.[154] These thus vanquished, after became tributaries as subjects and vassals. The fame whereof was bruited° far and near that there were few kings in those parts which requested not his amity, for all accounted him the lustiest° warrior in the world. And sooth° it is that in all Asia was never born so proud and fierce a Pagan.[155]

But he was gainsaid° by him, unto whose courtesy not only our lives and livings, but we ourselves stand thrall and subject, otherwise he had in few days made himself lord of the greatest part of all Asia. This Pagan° was a huge and mighty man, large limbed of the bigness of a giant, and so strong and weighty° withal that the strongest horse which was he could make to bow between his legs, any piece of armour how fine so ever it were he would bend and wreathe° in his hands easily as if it had been framed of wax.[156] This man, well knowing his own forces and estate and not contented with that he had gotten in few days, determined to invade the kingdom of Persia, to bring that also to his subjection. Into it he entered, and in a little time he conquered many cities, plaining° towns, and castles.

All this while the Prince Florion being in Babylon, the peers of his kingdom sent messengers unto him declaring the whole state of the country, how unable it was to make resistance without the levying of a new army and some foreign succour.[157] Then the prince assembled the royalest° army that he might in the land of the Sultan and shipped into Persia, there to give battle unto Africano and to punish by arms his enemies' intrusion.[158] But he reckoned without his host, for he had not ridden ten miles in his own kingdom when the mighty Africano came and pitched near with his whole army and in the first field discomfited Florion, the most part of his people being slain. The Prince Florion hasted° into Babylon, forever despairing to be revested° in his seigniories.° And Africano's power was so great that he well knew all the Sultan's power to be

---

[152] In *Espejo*, Florion's father dies at the age of 40.

Tyler omits the characterization of Florion as 'muy orgulloso' ('very arrogant / proud', I.117.14), instead describing his 'great courage'. This recalls her earlier alterations of Prince Edward's portrayal.

[153] The addition of 'as a knight errant' highlights Florion's affinity to the Christian heroes despite his Muslim faith. The unusual (for English romance) acceptance of a Saracen hero is discussed in the introduction.

[154] Media: an area of modern Iran inhabited by the Medes from the second millennium BCE. In c. 625 BCE the Median state was established. With Babylon, Lydia, and Egypt, it was one of the four major powers of the region. The reference here is anachronistic, since it was no longer in existence during the Christian era.

[155] While Florion and Africano are both Saracens, they are opposed to each other politically and ideologically. Florion shares qualities with Christian knights, while, in contrast, Africano is proud and vicious. These differences are invesitgated in the introduction.

[156] Unlike Trebatio and Briana who are exceptionally large and giant-like, Africano is a true giant, who exhibits all the negative attributes of the typical romance giant. The figure of the giant is discussed in the introduction.

[157] 'how unable . . . succour' is an addition.

[158] 'royalest' mistranslates 'gruesso' (thick, bulky, or rough). The same term is omitted from Chapter 15.153 and mistranslated in Chapter 17.27.

50 of little force to withstand him. The Sultan received him, glad of his escape, but yet sorry again for his people and disheriting° of his nephew of so noble a kingdom.

As they were thus sorrowful, within a few days after came into the court the third brother, Lirgandeo, which as the story sayeth, inhabited the Crimson Island. At his coming they were much quieted. He bade them be at rest and not take care for the kingdom of Persia, for that there was among the Christians a child born in the happiest° and most fortunate hour that ever knight had been born in, the which by good adventure should be brought to those parts, and by his noble valour and virtue should deliver the sultan° and the princess his daughter from death or from perpetual imprisonment.[159] Dispossessing the wicked intruder should place the Prince Florion in his lawful inheritance to his own great glory and the utter confusion of his enemies.

60 This done that Florion should enjoy his kingdom in peace and tranquillity all his life. Until then, he requested them to have patience, since,

'It is not yet', sayeth he, 'when these things shall happen'.

Lirgandeo was held for a very wise man, and they all believed his saying, for that at other times he had divined of many things which came to pass accordingly. But yet they knew not who that knight might be so strong as to resist the force of Africano, for he was reputed the bravest and most valiant knight of the world. And they were very desirous every day to hear of his arrival in their land.

Now not a month after this, the wise Lirgandeo counselled with the Prince Florion in secret, willing him immediately at that hour to take twenty knights of the best he had in the court and

70 himself and to embark themselves in a war ship, as it were to scour the coasts. Where, sailing in the Sea Mediterranean, Fortune should bring unto their power two little boys the most beautiful and excellent that ever he had seen.

'With these', sayeth he, 'you shall return to Babylon, for these are the nurses of your good hap'°.

The Prince, glad to please his uncle, chose out his knights and took leave of the sultan, departing from Babylon and passing through Asia the Less.[160] He came to a haven in Phrygia, where he put himself and his mates in a ship well purveyed of victuals and lately rigged and trimmed for some such voyage.[161] In this, with a prosperous wind he sailed, till at the end of twelve days, mounting on the tail-back° of the ship to look if perhaps he might behold the thing

80 of which the wise man had told him, it was so that he kenned° a far off a little bark in which the Gentleman of the Sun was driving towards them, and the waves rocking it on every side. It might be that this boat defended the burden naturally, as only following the course of the waves, but I rather believe that God, which had created him with so wonderful marks, took this care and keep of him until that Florion, espying the bark coming right towards him and the gentleman in it so beautiful and bright as an angel of heaven, no tongue can express the joy that now he promised himself touching the performance of that hope which Lirgandeo gave him to repossess his kingdom. His conceit° also as concerning the beauty of Donzel del Febo was that some one of his celestial gods had begotten him on some fair lady here on the earth. And therefore, as to a personage which did participate with the deity, he bowed himself, honouring and embracing

90 Donzel del Febo.[162] And upon his knees thanked his gods for the grace they did him in delivering into his hands one with whom they themselves might joy.

The beautiful young gentleman, which saw him so before him embased,° feared him not a

---

[159] In *Espejo*, Lirgandeo reassures them with news of a knight born in the west.
[160] Asia the Less: Asia Minor, also called Anatolia, the peninsula that constitutes the Asian portion of modern Turkey
[161] Nautical vocabulary is added to this and the following sentence.
  Phrygia: an ancient district in western-central Anatolia (Asia Minor), named after a people whom the Greeks called Phryges and who dominated Asia Minor between the twelfth and seventh centuries BCE
[162] Tyler adds the detail of Florion bowing to Donzel del Febo, suggesting the cultural perception of his faith's idolatrous practices of worship.

whit,° although the armour glistered, but with a joyful and pleasant countenance, colled° him and clasped his arms about his neck as if he had known him a long time. I do not think that the desire of safety made him so to fawn upon Florion, for they with whom he was erst° acquainted wore no armour.[163] But the Prince Florion took him up in his arms and kissed his white and roseal° cheeks as tenderly as if he had been his own child, making him to eat of the most delicate meats which he had then on board. The little boy, which was very hungry, fed very well, and from that time forth loved the Prince Florion more than any other, as it is natural in man to prefer those of whom they receive benefits. When the Gentleman of the Sun was well satisfied, the Prince Florion entered again into his own ship and hoisted sail toward Phrygia with a good wind.

CHAPTER 17

Prince Florion in his way homewards findeth by adventure the young gentleman Clavergudo, son to the King Oristeo of France, and bringeth him with the Gentleman of the Sun to Babylon[164]

The second day after the Prince Donzel del Febo had been thus taken into Florion's ship, they turned about towards Phrygia whence they first departed, and escried,° at three of the clock in the morning right against their ship another, the tallest and beautifullest° ship that they had ever seen, which the faster it sailed, the nearer it approached to their vessel, for the pilot° directed their course straight upon Florion's ship. And in short space they joined together. This ship, grappling with the other, by and by a chieftain getting upon the hatches commanded all in the other ship to yield as prisoners. Then the strong Florion, not knowing who they were, took a heavy and well steeled battle axe, and getting upon the shipboard made him answer on this wise:°

'What are thou knight so arrogant, which without knowing who we be would make us thy prisoners?'

'What may you be', said the knight, 'that you can acquit yourselves from the terrible Mambriniano, which cometh in this ship? Now, except you do this that I command you, all the world is not sufficient to make you a way to escape his hands. Until this day there was never born a man which hath made like effusion of human blood in this sea'.

'Then fain would I see this brave knight', answered the Prince Florion.

And scarcely had spoken these words when the devilish rover,° armed with a very great and heavy armour and a battle axe of fine steel in his hands, joined to the Prince speedily, and without 'God speed you!' laid at him such a blow upon the headpiece as might have cloven his head in pieces.[165] But the prince was deliver° and quick, and seeing the battle axe descending, the air beaten before it, he stepped aside and the blow fell upon the planks of the ship, which made a great piece thereof to fall into the water, quite shutting him from hope of a second blow. Then the bold Florion, closing with him, gave him a buffet with his sword upon his great and fine helmet that he made him bow his knees. And with the great weight of his body, scarcely might

---

[163] 'I do not . . . no armour' is added.
[164] Clavergudo is always called Claueryndo in the second and third editions. This variant is not enumerated in the textual notes in order to avoid repetitiveness.
[165] 'very great' mistranslates 'gruesso' (thick, bulky, or rough). See note 158.

In *Espejo*, Mambriniano is so big that he seemed to be a giant. By referring to him as a 'rover' Tyler alludes to the contemporaneous dangers represented by pirates and privateers, many of whose activities contributed to Anglo-Spanish tension.

this rover° arise, but he turned himself with great pain to strike the prince. There began a brave and terrible battle, either of their knights much amazed in beholding them.

Now well fare thy heart, thou valiant Florion, for thou much disappointed Mambriniano of his enterprise, and made him confess that in twenty years robbing on the sea of so many as he might find, he had never met knight which had put him in so great danger, nor fought with one of so great force. Thus they fought half an hour, and no man might judge who should have the better. The great rover° struck with all his force at his enemy, but the final hour of his own life now edging near him, so it was that the courageous prince avoided it. And as he was already entered into the good success of his voyage, having in his power the Gentleman of the Sun, so fired all with wrath, his colour, as a man might say, bewraying° his choler, he gave the rover° with both his hands such a blow upon the head that he felled him to the ground.[166] And before the rover° might get on his knees, he gave him another between his helmet and his neckpiece and laid him flat upon the planks of the ship. There the wretched Mambriniano, with his gluttonous desire, spit out his stinking and corrupted spirit.[167]

And the noble Florion rested not here, but with a brave and stout° courage entered in the ship and laid° about him on both sides. The knights of the rover,° to revenge their lord's death, wounded him on all parts. But, by and by, there boarded them the twenty knights of the prince, all chosen men of war, and helped their lord in such wise° that, in short time, the greatest part of their enemies were slain, and the rest, seeing their fall, yielded themselves to his mercy. The battle thus ended, the prince would see what was in the ship, for he believed that there was within great riches according as the dealings of the rover° had been.

There was much treasure found, but searching every place of it, they found in a cabin a knight of an indifferent° age, clothed with rich garments, and by his grave countenance seeming to be of good account.[168] And near unto him, a young gentleman of four or five years old, very beautiful and seemly arrayed in cloth of gold, and about his neck a collar° of gold set with rich and precious stones. The young gentleman was so gracious in his behaviour that if Florion had not before seen the Gentleman of the Sun, he had believed him to be the fairest and properest° gentleman that ever he had seen. And desiring to know who they were, he saluted them courteously, willing the knight to tell him who they were. He, which had already known Florion's great virtue in the battle that he had with the rover,° rose with the young gentleman from the place where he was seated, and using a humble duty to him, answered:

'Sir Knight, I am a prisoner to the rover° Mambriniano, which took me and this young gentleman at a place near a haven of the sea. And since God (by fortune) hath been so favourable unto you that in a righteous battle you have slain him, we remain now for yours to do with us that which shall seem best unto you. And we have good hope that with a knight of so great valour there cannot happen unto us so much evil as with him which took us prisoners'.

The prince accepted well that which he said unto him, and prayed him to go on in declaring who he was, for that by lack of knowledge he might foreslack° to do to them the honour that they merited.

Albeit now the knight wished that he might dissemble it for the danger which might ensue, yet in the end, putting his affiance° in the prince, he said unto him:

'Since it liketh you, Sir knight, to know who we be, only to please you I will tell it you, though I would gladly have suppressed our names till Fortune, somewhat more friendly unto us should have bewrayed° it. But know you that this young gentleman is called Clavergudo, and is the son

---

[166] The humoural reference is added.
  The name Gentleman of the Sun is preferred by Tyler, whereas in *Espejo* he is invariably referred to as Donzel (and later as Caballero) del Febo.
[167] His spiritual corruption is intensified in *Mirror*. The source explains that the sad Mambriniano, with such a hungry greed for robbery, ended his perverse life.
[168] Tyler adds the detail of the found treasure.

of the King Oristeo, King of France, only inheritor and successor of that great kingdom. And I have to name Armineo, being brother to the King Oristeo and uncle to this young gentleman. The whole order of this misfortune was in this sort: one day for to sport ourselves in the company of many other knights, we rode to a fair forest near unto the sea, and the knights which came with us, the most of them delighting in hunting, severed themselves for their disport° in such manner that the young gentleman and I, with only ten knights, were left in a fresh and fair harbour about a well near adjoining unto the sea.[169] In this time, while our knights followed their game, this great rover° Mambriniano, whether espying us or by chance taking land for fresh water we know not, but, with more than twenty knights, he beset us. And although we defended ourselves sometime, in the end, this gentleman and I were taken prisoners and our ten knights slain and sore wounded. Before the other knights, which hunted in the forest, might understand of it, he carried us to his ships, where it is more than a month that we have been in this manner as you have seen us, close pent up in this cage.[170] For my self, Sir, as I never hope for liberty, so I respect not my imprisonment. But for this fair young gentleman, my heart is sore wounded. I had rather suffer ten deaths than any such misfortune should happen to him, because that when such news shall be reported to his father he will bear it more impatiently than his own.[171] And that which worst is, to me only will he attribute this fault, since having committed his only son to my governance, I have given so ill account of him'.

Unto these words the knight lent many a tear sliding down his face, which well showed the grief he bore in heart. The Prince Florion, in great compassion, comforted him, promising liberty of return into his country when he would. But, by and by, remembering the words which the wise man his uncle had said, he called it back again. And instead of his first promise, he turned his tale to the narration of his own mishaps, being on this wise:°

'I thank you heartily for your courtesy in recounting to me the whole discourse of your imprisonment and of this young gentleman's captivity. And I call the high gods to witness what pain your misfortune hath caused in me, and how ready my power shall be to remedy it when I may. For I mean to give you liberty of return, and with my men to conduct you homewards into France, thus much occasioned in me by the deserts° of your estate. But Fortune hath been so contrary to me that except your return be delayed, I myself shall want my necessary help, the whole state of the matter lying thus, if it so please you to hear: I am by name Florion, King of Persia, my father deceasing which was king thereof, and so by just title as to his only son and heir, the crown of the kingdom descended to me.[172] This charge I sustained in mine° own person a good while, but being young and lusty° and in good age to follow arms, I was desirous to wander in the world. So leaving a governor in my kingdom, I travelled through diverse countries until the end of three years, at which time I took over into Babylon where I was matched with the daughter of the sultan, being mine° uncle. Thither° came ambassadors from my subjects, certifying me that the King of Media, the stoutest° pagan in all the heathen country, with main° force had intruded upon my kingdom. I, for to remedy it, gathered a great host in the sultan's land and transporting into Persia, at the first battle that I had with the King of Media, the greater part of my people being slain, myself was overthrown, and with great grief, by secret by-ways, recovered Babylon where I could willingly have died for pain and anguish. But one, mine° uncle, a very wise and learned man in [the] art [of] magic, recomforted° me saying that the time should come in which I should be restored to my kingdom with great honour and that for this it behoved me to await on the sea till I met with two little boys of excellent beauty with whom I should return to Babylon, for that they should be the principal cause of my redress. And so giving credit

---

[169] The setting recalls the scene of Donzel del Febo's misfortune, thereby furthering the parallels between the two boys.
[170] Their enclosure 'in this cage' is added.
[171] 'his father' replaces 'sus padres' (his parents), as in Chapter 21.
[172] He claims his kingship unequivocally, whereas in the source he admits that for a time he was called king.

to his word, I thus put myself in array for this adventure, where thanks be to the gods, all hath succeeded as the wise man forespoke° it. For within this three days I lighted upon one, being alone in a little boat, having in him (according to my fancy°) the very pride of all beauty. And the other must needs be this young gentleman Clavergudo, the fairest beside him that ever I knew. So as I have good hope hereby to re-enter into my kingdom. For this cause, I have in charge to bring these two to Babylon. And now, Sir knight, I beseech you to take it in good part, for he shall be as well entertained in the court of the sultan as in the court of the king his father. And when my good fortune will that my seat shall be established, he and you shall return into France with my ships, and my people, and myself also, if it be so convenient'.

When the prince had here stayed,° Armineo was well contended with his talk, taking him for a knight of great prowess. And although the long stay that the Prince Clavergudo should make in this country grieved him, yet with hope to return in the end, seeing it was not in his power to do otherwise, he subjected his will to the prince's command. And with courteous words rendered him thanks for the story of his adventures and for the offer he had made them, the pith of his answer being in few words this:

'Be it as you have said, Sir. For I deny not but the gentleman Clavergudo shall gain very much by his bringing up in yours and your uncle's so noble a court'.

With these proffers to and fro, Florion took Clavergudo in his arms, and entered in his own ship, Armineo following him. When Armineo had beheld within Florion's ship the young Donzel del Febo, you must not marvel though he blessed himself, for there was none which had had but a blush of him within his tender years but took him rather to be a celestial seraphim than a human creature and believed that this might not be done without some great mystery, as if the young gentleman showing in his infancy the comeliness of stature and other excellent qualities wherewith he was endowed, besides the strange finding him alone in the rage of the tempest, did well foreshow his nobility in time to come.[173] But when they saw him naked and the portraiture° of the Sun, with the brightness that it gave to the beholders, it was so strange that they called to mind Phaeton's fall out of heaven, comparing this young gentleman with Phaeton as if he had been Phoebus's son, like as Phaeton was. Although somewhat diverse again in this, for that Phaeton taking his father's chariot for his presumption was drenched in the sea, this young gentleman was preserved in the sea, as betokening some greater secrecy in nature.[174] Armineo was best apayed° to have the company of so excellent a gentleman for the Prince Clavergudo.

Now by the way, this may you learn: that although they could not tell Donzel's name, yet by the tokens he had upon him they named him the Gentleman of the Sun, somewhat in other terms in the Persian tongue, but in signification all one with the name that his mother's gentlewoman gave him in Hungary, being worth the marking that both Persians and Hungarians should so jump in naming him. But to make haste homewards they took the way to Phrygia, and with a good wind, ere° fifteen days, they landed there. And coming ashore, they sent harbingers aforehand,° as well to advertise° the sultan and Lirgandeo of the prince's coming as to purvey by the way of lodging for the estates, the two young gentlemen being not a little welcome unto Florion's two uncles, as you may read in the next chapter.[175]

---

[173] 'the comeliness . . . the tempest' expands the Spanish.
[174] In Greek mythology, Phaeton, the son of Phoebus Apollo (the god of the sun) is reluctantly granted permission to drive his father's chariot. He was unable to control the fiery horses that drew the chariot, which had disastrous effects on the earth. In order to stop the chariot and save the world, Zeus struck it with a lightning bolt and Phaeton fell into a river and drowned.

The brightness of his birthmark recalls Havelock the Dane's luminous mark.
[175] The concern for their lodgings and their welcome by the uncles are additions.

CHAPTER 18

Prince Florion with the two young gentlemen entered into Babylon and were there honourably received by the sultan

The Prince Florion needed not to have given intelligence to the sultan of his coming, for the wise Lirgandeo opened° all which had chanced as well as if he had been a party in the doing of it. So when the prince was in less than a half day's journey from the city, the sultan and his wise brother Lirgandeo issued out with a great train to receive him. And coming near, the wise Lirgandeo, espying Florion with the Gentleman of the Sun on his horse before him, in great joy rode apace. And taking him in his arms, spoke these words:

'Oh, ye° sovereign gods, immortal thanks be given unto you for the high favour you have showed unto us in bringing into our power this rare gentleman with whom you have imparted of your most secret graces! Oh, that mine° arms could once merit such a heavenly burden! Oh, how well may Babylon rejoice since he is thither° brought whose glory shall no less glister through the earth than the bright sun shineth in the world, who deserveth to have his biding° among the demigods for his valour and mightiness![176] Oh, how he shall erase out the memory of Ninus, and Xerxes, and all the pride of the Assyrian monarchs![177] From henceforth, Assyria, for being only the cradle of this gentleman's nursery, shall be famous throughout the whole world. From henceforth, men shall have so much to do to put in writing the worthiness of this gentleman that all the monuments of our ancestors shall quite die, and this man only shall be our table talk'.

The wise man thus as it were ravished and uttering his conceits° in great gladness by inter-breathings, the beauty of the child sometimes amazing him, and his divinity astonishing° the hearers, he kissed the young gentleman and held him in his hands till the sultan drew near. As the sultan approached, he delivered Donzel del Febo unto him and turned himself towards Clavergudo, embracing him goodly. But, in [no] more modesty of speech or less delight, he said unto him:

'You are welcome, noble and sovereign prince. I, knowing how well known your name should be in the world, had great desire to see you.[178] Albeit it shall be some grief unto your parents not to enjoy your presence, the time shall come when you shall give them greater comfort and pleasure. In the meantime, you shall not lose anything in being brought up in the company of this gentleman, whom you shall love so exceedingly that his love shall often extinguish the remembrance of your parents'.

Armineo, which was not far off, gave him great thanks in the behalf of the prince. Then they two rode together, devising of many things and many courteous words of good entertainment passing between them, until the sultan fell in talk with the young Clavergudo and Armineo, to whom he showed a friendly countenance in token of great good love.

These things thus done, they all held on their way to the city. And passing through towards the palace, there they were received by Balisea, princess and wife to Florion, making semblance of great liking to Donzel del Febo, whose excellent beauty and comeliness she well noted, and already concluded in her thought for a companion to her son, now of three years old, very large and beautiful, called Brandizel, which indeed after proved a knight so good as few better, being strong made, somewhat higher than his father, and of more puissance.[179] These three gentlemen,

---

[176] The divine gods of the Spanish become 'demigods'. In ancient mythology, a demigod is a partially divine being, including those of joint divine and mortal parentage, or humans who were raised to the rank of god.

[177] Ninus: in Greek mythology, King of Assyria, husband to Semiramis, and founder of Babylon
Xerxes: Xerxes The Great, King of Persia 486–465 BCE

[178] 'nombrada' (renown) is mistranslated as 'name'.

[179] Tyler adds Balisea's plans for Donzel del Febo to be her son's companion.

by the Princess Balisea's device, were brought up altogether in like suits° and like exercises. And so, from their youth their friendship increased with their years that in the end, as they themselves were at their full growth, so their friendship waxed so firm that neither the diversity of their professions,° nor the distance of their countries might in any wise° infringe it. These young gentlemen [were] thus brought up in Babylon: Armineo, which in all things was very wise and well learned, taught Clavergudo the liberal arts and instructed him in the true and perfect law of God, in such manner that although his education was among the Pagans, yet the prince was always a good Christian; the wise Lirgandeo, likewise careful° of the Gentleman of the Sun and of Brandizel, read unto them diligently what was convenient,° save that as he was a Pagan so he acquainted them only with Pagansie° in their religion, which error notwithstanding afterward they both renounced.

This was the training up of the young princes in the court of the sultan, as heedfully looked unto as if it had been in their parents' courts. But as their years multiplied, so they exceeded all others inferior in judgement, wit, discretion, goodliness of stature, activity, and all that which was requisite to such princes. But especially and above all his equals, Donzel del Febo surpassed, for attaining to the age of ten years he seemed to be more than fifteen both for wit and strength, courage and policy, and by the bigness of his body (being withal well featured), men gathered undoubtedly of his might. They made their argument thus: if he be so strongly set in his youth at ten years, what will he be at twenty? And truly, although his father, the Emperor Trebatio, was big of body, as the history hath already specified, being eight foot in height, yet Donzel del Febo over-reached him somewhat. And with all this maintained the prerogative of his proportion, so that I think our painters, as well Grecians° as Assyrians, had never the perfect knowledge to draw and finish the true proportion of man before they had the view of this knight.[180] His picture was sent into sundry parts as the noblest painture° that ere° was wrought. Besides this, there appeared in his face a majesty so grave and prince-like that it struck a fear of him into mighty princes. For all this, he was yet of behaviour affable and somewhat familiar, that he which know him well, albeit his mortal enemy, could not but highly commend of it. What shall I say? As the adamant° stone draweth to it the hard and sharp iron by his hidden virtue, so likewise this knight procured the love, as well of foes as of friends, and of as many as knew him and were conversant with him. And so th[ese] young gentlemen, Clavergudo and Brandizel, and other young gentlemen which were his playfellows were so glad of him that they could at no time be without him.

Now because we have more particularly to descend into this story hereafter and to describe the manifold graces of this knight, for these matters we will let them pass at this time. And remember you of his age of twelve years, at which time there happened that which shall appear in the chapter following.

CHAPTER 19

The delivery of the sultan by the Gentleman of the Sun

Many times, the sultan and the Prince Florion (with some other knights) for their recreations, rode on hunting into a thick wood, standing in a fair forest, seated somewhat near the sea, and plentiful of all kind of game, especially of wild boars and such like beasts. Now when the young gentlemen could sit their horses and were able to endure some travail,° they took them with them and, furnishing them with boar-spears in their hands, they appointed them to the chase. Some game there was killed before them, wherein they took great pleasure, but especially the

---

[180] As a young boy, he is also advanced as an example of beauty suitable for artists' emulation, see Chapter 14.57–58.

Gentleman of the Sun, which by himself wearied a wild bear and two boars so fierce as might have frayed° a right good knight.¹⁸¹ His practice was always to hunt alone, to have no man's help to the encounter with any wild beast.

And it was so that one day, the sultan would go to the same forest to delight himself there for certain days, taking with him the Princess Balisea, his daughter, and the train of many ladies and gentlewomen, and the most principal lords of his court, because the place was gallant and delectable, and replenished with variety of game, being, as I said, hard upon° the cliffs of the sea. For this cause there were reared up many pavilions there, and there was purveyed of other provision necessary for the household. He made his own tent to be pitched in a flourishing meadow next to a goodly fountain.¹⁸² There rested he one day, solacing himself among his knights, for the first day they went not out to seek their game. The next day, early in the morning, the Prince Florion, the young gentlemen, and the most part of all the knights took their way through the forest, climbing up a steep hill, and parted themselves into diverse companies, some to raise° the game and others to be at the receipt,° the sultan and the princess with her ladies, and only fifteen knights remaining in their tents as unmindful of any danger if any should happen. The sun being almost at the highest and his beams more direct, the sultan with the princess, his daughter, and her gentlewomen left their tent and came to the fountain, the water being clear and the place well shadowed with trees, there in the quiet shade to abide the coming of the Prince Florion and the young gentlemen to dinner. In the meantime, the gentlemen sewers° prepared the cupboard, and the cooks made ready for dinner.

The tables being spread upon the green grass, and every man attentive to his function —the officers to their charge, the knights to their game, and the sultan with the princess and ladies to refresh themselves in the cool air — there came in place a mighty and woeful° giant, with more than twenty knights after him.¹⁸³ The ladies screeched out, but there was no remedy, for the giant with his knights took the sultan, the princess, and most of the gentlewomen, and conveyed them into a chariot drawn by strong horses which they brought with them for the same purpose. With the outcries of the ladies, the knights which were in the tent issued, and seeing their lord and the princess with her ladies so carried away perforce° — albeit this they did more for shame than through hardiness — yet they made towards the giant with their swords and began to compass him about.¹⁸⁴ But they so ill performed their duty that in short time themselves were either wounded, slain, taken, or put to flight, and their lord, for lack of rescues, was bound and fettered. The giant, having his prey, with all the haste he might, took toward the sea, where he had a good ship in readiness. The lamentable noise which the ladies made was such that it beat through the air unto the skies, and yet could not penetrate so far as to Prince Florion or his knights, either that they were so eager in the pursuit of their wild boars that they marked it not, or that the cry of the hunters was so loud that it drowned the other.¹⁸⁵

But the young Gentleman of the Sun, losing his company and well mounted upon a light horse with a boar-spear in his hand, being also clothed in a hunter's weed° of green cloth of gold and a hat to keep down his yellow° hairs, rode roaming about the wood to seek some beast upon whom he might try the steel of his boar-spear.¹⁸⁶ And taking this way and that way without staying° in any place, he met with a knight sore wounded by the giant, which rode piteously to call the Prince Florion and his knights for succour to the sultan and the princess. As Donzel del Febo saw him thus arrayed, he asked what he ailed.

---

¹⁸¹ In *Espejo*, he kills the bear.
¹⁸² The location recalls the pleasant sites in which earlier misfortunes occurred, as in Chapters 15 and 17.
¹⁸³ Tyler adds the mention of the specific functions and the officers' tasks.
¹⁸⁴ In the source, the sultan also cries out.
¹⁸⁵ Their cries reach heaven in *Espejo*.
¹⁸⁶ In *Espejo*, he is greedy for prey. The alteration recuperates his behaviour from any connotation of sin.

'Alas, Gentleman of the Sun', said the knight, 'the sultan our lord and the princess are taken prisoners by an ugly and monstrous giant, and by the haste he maketh, I guess he is already near unto the sea!'

The Gentleman of the Sun much lamented such news, and with a noble and heroical° courage, which by nature now enforced° itself forward, he prayed the knight to guide him on the way towards the giant. The knight, thinking it an unfit match and beside his purpose to turn back with him, for he thought him too young for such an enterprise, would not stay° but rode on faster. The gentleman moved with this that the knight set so little by him, yet said nothing. But not tarrying for more company broached his horse with his spurs that he made him spin° the same way in which he had seen the knight before.[187] The haste he made is incredible, for before the giant had recovered the sea he overtook him in a plain amongst his knights and the chariot in the midst. The giant was hindmost on foot with a great battle axe of steel in his hand, so that it might have dismayed one to see his fierce and cruel demeanour. When the Gentleman of the Sun had got a sight of him, with greater force than before, he spurred his horse making way through the green meadow as fast as if he had been driven by the rage of tempest and thunder, and crying aloud:

'Stay,° stay!'°

The giant and his knights, hearing the noise that he made and the sound of the horse feet galloping in such haste, turned their heads aside to see what it meant. And amongst the rest, the sultan likewise looked behind him. And espying him to be the Gentleman of the Sun with only a boar-spear in his hand, he much pitied his case, for he thought surely Donzel should never escape death or durance.°

The loathsome giant, wondering at the young gentleman coming toward him with great fury, lift[ed] up both his hands to his head, and there staying on foot as he was, made a fierce and stern countenance of disdain till the young gentleman approached.[188] But the noble and valiant Donzel del Febo, born for the achievement of greater adventures, with a furious mood as it had been thunder, drew near.[189] And with his boar-spear in his hand, being very strong, sharp and well-steeled, with all his force he shoved it into the breast of the giant, that although he had a breastplate of fine steel a finger° thick, yet the spear entered and issued out at the shoulder all begored° with blood.[190]

Thus the giant fell down dead on the ground to the great abashment of all those which saw him, judging that Donzel del Febo had been then let down from heaven to do this feat, for in their fancies° not the thunderbolt which by the renting of the clouds driveth the winds before it might ever give a more sudden or more forcible blow than that which Donzel del Febo gave the giant.[191] Especially, the knights of the giant's retinue, not witting° who he was, imagined that their own gods had sent him down from the heavens for the more notable chastisement of their lord's cruelty. Now some of the knights hearing a rushing a far off in the wood and thinking it to be the sultan's people, their master thus slain, without having care of chariot or prisoners took them to their heels with more haste by half than good speed; for one letting the bridle slip and for fear not able to guide his horse, by the stumbling of his horse had so sore a bruise that this horse rising, he lay still on the ground tormented with the fall.[192] And those which got to

---

[187] In the source, the horse galloped with such speed that he seemed to be a flying bird: his hoofs did not even disturb the grass beneath him.
[188] Rather than lifting his hands, in the Spanish text, the giant raises the steely and sharp hatchet.
[189] In *Espejo*, Donzel del Febo was 'raised' rather than 'born' for the adventures.
[190] The English unit of measurement, 'finger', replaces the Spanish 'six sheets of steel'.
[191] The Spanish giant is cut in half.
[192] Tyler makes explicit their fear for their master's death.
  'more haste . . . speed' is proverbial, Tilley H197.
  In *Espejo*, 'one' fears that a thunderclap will issue from the ground and strike him.

the sea, themselves being past danger, nothing sorrowed at the death of the giant for they hated him and served more by compulsion than with good will.[193]

This trouble in the giant's men made the Gentleman of the Sun make no account of them. Wherefore, alighting from his horse, he went towards the chariot where the sultan was with the princess and ladies and unbound them. The ladies, when they saw him, were no less glad of the proof of arms in Donzel del Febo than of their own delivery. But the sultan, embracing him and kissing him with great love, said unto him:

'Oh my son, now I know assuredly that the mighty gods highly favour you and that only by miracle you have been brought to Babylon as to give succours to me and to my children! Now do I firmly believe my brother Lirgandeo, who long before prophesied of the great marvels of your valour: since that being so young and tender and in the maidenhead of your strength — it being never before tasted upon an enemy — you have begun so well as I have known no knight in his perfection matchable.° And truly, this is the accomplishment of your first adventure, as my brother foreseeing it told me, that you should rescue me and my daughters from death or imprisonment. And I hope as well in the immortal gods that the second shall be likewise finished: that is, the kingdom of Persia, so long withheld by a false usurper, may by you be redelivered to the Prince Florion'.

'My lord', answered Donzel del Febo, 'I have not as yet done the thing in your service, neither in my life may hope to compass which may counter-peise° with my good will in this behalf. And truly, the duty which I owe to your good grace, my lord, to the Prince Florion, and to my lady, the princess your daughter, daily so augmenteth as more than that duty I cannot owe unto my father, to the discharge whereof notwithstanding I stand bound to your goodness, not only of courtesy but in conscience'.[194]

And so humbled himself before the sultan. But the sultan again embraced him and they two helped the ladies out of the chariot. The ladies were desirous to know who the giant was, and what should be the cause why he so assailed them. Therefore, the sultan and the Gentleman of the Sun made toward the knight of the giant's, which was fallen to the ground. And as they took off his helmet to give him air, they fetched him out of his sound.° And setting him on his feet they demanded of him who the giant was, and why he came to take them prisoners.

The knight, seeing it behoved him to say the truth, made answer shortly thus:

'You shall understand, my lords, that this giant was called Brandafileo, lord of the Towered Island, which is in the Great Ocean, at the mouth of the Red Sea. This island is so strong and invincible that, being within, he need not fear all the world if they had bent their force against him. And being proud upon the safety of this island, he did much wrong to the nations round about him, spoiling and robbing all Arabians, Ethiopians, Egyptians, and the Garamants of Inde, and finally so many as he might come by in the great west seas and [ ] the Island of Taprobane.[195] And by long continuance in this trade of roving,° he is become so rich of captives and treasure that no island is comparable with his. Now the cause wherefore he came into this your land was for that in the time that the mighty Orixerges, your father, reigned in Persia, the father of this giant, called Briontes, then being lord of the Towered Island. By occasion of Briontes's evil life, your father and he fell at variance, wherefore the king your father sent out his whole navy to subdue this island. But being not able to conquer it, he gave them notwithstanding in charge to lie in the out-creeks,° awaiting when he came forth from the island and so to set upon them. One time, the giant making a road out for a like chevisance° a far off

---

[193] Tyler adds the explanatory clause, 'themselves being past danger'.
[194] The expression of loyalty, 'to the discharge . . . conscience', is an English addition.
[195] Garamants of Inde: from 500 BCE to 500 AD, the Garamantes lived in Fezzan in the Central Sahara of Libya. They are mentioned by Herodotus and appear in contemporaneous Spanish texts such as *Amadís de Gaula* and *Reloj de príncipes* (*Espejo*, I.145).
Island of Taprobane: Sri Lanka

from his own island, the king your father dogged him with his ships, and as he returned, met him in the half turn. And for all the havoc he and his made of your father's soldiers, in the end, killed him. This Brandafileo, his son, then being a child of tender age, yet so soon as he was of years to be made knight, he greatly longed after the revenge of his father's death. And because he could not work his mischief on the King Orixerges, being then dead, at the least it would ease his stomach if he might wreak° mischief on you, his son.[196] And for this cause many times he hath sent spies into your land to be advised by them when he might have opportunity of vengeance. And learning of your coming to this forest for your disport, he hath now lain more than a month in secret expectation of so good luck as to take your person. This time, he had found to his contentation,° had not this gentleman been, who now hath made sufficient pay to Brandafileo for his month's hire. This is all, my lord, which I can tell you as to your demand. And it is truth which I have told you, as I certainly believe that if ever he had clean carried you from hence you should not have escaped from death or bondage, for so he had determined'.

The sultan mused at that which the knight had told him, and weighing the great danger wherein he was like to have fallen, he ceased not to give thanks to his gods and to the Gentleman of the Sun for his safety. At this time Prince Florion came with more than thirty knights, running their horses so fast as they might because already they had heard the news. And coming where the giant lay dead, viewing well the wide and mortal wound, they highly commended of it and could not judge by whom he had received it. But very joyful to see the sultan and his princess out of danger, leaping from their horses, they came towards them. Then Florion, excusing his long absence by the ignorance of the fact, desired to know who he was which had so gently bailed° them from the giant.

The sultan answered on this sort:

'Ah, Florion! Florion, now we know your uncle Lirgandeo's divinations as touching this Gentleman of the Sun to be sooth° and steadfast, for we have well approved his valour. And know you that he alone, being the only man which came to succour us, brought to ground the giant Brandafileo by one only blow with his boar-spear, riveting, as you see, his coat armour,° and ridding us from so dangerous a foe, making his entrance to knighthood the strangest that ever was heard'.

Florion, giving back either as wondering or not crediting his uncle's speech, was still urged by the sultan, who told on forward as Brandafileo's knight had confessed. Florion, yet as it were half in a mammering° which part to take between the gentleman's youth and his courage, disputed rather the impossibility by means of the hugeness of the giant, his strong armour, and the number of his knights.

In the end, he overcame himself by remembrance of Lirgandeo's report, and thanked the gentleman on this wise°:

'Oh, my right noble and beloved son![197] I grant that not my force, but the mighty winds and swelling waves, by the ordinance of my gods, have given me power over you, for that by your sovereign bounty the wrong which is done to me by the tyrant shall be revenged and I shall recover mine° own kingdom![198] Oh, how happy was the day and the hour fortunate in which I found you, since my gods have reserved you for so great benefits towards me and the release of mine° uncle!'[199]

With these and many other words, Florion wept for great pleasure to think of Donzel's magnanimity.

And in this time, the other young gentlemen, his companions, came riding from hunting and saw the fierce giant lie dead by the way. They enquired after the manner of his death, and hearing

---

[196] The medical imagery applied to the giant's emotions is added by Tyler.
[197] The memory of Lirgandeo's report is not mentioned in the source text.
[198] He is referred to as 'king' rather than judgementally as 'tyrant' in *Espejo*.
[199] The release of the princess is omitted from his speech by Tyler.

it to be as you have heard, the one took great pleasure in it and the other, with an honest emulation of the fact, wishing it to himself, according to the diversity of the good will they bore unto the Gentleman of the Sun. Then they came altogether to their tents, where they made but a hunters' breakfast, for ere° dinner was half done the sultan commanded to horse to return to Babylon.[200] And so they all on horseback, the princess and her gentlewomen on their palfreys, and the lusty° knights on their sturdy rouncivals, took the way towards the city, laying the mighty giant upon a horse, his head and feet trailing on the ground.[201]

When they were within the gates of the city, all that which had happened being published, all the citizens and other of the court were in contrary arguments about the hugeness of the giant and the courage of the Gentleman of the Sun, thinking it an impossible matter to be brought about by one of so few years.[202] But from that time forth, although before likewise they loved him, yet now they made much more of him. And the sultan, with the princess and all the courtiers, held him in great account always. Notwithstanding the report of men and the high extolling of his acts to his own face, the Gentleman of the Sun kept the same tenor of life, not bearing himself anything upon his good fortune; but rather as the winds increased which promised him safety and honour and as his fame was more blazed, so he struck his sails and became more lowlier.[203] This, his humility, made him much more to be loved as the sprinkling of water augmenteth the flame in a smith's forge.[204]

Clavergudo, at this time egged on by Donzel's good hap° and being of riper years, sued° to be made knight.[205] But the wise Lirgandeo, foreseeing somewhat and to have him keep company with Donzel del Febo and Brandizel, withstood his purpose for that time. Clavergudo was but about fourteen or fifteen years of age, but he was so comely and nimble in all feats of arms that there was not a knight in all the court which outpassed° him.[206]

In this manner were these two gentlemen brought up in the sultan's court, with great magnificence as if they had been in their father's courts. And above all, they were so thoroughly instructed in learning that there were none able to come in controversy with them.[207] All this equal to both, notwithstanding the difference of beliefs which shall be alike ere° it be long: Clavergudo, which was guided by Armineo his uncle, was a Christian; and the Gentleman of the Sun believed in the law of the gentiles, as the wise Lirgandeo had taught him. Lirgandeo himself being bred and brought up in the same error by his father, for all his great cunning was not able to find out the vanity of his false gods.

Oh, the providence of God! How much be we bound to Thee and how ill do we acknowledge thy great goodness in suffering us to be [ ] Christians when thousands [of] wise men and mighty monarchs die in the law of the gentiles, not all their power available to save their souls, and their learning not worth a rush° for the displaying of the falsehood of that law wherein their fathers have nuzzled° them![208] And shall we Christians think that our knowledge can pull us out of hell, if not the wisest of the earth, I mean the learned gentiles, could once reprove their own law and

---

[200] The meal is not mentioned in the source. A hunters' breakfast is a large meal, see Tilley H826.
[201] rouncivals: Roncesvalles is a village in northern Spain and the site of the Battle of Roncesvalles (778), described in the epics *La Chanson de Roland* and *Roncesvalles*. The place name Roncesvalles came to be figuratively used 'to denote something huge or monstrous, probably with allusion to the legend of Roland' (*OED* 'rouncival'). Tyler seems to be combining this figurative usage with the noun 'rouncy', which denotes a steed or a horse used especially for riding (*OED* 'rouncy').
 The evocative detail of the giant being so big that his head and his feet dragged on either side of the horse is excised.
[202] There are no 'contrary arguments' in the Spanish, which instead alludes to their strange fear.
[203] Tyler specifies that it is notwithstanding 'the report . . . face'.
[204] The imagery of the elements — wind, fire, water — and the smithy are all added by Tyler.
[205] The theme of jealousy is heightened by Tyler, as explored in the introduction.
[206] *Mirror* specifies his age; in *Espejo* he is portrayed as young.
[207] *Espejo* explains that no one 'had advantage over them', which makes more sense.
[208] The language in *Mirror* is much more judgmental. *Espejo* merely describes their beliefs as 'false'.

know the only and true God? As for example, this Lirgandeo was so wise and well learned that not Artimodoro, nor Rogel, nor Turk, nor Saracen, nor Jew, nor Christian came ever near him.[209] And yet, because he had learned that law from his cradle and wanted the gift of God for the true understanding of his will, he wallowed still in his error as the sow doth in the mire, till God, having a regard of the Gentleman of the Sun and minding to make him a true Christian, did by His means convert the wise Lirgandeo to the knowledge of His will and pour out His grace abundantly upon the whole kingdom of Persia, according as more largely shall be recited. But to return, the two young gentlemen, albeit contrary in professions,° yet in friendship and good will were conformable, as shall be declared in this story.

CHAPTER 20

An adventure in the court of the sultan, which befell to the young Gentleman of the Sun

The sultan and the Prince Florion, with all the knights of his court, greatly prayed their gods that the Gentleman of the Sun might come to his full age to be made knight; for that only they stayed° their voyage into the Kingdom of Persia, for his cause as willing to have him with them for the great prowess which rested in him.[210] And they thought their stay not overlong, seeing it was not unlikely that which the wise Lirgandeo prophesied of him: that he should be a valiant knight and that, without him, their entrance into Persia were to small effect. For this cause, they employed their care in the advancing forward of the Gentleman of the Sun. This gentleman, now being of the age of sixteen years, was so high and well fashioned that he wanted little in stature of any man.

One day, Prince Florion, with many other knights, being abroad at the river to fly° at a fowl, the young gentleman staying in the palace. The sultan, with many of his knights and gentlewomen, took their pastime in one part of his great palace where entered in at the gates six ancient knights with white beards hanging down to the girdlesteads° and all armed save the headpieces, compassing on each side a gentlewoman fair and young, clothed all in mourning apparel and having a crown of gold upon her head. This lady was led by a knight great of body, well and strongly proportioned, and armed at all points with a rich and strong armour. This knight, lifting up the visor of his helmet, showed himself to the sultan, where they perceived his face to be very foul and fearful, of colour more tawny and sunburnt than coal black, his eyes flaming in his head, his nostrils wide and large, broad lipped, and his sharp fangs issuing out of his mouth like boar's tusks and reaching to his chin, so that there was no man living but might have been afraid of his fierce semblance.[211] But besides this, he was so high that there was not any in that place whom this knight exceeded not two span-fulls° at the least, and in making of his body he was so large and well quartered, more than the compass of two knights.

Having thus entered and set himself to view, those which were present had enough to occupy their eyes: either on the ugliness of the giant or the beauty of the gentlewoman. But the gentlewoman kneeled before the sultan to have kissed his hands. But the sultan, taking her by the hand, raised her up, doing her the honour he thought it convenient in that she appeared to

---

[209] Rogel de Grecia: Amadis of Gaul's relative and the eponymous hero of the eleventh book of the cycle of *Amadís de Gaula* by Feliciano de Silva (1535). Rogel's adventures are continued in Pedro de Luján's *Silves de la Selva* (1546), the twelfth book of *Amadís*; and in Silva's *Cuarta Parte de Don Florisel de Niquea* (1551), the thirteenth and final book of the series. These romances were not translated into English. Tyler would have read them in Spanish or French.
[210] Their appeal to the gods is added by Tyler.
[211] Several horrific details are omitted from the source, including the fact that his nostrils were wide enough to each accommodate a hand.

30 be a lady of great birth. She, with tears distilling down from her beautiful eyes and watering her crimson cheeks, spoke unto the sultan on this wise:°

'The heavenly and immortal gods maintain and increase thy high estate, most puissant and mighty Sultan of Babylon. Know for certainty that uncertain Fortune, never constant to any, hath in such manner showed herself cruel and adverse to me that she only not sufficed with the death which my father, and mother, and many of their subjects have received for my sake, she ceaseth not daily to afflict me and to bring me to so low an ebb, that being defeated of mine° own inheritance, I am yet fain to wander through the courts of mighty princes to find some good and pitiful knight, which bewailing my mishap, will ease me of the great travail° I daily take to save my honour.[212] For if you will suffer me to lay open my case, the whole story is thus: I am
40 right inheretrix° of the Island of Cyprus, where my predecessors reigned long time with much joy until that their good hap° was hindered by my beauty.[213] For having brought me into this world with the beauty wherein you see me, which I would to our gods had either perished when I first was swaddled, or else had never been known, that none might have taken delight in it. So soon as my beauty was sounded abroad, this knight here present — King of the Zardians, lord of the Island of Zardia, called Raiartes — hearing of it, came to see me.[214] And so soon as he came, he was taken with my love.[215] And demanding° me for wife, was denied it of my father. Wherefore, very angry, returning to his Island of Zardia, with a great army of knights he came against my father, and at the first field killed him and murdered all his people, and in short time became lord of Cyprus. My mother, seeing my father dead and her land wasted, died for grief.
50 I remained alone, without company, till such time as Raiartes came to the palace where I was. I knew to whose power I was become servant, and fearing that he would have forced me, determined by ending my life to make myself free from his subjection, esteeming it far better to die with my parents than [remain] alive to bewail their deaths.[216] And having no better leisure nor means to achieve my purpose, I leaped up to a window, the highest in the palace, thence to have thrown myself down if Raiartes, seeing me in this plight, had not prayed me not to do it, promising, if I forbore that to do the thing that I commanded him. I, resolving upon death, told him that unless he granted me one gift, I would be mine° own executioner. He, to save my life, promised it, whereby I left off from putting that in practice which I had contrived in my thought. By this means, Raiartes had me in his power. And having the whole island at his commandment,
60 he carried me contrary to my will into his own country with these aged knights, my near kinsmen. There, he requested me of love and prayed me to accept of him for husband. What should I do?[217] He was importunate° in his demand° and I remained in his danger,° so that to put by the execution of his desire, I had none other remedy but to answer him that so soon as he had performed the promise which he made me, I would satisfy his whole intent. This hearing, he was well content. And so, I told him that he should carry me for the space of a twelve month into all places whither° I would, and if in the meantime I found a knight to defend my right by fighting against him, he should grant the battle with condition that if my knight vanquished him I should be free from his demand and my land at quiet. Otherwise, if he had the upper hand, I from thenceforth to be at his commandment and he do what ever liked him. This knight, most
70 noble sultan, counselling with his strength and thinking all men's virtues inferior to his, took upon him the quest, glad by such means to manifest his power. And so, he carried me from the

---

[212] Her desire to preserve her honour is added by Tyler.
[213] Her status as 'inheretrix' is added in *Mirror*. In *Espejo*, her misfortune arises from her birth rather than her beauty.
[214] Zardia possibly refers to Sardinia (*Espejo* I.154).
[215] 'he was taken with my love' signifies that he was 'taken with love of me'. Accordingly, the Spanish text explains that he was 'enamorado de mí' (I.20.2–3).
[216] Although suicide was a sin, there is a lengthy tradition (dating back to Lucrecia's suicide in classical Rome) of women killing themselves in order to avoid sexual dishonour.
[217] The addition of the rhetorical question increases the pathos of her speech.

Island Zardia more than half a year past, in which time yet I have not found a knight to undertake my quarrel, and yet I have been in the courts of mighty kings and other great lords. Now seeing the term set between us is more than half expired, for my last refuge hither am I come to thy court to prove if here my good fortune should be such that I should find in it that which I have so long sued° for in other courts'.

Here she ended with sighs and sobs out of measure, thereby uttering the sorrow she had in her heart and the grief for to love such a knight, which moved great compassion in both sultan and others of his company. But there was no knight which would answer for the Princess Radamira (that was her name), and yet there were many in the sultan's presence.

Then, in great pride and with a fierce look, this terrible Raiartes spoke unto her:

'What knight is there in the world so foolhardy and presumptuous, Radamira, which for thy cause dares enter into lists with me? Yea, be it that both right and justice were right and clear on his side. And are thou not quite devoid of reason to leave undone that which I beseech thee. Besides, valuing thy beauty with my bravery and thy pride with my puissance, I shall seem to set too low a price on myself if I enjoy thee. And if there be any knight here which will say the contrary, I will soon make him recant his folly'.

Raiartes, having said thus, knit his brows and made such a grim countenance that all they feared him which beheld him, and there was not a knight there so hardy as to answer anything in the Princess Radamira's behalf, as if it had been mere sin in a gentlewoman stranger's right to hazard their person upon a devil rather than upon a human creature. Every man was still, to the no little grief of the sultan in that his court received such disgrace.

But the Gentleman of the Sun, sitting by and moved with compassion towards the gentlewoman, arose on his feet and made answer to Raiartes, saying:

'Sir knight, it is a great blasphemy to knighthood to say that in the whole world there is not a knight which dare fight with thee. Thy lie is loud,° and thou does against all reason enforce° this princess to marry thee. Be thou sure that if I were a knight, I would suffer a thousand deaths rather than such reproach should be offered to a gentlewoman, for thy brown beauty is not fit to be her playfellow'.[218]

And saying thus, he set himself down again.

Raiartes, mad angry for these words, turning towards him and rolling his eyes with great rage, answered:

'If thou were as strong as thou are foolish, thou weak youngling, I would make thy life and thy words end at one time. But they say commonly that women and those which are not able to wear armour are privileged for their speech and may talk without controlment'°.

And so Raiartes left him.

But the courageous gentleman, not being able to bear that contumely,° in his anger rose from where he sat, and coming to the sultan, kneeled before him beseeching his grace to grant this one suit, the first which in his lifetime he had made. The sultan, little thinking what he would ask and loving him so well that what thing he demanded° it should have been granted, willingly said, 'Yea', and bade him say on what it was that he desired. The Gentleman of the Sun said:

'My lord, that which I require is that you make me knight, because it is high time that I receive it. I do not think myself so young as to put up wrong at any man's hand'.

Those which were present were much troubled at the request of the Gentleman of the Sun, foreseeing the end, which was to answer the bold Raiartes. And the sultan was greatly sorry to have been so rash in making promise before he had known his suit, wherefore he sat still without speaking 'yea' or 'no', devising only how to satisfy the young gentleman and to quit° himself of his promise.

The Gentleman of the Sun, doubting lest the sultan would linger and delay the time, very angerly° said unto him:

---

[218] The racial slur is not present in the source text.

'If I cannot obtain this at your hands, my lord, I swear by the high gods that during my life I shall not be merry, and I will go serve some other lord which more liberally will consider of my requests'.

The great sultan, loath to disquiet the Gentleman of the Sun, whom he saw attent° upon this matter, albeit his promise grieved him much, answered him thus, saying:

'Assuredly, Donzel del Febo, if you had demanded any other thing of me more profitable for yourself, doubt you not but you had been in possession of your desire by this time — yea, had it been the greatest part of my kingdom. But because I see you are of tender years and that the time is not yet for you to support the burden of armour, I would wish you to refrain and let fall your suit for this time. Or, if you will not otherwise be persuaded, hold you; I yield unto you. Watch this night in your armour, and tomorrow at daybreak I will give you the order'.[219]

The Gentleman of the Sun took him at that word and very joyfully kissed the sultan's hand for his gracious favour. Then, from thence by soft paces, coming to Raiartes, he said unto him:

'Now that I have licence to parley° with thee as a knight, I will answer thee, Raiartes, to the words which thou have said unto me. And so, I tell thee that if the Princess Radamira will put her quarrel into my hands, I will defend her right and take the battle upon me. And be it that the Princess Radamira dare not commit her right unto me, yet I say that to be avenged on thy reproachful speeches, which thou have blown forth, I will fight with thee and make thee to know that thou are more unjust and foolish than valiant and courteous as knights ought to be'.

The Gentleman of the Sun here ended, and the grim sire Raiartes began a laughter with these words:

'Indeed, if all folly were force, many knights were courageous and strong, for most of them are too venturous.° And if thyself were of as great ability as thou are of forwardness, the Princess Radamira should end her quarrel by tomorrow night. But thou deceive thyself. And albeit I am half ashamed to take the battle against a knight never before acquainted with armour, yet, because thou shall not want due correction for thy folly, I accept the battle which thou offer, as well for the one cause as for the other'.

As this talk was at the hottest between them, the Princess Radamira beheld the Gentleman of the Sun very earnestly, noting as well his years as his person. And albeit he was then beardless, yet she thus conceived of him that he was of noble courage and very strong, and besides this, there appeared in his face somewhat which she judged more than manlike.[220] And as she was wise, so her heart gave her that this young gentleman had some divine blood in him, which she thought to have descended from some of her false gods. So neither lightly nor wantonly moving, but with great discretion and wisdom standing in the same place and musing what she ought to do. In the end, no other knight answering the challenge for her, not altogether out of hope, she agreed to put her quarrel into his hands by deliberate counsel, concluding if he were murdered, herself to follow after. And so she spoke to the giant on this wise:°

'Raiartes, since this gentleman with so good will proffereth himself to maintain my right against thee, I am very well content to put my quarrel into his hands. And from this time forth, I will not seek other knight'.

The beautiful Princess Radamira doing thus, the fierce Raiartes was sore moved to see that she made so little account of him and so much trusted the boldness of the young gentleman. And foaming at the mouth like a wild boar, he was not able to speak one word for the fury and choler which boiled in him.[221] The Gentleman of the Sun thanked her goodly for the acceptation° of his pains in her name.

In this manner, the battle was put off till the next day, but the Gentleman of the Sun was not

---

[219] The 'order' is the order of knighthood.
[220] A reference to his largeness is omitted here.
[221] The description of him as choleric is added by Tyler. She tends to pathologize her characters' emotions by adding the medical language of humoural theory.

so glad to have occasion offered to be made knight as the sultan and his friends were sorrowful to have him fall into this danger, which they imagined to be too sure because of the strength of Raiartes and the youth of the Gentleman of the Sun; they thought it a desperate case for him to wage this battle with the safeguard of his honour. Then the young gentleman Clavergudo, being of more years than Donzel del Febo was, repented that he had not answered for the princess, both because he thought it a blemish to his honour to have excused himself from such a matter; and his age was more than Donzel del Febo's was and so might better acquit himself against the force of Raiartes. And especially fearing the peril of his friend, he would needs have taken the battle out of his hands, but perceiving the unwillingness of the Gentleman of the Sun, he would speak no more of it.

At sunset, Florion came from hunting, and hearing of the battle which was appointed, he was very sad for Donzel del Febo's sake because of Raiartes's force and Donzel's weakness.[222] And so, he took upon him to persuade Donzel del Febo to give over the battle and put it upon some other in his right, if it so pleased him.

But Florion and Clavergudo were both beguiled in Donzel del Febo, albeit either of them were such knights as of the one hath been rehearsed and of the other shall be showed you hereafter. Raiartes was strong as his like scarcely among the Pagans, and it might be it would ill have proved with them two, as a man would have sworn it only by the tenor of Raiartes's countenance, no man beholding him but with the same good will which they bore unto the devil.[223] And if Florion and Clavergudo desired this battle, it is to be thought it sprung of their love towards Donzel del Febo rather than of any comfort their courage gave them to win honour in the battle.

But the day was spent, and things necessary for the battle were in providing. At night, Lirgandeo the wise, coming from the Red Island, took landing at Babylon. And meeting with the Gentleman of the Sun, he told him that many days had passed since he knew of the conflict between Raiartes and him, and therefore, had brought certain armour for him. And so he commanded his squires to untie their two packets. Out of the one packet, Lirgandeo took a white armour wrought with beams of gold descending from his helmet, wherein was graven a face so fair and sheen° that it shed out beams as the sun, and scarcely for the brightness might a man behold it. And out of the same, he took out a sword, all garnished with gold and embossed with precious stones, the pomell,° scabbard, and chape° being so rich and curious that none there was which praised not the workmanship. Out of the other packet, he drew out another white armour pounced° with flour-de-luces° of gold and another sword, both which he gave to Clavergudo, bestowing the other upon Donzel del Febo.

With these good armours, the two gentlemen were well apaid,° especially the Gentleman of the Sun, which more esteemed of this gift than of all the seigniories° of the earth. And so he continued his charge for the morrow° battle, very confident on his own part, but to the no little dismay of his friends, chiefly of the Princess Balisea, which would not his destruction for all her father's lands.[224] The Princess Radamira, in the meantime, not fully settled in her thought, drove out the night neither merrily nor dumpishly but very heavily, as abhorring nothing so much as the company of Raiartes. Her flesh would tremble often and quake for fear, mistrusting Donzel del Febo's good fortune for the perfecting of his charge, his years being clean contrary to all good hope.

---

[222] He fears because of Donzel del Febo's youth in the source.
[223] The association of Raiartes and the devil is absent from *Espejo*.
[224] The description of his confidence is added.

CHAPTER 21

Donzel del Febo is dubbed knight and overcometh Raiartes

The next day in the morning, the Gentleman of the Sun, with his rich harness buckled about him, was brought before the sultan and all the knights and gentlemen in the court.[225] When he was thus bravely armed, he showed greater and stronger than he did unarmed, and none of them which saw him would have judged him of so young years. And when he came before the sultan, thus accompanied with all the principal knights and gentlemen of the court, the Gentleman of the Sun kneeled down and humbly craved to be made knight. The sultan, with tears flowing from his eyes, embraced him, greatly rejoicing to see him so comely in armour.[226] Then, taking the rich sword which the young gentleman held naked in his hand, he gave him three blows on the crest of his helmet. And so sheathing it again, girded it about Donzel del Febo's loins. And with these words blessing him — 'The high gods defend thee with their mighty hand!' — he bade him arise knight, and then made him swear to the observance of all the orders of knighthood, which done, the young gentleman kissed the sultan's hand, and all the hall rang with the noise:

'Our gods defend the sultan!'[227]

This was in the morning but before dinner was clean done and the tables taken up. The hour was near wherein they ought to perform the battle, and Raiartes, richly armed and mounted upon his horse, traversed up and down before the palace, where the ladies, which were bestowed in the windows to behold the fight, were afraid, for in their seeming by the hugeness of his body and his fierce countenance, he was the bravest knight in the world.[228] And his harness covered in him the deformities of nature.[229] The Princess Radamira, in her mourning weed accompanying the Princess Balisea, was in a great bay window, and seeing Raiartes so great, strong, and well-horsed, she changed her colour, without hope to remove Raiartes's love, and there fully appointed with herself rather to murder herself than to be in his power. For his filthy and ugly shape was such that what gentlewoman in the world could have afforded him for love?

When the sultan and other knights took their seats as judges of the field, the Knight of the Sun, departing from the palace, was conducted by diverse knights to his tent, and there, sitting upon a lusty° courser,° he pranced a while before the sultan. His horse was all covered with rich harness, in which were enchased sundry precious stones, all — both horse and harness — of the sultan's gift. Himself being clad with his bright armour, his umbrere° pulled down, and a mighty spear in his hand, so big as they all marvelled at his good making.[230] When Chevaliero del Febo stayed,° Raiartes drew near, and with a proud voice said unto him:[231]

'Thou presumptuous knight, what would thou give now not to be here alone with me? Do thou not think it no wisdom to adventure thy body where there is no hope of safety?'

'Assuredly Raiartes', answered the Knight of the Sun, 'hitherto I have not seen the thing wherefore I should repent me of my enterprise, and hitherto I have had more experience of thy vain and foolish words than of thy great and valiant prowess'.

Raiartes was fel° angry at this. The foam° staring° through his visor, [he] would have run upon the knight, but, being awarded by the judges to the lists while the trumpets sounded, he groaned out thus much to himself in the cursing of his fortune:

---

[225] The source text specifies that he is there to be knighted.
[226] *Espejo* reminds us that the sultan is upset because he fears for the great dangers the Gentleman of the Sun is about to face, which intensifies their relationship.
[227] The outcry of support for the sultan is unique to *Mirror*.
[228] In *Espejo*, the setting is the plaza in front of the palace, which reflects the architectural design of Spanish palaces.
[229] Tyler adds this sentence in order to explain the ladies' admiration for the enemy.
[230] A sentence further describing his behaviour is omitted.
[231] 'Chevaliero' signifies 'knight', from the Spanish 'caballero' and the French 'chevalier'.

'Oh, how doth Fortune envy my felicity in prolonging the time thus that I cannot, so soon as I would, dispatch this wretched knight!'[232]

Saying this and somewhat else the trumpets stayed.°[233] And with great rage, he ran towards the Knight of the Sun. But the knight, bearing his shield before him, with his spear in his hand, met Raiartes with all his force. With the violence of this course, the ground shook under their horses, and this first journey burst their great spears into small shivers.°[234] Raiartes, with the strong encountry° of the Knight of the Sun, doubled and fell over the arson° of the saddle, his horse carrying him out of the press to blush without company, for never in his lifetime had he received the like blow.[235] But when he recovered his seat and saw the Knight of the Sun not stirred in his saddle and now with his sword in his hand coming toward him, he drew out his sword, which was broad and heavy, in great choler to receive him, thinking for a surety with the edge of his sword to supply that which had failed in the point of his spear.

Both of them mad angry, Raiartes, to amend that which he had marred in breaking his spear, and the Knight of the Sun, to revenge the proud words which Raiartes had spoken, their first blows were such that their pavises° were hewn asunder and fell to the ground, the other part they after threw from them.[236] And gripping their swords in both their hands, they hit each other such blows upon the helmet that flakes° of fire issued after them. By this time, neither of these knights were well pleased with the other, and they let drive so each at other that in short space they made plain their singular manhoods. And they which saw it judged it to be the bravest battle which they had ever seen between two knights. The valiant knights, with malicious eyes sorrowing each at other's welfare because their armour was so good that no sword would enter, were much more wood,° laying about them without order and caring not where they hit, so they might see the blood spin as fast as the sparkles° increased.[237]

It was now half an hour since the battle began, and Raiartes, well feeling the courage of the Knight of the Sun in that he had gotten none advantage over him in all that time. Now with what courage fought he, think you, being beside himself for the desire of the lady? At that time, he doubted whether this were the Gentleman of the Sun, whom before he had continued, and, if it were not he, yet he marvelled in himself who this valiant knight might be.

In the meanwhile, the sultan and Florion, with all the beholders of the battle, were astonished at the great prowess and valour which the Knight of the Sun showed against Raiartes. They thought truly that he would prove the best knight of the world since in so tender years he was of great virtue. The Princess Radamira, which looked on this battle before half against her will for fear, now viewing how well her knight had behaved himself against her enemy, with greater joy and hope, she gazed on him and often prayed her gods to grant him the victory.[238]

But as I told you, Raiartes, seeing his adversary so valiantly bear himself against him and not being able to govern his ill will, he lifted himself up in his stirrups and lent the Knight of the Sun a blow with all his force, that although he could not cut his fine helmet, yet he made him bow his head to his horse neck, being blinded with the continual sparks of fire which came out of his headpiece. The worthy Knight of the Sun, coming again to himself and sitting surer in his

---

[232] The substitution of 'foam' for 'smoke' likens Raiartes to a rabid animal.
[233] Here, in the source, the trumpets begin to sound.
[234] The scene is much noisier in *Espejo*. In addition to the music of the trumpets, the knights charge like thunder and clash with violent noise.
[235] The phrase 'his horse . . . without company' corresponds to the Spanish assertion that he passed through, very frightened of the terrible encounter.
 'arson' (saddle-bow) is a false cognate of 'arcon', signifying 'chest'.
[236] The source text explains that they discarded their shields because they no longer provided them with any protection.
[237] 'The valiant knights . . . welfare because' is added to *Mirror*, while battle descriptions are omitted.
[238] The translation is confusing. The source recounts how Radamira had previously been wracked with extreme sadness and fear.

saddle, returned the like blow to Raiartes, so that Raiartes lost his memory and received another blow on his bulk against the saddle-bow, which made the blood gush out of his mouth and nostrils. And the Knight of the Sun followed him to have unhorsed him, but Raiartes recovered, and, ere° the Knight of the Sun could hit him, he gave him on the left shoulder a mighty blow, that with the weight thereof he had fallen to the ground but for the embracing of his horse neck. Again Donzel del Febo repaid him with a *plus ultra*, the surplusage° more than an ordinary interest.[239] And they wounded each other, mangling themselves pitifully. And the clashing of their armour was so great that it rang like bells in all the city.

This was the second hour of the fight and the match was equal, not being known who had the better hand. Raiartes not greatly pausing, but in his anger reviling his gods, said unto himself:

'Oh, immortal gods, how little is Raiartes beholding unto you if a man is able to resist his might? Why, if the report of my valiant deeds and noble prowess made known in the heavens causeth you to malign my state, come you down and fight with me, for I had rather be vanquished by your deities than to be yielded to man's strength? But what can I think? Either then that this knight is one of you, for the love of Radamira to take her right in hand, or at the least some fiend of hell in likeness of a knight minded to quell me. But seeing this is the issue that if I lose the day I must lose Radamira also, let him win her and wear her, for be he what he may be, he shall get no honour at my hands'.[240]

And so saying, he stroke his adversary so sore on the breast that he bruised his cuirass° and put him in great danger. Chevaliero del Febo, not a little abashed at the great force of Raiartes this being the first battle that ever he had fought, thought in himself that if all the knights in the world were like him he should get but small praise. And therefore, to embolden his courage, he rated° himself on this wise:°

'Am I he of whom the wise Lirgandeo hath foretold so much? Am I he without whom the Babylonians dare not set foot into Persia? Am I he for whom they have thus long time waited?[241] Certainly, if this be all which I shall be able to do, shall not all happen contrary to that which the wise man hath said? Shall not the Babylonians be mocked of their hope? Hath not one only knight much endamaged me? What shall the whole multitude of the Persians do, and the puissance of the giants which shall come to assist them? Had it not been better for my credit not to have been born with so great fame as the astrologers have foreshowed than in so short a time so much to be troubled? Oh, Sultan of Babylon and you others which are judges of the field, are you not ashamed of me that in my first battle and the first fruits of my knighthood I am at the point to become recreant? But recreant I will never be!'[242]

And so, as it were blowing the coals of his anger when he was on alight fire, he set Raiartes in such a heat with his thick and mighty strokes that the unlacing of his helm and unmailing° of his armour could scarce give him breath enough.[243] Raiartes then thought that his enemy's strength increased, yet not altogether foundered.° He answered him as well as he could, that the battle seemed to be more fierce at that time then at the beginning. The hour clock hath smitten thrice since they entered the lists, all much marvelling how they were able to endure so long.

The sultan said to Florion and to the wise man which sat by:

'Certainly, if I had not seen it with my eyes, I should hardly have believed that a knight of so young years as this Knight of the Sun is might have had the force so to endanger a worthy

---

[239] The Latin expression *plus ultra* (more beyond) coupled with the fiscal language imbues the sentence with the tone of a legal, official document.
   'plus ultra' was the motto of Emperor Charles V.
[240] Proverbial, Tilley W731.
[241] The addition of 'Am I he' extends the anaphora.
[242] The final exclamation, added by Tyler after the pysma (the series of rhetorical questions), is a forceful avowal of strength.
[243] The imagery of wind, heat, and fire is added.

knight. For you know how the hours are passed since they began the combat, and how yet he abideth many blows and still seems as fresh as he was when he first came forth'.²⁴⁴

The wise man answered:

'Yea, my lord. But if you knew with whom he doth fight, you might with more reason marvel at it, for Raiartes is one of the strongest and worthiest knights that is among the pagans. And his pride is so great that he alone would not refuse to join with a hundred knights, and would well think to have the mastery of them all before he would be taken'.

Thus, the bench was not idle.²⁴⁵ And the Princess Radamira very busily attended upon her knight, and watched every turn more than half joyfully, speaking thus unto the Princess Balisea standing by:

'I believe for a certainty, Princess Balisea, that our high gods, now at length cloyed° with my mishaps, have provided this knight for me; for in respect of his beauty and great bounty he seemeth rather heavenly than terrestrial'.

'Yea, so I think', then answered the Princess Balisea, 'and that not only for your succour, but to aid me and my cause, the gods have sent him hither, for by him I look to be Queen of Persia'.

'Do you so, madam?' said Radamira.²⁴⁶ 'Now I pray our gods that he will escape this battle to fulfil your heart's desire. And truly, if he become victor, not only I shall be avenged on him for my father's death, but I will make account that I am now risen from death to life, for sooner had I purposed to kill myself than to lie in Raiartes's arms'.²⁴⁷

But all this while, the good knights plyed° the combat, fighting courageously till they were fore-wearied,° everyone misconstruing the event. For Raiartes, seeing that the longer the battle lasted, the farther he was from the victory, with all the force he might, he stroke the Knight of the Sun such a blow on the helmet that his senses were bereft him. And had he not taken hold of the saddle-bow, he had kissed the ground.²⁴⁸ So the fray was renewed.²⁴⁹ But the Knight of the Sun gave Raiartes another blow as strong, which bewitched his understanding, for his horse carried him about the field, tossing him on the pommel° of his saddle as if he had been dead. The Knight of the Sun, thinking it no glory to smite a man half dead, pursued him not. But Raiartes, reviving his face all bloody, with both his hands hit the Knight of the Sun upon the headpiece that if the helm had not been the surer, it had riven° him to the belly.²⁵⁰ But the stroke amazed him and the gor[y] blood ran out of his mouth and nostrils. And his horse, feeling part of the great blow, carried his master from thence, the good knight lying upon the crupper of his horse in an ecstasy° as if he had been quite dead. Raiartes hasted° to have given him another blow. Those which saw it were very sad, but none were ever so woefully-begone° as was the Princess Radamira, who with great grief, turning herself from that sight and fell on weeping bitterly.²⁵¹ But Raiartes had not followed him four paces with his horse when the good knight started up, and feeling his face wet with blood, in great fury spurred his horse and met Raiartes with such a blow that the fine helmet could not deny him passage, but that he clove Raiartes's head in sunder.°²⁵²

Here, the shout of the people and the Princess Balisea's calling her awaked the Princess Radamira, as it had been out of a sound sleep and little looking for so good news. And the good knight, Raiartes being dead, put up his sword into the sheath and demanded of the judges if

---

²⁴⁴ The source text asserts that four hours have passed, which Tyler omits because the narrator has just explained that the battle has lasted for three hours.
²⁴⁵ 'Thus the bench was not idle' replaces Florion's reply.
²⁴⁶ Radamira does not pose a question in *Espejo*.
²⁴⁷ Tyler translates 'padres' (parents) as 'father's', as in Chapter 17.88.
²⁴⁸ The metaphor of kissing the ground replaces the prosaic 'derribato' ('been knocked down', I.174.26).
²⁴⁹ This sentence is added.
²⁵⁰ Tyler omits descriptions of the bloody and swollen condition of his face as well as the continuation of the battle.
²⁵¹ Her sadness and tears are augmented.
²⁵² Again, the thunderous quality of the charge is omitted, but the personification of the helmet is added.

there were ought else to do to make the princess free. The princess heard this gladly.²⁵³ And the judges answered him, 'no', for that sufficed which he had done. Then with the noise of instruments and much honour, the judges led the Knight of the Sun from that place to the palace, where with great joy and pleasure of the sultan and Florion, he was well received, they showing as much good will to him as if they had never enough in making of him. The gentlemen, Clavergudo and Brandizel, glad of their friend's conquest, helped to unarm him. Then, the Princess Balisea came. And the Princess Radamira, doing her duty to the Knight of the Sun, and as not able else to requite the courtesy he had shown her, she offered to him both her lands and her person, the better to serve him.

Thus, they took their rest many days, and the good knight was much honoured of them all. And there was a great feast made, and diverse jousts and tourneys there proclaimed for the dubbing of Clavergudo and other gentlemen knights. At this feast, the Prince Clavergudo behaved him best, so that all men judged him to be a valiant knight.²⁵⁴ And after this, the Princess Radamira, minding to return, desired a safe conduct of the sultan, who sent with her a hundred knights and other men of war which saw her safely landed in her country and in full possession of the crown. For after they knew that Raiartes was dead, willingly they gave her place, and the princess remained lady of it, although not very free of her thought from the Knight of the Sun, whom she loved so well that in long time she forgot him not. And it fell out so that in the end she pleasured° him, wherefore he gave unto her a mighty prince for husband, as shall be declared hereafter.²⁵⁵

CHAPTER 22

Africano, King of Media and Persia, inferred war° upon the Sultan of Babylon

The history hath told you before that the strong and mighty Africano, transporting° from Africa into Asia, by his force and valiance° made himself Lord and King of Media, and after entered into the Kingdom of Persia, conquered it, and overthrew Florion, coming to succour his own people. After which time the Prince Florion, recoiling back to Babylon, there remained very sorrowful and without hope to recover his kingdom.

Now the story returneth to the same Africano and sayeth that when he had appeased the people and brought these two kingdoms in quiet subjection — as this is an imbecility of man's nature, ever coveting to amplify and enlarge our possessions — so this stout° and proud pagan,° not content with that which he had already got by disorder and rapine,° he adventured yet farther to win Babylon with all the kingdoms of the Assyrians bordering in those parts, reckoning himself already in possession of them for the power of the sultan was insufficient to repulse his forces, hoping moreover to add to his dominions all those countries lying in the coast of the Middle Earth Sea.²⁵⁶ For this cause he assembled his power, as well Medians as other his subjects. Having this great army in a readiness, yet trusting more in his own person than in all his people, he took the way toward Babylon, minding not to stay° till he came near to Babylon.

This was some days after the combat which the knight had with Raiartes. And as it fell out, it was at the same time as the sultan and the Prince Florion were devising of the order which they should take for to recover the Kingdom of Persia that the news came how the puissant Africano was on his way with a huge army toward Babylon. For which cause they were cast

---

²⁵³ The mention of her happy reaction to the news is added.
²⁵⁴ In *Espejo*, he is deemed one of the best knights in the world.
²⁵⁵ 'pleasured him' translates 'did him service'.
²⁵⁶ The Middle Earth Sea: the Mediterranean

into double doubts, seeing that the enemy whom they purposed to find abroad came to seek them at their own doors. Well, with great care and diligence they began to prepare all things necessary for the welcoming of such a guest: by gathering his people out of all parts of the kingdom, raising the walls higher, and fortifying the towers once built by Semiramis, all which would little have helped the great Babylon against the power of Africano, if the puissant° arm of the young Greek had not defended it.[257]

But thus, the Assyrians were almost at their wits' end, not knowing how to repel him, for the bruit° of his fame was greatly noised.° The Sultan of Babylon, well-experimented in warfare, commanded all which could bear armour to come to Babylon, that his forces being united, he might be of greater power against his enemies. Africano stayed° not till he came to the very walls of Babylon, where he gladly beheld the city; because of the fame it had to be so great and so well-peopled, he highly commended of the sumptuous edifices and high walls enclosing it, which enflamed his desire to be lord of it.

Presently, he made to pitch his tents in a large field, environing the walls as far as he might, for it was impossible to compass them round about with two of Xerxes's armies.[258] He had in his camp 20,000 knights, and 30,000 horsemen, and two strong giants beside, the one of them called Herbion and the other Dardario, through whose force he thought to have overcome the Assyrians.[259] So soon as he had trenched round about his camp and provided for the safeguard of his army, before he would enterprise any farther, he sent a messenger with a letter to the sultan, containing this that followeth:[260]

'I, the great and mighty Africano, King of Media and Persia, send greeting unto thee, Sultan of Babylon, son of Orixerges.

Know that the report of thy city of Babylon hath procured me to cut° the seas and to arrive in this country, rather with desire to have it as mine° own than for any pleasure to offend thy person or molest thy people, for thy father and mine during their lives were great friends, which friendship I would willingly should endure between us if thou will as willingly satisfy my desire.[261] Albeit, I am content in recompense thereof to give thee the Kingdom of Persia or Media, chose thee whither.° Now thou know my whole meaning. Fail not to accomplish my desire, for unless I have it with thy good will I will force thee thereunto maugre° thy ill will.

Farewell'.

The messenger, coming to the gates of the city, was let in, and being brought into the palace, he delivered the letter to the sultan in the presence of Prince Florion and the other knights of the court. The letter was read, and they all said that in great pride the Pagan had so written. But because Prince Florion and the most part of those which were there knew the strength and power of Africano in the battles fore-passed,° they would not make answer nor speak a word until they had heard the sultan's mind. Being in this order all hushed, the Knight of the Sun rose up and demanded licence of the sultan to give answer to the messenger. The sultan granted it him. Then, the Knight of the Sun, advancing his voice that it might be heard spoke to the messenger thus:

'Return to thy lord, for it is now too late to answer his letters! But in the morning my lord shall call his counsel and shall send thy lord an answer by one of his knights, to whom he must give credit in this behalf'.

Thus the messenger dispatched from the sultan went to his lord, who little delighted in the foreslowing° of the sultan's answer, for he less weighed the sultan's power. Therefore, he

---

[257] Semiramis (fl. 9th century BCE): Assyrian queen and legendary heroine, who founded Babylon and conquered many territories in Asia
[258] Xerxes: Xerxes The Great, King of Persia 486–465 BCE
[259] The army in *Espejo* consists of 20,000 horsemen and 30,000 foot soldiers.
[260] Marginal note: 'Africano's letter'. The note is formatted like a chapter header in the 1599(?) edition: it is centred, preceded by a paraph mark, and set in Roman type.
[261] Tyler mistranslates 'traido' (brought) as 'cut', possibly as the result of confusion with 'trozo' (a piece).

determined in few days to destroy the great city, burning and wasting all. For all that, that he wished rather to have been owner of it by exchange or covenant than by raising and battering the walls which were so goodly.°

The messenger avoiding the palace, the Knight of the Sun directed his speech to the sultan in this wise:°

'Since your Excellency well understandeth the arrogancy° and high disdain of Africano and hath given me in commission to devise the answer, I humbly beseech your grace to be content therewith if tomorrow in the morning, I alone take upon me this message to satisfy him, as shall seem best unto me and according as his pride deserveth'.

When the knight had so said, the suit which he made grieved the sultan very much, although the great exploits which he had already done and which were divined to be done by him somewhat abated his grief.[262] Yet greatly preferring the valour of Africano above that which he had heard of all the princes pagan, for there might none be compared to him, he put off the Knight of the Sun for that time with this answer: that he would not have him to hazard himself in such danger until he had grown to more ripe years. But if the sultan was in any perplexity for love to the knight, much more was Prince Florion troubled, which had had experience of Africano's puissance and had seen Africano in his own person demean himself so lustily in the battle between them that he thought him to be unparagonized° for manhood. And therefore he was more than unwilling that the knight should alone deal in this matter, albeit he had well and worthily acquitted himself against Brandafileo and the strong Raiartes; for it was not a thing convenient in his judgement that he, being as yet of tender years, should prove his body upon Africano.[263]

But were it that the sultan and the Prince Florion were loath of this, as at the first it appeared, yet they thought it best to dissemble their conceits°, lest the knight should take displeasure at their little account of him. And therefore, in the end, after some consultation had with Lirgandeo, with a mild countenance, the sultan agreed to the knight's request, saying that he would put into his hands both his honour and the cause, to the end that he should answer Africano as best should like him.[264]

The Knight of the Sun would have kissed the sultan's hand, but the sultan embraced him.[265] And there, it was solemnly enacted that the next morrow,° the Knight of the Sun should be the only messenger. Clavergudo and the Prince Florion lay at him earnestly to bear them in his company, but he shifted them off with this: that it behoved him to be alone for the answer which he should give to Africano.

CHAPTER 23

The Knight of the Sun maketh answer to Africano as to his letter

At the day peep before the gray morning, the valiant and worthy Knight of the Sun got him up. In the meantime, while he ought to execute his charge, he armed himself with that armour which the wise Lirgandeo had bestowed on him and so stayed a great while until it was past broad day, every minute in this time seeming an hour, and every hour forty, for his magnanimous stomach always coveted to put himself in praise, where to exercise his valour.[266] And so, when it was now time, casting a fair horn about his neck tipped with gold, and having a horse under

---

[262] The sultan's paternal affection and fear for the Knight of the Sun are omitted.
[263] The other knights' fear is omitted by Tyler.
[264] The consultation with Lirgandeo is added.
[265] In *Espejo*, both the kiss and embrace occur with great love.
[266] Tyler adds the clause 'and every hour forty', thereby emphasizing his impatience.

him the best that the sultan had — as the night before he had taken his leave of the sultan and the other knights of the court — so he privily° put himself on his journey without being seen of any of the court.

And making those gates of the city to be opened which were shut to Africano's camp, he rode through. And by soft paces, coming within a bowshot° of Africano's own tent, he winded° his horn so loud that it was easily heard in both the enemy's camp and the city of Babylon. Immediately, the sultan, the Prince Florion, Clavergudo, and other knights cried 'Alarm!°' and issued forth of the gates in battle array to see what the good Knight of the Sun would do. And by and by the walls and high towers were full fraught with as well nobles as commonalty°.

The King Africano in his tent, busied about other matters, hearing the shrillness of the sound was somewhat disquiet[ed], not thinking any knight to have had the hardiness to summon him to the battle. And desirous to know who he was, he called before him one of the two giants which came with him named Herbion, a strong man and King of the Camarians, a little region adjoining to Media. To him he said:

'Take thy horse and armour and ride toward that knight which hath winded° his horn, and fail not for any entreaty to bring him before us, here in our presence, to declare his message'.

The giant, having his charge, delayed no time, but hastily arming himself with fine steel, he took a strong spear in his hand and rode toward the Knight of the Sun, who in the midst° way abode his coming, very glad when he saw so great a giant come against him as desirous to purchase honour upon his likeness. But the giant said unto him:

'What are thou, knight, so bold and venturous that has in such wise° disturbed our camp with the noise of thy horn?'

The Knight of the Sun replied:

'I am a knight of the sultan's, which come to the King Africano to make him answer to the letter by him sent unto the sultan. Now return you back and tell him I am here to do my message. And if he will hear it, bid him come armed and well horsed, for otherwise I will not make him answer'.

The giant, very scornfully took up a great laughter, and giving the knight a little souse° on the helmet with his gauntlet, he said unto him:

'Now, I tell thee that thou are the maddest knight in the world to challenge him to battle, at the only hearing of whose name the greatest part of all Asia doth tremble. And if thou were not a simple fool, thou would not in such sort discover thine° impotency. If thou have any message to the King Africano from the sultan, come with me and thou shall be brought to his presence, for he is not such a one as to come into the field against one sely° knight'.

'The King Africano himself must hear my message', said the Knight of the Sun. 'And he must hear it armed, for otherwise, I will not open it'.

The strong Herbion was angry at the knight's words, and thinking him to be but as other knights were or amongst the meanest,° he offered to have set the knight beside the saddle and so to have drawn him perforce to the king, showing herein no less pride and disdain than the greedy falcon doth in the pursuit of the simple pigeon, to carry it to the air among the young ones. But his lot was far otherwise, for the knight, perceiving his intent, turned the point of his spear and struck him so strongly on the chest that though his armour was good, it entered a little and left him windless for a time. Herbion thought himself now not well at ease. And therefore returning to himself, he never studied at the courtesy of the knight in sparing him in his trance, but taking one part of the field and broaching° his horse with the spurs, his spear being in the rest, with deadly rage he ran against the Knight of the Sun, who was nothing slow in the receipt. Their shocks were such in their meeting that the heavy spear of the strong Herbion brake into shivers° in the fine helmet of the Knight of the Sun, not diseasing° him. But the Knight of the Sun hit the giant with such dexterity that he overthrew him. And the great weight of his body made the giant wear his neck on the one side like a fiddler, which was no little pain unto

60 him. Yet he got upon his feet, rising with much ado.²⁶⁷ Then the Knight of the Sun, finding him uprisen, bade him defend himself. The giant answered that he could not:

'Therefore do with me what you will'.

The Knight of the Sun said:

'No, but return to the King Africano, thy lord, and tell him that a knight of the sultan's doth await him here to make answer unto his letter. And if so be he be minded to hear it, will him in his armour to come forth, for in no other order will I utter it'.

The giant answered he would do it. And not being able to sit on horseback, he was compelled to go on foot through the camp, driving in his thought the remembrance of the knight's prowess so that he was persuaded that not twenty knights Assyrians could have done him so much harm
70 as this one knight had done. The sultan, with the Princes Florion and Clavergudo, were no less amazed in their contemplation to behold the event of the first welcome, and they gave great thanks to their gods for sending them so good a knight.

Herbion came before the King Africano his lord and, without failing in any part, declared to him that which had chanced with the knight and the message which was sent by him, moreover telling the king that he thought that knight the strongest knight in the world, for that with these two blows which he had given him he had thrown him to the ground and might have killed him.²⁶⁸

The King Africano, not a little sorry to see the strong Herbion so ill entreated and abashed at the force of one only knight, would thereupon have put on his armour to have been avenged on the knight and to hear his message. But the other giant then in presence called Dardario, and
80 much about Herbion's pitch, being of no less value than the first, in his choler menacing the knight, swore a great oath that he would bring the knight bound hand and foot unto the king.²⁶⁹

Wherefore, taking a great horse, he passed through the camp. And approaching near the Knight of the Sun, he would not salute the knight, but, as his anger was thoroughly kindled, with a great spear as big almost as a pine tree, he prepared himself for the career.° And the worthy Greek, knowing the giant's errand, did the like. And spurring his horse, he came unto the close.° The great spear of the giant was thought to have pierced the harness of the knight, by reason of the few shivers° that it made; but it did not so.²⁷⁰ And contrariwise,° the knight's spear, couched with great dexterity, entered through the body of the great Dardario, a great part of the staff appearing at the shoulders. By this means, the monstrous giant fell dead from
90 his horse with such a groan as the tall cedars of Libanus make, being rent° up by the root.²⁷¹

The Babylonians rejoiced exceedingly at this, but Africano was all enflamed with choler to see his giant slain with one only blow. And knowing that to himself alone this base° was bid, in great rage rose from the seat where he sat without speaking a word, and entering into his tent armed himself with sure armour and chose him a very strong spear, not tarrying for squire or page to help him.²⁷² In this anger he was so terrible that none of his people durst° come near him. And so, with a most fierce and cruel countenance, he armed himself.

So soon as the pagan had buckled on his armour, immediately there was brought him a horse such a one as could have carried ten armed knights, as I think of the same breadth whereof the horse of Troy was.²⁷³ The trappings of the horse as well gold as the stirrups and all his armour

---

²⁶⁷ The evocative simile, comparing the giant to a fiddler, is added by Tyler.
²⁶⁸ Herbion's emotional reaction to the events is omitted.
²⁶⁹ The humoural language is added.
²⁷⁰ Tyler specifies 'but it did not so', clarifying her source.
²⁷¹ Libanus: Lebanon. The cedars of Lebanon are mentioned on numerous occasions in the Bible. This may be an allusion to Isaiah 2.13 where the trees are a metaphor for pride.
²⁷² In *Espejo* his anger is accentuated: fear and terror are invoked; he has a furious spirit; sparks seem to escape from his eyes; and the fierce battle is described in greater detail.
²⁷³ Horse of Troy: at the end of the Trojan War the Greeks built a huge wooden horse capable of containing many armed men. They presented it as a gift to the Trojans, who naively accepted it. At night, the armed men exited the horse and opened the city gates, enabling the Greek army to enter Troy, destroy the city, and win the war.

100 set with precious stones, that he might well seem a great lord, which was master of such armoury. But this was the strangest sight: that Africano set upon so mighty a horse made him notwithstanding to bow and double under him. But to go forward, Africano, taking the greatest spear which might be had, rode with a soft pace towards the Knight of the Sun.

The Knight of the Sun saw him come from amongst his people and thought presently that he was the King Africano, as well for his rich armour and his horse so curiously barbed° as the tallness of his personage which he very well noted to be not far dissonant from the common report. So he beseeched his gods from his heart to be favourable unto him against so strong a giant.

Africano well viewed the Knight of the Sun, his stature and making, and upon these premises
110 inferred thus much: that well might he be a man of much force, which so well showed it in his exterior countenance, and much more in his deeds and valour. But coming nearer unto the knight, as his custom was little to regard the whole world, so with a proud and disdainful voice, he spoke unto the knight:

'Thou miserable and wretched knight, thou say thou are a messenger and bring a message unto me; thou have slain the giant Dardario and almost the strong Herbion, which two had been sufficient to have beat down the walls of Babylon. I swear unto thee by my gods that if all the world were given me for thy ransom, thou should not escape the death!'

The Knight of the Sun, embasing° his voice, mildly answered:

'If I have had to-do with thy giants, Africano, they were occasioners° of it themselves, for I
120 came not hither to other purpose but to make thee answer in the behalf of the sultan. And if I came only to seek thee, thou ought to have been first which should have presented himself to me and to have heard what I would have said, and to have heard me as a messenger, and not to attempt my death as a known enemy. Now that thou are come, Africano, I tell thee why I am come. Hear it if thou will! The gods, which have preserved me from thy giants have reserved me to fight with thee. But listen on, *et cetera* . . .'

Here the rage of the pagan stopped the course of his talk. And the mighty Africano, smiting his hand on his thigh for anger, lifted up his other hand also to have buffeted the knight. But a better mind overtook him, that he thought it reason to hear the sultan's answer before he should condemn the messenger. And so staying,° he had him tell on quickly:
130 'For I will well punish thy offence, whatsoever answer the sultan sendeth me'.

The Knight of the Sun, wishing the battle with all his heart, said:

'Then know thou, Africano, that thy letter being received and read in the presence of my lord, the sultan, after consultation had, my lord sendeth thee this answer by me.[274] Albeit before this time thou are notoriously defamed for a tyrant in that thou has falsely and fraudulently encroached up many kingdoms, yet he never thought thou would have enterprised the usurpation of the most sacred Assyrian Empire, an empire consecrated to the gods and claimed by them as their right, and in their right governed by my lord's ancestors as lieutenants to the gods and their fee-farmers.°[275] And therefore, though peradventure° the open wrongs done unto men the gods do often pardon and wink at, yet seldom leave they unrevenged the injuries offered
140 to themselves. And as it is to be thought, so manifest a contempt of their divine power shall not escape them. Besides for the city of Babylon, he letteth thee to understand that thyself are not ignorant that it is his and that he hath right to it as heir to the King Orixerges his father on that part of his livelihood, and that thou had no title nor colourable° show to demand it. Wherefore, if it be so that thou will take it against all reason from him, he telleth thee that he can no less do than defend it from thee and the whole world. For having right and justice on his side, he little feareth the invasion of man'.

---

[274] The consultation and his role as messenger are not mentioned in the source.
[275] 'and claimed . . . fee-farmers' is added.

Delivering his message in this form of words, the Knight of the Sun said:

'This is the sultan's answer'.

And pausing a while, he began again thus:

150 'And I, Africano, craved of my lord to be the messenger, for I would thou should know how dangerously thou offend the divine gods in entering upon the Kingdom of Persia, and disinheriting the Prince Florion, the legitimate and only lord of that kingdom. Now therefore, thou should well do to surrender thy claim into his hands and content thee with the revenues already received and the unjust detaining of his right so long time. If thou will do this not for my sake, but for the high gods against whom thou have heinously trespassed, thereby thou shall pacify the gods and lose the name of a tyrant, so odious and so detested amongst men. If thou will still persevere in this, thy tyrannical obstinacy, I utterly defy thee to the death and certify thee that either I will slay a tyrant, or upon a tyrant I will be slain'.

Whilst the Knight of the Sun amplified at large upon this point, Africano, albeit very angry,
160 yet marked him from top to toe, weighing with what confidence he had discharged his charge, sometimes quietly admonishing to amend and otherwise threatening and defying with a fierce semblance. But as he cared neither for God nor man, so he swallowed up the knight's words, reputing the knight for a fool, for he thought his name only to able to affray° any knight, thus he replied:

'Were thy hands, foolish knight, as good to fight as thy tongue is fine in preaching, I would not marvel though thou had the hardiness to defame Africano. But I will curtail thy copy° with this currish answer.[276] Prepare thee to the battle and take this promise at my hand: that if I be overcome, I will leave to Florion not only the kingdom of Persia, but also all that which I myself have of possessions in Asia'.

170 And so saying, Africano made against the knight. But the Knight of the Sun, wisely to order his affairs, answered him saying:

'Stay a little, Africano, and hear that which I say. Thou know that already this day I have twice fought with two of thy giants and am fore-wearied.° If now I fight with thee and thou subdue me, what honour shall thou get thereby? Will not men say that thou took me at the advantage, when I was hurt before or wearied as I am? Appoint that our combat be tomorrow and that assurance be had of this condition on either parts, and say thou the same before the principal of thy army: that if perhaps I should slay thee in this battle, the sultan should not need to have a new skirmish with thy people'.

This devise of the knight was sore against Africano's mind, for he would willingly have purged
180 some part of the choler which he brought with him boiling in his stomach.[277] But seeing this avoidance could not be at this time made with the warranty of his honour, he granted to the conditions and thus answered him:

'Let it be so as thou say, foolish knight. I will do thee a pleasure in delaying the time of revenge of my knights and thy foolish words. But since I may not refrain my anger, having thee before me, return hastily to the city and I will to my tent'.

And with this, he turned the reins of his horse and came to his pavilion, where he fed upon melancholy all the day, not speaking to anyone. The Knight of the Sun deferred the battle till the next day, not for that he was weary, but to advertise° the sultan of that which was agreed upon.

190 Now the rather to assure himself, [he] returned to the city, where he was received with great joy and pleasure of all his friends. And being within the palace, he told the sultan to what issue he had brought the matter. He was very joyful by reason of the wise Lirgandeo's prophecies,

---

[276] His disregard for divine opinion is an addition; in the source, his prideful condition makes him care little for the whole world.

[277] The choler that creates heat boiling in his stomach and his subsequent melancholy, both of which medicalize his anger, are added by Tyler.

which he hoped then to be accomplished. And partly doubtful of the success, because Prince Florion knew Africano's strength was such as few were able to resist it, he would have had him not to deal in this adventure alone and requested him to join unto him some other companions, namely Prince Florion and Clavergudo, which themselves laboured greatly. But he gave them thanks and excused himself, with this that it was so decreed. But sayeth he:

'There may be a time wherein you may employ your forces'.

For he knew the people of Africano to be so hardy that if perchance their lord should be slain or be in danger, they would either succour their lord or work his revenge upon the conqueror. Therefore, he willed them to be in a readiness. So these two knights gladly accepted that charge, and all that day chose out of the people those which should the next day keep the field with them to be at hand for succours to the knight if any treason should be compassed against him. The Knight of the Sun took his rest merrily till the day wherein he prospered, as you shall now hear.

CHAPTER 24

A cruel battle between the Knight of the Sun and Africano, with the discomfiture of Africano's host

So soon as the day appeared, the noble Greek arose from his bed. And he being now ready to arm himself, the sultan, the Prince Clavergudo, Florion, and other knights his friends came into his chamber, which all helped to arm him. When he was all armed, the wise Lirgandeo came in also with a helmet in his hands, the richest and most precious that ever was seen, and the strongest also and the best wrought that ever came on knight's head; for that the wise man had made it by observation of signs and planets in such aspects that no sword how good so ever might enter into it. And he had been more than twenty years in making it, to have the true conjunction of the celestial bodies which were apt for the operation of it. Besides all which, he had fetched from far countries the stuff whereof it was made, for it was no common metal. This helmet was for workmanship so exceeding, as for it only Lirgandeo won his spurs and was commended above all the learnedest° and wisest magicians, for none other having not attained to the like perfection in astronomy or [the] art [of] magic could have ever made it.

Now, as I said, coming into the chamber where the Knight of the Sun, the sultan, and the rest were, and showing his helmet, he drove them all into a wonder at the beauty and richesse° of the helmet, for although they knew not the hidden virtue of it, yet for the bravery° of the stones they judged it valuable to a king's delight.[278] He bore in it a field azure of the likeness of the element in most quiet and peaceable manner, not troubled with wind or clouds.[279] In the chief, there was a sun gilded, spreading his beams all over the helmet, as it were the mantling,° somewhat besides good armoury, I think, but well fitting for so gorgeous a piece of armour.[280] The sun shined so bright that it almost dazzled the eyes of the beholders. This helmet christening him now by the name of the Knight of the Sun, as the sun in his left side named him the Gentleman of the Sun when he was first found in the sea by Florion.[281]

The wise man came unto the knight and took from him the helmet which he had already laced on and put this other, saying:

---

[278] The sense of the original is that it would be desired by any king or emperor.
[279] The 'element' refers to the air, here symbolized by the sky. The 'field' of the shield is the background. The 'chief' is the horizontal band that extends across the top edge of the shield. This chief is wide since it is 'charged' (decorated) with the image of the sun.
[280] 'as it were . . . armour' is added.
[281] Tyler adds the reminder of his birthmark and his naming.

'My lord, you go to fight with one so strong and valiant a knight that neither may I report it for the strangeness, neither can you give credit unless you have trial. Now though the helmet you have is very good, yet being hacked and bruised with the terrible blows of the strong Raiartes, it is not such a one as may resist the weighty strokes of Africano. But this which now I give you, make much of it, for I knowing that this battle ought to be fought by you in the right of my nephew the Prince Florion, have this twenty years and more busied myself about it and fully finished it not past a year since'.

The Knight of the Sun triumphed now to be made the master of so rare a helmet and in so needful a time, saying to Lirgandeo in thankful wise° that he accepted better of that helmet than of the whole world if it were given him.

'You do not amiss in so doing', answered the wise man, 'for I tell you, the time will come when you shall make exchange of it unto a knight stranger, far born out of these countries. And I do not marvel, though you shall then make merchandise of the headpiece which now you so highly regard, for at that time you shall sell the most precious thing that ever you had for a worse thing, which shall bring you to the jeopardy of death a thousand times, and neither shall wit nor might, cunning nor courage, help you to avoid this chance'.

The Knight of the Sun stood looking upon the wise man as not witting° to what end those words tended. And studying a long time, he thus gainsaid° it:[282]

'Of things to come, I have naught to say, but to refer such things to the providence of our gods. But of things which are already come, thus much I say: that I know nothing in the world for which I would lose this helmet given me in so good opportunity'.[283]

But the morning being far spent, they left off for that time and departed all from the palace towards the sultan's army. And setting their people in order, they passed out of the gates with all things prepared for to keep the field.[284] The Knight of the Sun — accompanied with the sultan and the other two princes, Florion and Clavergudo, Armineo, and the wise Lirgandeo —rode to the place appointed for the execution of the conditions concluded upon.

The great Africano was in place before, expecting his adversary, whom, when the knight espied, he rode against with only two knights of the most principal in the sultan's host. The Knight of the Sun saluted Africano courteously, but Africano being of a stubborn and discourteous nature, gave him the resalutation° in this manner:

'Thou ought to have come earlier into the field, to the end our battle might have been sooner dispatched. But tell me now quickly the articles of the agreement to be made. And spend no more time, lest we take another day of respite'.[285]

'Nay, there is no more to do', answered the Knight of the Sun, 'but that of thy part two of thy knights be judges, and for my part these two knights, Clavergudo Prince of France and his uncle, here present shall sit with them. Before them, take an oath for the performance of that whereof thou made me promise being alone with thee'.

'I am well contented with this', said Africano, 'and now I swear the same: that if I be either slain or yielded, the Kingdom of Persia shall be redelivered to Florion, and this I command my knights to see avouched°'.

So soon as he had said this, he gave back and the Knight of the Sun did the like, the judges assigning a place for the combat. Now are the two couragiousest° knights of the world left the one against the other, with so fierce and manly countenances that it might have dismayed the spectators.[286] When the sound of the trumpet had summoned them to the battle, the two strong knights, girding their horses with their spurs, rode the one against the other with such violence

---

[282] In the source, rather than oppose Lirgandeo, the Knight of the Sun is confused by the wise man's speech.
[283] In *Espejo*, he possesses knowledge only of the present moment and not of the past.
[284] Specifics of the preparations are omitted.
[285] Africano's pride rather than his stubbornness is highlighted in the Spanish text.
[286] Tyler renders 'aspero' (surly) as 'manly'.

as if the clouds had rent° asunder by the outbursting of the thunderbolt.²⁸⁷ Their great spears, broken upon their armour, flew in small shivers,° and they rode one by the other as quietly as if no shock had been made. Africano the pagan, not acquainted with such encounters° and always wont to unhorse all knights whom he met, seeing the knight prepared for the second journey, marvelled much who this strong warrior might be, whom before this time he had not proved nor yet ever heard of.

But lightly casting these things in his mind, as at a sudden he drew out his sword and turned towards his enemy which was then ready for him. They struck each other such heavy blows, that warding them on their shields, although they were of pure steel, yet they cleaved them in the middest° and their swords lighted on their helmets, driving out great sparkles° of fire before them. The great Africano gave the Knight of the Sun upon his helmet such buffets, and with such force, that every man would have judged it had riven° the headpiece. There the cunning of the wise Lirgandeo well appeared, for it was not possible for iron, steel, or adamant stone but to have yielded to that stroke.

But what think you that the Knight of the Sun did when he thought that he had clean lost his hearing by it, and said to himself that not without good cause Africano was greatly feared among the pagans? Nay, to the no less marvel of both hosts, the Knight of the Sun let drive at Africano with such force as it was to the no small admiration of all men that he hewed him not in pieces. But you must learn that when Africano passed by sea from Africa into Asia, it was his chance to sail by Lemnos, where Vulcan's forge was.²⁸⁸ There he heard of Vulcan's cave where his storehouse was, and entering into it, he achieved strange things not here to be recounted, and gained Vulcan's armour wrought with his own hands, the best in all the land. This when Africano tried often times to be very good, whereof he was well pleased: from that time forth he never fought with other but with that. Now, albeit this headpiece was well framed from being cut, yet the Knight of the Sun's blows were so heavy that oftentimes Africano wist° not where he was, and recovering, would say unto himself:

'What is this? I believe the strength of the whole world conspireth with this knight against me. And if it be not so that he is of the offsprings of our gods, yet am I sure that he is no man'.

But among all the great blows, which the Knight of the Sun lent to Africano, there was one at the fore-end° of the battle upon the top of Africano's helmet, the sword not entering but sliding down upon his shoulders with such force that it made him lean all his body upon the horse neck, whereof if he had not taken hold he had fallen to the ground.²⁸⁹ Then the pagan, sure enough yet in his saddle and his force redoubling as his anger increased, smote at the enchanted helmet that he made the knight confess in his thought that his helmet was his good borrow.°²⁹⁰ The blow sounded throughout all the field as if it had been a bell. And the Knight of the Sun, with the weight of the blow, neither bolt upright nor full declining but staying upon the arson,° drooped as half dead. But the blood gushing out of his nose fetched him again quickly, ere° that Africano could come within him.

Now, seeing it time to defend himself from his adversary, he stood upright in his stirrups and with both his hands struck at Africano so that if the workman had not been more to blame, the blow had made peace between them; but for all the workman's craft, the weight of the blow bruised the helmet, which was the cause of Africano's speedier death.

Africano, benumbed of his senses, the blood straining through the joints of the helmet and he sitting in his saddle as half dead. The horse, sore daunted with the blow, stood still

---

²⁸⁷ The image of the thunderbolt, added to this sentence by Tyler, stands in for a series of clauses describing the thunder and sparks of the battle omitted from the subsequent sentence.
²⁸⁸ Vulcan's forge: after his expulsion from Olympus, Vulcan set up a forge on (or near) the Island of Lemnos. He was renowned for the quality of his workmanship.
²⁸⁹ *Espejo* speaks of a blow with two hands, and not the 'fore end of the battle'.
²⁹⁰ A lengthy discussion of the helmet's virtues is excised.

till Africano revived. And in the gathering of his strength, outbrayed° thus much in his thought:

'O, infernal furies, are you not all hired against me? Or is it credible that either Jupiter, or Saturn, or Mars, or all the gods may have the like force as this young man's?'

But Africano's heart failed him not, albeit his words outraged, for he followed the Knight of the Sun, who attended him speedily.

Then the Prince Florion said to the sultan his uncle:

'We make great account of the travails° of the ancient Assyrians our forefathers and of the Grecians,° with whom our countrymen joined at the expedition of Troy, but I cannot think that ever two so strong warriors have been as Africano and Raiartes'.

'You may boldly justify that', answered Lirgandeo, 'for there was never until this day a battle between two knights so valiant and sharp as this is, nor yet ever two so hardy drew swords against each other; although things before done carry a greater burden of authority than that which we ourselves can testify'.[291]

But the jealousy which Clavergudo had over the Knight of the Sun was not a little to be judge of so valiant behaviour, not that he had an ill eye towards his friend's good fortune, but either wishing to himself the like trial or desiring to adventure with his friend; although not many days ended ere° he had his fill to his contentment.

Africano's people looked ever for the victory, greatly forethinking° them that any one knight should make resistance to their lord, as having experience in themselves, which all shook for fear to see him angered.[292] Now it was more than two hours since the battle began, and then Fortune, always fickle and unstable, which had of a long time one even with Africano, now played her part in her kind and, as already weary of his company, turned her tale and struck in another way, desirous to show the great swiftness of her ever-turning wheel and minding the sudden overthrow of those which too much trust in her.[293] For Africano, desperately determining to break up the fight one way or the other, once again hit the Knight of the Sun upon his magical helmet that he took quite his memory from the knight, the sword and the reins falling from him, yet the sword hanging by a long string at the pommel° was not out of his reach. But the horse, having the liberty of the reins and feeling his part of the blow, flung up and down the field with his master, the strong pagan following to have unhorsed him. But how dear was this blow to Africano, for it cost him no less than his life! For the valiant Knight of the Sun, never stained° in fight, became wood° mad for his hurt, and in great rage took his sword in both his hands and repaid the borrowed blow so surely upon Africano's head that not Vulcan's well-tempered steel could forbid the passage, but that it quartered the helmet and made the brains sprinkle on the ground. Now sound ye° trumpets, for in this wise° is the great Africano brought to ground, ending his life in such sort as is fatal to tyrants, whose death commonly is cruel and bloody![294]

This the sultan and those of his part seeing, made such joy as cannot be told; but on the contrary side, Africano's people made great lamentation.[295] And reckoning little upon that which their lord in his lifetime had commanded, because they were greater in number than their adversaries, they joined together on heaps *sine*° discretion, and without a guide made an assault upon the knight and his adherents. But they, not taken at unawares, received them accordingly. These were the sultan, the Prince Florion, the Prince Clavergudo, and Armineo, with the Knight

---

[291] Lirgandeo's comment offers a powerful counterpoint to the widely-accepted belief in the authority of history.

[292] The source text specifies that they think the defeat of Africano to be impossible.

[293] 'turned her tale' is proverbial, Tilley T16.

[294] The addition of 'Now sound ye trumpets', places the victory within a religious context. In the Bible, the sound of trumpets punctuates moments of war and liberation and it is also linked to the Resurrection (see Psalms 81.3–5; Joshua 6.4–20; Zechariah 9.14–16; 1 Corinthians 15.52; Revelation 8.2–11:15).

[295] The image of the decapitated Africano on the ground is omitted by Tyler.

160 of the Sun, in whose company they were the bolder. And coming to the forward in the foremost rank, they find of the stoutest° and principallest° knights that Africano had. These four encountered them and unhorsed as many as they came against and, breaking through to the thickest throng, they wrought wonders. Especially the Prince of France, desirous to get honour in the first head of his knighthood, shoved into the middest,° beheading some and maiming° other some, making as it were a lane before him to pass through, so that the wise Lirgandeo said openly that now his outward sight did well witness the self same thing which his art had showed him in casting the constellation of this knight: for he was a valiant knight, and the slaughter he made was nigh hand° comparable with that of the Knight of the Sun.[296]

Upon the left wing, Prince Florion tried his manhood, having near unto him the sultan, where
170 be it that otherwise to a strong giant as Africano was he was inferior, yet among the other people he was as proud as a ravenous wolf among a flock of sheep.[297] The sultan and the good knight Armineo did their part, but what would all this avail unless the Knight of the Sun had beaten the way before them with his sharp sword, slaying so many as it was easy for the followers to keep the trodden path?[298]

And now at this time, the sultan's army, appointed for the guard of the Knight of the Sun, came to the battle, and finding Fortune so courteous at their coming, they refused not her gentleness, but following her command, made it a bloody conflict for the adversary. But, yet a man may rightly say that the Knight of the Sun delivered that day the Babylonians from death or bondage, for if he had not overcome Africano, not the high walls of the Queen Semiramis
180 could have kept Africano out from enjoying the city.[299] But their lord being slain, and they left without a head, their courage was so quailed° that ere° two hours passed the greater part of them was slain likewise. And of those which remained alive, the most part fled by one and one, the Assyrians pursuing them till the sultan commanded the retreat to be blown, fearing to be overtaken by the night. By this means some escaped to their country, most of them being inhabitants of Media, where also was the abode of Africano's son called Brandimardo, not being able for years to be made knight, and therefore going not out with his father to the war.[300] These, so soon as they came home, crowned Brandimardo and incensed him to the revenge of his father's death. For although he was of years young and tender, yet was he very strong and of a lusty° body, being like unto his father as well in stature as in qualities. And indeed, being
190 continually laid at by his father's subjects, passing into Greece, he behaved himself manfully as shall be showed you.

Well, the sultan and those which were with him, as you have heard, returned in joy and pleasure, and highly magnifying the noble Knight of the Sun.[301] So, as this discourse as an argument of great good will canvassed between these knights and princes brought them, ere° they were well aware, before the palace gate, where the Princess Balisea welcomed them with torch light. The first whom she embraced was the Knight of the Sun, to whom she said on this wise:°

'Sir knight, we have great cause to give thanks to our gods for your hither arrival. First you delivered my lord, the sultan, and me from death, and now you have set all us free from
200 sorrowful captivity'.

'But madam', answered the Knight of the Sun, 'to my lord the Prince Florion and to these other knights you ought to attribute this, for they are those which have destroyed Africano's host'.

---

[296] The 'maiming' in *Espejo* is explicitly rendered as cutting off arms and slicing others through the middle.
[297] The wolf's pride and the danger he poses to sheep are proverbial. Cf. Tilley S300, W602.
[298] References to Clavergudo and the Knight of the Sun as the greatest knights in the world are omitted.
[299] Tyler omits the mention of his salvation of the Assyrians.
[300] *Espejo* indicates that those who remained after the battle were able to return to their lands.
[301] The reunion is more elaborately narrated in *Espejo*.

Then the princess turned to Clavergudo and thanked him likewise for his pains in the defence of her father's city, and so to the rest in that order which best liked her. After this they supped in the great hall, continuing there their sports till bedtime, as likewise the citizens well showed their good liking of the victory by bonfires and other revelling sport.[302] The next day, they ordained that which followeth.

CHAPTER 25

The Knight of the Sun [and] the two princes, Florion and Clavergudo, with a great host enter into Persia and there put Florion in possession of the crown

The next day after dinner, the sultan himself entered into the counsel chamber, and other affairs being laid apart, the wise Lirgandeo made this oration:

'It is apparently known unto us all how bountifully our high gods have dealt with us, as well touching my lord the sultan as the Prince Florion and the whole nation of the Assyrians, in bringing to this court the Knight of the Sun and the Prince Clavergudo, who by their notable virtues not only have kept this city from sacking, but also, as we make account, have left the realm of Persia naked for resistance, not one spear remaining to be tossed against us. For the attaining of either of these things we are not ignorant how weak and unable we were, that were it not for these two young gentlemen, not only our home-bred power, but also thrice as many of foreign succours could not have hindered Africano from his purpose.[303] Wherefore I think it convenient that since the gods have granted us this victory and that we have the wind at our backs, that we follow our good Fortune while we have her, lest by overslipping° the opportunity we too late repent our too much daintiness. My meaning is that with such speed as may be, the Prince Florion and these lords depart the realm into Persia, there to make claim of his right by arms whilst every man is occupied in complaining of his own harms.[304] For, although as yet there dare no man stand against us, yet for a certainty there is a King of Media, Africano's son, which ere° it be long will be our heavy neighbour. He is not yet made knight, but his destiny fore-showeth us that if he once come to board in Persia, we shall be no less disquieted with his company than we were with Africano his father'.

The wise Lirgandeo made an end of his oration, knitting up his matter with this clause: that it were not out of the way to advise themselves, notwithstanding for good reasons this was his judgement.[305]

They, which would never contrary him in any point, took no further respite, but consenting to the effect of Lirgandeo's oration concerning the conquest of Persia, took this order: that Prince Florion, the Knight of the Sun, Clavergudo, and Armineo, his uncle, with 15,000 knights and 50,000 footmen, within ten days should prepare themselves for this adventure, the Princess Balisea abiding with the sultan, her father, till the kingdom were well settled from tumult and the prince in peaceable fruition of the crown.[306]

This they dealt in effectually, for within the compass of the days limited, they left Babylon, the sultan and the princess only comforted with the hope which Lirgandeo made promise of. The 15,000 knights with the footmen by long journeys entering into Persia and coming near unto one of the chiefest° cities of the kingdom, there in the plain, unloaded their carriage to erect their tents there. But the citizens — having understanding of Africano's death by the

---

[302] The celebrations are condensed in *Mirror*.
[303] His fearful memories of Africano are omitted.
[304] The specific necessity of going to claim their rights at this moment is added.
[305] The final clause of his oration is added.
[306] The army is smaller in the source: *Espejo* lists the participation of 10,000 knights and 5,000 footmen.

fugitives in the last discomfiture of Africano's host and thinking it not safety for themselves to rebel against their liege and natural lord Florion, especially he having the aid of the whole flower of Babylon — set their gates wide open for his army and sent of their worthiest knights to Florion's tent to invite him to his own city and to crave pardon for their former revolting in that time when they were left destitute of man's succour, not being able of themselves to withstand the force of Africano, and also excusing themselves that they had never a guide to conduct them into the field against so strong an enemy, having in his power the greatest part of all Asia.[307]

The prince, lightly excusing their fault, easily condescended unto their requests and, being glad of so good entertainment at the first, the next day rode into the city with the joyful acclamations of the whole multitude. There he resumed the crown and sceptre, and being in quiet seizure, the subjects of the realm, by the fame of his thither° arrival, came form all parts to do him homage, so that in half a year's space all the principal cities of the kingdom submitted themselves, and there was left no more memory of the usurper's name.[308] The King Florion, seized of his land in such a friendly manner, now took counsel how to have the queen, his wife, conveyed thither.° And for that it was requisite that the king himself should tarry behind; for the appeasing of all tumults if any should arise in so raw a possession, he gave the charge of fetching the queen with all reasonable pomp unto the Knight of the Sun and the Prince Clavergudo, they to take with them 200 knights for their safety. They took it gladly and freighted their ships with necessary provision and other furniture° for war, determining to travel by sea the sooner to come unto their journey's end.

When everything was in a readiness, the knights took their leave of King Florion and the wise Lirgandeo. But the wise man, not refraining from tears and lovingly embracing the Knight of the Sun, burst out into these speeches in such sort as the sibyls in ancient time were wont to read men's destinies:[309]

'Noble and worthy knight, you are determined to see Babylon, but you are uncertain whether ever to see it or to return to Persia. And as little know I what shall befall, for truth it is that all the heavenly spheres warrant more unto you than to any knight.[310] What that is, it is kept from me. I cannot find the entry thereunto, wherefore I am in doubt of your hither return. But if the fates or otherwise the course of the stars, which impose a necessity to man, carry you beyond the compass of your will into a far country where there shall be greater need of your presence, grudge not at it, but give thanks to our gods, for all shall redound° to your honour and the magnifying of your lineage. This I tell for a surety: that you shall never do the thing in your life whereof you shall take like pleasure as in your two first adventures undertaken for two knights strangers, whom notwithstanding you shall not know till time and place discloseth them unto you. Of your lineage, I will report nothing, for it is ordained by the gods that by the mouth of one of these two knights of whom I have spoken, your whole parentage should be laid open, before which time you shall be at mortal defiance. For the shutting up of this speech, the remainder only is that I make offer of my service unto you, whereof I hope it shall be needless to make a profession in words, seeing I am thereunto bound by your manifold friendships towards my kindred. In a word, Lirgandeo shall never fail you in the thing wherein either his wealth or wisdom may stand you instead. And the day shall come wherein you, being in the country where you were born and amongst your own parents, shall account them all for enemies, and yet no man shall take your part but only Lirgandeo, which for that time shall save your life. And I hope that this service shall not be the last in account or the least in value which I will do unto you'.

---

[307] In *Espejo*, they immediately acknowledge Florion as their king and they kiss his hands in greeting.
[308] The disappearance of his memory is added by Tyler.
[309] Sibyls: prophetesses in classical legend and literature, who uttered predictions in ecstatic frenzy
[310] Five lines of text are omitted, in which Lirgandeo outlines the machinations of fate.

The wise man ended, and they all which were present wondered to hear him so divine of things to come. But the Knight of the Sun, not understanding the tenor of this prophecy, wisely referred all things to God's providence, thanking the wise man for his great care over him. Now, when on all parts all courtesies were performed and that the King Florion had commended them to his gods, they embarked themselves, and spreading their sails, followed the way towards Babylon, as the chapter following shall declare.

CHAPTER 26

The Knight of the Sun and the Prince Clavergudo, being in their way towards Babylon, were divided by a sudden adventure

As already the noble and knightly deeds of the Knight of the Sun did bud out and were likely to flourish more hereafter, so now not only the celestial influences, but the confluences of the tempestuous winds also and the sea itself became so careful for his advancement that there failed nothing of that which might work his preferment. For so it is that when anything is forced by the stars as to succeed prosperously unto a man, albeit mountains of adversity impugn and assail him, yet can they never expunge his good fortune, but in the end he recovereth his quiet rest maugre° the malice of misadventure.

And so the issue declared in the Knight of the Sun, for the ninth day after that the Knight of the Sun, Clavergudo, and those which were with them had sailed in the Persic Sea, that night attached° them overcast with dark clouds without any stars appearing.[311] Whereby the mariners construed the roughness of the weather on the morrow,° and therefore guided towards land to cast anchor in some good harbour till the storms ceased. Ere° the dawning of the day, they discovered a dock not far from the continent, in their seeming very commodious, but indeed very dangerous, as it proved. Entering the dock, they scarce had leisure to throw out their anchors, but two other ships joined with them to seek some safe road out of the tempest. These, which last got to the port, were very desirous to know what the other might be, and therefore, an armed knight so huge and great as if he had been a giant, mounting on the shipboard,° called aloud unto them to answer him. Some of the other ship, hearing him in this wise° crying, leapt upon the hatches saying:

'What is it, Sir Knight, that you would have?'

'Marry,° I would know', answered the knight, 'what you are and whither° you will'.

One of the company, being stout° and of ill behaviour, and supposing this knight to be some giant of that country minding to set upon them, made him answer thus:

'Return to thy dwelling, and be not careful to know them which know not thee! Otherwise, assure thyself, here are knights which will chase thee hence in such sort as it shall well grieve thee'.

The strange knight, stomaching this rudeness, said again:

'Assuredly, knight, thou are some villain born or of base birth, since in such order thou reward me, demanding only upon courtesy. But seeing I cannot learn it of thee with thy good will, I will compel thee thereunto with thine ill will'.

And saying no more, he drove at the knight so strongly that he clave both shield, helmet, and head unto the eyes.[312] Oh, what a mischief doth ill speech breed unto man! And how inexcusable was it in this knight when he redeemed this frank speech with his own life and sold to make payment the life of many others? Another knight, seeing his fellow slain, stepped into his room

---

[311] Persic Sea: Persian Sea
[312] Details of their armour and the fight, here and in the descriptions below, are excised from the original.

and smote at the stranger, where by the clattering of their harness, the din was so great that it raised the people on both parts by clusters.³¹³

And there was a great fray betwixt° them, the Knight of the Sun nor Clavergudo witting° of it till the great knight had overthrown and put to death five or six of those knights which came nearest to hand. The Knight of the Sun, seeing his knights so destroyed especially by this great knight, leaving the others, bent his force against him and struck him a blow overthwart° the headpiece, making him to abate his courage. The great knight answered the loan, and the battle was very hot between them; for though the night was dark, yet they knew where to hit as well by the flames which sprang out off their helmets as the clashing of their armour.³¹⁴

Clavergudo put himself amongst the thickest, and at his first good-morrow° slew ten knights. And then, not finding with whom to fight, he leapt into his enemy's ship with his uncle, Armineo, where he felled more than thirty knights. And the skirmish began afresh, either part willing to help theirs. And the four ships grappled together so that the fight would have been dangerous if it had lasted longer.

But half an hour and a little more overpassed,° the tempest which before threatened to appear now outraged, and the port not very sure, the four ships were divided by the storm, everyone withdrawing himself to seek succour. Now in the ship, wherein the Knight of the Sun and the great knight fought, there were no more knights but they two, for all followed Clavergudo into the other ships. The two knights left alone were so earnest that they took little keep° either of the tempest or of their danger. The success of the battle was doubtful, sometimes inclining to the one part sometimes to the other, neither part quailing,° but gathering their strengths to them by the emulation of each other; for the Knight of the Sun verily believed that except his enemy had been some such as Africano was, he could never have abided those mortal strokes, and the other knight thought as well that no man's force could be matchable° with the knight's. And either of them both had better cause to thank Lirgandeo's kindness, especially this strange knight at this time, for had not his armour kept out the edge of the other knight's armant° sword, he could not have prolonged the battle till daylight; yet at that time he was so overmatched that if a sudden adventure had not broken up their fight, he had ended his life in that place.

But when it was broad day, by this the battle surcease,° that the strange° knight knew the devise of the sun upon the Knight of the Sun's helmet, which when he espied, letting his sword fall and lifting up his beaver,° he cast himself at the knight's feet with this speech:

'Oh, my lord, the Knight of the Sun, pardon! I pray your friend[ship], who by mere ignorance hath made upon your person, and who acknowledgeth in you such sovereign virtue as may not be in other but in those to whom our gods have imparted of their goodness. For if the day had lingered or that the morning had not been somewhat clear, I should have received a full payment for my rashness'.

And saying this, he would have embraced Del Febo's knees. Now the Knight of the Sun, so soon as the other's visor was pulled up, knew well that he was the Prince Brandizel, whom his father not willing to make knight before his years were more, had left with the sultan in Babylon; for he was scarcely eighteen years of age, yet being in armour he was as big as you have heard of.³¹⁵ And taking courage upon his stature, in his father's absence he lay at the sultan, his grandfather, to be dubbed knight, thinking it long till he were with his father and his great friends, the Knight of the Sun and the Prince Clavergudo.³¹⁶ So, after that he had obtained his suit of his grandfather, he demanded licence of departure of the sultan and the Princess Balisea,

---

³¹³ The phrase 'raised the people on both parts by clusters' is unclear; *Espejo* describes how the noise of the fight forces the crowd into distinct groups in support of their chosen knight.
³¹⁴ The term 'loan' translates the Spanish 'respuesta' (reply). Tyler here invokes an economic lexicon to describe the exchange of blows.
³¹⁵ He is referred to as a giant in the source.
³¹⁶ His longing to be with his friends and family is added.

his mother, to pass into Persia, which was granted him and two ships charged with two hundred knights to convey him thither,° where after the fourth day's sailing that chanced to him which the history hath recounted.

But to return, as soon as the Knight of the Sun knew his dear friend the Prince Brandizel, very glad to have found him so valiant and hardy, he embraced him heartily. And so they communed° of their own affairs and the desire that each had to see others. But as they began their several° stories by interchange of speech, first one and then another, the mariners cried that the ship rent° in pieces. So some leapt into the water, and others threw out planks to save themselves by. And the Knight of the Sun, finding the cock-boat° near unto him, let it down into the water by a cable. And calling the Prince Brandizel, he leapt into it first himself.

Thus much is ordinary in the course of worldly things, but that which is to come is beyond the credit of a story, as it were an extraordinary miracle. For when the Knight of the Sun leapt into the boat, the cable rent° in pieces. And with the force of the jump and the rage of the winds together, the boat launched into the depth, that the Prince Brandizel could not follow him but got into a little boat which the governor° of the ship had before taken. But by and by after these princes had thus escaped, the ship wherein they had been tore in pieces with the storm: some being drowned, and other some in no little danger as the waves began to swell, so ever prognosticating of their own deaths.

The Knight of the Sun, sailing alone in the vessel and in such fear of destruction, was not so stout°-hearted as to contemn° the senseless element, but confessing the imbecility of man's power subjected under these weak things as fire and water, besides casualties infinite more, he commended himself unto his gods by earnest prayer, not yet only for himself, but also for his friend Brandizel, not being able to divine of his deliverance. Sitting thus in the boat, all pensive till the winds were somewhat allayed and the sea waxed more calm, afterwards he looked about him and saw that he was out of danger, with other two things which made him more to marvel: the one was the great foison° and plenty of all victuals, sufficient to a man for many days; the other was the swiftness of the boat in the sea, having neither sail nor oar to rule it.[317] And musing of this in his thought, he conjectured presently that it should be done by Lirgandeo. And therefore, as very glad of such a man's friendship in so needful a time, he gave him thanks as heartily as if he had seen him there.

In this order, he was upon the sea many days without knowing whither° the wind would drive him, till that from out of the Persian Seas he came into the ocean, and so coasting the whole country of Asia lying upon that sea, he was carried into Africa, which stretcheth upon the wide West Seas, in which country the history leaveth him till another wind serveth. Now, it proceedeth with the story of his friends, Brandizel and Clavergudo, who were on the seas tossed in like manner.

Clavergudo, as the story told you, boarded his enemy's [ship] with fifty knights in his company and made great havoc of them, so that he had not left any of them alive if the storm had not risen so greatly, for the winds were so outrageous between them. And when they could stand no longer on shipboard to try it out, they left not off to ask who each other was: the one party said we are Babylonians; and the other, we are Persians. All this happened in good time, for when they knew each other they fell not again to quarrelling, but they agreed to empty their ships thereby to avoid the danger.[318] So Clavergudo having now leisure to look about him, the battle being ended and not finding the Knight of the Sun nor the Prince Brandizel withal, remembering how he had left them twain in fighting, was greatly afraid lest that the Knight of the Sun should endanger the prince before the one should know the other. Therefore he beseeched God like a good Christian to deliver them both and to make them know each other, thereby to make greater

---

[317] The comparison of the ship to a flying bird is omitted.
[318] *Espejo* refers to their sadness following the battle. The English translation, 'but they . . . the danger', is confusing.

account the one of the other. And it is to be thought that this his prayer was heard, for the second day following, the storm slacked and the ship wherein they sailed arrived to a port not far from a place where they were newly rigged.

There they had not stayed° an hour but that they saw the boat in which the Prince Brandizel was. The mariners in Brandizel's boat, not being perfect in the haven, would not venture to take landing there, but coasting along they passed by the ships to find some more safe place to land in. The prince was ascried° by his men in his ships, and therefore they made signs unto the governor° to steer towards them. So the governor,° understanding the tokens, guided thither.° The Prince Clavergudo and his uncle Armineo, standing on the hatches ready to welcome the Prince Brandizel, between whom there were showed tokens of great good will, and each made much of other as two faithful friends. But questioning about the Knight of the Sun, the Prince Brandizel declared the manner of their parting and the danger wherein he had left him. This caused great sorrow in them, for they loved him as dearly as any father his children, or any wife her husband.[319]

And to assuage their grief, Armineo remembered unto them the words which the wise Lirgandeo had spoken to the Knight of the Sun at his departure, whereby they were persuaded that his departure by such a chance was but for the achievement of things more worthy of him alone, and for whom only they were reserved. Now having stayed in this haven two days to repair their ships, when they were in a readiness, they sailed towards Babylon where they were goodly received of the sultan and of the queen, both very joyful of the news as touching Persia and the King Florion's peaceable possession, and again as sorrowful for the loss of the Knight of the Sun and the peril of death wherein Brandizel saw him last. But in short time after, there were letters received from Lirgandeo containing the certainty of his safety, the manner of his escape, and the affairs wherein he was employed, which last point bred a great desire in Clavergudo and Brandizel to stray through the world and to exercise the feats of arms.[320]

And a while after they had rested themselves in Babylon, they brought the queen to Persia by land, for they would no more adventure the seas, especially having the queen as part of their burthen.° And the history bringeth them on their way as far as Persia, whence it returneth towards Hungary to matters of like importance wherein the younger son of Trebatio had to deal, whose prowess is no less worthy my pains than his brother's valour is worthy of your remembrance, for he surpassed all other knights in loyalty and might, being equal to Donzel del Febo in all points, as hereafter you shall hear.

CHAPTER 27

The Princess Briana discovered to Rosicleer secretly that he was her son

The story left the Princess Briana strangely afflicted and tormented with the double loss — both of Prince Edward, her husband, and Donzel del Febo, her son — which grief no doubt had quickly killed her had not a nymph given her comfort at the well in the orchard as it hath been showed. But yet, it somewhat eased her melancholy that she had the fair and courteous Rosicleer, in whose only company she was wont to beguile her mishaps, and by his means to forget her miseries. For he was so gracious as that he was beloved not only of his mother, but of the other gentlewomen also, which might not one minute spare his company as if he had been child to everyone.

This Rosicleer, when he had attained to the age of twelve years, removed out of the monastery to a house hard by where his nurse° Leonardo kept, whom he thought to be his father. Here he

---

[319] Tyler extends the analogy by mentioning the wife's feelings for her husband.
[320] 'to exercise the feats of arms': to perform knightly adventures

was diligently instructed in all good literature and in the exercise of arms, both to be able to be a good counsellor in peace and as good a warrior in battle.[321] Over and besides the knowledge of the tongues, wherein Leonardo was very curious° as having travelled for his knowledge through the most parts of Europe and Asia, being thereunto both wise and well learned, Rosicleer was of such pregnant wit and so ripe of capacity that he little needed the help of a teacher. And to that which his nurse° read, he added by his own industry somewhat, that he became so profound in these studies as if he had been studied in them all his life time at Athens.[322]

But remaining thus under the governance of his supposed father till he was fourteen years of age, he then was so high and big made that few in that country were so tall. And being at this age, he was able for strength to do that which three knights together were unable to do. The princess, knowing of his strength, forbade him her father's court and would not suffer him to forego the monastery, for she feared lest the king hearing of his towardness° should enquire after him and so retain him in his service.

For this cause Rosicleer, thus kept in at this age and thus strong, became very sad for his so straight enclosure as if he had professed already a vow in some cloister. And his mind ever ran upon his desire to be made knight, to the end he might experiment the adventures of the world and learn by proof that which he had often heard by rehearsal. Hereunto, having no hope nor help by this restraint, it abated his cheer and increased his sadness. Leonardo, his nurse,° marking in what plight he was often, demanded the occasion of his heaviness, but could by no means wring it out of him. And so one day, talking with the princess, he told her that unless she found a remedy for her son, his thought would annoy° him.

The princess, very pensive at that which Leonardo had told, commanded Rosicleer to be brought before her presence. Rosicleer, coming into the presence of the princess, kneeled down and humbly asked what was her grace's pleasure. The princess, bidding him stand up, spoke thus:

'Rosicleer, thy father, Leonardo, telleth me thou are never merry. Now therefore open to me the cause of this thy heaviness. And if thou want ought which thy father cannot supply, utter it freely and I will provide thee of the remedy to have thee contented'.

Rosicleer, hearing the words of the princess, kneeled down again and said:

'Madam, I kiss your hand for the sovereign grace you show me in having such compassion on my grief. And I am well assured that if it were for anything whereof I have need, your ladyship would furnish me of it as hitherto you have done. But if I be sad or solitary for anything which grieveth me, it is not for need of any necessary provision. For I thank your goodness, I have had it hitherto abundantly considered by your highness without my speaking. But it is for that in respect of my age, the life which I now lead is more like a gentlewoman than a young man, which made me desire to be dubbed knight and to wander abroad for to seek adventures. Now, for that I know your ladyship's pleasure to be the contrary, as neither willing to depart without your licence nor daring to utter my desire unto you, I cannot do less but be sorrowful, for I want the remedy of satisfying'.

When Rosicleer had thus said, the princess, feeling already in him the heroical° stomach of his father, Prince Edward (as she thought), and calling to mind the continual casualties of knights errant, burst into tears in great abundance, which occasioned great ruth° in the young Rosicleer, but that he durst° not demand the reason. After a while, the princess, to withdraw her son from his thought or by some means to remit his grief and to comfort him, stretching her arms over his neck, said unto him:

'Oh, my son! Rosicleer, already thy valiant heart doth manifest that which so long time for mine° honesty sake I have concealed: this is that thou are the son of my lord and lawful husband,

---

[321] The addition, 'both to . . . in battle', invokes the qualities of the ideal gentleman.
[322] Athens is reputed to be the seat of culture and education, due to its dominance in classical Greece.

the Prince Edward, begotten in wedlock, but my parents unwitting° thereunto.[323] Thy father's likeness in other qualities thou do well resemble, albeit his favour is clean out of my remembrance. Thou cannot be content with the life which thou now leads, void of all danger, but covet to be made knight and to jeopard° thy person in the search of adventures as thy father did. This if thou does, so that I may not behold thee every day, from that time make account of me as dead. For my great misfortunes together, with the double loss of both of thy father and thy brother, in that order as thou has known, hath by thy only presence been born out and supported. And now, deprived of this support, must I not yield my back to the burden of continual woe and misliking?°[324] Behold then, my child, the extreme grief wherein thou finds me. And for that as yet thou are young of years, do away this affection for a time, and hereafter when thou shall be of more strength and better able to undertake the enterprise of arms, I will so travail° with the king, my lord, that he shall dub thee knight and thou shall have horse and harness at my charges, conformable to thy estate. In the meanwhile, rest thee here, for it may so be that I shall in that time hear some news of the Prince Edward or of Donzel del Febo, which if it so fall out, then shall thy absence be less grievous unto me'.

When Rosicleer heard the secret which the princess his mother bewrayed° unto him, he was well apaid° as touching his thought of being made knight: before the baseness of his foster father hanging in his light, and now he reckoned the rather to undertake the highest exploits whereto his heart drove him.[325] And kneeling down before her, he kissed her hand for the secrecy which she concionated° with him touching his true original.° His mother, by the outward joy he made, supposing his former thought to be put out of conceit° was very glad.

But the princess was deceived in him. For Rosicleer, hearing himself to be named the son of so mighty princes, if before he wished to be made knight, either of a wanton delight or for some greater occasion, now he thirsted greedily after knighthood, as thinking himself bound in conscience to advance his lineage in the right of his parents. And his care increased how to steal from thence. This care he covered the best ways that he might, and stayed with his mother comforting her in all that he could, until that the princess went to her lodging and he returned with Leonardo, who only heard that which the princess had declared. But from that time forth, as I say, he canvassed in his thought to and fro the secret means of his escape, which he thought though perhaps at first it might wring some tears from so tender a princess, yet in process of time would as well dry them up, his valour making amends for his sudden departure.

CHAPTER 28

Rosicleer departed from the Monastery of the River without the knowledge of the princess, his mother

Eight days after Rosicleer knew himself to be the son of the princess, his lady, he abode with Leonardo, casting how he might convey himself from thence without the knowledge of any man. In the end, one night all the household being on sleep, his lodging standing in one corner severed from the gentlewomen's chamber, he took a sword which his nurse had given him and, out of a window looking into the garden, he vaulted down. And coming to the porter's lodge, he requested a horse of him, whereon sometimes before he had ridden, saying unto him that his

---

[323] The translation stresses his legitimacy, but neglects to disclose that she is his mother, which is the essential information revealed in the source.
[324] *Espejo*'s reference to her maternity is again omitted.
[325] The Spanish text makes no mention of his previous worry that he was not highly ranked enough to be made knight.
  'hanging in his light': hindering him

10   lady the princess had sent him on a secret message.³²⁶ The porter believed him and saddled a horse, commending Rosicleer to God, who from thence rode so fast that by the morrow° he was beyond hue and cry.°³²⁷

    Before noon, the princess sent for him, but he could not be found. Then the princess, guessing what it might be, was so sorrowful that it little failed of her death, which assuredly she had not avoided but that there came to her remembrance then that which the nymph had foretold her in the Fountain of her Loves as concerning her losses.³²⁸ And so with some little lingering hope for the return of fortune, banishing all delights, she shut herself up close in the monastery, more like an observant vowess° than a stately princess, whence also she never departed until that God had permitted her to recover her husband, as shall be told you.

20   But to return unto Rosicleer, being neither sick nor well at ease between the conceit° of his mother's grief and the hope of being made knight by some adventure, he gave himself unto the quest of seeking Prince Edward and Donzel del Febo, his brother. And therefore, his intent was to pass into Great Britain to see the King Oliverio, his grandfather, as he had heard, and by some good hap° to be made knight.

    In this journey, he made so great haste that in short space he entered into Almaine and there, travelling by the ignorance of the way, one day he lost himself amongst the mountains, which were thick of tall wood and other lower bush, seeming to be no way unto him.³²⁹ And he strayed so long not finding his way, that the sun was set ere° he knew how to get out. Wherefore, having no other remedy he climbed up to the top thereof to take a view of the place on each side, and

30 he saw beneath him a deep and large valley as it were a mile from thence, environed with steep and high hills in which there were some castles and other buildings very fair and goodly.

    Now that it was night and that this was his only refuge, he made his horse easily descend the hill, at the foot whereof he espied a savage bear running from the town with a child in his mouth of two years old. The child cried so pitifully that Rosicleer took great compassion of it. And seeing it even at the point to be devoured, he ran his horse with great fury towards the bear. The bear, nothing affrighted at the noise of the horse, stood still with his prey in his mouth, and he so glared with his eyes, setting his foremost paws for his defence, that although Rosicleer spurred him, his horse yet would not approach nearer.

    Then Rosicleer alighted, and fastening his horse to a tree, with his sword drawn, went toward

40 the bear. And the bear, seeing him so make towards him, let the young child fall upon the ground and began to buskle° himself to the fight with such a loud groan that he might have feared° a right good knight. But Rosicleer, as it were dedicated to greater purposes than to be murdered by a bear, was nothing appalled at this. But when the bear snapped at him to have gripped him between his arms, he gave the bear a blow cross the reins° of the back, that the bear almost hewn in sunder° fell dead to the ground.

    Rosicleer, by and by, wiping his sword in the grass, put it up in his sheath and to the child he went, which lay crying on the ground, being also in his seeming both beautiful and pleasant, and therefore likely to have been taken from some of those castles in the valley.³³⁰ By the time Rosicleer had ridden a mile in the valley, he saw therein situated many castles and edifices so

50 near together as that the valley seemed to be well peopled. And taking his way to the nearest, he saw two young men and an old man with battle-axes in their hands and in their armour, ride in great haste as somewhat disquieted. As they came near to Rosicleer and saw the child whom they sought for, they were very glad. And well eyeing his good proportion and beauty said:

---

³²⁶ In *Espejo*, he requests the horse of 'el florestero' ('the forester', I.235.15), and not the porter.
³²⁷ In *Espejo*, Rosicleer commends the forester to God.
³²⁸ A sentence in which she ponders the veracity and consequences of the predictions is omitted.
³²⁹ Almaine: Germany
³³⁰ In the source, Rosicleer picks up the toddler, who, since he cannot speak cannot reveal his origins or what happened to him. The relation of their journey to the village is likewise omitted by Tyler.

'God reward you, fair gentleman, for you have rid us of a great part of trouble which we should have suffered in seeking this child. And we pray you, on your faith, how you came by him?'

Rosicleer, saluting them courteously, told them that the child was carried by an ugly bear, and that he was fain° to set the child free by slaying the bear.

The men, more amazed at this, gave him great thanks and certified him that the most ancient in that company was the child's father and that the other two were his brothers, and that they, walking on the battlements of their castle, the child stood at the porch, from whence the bear had carried him, and neighbours espying it, had told which way the bear ran.[331]

'Upon this, we prepared ourselves, although we are sure that if you had not succoured him before, we should have come too late for rescue'.

Rosicleer then delivered the child to his father, whom the father kissed with so great love as if he had seen him newly raised from the dead.[332] Then the ancient man, making his preface with a great sigh, said:

'Beautiful gentleman, if you know how plentifully God hath bestowed His blessings upon us on the one part and how justly He hath scourged us for our offences on the other part, you would not so highly commend of the fruitfulness of the soil as greatly bewail the misery of the inhabitants enduring such torments as were never greater in the land of Pharaoh'.[333]

'What great visitation is this?' said Rosicleer. 'You make me muse on it'.

'This plague', replied the old man, 'is so insupportable that diverse times the indwellers° have forsaken their country and abandoned themselves to wind and weather, to avoid the inconvenience of this place. But for that, all my living lieth here, and in other places I have nothing whereby to maintain my degree. I drive out my days here in sorrow. The valley of itself is fat, delectable, and wholesome, and so large that it containeth more than 2000 castles and other houses, all divided as you see. But I pray God our fullness of bread be not our just undoing as it was to the Sodomites.[334] For we had a prince and lord over us in times past good and gracious, but as God hath provided for our misliving,° in our time very cruel and vicious. He hath to name Argion, who according as his power, by reason of his exceeding wealth which the country yieldeth, is not to be contraried.° So, I believe of life he is the most perverst° and wickedest under heaven. For among other his devilish and detestable customs which he ordinarily observeth — and besides the impoverishing of his poor tenants, racking them shamefully to enhance his treasury, and besides the daily ransoming of his neighbours' lives and goods at his pleasure, for every little displeasure conceived against us — this is one the most ungodly of all: that every week, he enjoineth° us to find him a gentlewoman for his carnal liking.[335] This use he hath frequented this four years, so overawing us and murdering such as make denial that now there are none to make resistance. And his fact now grown unto a habit by our patience perforce,° and his force in spite of our patience is nothing strange unto us, that now all of us obey his hest° in being bawds unto our children, so that it would rive° a man's heart asunder to hear the fair damsels curse the light into the which their parents brought them only to fulfil the shameless lust of so tragical° a tyrant.[336] And to my share it is fallen, that having one only daughter — the fairest in all this valley — since she hath been fifteen years of age, I have every day expected her sending for. If I ought could remedy it, I would either murder my daughter or banish her my country to release her of so great an infamy, but Argion is so wicked

---

[331] In the source text, the child is alone in the field in front of the door, rather than on the porch.
[332] A long passage in which Rosicleer is offered, and accepts, their hospitality is omitted.
[333] Land of Pharaoh: Egypt
[334] Sodomites: people of Sodom and Gomorrah, notoriously sinful cities in the Old Testament Book of Genesis
[335] 'racking them . . . ungodly of all' is added.
[336] The translation increases the pathos of the people and the sinfulness of the ruler.

and devilish that this will not suffice him, but rather if he be defrauded of his bargain, we shall all die for her sake'.

Here, the ancient man was so overtaken with grief that he might not utter a word more. His name was Balides. Rosicleer, angered at the heart to hear of the malice of the wretch Argion, would have given away the possibility of his livelihood to have been made knight, only to have set the land free from so intolerable slavery. And therefore, he appointed with himself when he were made knight in England, to return hither and to wage battle with Argion.

And so still devising of such things, he came to the castle of Balides, where he alighted and was friendlily entertained by the ancient man's wife and the young gentlewoman, their daughter named Liverba, both greatly praising Rosicleer's good favour and feature of body, but much more his courage when they understood that he had delivered the child by killing the bear. Rosicleer, seeing the gentlewoman fair and proper and yet very sad for that Argion had sent her word that he shortly looked° for her, was greatly moved, and the rather for that he knew not how to acquit her.

Balides, at his first coming in, commanded the supper to be made ready, in the meanwhile taking Rosicleer aside to a window opening into the valley, and questioning with him of his birth and of the adventure which brought him thither.° Rosicleer answered:

'I am born in Hungary and I am to travail° about my affairs into Great Britain. And being on my way this morning, I lost myself in the wood, which was the occasion of my hither coming'.

'In good time came you this way', said Balides, 'for by you I have recovered my son'.

And talking of such like matters, they passed the time till supper was ready.

CHAPTER 29

Rosicleer, in Liverba's name, slayeth Argion and removeth the Jews[337]

The supper being ready, Rosicleer with Balides, his wife, and children sat at the table, but there was little discourse at the board°, save that the beautiful Liverba felt so great grief in the remembrance of Argion's message that in lieu of meat she fed on tears, and her parents helped to bear a part with their sighs, which made it a very melancholic supper unto Rosicleer.

And in the neck of this, ere° the cloth was taken up, they heard great rapping at the gate. And looking who they were, they saw more than twenty knights and other serving-men° with torches in their hands at the gates. Those of the house demanded what they would. One of them answered:

'Tell Balides that Argion, our lord, hath commanded us to bring Liverba by and by, for he tarrieth for her to have her company this night'.

Oh, how unwelcome was this errand° unto the parents and how pitiful unto the gentlewoman, which swooned at the hearing of Argion's name! And all the household wept bitterly.

Rosicleer, for company moved to great pity, with the best courage that he might to give remedy unto this outrage, devised a present shift and bid some of the servants to tell those which were without that they should stay a while until the gentlewoman were in a readiness, and after that, that she should be sent unto them. Then he made the costliest apparel which Liverba had to be brought unto him and clothed himself with all, making for his head a periwig° of Liverba's hair and binding it with a little chain of gold; so that being thus readily arrayed he was so beautiful as no gentlewoman thereabouts might parage° him for grace or favour. His host and hostess were amazed in beholding him so well bear out the credit of a gentlewoman in his

---

[337] The removal of the Jews is added to the chapter title, which is very odd since there are no Jews in the chapter, or anywhere at all in the romance.

disguised habit, neither yet knowing what he meant thereby nor yet minding to learn it of him unless he first declared it.

But so soon as he was thoroughly arrayed in this wise,° he softly rounded° his host in the ear, saying:

'My friend, your mishap and the thraldom of this land hath had such force over me that having hope in God which brought me hither, I will take upon me to be Liverba and will go with these knights to the castle of Argion. When I am alone in his chamber, I will behave myself, God willing, that I will free you from this man's tyranny. [F]or, although I be slain in the execution of this enterprise, yet it were a small damage in respect of so great a cure. But I would have you Balides, your sons, and your other acquaintance, and friends to arm yourselves likewise and lie covertly a little from the castle, where if you see that I make you any tokens by the light at a window make account that Argion is slain and be not afraid to come near the gates, which I will set open for you. And so, with little ado we shall make ourselves lords of his castle. When this is done, we will publish it abroad to the inhabitants of the valley, which being certain of Argion's death will rise to our succour'.

Balides looked wistly° upon Rosicleer and wondered at his courage, for he being so young, it was in his fancy° the boldest match which he had heard of. Yet, though it was impossible, as he thought, to come to their purpose, for that he saw how willingly Rosicleer had made this offer, he consented to call his friends, esteeming it far better to die in such a quarrel than to see and suffer so great a mischief. The gentlewoman Liverba, being made privy° thereunto by her father, kneeled down before Rosicleer, and shedding abundance of tears said unto him:

'The God which created both heaven and earth grant you, fair gentleman, so good hap° that both this land may be acquit from this tyranny and I delivered from this villainy'.

The knights, which were without, hasted° to have the gentlewoman with them, and so Rosicleer, putting a sword under his kirtle° closely° and surely that it could neither be perceived nor fall from him, he took his leave of Balides, his wife, and his daughter. Balides, wishing him well and commending him to God, accompanied him to the gates where the knights were attendant, and there poured out so many tears to the outward sight as if it had been his daughter. The people, without having a glimpse of Rosicleer by the light of the torches, took him to be the fairest gentlewoman which they had ever seen, and very glad to bring so good tidings unto their master, they set him upon a palfrey provided for the purpose. Only they were aggrieved at the time, which was so short that they could not sufficiently gaze on her. Their whole talk by the way ran upon this: that it were for Argion more convenient to detain her for wife than every week to seek a new.

And laughing at their own devices,° they came to Argion's castle, being very great and of building the most sumptuous in the valley as it had been a king's palace. In this they entered, and helping the feigned Liverba from her horse, they led her up a pair of stairs into a chamber where Argion awaited her coming. Rosicleer, keeping a demure and sober countenance, drove Argion into a great amaze° at his beauty that, greedily beholding him, he arose from the place where he was set and embraced him in these terms:

'You are welcome hither, my Liverba, for you make me right glad to have your company. And for that your beauty is more than the rest, I will do you more honour than to others'.

The feigned Liverba countenanced out his counterfeit with grave behaviour, only fixing his eyes upon the ground without answering a word, save that he thought upon his purpose, which he knew would be somewhat dangerous in that Argion was strong, foul, and fierce of look more than ever he had seen any. Argion took him by the hand and placed him next himself, demanding first how her parents did. And from thence he fell to more amorous delights, still staring on Rosicleer's beauty, which thoroughly kindled his lust. And he desired her to unclothe herself and to come unto him into the rich bed. This supposed Liverba, framing a shamefast° and bashful look, with a low voice gently answered him that unless he commanded his servants to avoid the chamber and the doors to be fastened, she would not be seen naked in that company.

Argion, taking it to be an argument of great honesty, did off his clothes first and leapt into his bed, commanding his people to go out and shut the doors after them. They, lighting a great candle set on a candlestick of silver, went out. And there remained only this Liverba with Argion, leisurely unclothing herself to delay time. And that the servants should mistrust naught by hearing a bustling in the chamber, first she put off her upper gown, then to her petticoat. And so she stayed a while, Argion calling on her to dispatch quickly, as if the greatest part of his delight had been to come.[338]

Rosicleer, thinking it now time to discover himself, and that the hour was already come wherein God almighty would the wicked Argion to be chastised, cast of his long garment and turned himself into his doublet and hose. And having his sword drawn, he came to Argion's bedside, saying:

'Come out of thy place where thou are, thou foul lecher, and come to rejoice thee of Liverba's love, for very bitter shall this night's rest be unto thee!'

Argion, which beheld him, rose up lightly. And taking a sword which hung at his bed's head, went towards Rosicleer to have caught him in his arms. But Rosicleer with his naked sword watched him, so that he smote the neck from the shoulders, the head beating against the wall and the body falling headless to the ground.[339]

This done, Rosicleer quietly sat down in the same place, and thus remained till the greater part of the night was spent. Balides now in this time had not forgotten his charge, and having talked with more than twenty of his friends as concerning their intent, he easily persuaded them to this enterprise. So, having them in his company with his sons, he lodged near to Argion's castle, only looking for a sign which Rosicleer should make them out at a window, which when Rosicleer had for a time neglected, they suspected the unlikelihood of the fact and had returned closely° to their homes, if that Rosicleer had not then, taking the light in his hand, opened the doors of the hall and showed the torch out of a window. Then they knew what had happened and went joyfully toward the castle. Rosicleer coming down, opened the gates so that they all entered. And lighting many torches which they brought with them, they cast themselves into several companies to search every corner. And ranging without fear throughout the castle when they knew that Argion was slain, and killing so many as they found that indeed though there were more than a hundred knights and other servants within the castle, yet all were slain before they could purvey of armour or think of remedy, in such sort that in the castle there was no one left to take Argion's part.

At Argion, may the stout° lords and untamed tyrants take example of their ends, and make it a benefit of his fall.[340] For although God sometime forbore° the wicked, giving them space of amendment and repentance, yet when they can in no wise° be reclaimed, his justice must of necessity correct them in the manner that both their bodies repay in this life their trespasses with cruel death and perpetual dishonour, and their souls in the other world receive double disgrace and horror of conscience for their misdeeds. How many great lords and tyrants have we read of to have been in the world? And how few or none have we heard of unpunished? Which can be no other thing but that the divine providence hath so ordained it some to be chastised for the misgovernment of themselves, and other some to amend by the terror of others' destruction.

Well, the tyrant Argion thus being slain with all his people, Balides and those which came with him, for his great prowess in killing Argion sued° unto Rosicleer to acknowledge them for his subjects, as they all would willingly obey him for their lord. But he severally making semblance of great love to every party, made them to rise, advising them on this sort: that for their deliverance they ought to attribute it unto God with hearty thanks, for it which by his

---

[338] The added irony creates complicity between narrator and reader at Argion's expense.
Rosicleer is referred to using female pronouns until he discloses his identity.
[339] He struck him, not watched him, in the source.
[340] The moralizing is added in *Mirror*.

goodness had provided that the evil lust of wicked Argion should last no longer. But for that they called him their lord, he said he would be their friend. And nevertheless, since they requested him thereunto that he would not refuse their proffer not for himself, but indeed to give order to that which should succeed for the quiet government of the seigniory.°

This done, Balides sent for his wife and his daughter, Liverba, with his household. They, coming before Rosicleer, gave him thanks for this great good turn in procuring their safety. He received them with great pleasure, and they made merry all that night.

The next day, they devised for the publication of Argion's death, which Balides made to be known to the most principal in the valley. They, all very desirous of such news, came to the castle, where knowing the manner of Argion's end, much praising the strength and boldness of Rosicleer, withal seeing him so well-favoured and of so young years. They ceased not to give him thanks for the good which he had done, so that Rosicleer, somewhat blushing at it, forbade them to speak more of it but to attend their own affairs; for the valley being so replenished with dwellers, all of them were not found but for fear or favour were Argion's claw-backs.° These they had to-do° withal, and in the end subdued them. After wanting a governor, they besought Rosicleer to abide with them and to take oaths of their allegiance towards him, for since that by him they have been restored to their ancient liberties, they thought him to be an able maintainer of their franchises.

But Rosicleer made them answer that at the suit of Liverba, Argion was slain, and that he, moved with pity upon her, had enterprised° it for her sake. If therefore he had deserved ought, he wished them in respect thereof to make Liverba mistress of it, and for the establishment of her possession to match her with the chiefest inheritor of land and sea amongst them. This, if they did for his sake, he should account it not only a satisfaction on their parts for the pleasure he had done them, but also a bond for a further good turn if it so lie in his power. They, debating upon this matter, were all contented with it and promised all their abilities to do his command.

So among them there was a knight called Brandidonio, the chiefest° of all the valley, a proper and honest gentleman, lord of three great castles, and beloved of all the country for his bounty and courtesy.[341] Him they chose to marry with Liverba, their lady. Rosicleer, very well pleased with this gentleman's noble disposition, concluded° upon the marriage, so that in four days, the lord Brandidonio and the fair Liverba were created lord and lady of the valley, and in token of obedience, took the oath and assurance of their subjects, where they lived long time in quietness, their subjects as well at ease to have such governors.[342]

CHAPTER 30

Rosicleer departed from the Valley of the Mountains, meeteth with two princes christened, and by adventure is carried from them again

Rosicleer remained four days in the Valley of the Mountains, for so it was called, to solemnize the marriage between Brandidonio and Liverba, whereat the tenants of the valley being present and seeing his personage so tall and goodly and joined with so good grace and gentle behaviour, judged him a person rather celestial than mortal, and believed that God had sent him for their deliverance from the miserable subjection wherein Argion had held them. So they reverenced and honoured him as if they had seen in him some undoubted image of immortality.

But Rosicleer, this marriage being finished, having no more to do, made to assemble the

---

[341] In *Espejo*, he is young and handsome. The qualities attributed to him in the translation are more desirable in a leader.
[342] The Spanish chapter concludes by affirming that all their lives they were obeyed and served, and that they gave thanks to God and to Rosicleer who delivered them from subjection.

greatest of the country, unto whom he said that he had vowed a voyage which might not be left off, and therefore, now at his departure, he prayed them to accept well of his so short tarrying and, in his absence, to do the honour diligently to Brandidonio and Liverba, which was due unto their liege lord and loving lady. They, overcharged with grief for the lack of him whom they loved as their nigh kinsman, layed° to stay° him by gifts and other offers.[343] But when it booted° not, they swore faith and obeisance towards their lord, and for a remembrance of their love they forced upon Rosicleer a horse which was Argion's: a very tall and strong horse which he refused, not as being very commodious to travel with.[344] And then after this, took his leave of Liverba, her father and mother, and Brandidonio, her husband.[345]

Being ready to mount on horseback, a younger brother of Liverba's called Telio, throwing himself on his knees before Rosicleer, besought him to grant him his suit, which Rosicleer willingly promised, bidding him say on. Telio then said:

'Sir, since you are to travel alone and have none to serve you by the way, may it please you to show me the favour as to retain me for your squire?'

Rosicleer, well pleased with the good affection which Telio bore towards him, embraced Telio with much love and thus made answer:

'Telio, thou are beforehand° with me, for I have given thee thy request so that I may not excuse myself of my former promise, although I would advise thee rather to tarry at home in the delights of thine own nation than to put thyself in danger in a foreign and unknown country'.

Telio, gladder of this than of a good purchase, prepared all things ready for their journey and took his leave of his father, mother, and kinsfolk, who were nothing miscontent° of his choice, for that the company was such as every one could have wished his room°.

Rosicleer and Telio took on their way, neither speaking to other for the thought of their so loving parting from their friends, which as yet stuck fresh and green in their remembrance. And sooth° it is that within a while after Rosicleer's departure, to the end the strangeness of their delivery might be renewed by their posterity and no age should leave to speak thereof, they founded a house of religion with a fair temple, wherein at the one side of the high altar they erected a pillar of marble, very fair and curious, bearing the true counterfeit° of Rosicleer with the history of Argion, the freeing of Liverba, and all that consequently followeth in that story, so that in long time after this monument of restoring the inhabitants was found by our age in the pursuit of adventures in that country.[346] Brandidonio and Liverba here ruled long time in peace and tranquillity, and from them descended all the lords which since have had the governance of that valley.

But from thence to follow Rosicleer on his way, the history sayeth that with his squire Telio he travelled so long through Almaine that he came to a haven of the sea in a manner direct against Great Britain in Picardy, where there were two great and fair ships tarrying for the wind to coast over into England.[347] Rosicleer, hearing of this in his inn, went out of his hostry° to the haven's mouth, there to speak with the master of the ship for to become a passenger. And coming thither,° he saw many knights and other servants by likelihood of some worship pass to and fro, which made him think it was no merchants' vessel; but yet he entered the ship.[348] And there, espying two knights, young men, richly apparelled and placed in two several seats, to whom the other knights in the ship made their obeisance,° he turned his face to have gone out again. But the young knights, seeing Rosicleer and greatly delighted in his beauty and comeliness of personage, called to him. Rosicleer, turning towards them, made low reverence as unto so great

---

[343] Their entreaties to Rosicleer are recounted in much greater detail in *Espejo*.
[344] Rather than force the gift upon Rosicleer, in the source he requests the horse.
[345] The tears and embraces of the extended departure are deleted from the Spanish source.
[346] The historicity of the narrative is reinforced through the erection of a monument that can be 'found by our age'. The immediacy is absent from the Spanish text, which stresses the memory of the liberation of the valley.
[347] Almaine: Germany
[348] His suspicion of the boat's function is added to *Mirror*.

estates. The knights receiving him with as great courtesy, demanding of him gently what countryman he was and what he sought there. Rosicleer, looking upon them, sadly and soberly answered:

'I am come, my lords, from the Valley of the Mountains, and I am desirous to see Great Britain, for my affairs which lie in that country, whither,° as I have learned by others, your ships are prepared. I am therefore to beseech you to do me the pleasure as to grant me passage in your company'.

They — well contented withal, for that he was a young gentleman excelling in beauty all those which they had seen — told him they were willing thereunto, and that if he needed ought unto his journey they would minister unto his wants. Rosicleer gave them many thanks for this their courtesy. But they demanded farther how he was called and of what lineage he came. To the first, Rosicleer answered that his name was Rosicleer and, minding to cut off the rest, he desired them to spare him for the other at that time and to content themselves with this that he now came from the Valley of the Mountains, wherefore they believed that he was naturally born there.

By this means, Rosicleer was entertained with these lords and grew farther in acquaintance with them that he knew the one to be Bargandel, the Bohemian cousin germane° to the Emperor Trebatio and eldest son to the King of Bohemia; the other to be the Prince Liriamandro, brother to the Princess Briana, both of them of his nigh° kin.[349] The fortune which linked and conjoined these princes in this amity was this: the King of the Great Britain, called Oliverio, considering that the loss of the Prince Edward, his son, noised through his empire for fifteen years space,° had so appalled the courages of his knights that neither feasts were made, nor tourneys proclaimed, nor any disports° used with gentlewomen in his country whereby to fire the hearts of young men to the deeds of arms.[350] But that either all of them overcome with grief and mourning still for his son, forsook to wear armour; or else such as their own good natures pricked forwards to try adventures, departed out of his realm, in other regions to become famous. So that the Kingdom of England was very naked of able knights to defend it, whereas before it was best known in all the world for knighthood and chivalry.

The king, I say — wisely casting° of these things, did not now so much lament the lack of his son as fearing the inconvenience which might ensue by the want of good soldiers if any enemy should arise — provided against this mischief on this sort. First, taking the advice of his counsel therein, he caused to be proclaimed through every shire and market town that such knights, his subjects, as either were already departed or now were in mind to depart the realm for to serve in other princes' courts, should return to their homes by a day prefixed in the schedule, upon pain of his high displeasure. This proclamation divulged abroad by the sound of a trumpet, as many as heard of it either by their friends' letters or by the rumour spread in other countries, returned speedily so that the king, in a solemn triumph, taking the muster of his special knights, found himself sufficiently furnished. Now, the second care was how detain them at home. And for this, he devised with his counsel to make a high feast in the city of London with jousts and tourneys for all knights adventurous, both Englishmen and foreigners, and to ordain such prizes as might invite noble princes thither.°[351] This thus agreed upon, the King Oliverio, a year before that these feasts should begin, directed his letters to all princes christened and otherwise as far as Turkey, certifying them that he had appointed jousts to be held at the city of London, and prizes for the best doers, and that thither° it should be free for all knights to come and try their forces. The prize was a massy° crown of gold, all set with pearls and precious stones, valued by all men's deeming at the price of a great city.[352]

---

[349] *Espejo* reminds us that Briana is Rosicleer's mother.
[350] The British knights' sadness is highlighted in the source.
[351] Tyler adds the long section: 'upon pain ... and foreigners'.
[352] The value of the prize is augmented by Tyler, thereby increasing the prestige of her native country.

The news hereof by the king's letters spread over all countries enticed these two princes likewise, being but of young years, to crave to be made knights by their parents° and to travel towards England. So having obtained their purposes, either of them prepared for his journey and met together at one time in this haven, neither of them knowing other nor of their intents. Whereafter° they had knowledge each of other and had concionated° about their enterprise, they determined to go together as friends, and had stayed° three days for the wind ere° Rosicleer's coming, whom good Fortune drove unto the same coast there to make an assurance of perfect friendship between these three, like as she had erst° done between Donzel del Febo, Brandizel, and Clavergudo. This knot between three being the more insonable° as both it hath more hope of succour by the greater number, and represents in my fancy° the figure of the triangle in geometry with this posy:° every way the same.[353] This amity by degrees increased as their acquaintance augmented, for Rosicleer's conversation was so good that they were very glad to have his company. But they lost him ere° they had thoroughly found him, and as no pleasure in this world may dure;° so at the time when these two princes most joyed in Rosicleer's company, their pleasure was overturned and their delight converted to mourning. For the next day, the wind blowing very calm, the mariners hoisted up the sails and plyed° their tacklings° so merrily that with great liking of them all they rode easily, yet not so as they could attain to the haven in good speed.

But that one evening when the moon shone bright and the waves of the sea were still and quiet, the two knights with Rosicleer between them leaned over the sides of the ship, rejoicing all three at the brightness of the stars in the firmament and at the delicate rumbling which the wind made in the bottom of the water. This was so pleasant unto them as that in this contemplation they spent the third part of the night, about which time they heard the cry of a gentlewoman as it might be in some distress.

Then they looked about them and espied a little crayer° coming towards them, in which there was a wild man, for making a giant, fierce of countenance and all hairy of body, of manners savage and cruel, having in the one hand a knotted club with pikes at the end of iron, so heavy as a less man could not lift it. And in the other hand haling° a fair gentlewoman by the hair, her face all bloody with the blows he gave her and punches with his feet. The giant still cried:

'Turn thy boat, thy false and traitorous enchantress, or I will make thy life to answer it me, in that thou have kept me so long from it!'

The gentlewoman never answered him, but continually prayed unto God for succours.

This they both heard and saw easily by moonlight, for the boat approached to their ship and the two other gentlemen were much abashed to see so wild a giant so near unto them, for they had never seen his like before. But the noble courage of Rosicleer could not be so countermanded° by the giant's hugeness as to suffer such villainy towards any gentlewoman. And therefore, setting his foot upon the side of the ship and taking his sword in his hand, he leaped into the gentlewoman's boat. Nature, as it were, willing to manifest her own works and to discover the secret graces which she before had covered in his comely personage, for so as if he had long time experimented the danger of conflicts, boldly he took upon him this adventure. At his first coming into the boat, he struck not the giant, but with great moderation and more discretion than was needful (but that he was very circumspect and in all things lowly), he said unto the giant:[354]

'Leave off, giant, to entreat this gentlewoman in this sort! And weigh well, that it is great shame to a man for to lay his hands upon a woman'.

The great giant, little respecting this courtesy, left the gentlewoman to have taken up Rosicleer and to have thrown him into the water, but Rosicleer perceiving him, put his naked sword poignant° before him. The giant rashly ran upon the sword, that it entered a little, and therefore

---

[353] 'whom good Fortune ... Every way the same' is added to *Mirror*.
[354] His positive virtues are emphasized by Tyler.

mad angry at his wound, he gave back, lifting up his great bat with both his hands to drive at Rosicleer. But Rosicleer, as destined to greater exploits, watching the blow, started aside and closing with the giant, thrust his sword into his guts. Rosicleer pulled out the sword hastily to have given him another blow, but the giant fell upon the planks, gasping for breath. Then Rosicleer stepped unto him and with main° force tumbled him over shipboard, where he lay drenched in the sea.

All this the two princes beheld and wondered at the great courage of Rosicleer, but not a little diseased° in that they could not help him. For when he leaped into the gentlewoman's boat, they cried aloud to their knights to let down their ship-boat° into the water, but it could not be: before that the valiant youth had drenched the giant in the sea and that the gentlewoman's boat rode with such swiftness, as in short time they lost the sight of it, with so much grief unto both these princes as they might scarce speak the one to the other. For when they compared together the shortness of time in which they enjoyed him, and in that short time the great prowess which he had showed before them, they could not easily ascertain themselves whether they had dreamed of such things or seen them waking. But if so be they were not beguiled either by a dream or some fantastical illusion, I dare warrant they thought that in regard of that which God had wrought by him, he could not be but of noble estate. Well, when there was no hope of following, they haled° up their boat again to keep their course towards Britain, having hope to meet him there, otherwise appointing with themselves if they there failed, to go in quest of him.

I may forget to tell you of his squire, Telio, but you may easily think of his pains by the love he bore his lord. And I will leave him to your several considerations of yourselves in like cases, being far from your country and farther from your friends, whom you have preferred before your country, the rather to accompany these noble gentlemen unto the coast of England, which in their way still kept on their former ditty, ever talking of Rosicleer: either commending his good grace, or bewailing his departure, or blaming their own misfortunes, or extolling his strength. And ever the foot of their song was: 'what should the swiftness of the boat mean, and our sudden acquaintance?'[355] Unto the depth whereof, because they could not reach, thereby to quiet themselves, their sorrow redoubled by misjudging the worst.

In the end, the wind was so good that it set them on land in the Great Britain not far from London, where the king was resiant.° Where as soon as they came on shore, before they presented themselves to the king, they dispatched out one of their ships with some of their knights and Telio, Rosicleer's squire, to coast the same way which Rosicleer was gone, to the end, if Fortune were so favourable, to bring some tidings of him. Afterwards, themselves with the majesty that doth belong to so great princes, took towards the great city, viewing on every side the great assembly of people, all the fields and highways, besides towns and hamlets taken up for knights, as well strangers as natural, and an infinite number of ladies and gentlewomen, coming only to see the tourneys. The two princes sent two of their knights beforehand to give understanding unto the king of their coming. The king, glad to have the presence of so noble princes at his high feast, with a great train of knights met them without the city, and coming towards them, embraced them with great love.[356]

The story leaveth to recount the words of courtesy which passed between them, and sayeth that they entered into the palace with the king, and were lodged in one quarter thereof, himself keeping his new guests company that night and talking with Liriamandro as concerning his daughter-in-law, at whom he learned the whole state of Hungary with the appendices as touching that matter, which in some respect made him very sorrowful to hear of the continual affliction wherewith Briana tormented herself in the Monastery of the River. And he was as greatly abashed° to hear that in Greece they knew as little of the Emperor Trebatio as in England he

---

[355] The loneliness resulting from being distant from home is added by Tyler.
[356] Descriptions of their encounter and of the hospitality they receive are omitted.

heard of the Prince Edward.³⁵⁷ Then Liriamandro, espying the king somewhat inquisitive, proceeded farther with his talk, in declaring the adventure which had joined him and Bargandel, and how that they two met at the haven with a gentleman called Rosicleer, and so consequently of the battle with the giant. The king, hearing of so many virtues in Rosicleer as Liriamandro did his uttermost to set them forth, greatly wished to have seen him. Here, the story leaveth the king and these princes to the providing of things necessary for the tilt, and goeth on with Rosicleer, whom these princes left upon the main° sea.

CHAPTER 31

Certain accidents which befell Rosicleer after his departure from the two princes

Rosicleer made an end of the battle with the giant, and the gentlewoman, so well revenged by his means, kneeled down before him to have kissed his hand and to give him hearty thanks for his great friendship showed in working her delivery from the terrible giant. Rosicleer took her up and demanded of her what she was and by what adventure she was brought into the giant's hand.

The gentlewoman answered:

'Know, my lord, that I am named Calinda, daughter to the wise man Artimodoro (of whom peradventure° you have heard [spoken of] before this time), inhabiting in an island not far from hence in the midst of the sea, which may never against his will be seen of anybody. This wise man, my father, having sent me on a message in this boat to a friend of his, lord of an island not far hence, my fortune was such, that when I returned by this giant's island, there entering on land for fresh water, I was espied by this giant, who made to me to have taken me, but I fled towards my boat, which I could not recover so soon but that he entered with me.³⁵⁸ But as he shoved to land, my boat drove backward into the stream and had lost the sight of his island. The cruel giant, seeing this and thinking that I had done it by my knowledge, would have killed me, and entreated me in such sort as you saw. Now as for the lightness° of the boat, sir, I believe', sayeth the gentlewoman, 'that it is guided by my father's art and that we are on the way toward his island. Whereat, gentleman, I beseech you take no thought, although you have lost your company. For I doubt not but that by my father's cunning you shall be joined, and then my father shall serve you loyally for the mercy you have shown me'.

Rosicleer much wondered both at the gentlewoman's speech and at the giant's cruelty without good occasion, and especially at the incredible swiftness of the boat, sailing in the sea faster than a bird flyeth in the air, which made him judge Artimodoro to be a very wise man in that he had so great authority over the sea.³⁵⁹ And therefore he rejoiced himself upon hope to see the wise man at whom he might demand some news as touching Prince Edward, his father, and Donzel del Febo, his brother. And for that, he questioned with the gentlewoman many things as concerning her father, of whom he learned many things.³⁶⁰

Now as they talked of these things, the boat stood still as it had been landed. Rosicleer, much abashed thereat, looked on every side what it should be that stayed° it and gaged the water with a pole, but he perceived nothing, wherefore he thought that peradventure° under the boat in the place there lay some adamant° stone, of the virtue whereof he had read before times that it

---

³⁵⁷ *Espejo* erroneously mentions Hungary rather than England, which Tyler corrects.
³⁵⁸ In contrast to *Mirror*, the source text specifies that the giant did not catch her. This is because Tyler mistranslates 'no me alcançasse' ('he did not catch me', II.265.14) as 'he entered with me'.
³⁵⁹ Despite omitting this image twice earlier, Tyler here adds the simile comparing the boat to a bird flying through the air.
³⁶⁰ The sentence, 'And for that . . . many things', is added by Tyler.

draweth iron unto it and stayeth° the ships which sail over it. And as he was much perplexed in his thought, not knowing now to remedy it, he saw before him a little island, the freshest and most delectable that in his life he had seen, and the boat already fastened to the bank. Then, the gentlewoman bade him not to fear, but to come out on land, for the island which he saw before him was her father's island. This was strange unto Rosicleer, to see the liquid sea so soon converted to solid earth, but he made not strange to come on land at her bidding, where, by and by, the wise man met them: a man by seeming very aged, his beard all white and reaching to his waist, with a little white rod in his hand, as some token either of his honour or profession. The wise man, for the great pleasure he had to see Rosicleer, said unto him on this wise°:

'Right noble and most worthy Rosicleer, you are welcome unto this my country, for by your coming I have been more at my heart's ease than during my life I have been. And many years passed have I longed for your presence. For although I knew for a certainty that hither you should come, yet the time when, I knew not, which hath hitherto been concealed from mortal men and only made known to God himself. I knew, likewise, so soon as my daughter Calinda was born that she should be set free from cruel captivity and perpetual dishonour by you only, but the manner how was not revealed withal, only that it should be when the providence of God, directed by His will, committed the execution thereof to Fortune. Thus, may we men, for all our cunning, neither alter the course of things appointed by destiny, nor yet find other remedy than is permitted by the foreknowledge of God, as this my daughter could never have been saved, but only in that same manner as you gave her succour.[361] The reason was, because my knowledge could not wade so deep as to foresee everything concluded by destinies, the self same thing being subject under the line of destiny that I should not perceive it. So, my daughter went on land unto the giant's island, which I neither foresaw to prevent nor could have prevented if I had foreseen. Yet that which was in my power, I so ruled the boat that it came to your ship, thereby to have relief at your hands for my care. This have I told you at large the inability of our cunning against the influence of the stars, whereby you may perceive how much I am beholding unto you, the rather to make bold upon my service if in any respect either my art or my armour may do you pleasure'.

Rosicleer, attentively listening unto the wise man's discourse, in the end gave him great thanks for his so liberal offer, promising likewise the service of his body (for other thing he had nought) to do his command in any matter reasonable. With this the wise man took him by the hand and lead him toward a great and beautiful palace seated upon the shore. Rosicleer, with a curious eye, gazed on each part of the palace, so situate in an unknown island, and was never content, for indeed the subtlety of the workmanship surpassed far the craft of masonry in our days.[362] But here he abode two days with Artimodoro, served of delicate viands° and strange devises, able to quicken° a dead man's stomach, being here better pleased with his entertainment than he was ever otherwise.

One day, sitting at the board with Rosicleer, the wise man espying him occupied in his thought about his journey to England, sported with him in this sort:

'Rosicleer, I see well this country breedeth not such things as may content your appetite and I hold you excused, for your desire coveteth after Mars and martial feats, wherefore as my learning showeth me, your lust° carrieth your stomach into England, there to be knighted. Truly, fair sir, you have good reason thereunto, for the time is at hand wherein your knighthood must be manifested. But for to do you honour, I myself will attend you thither,° in respect both of your friendship past towards my daughter Calinda, and other greater matters to come which I hope shall be accomplished. I know not indeed the time when it shall be, neither the manner how, but this I know: that by your means I shall once escape the death. Now, as well for your own sake, being f[rom] the very moment of your birth illumined with more than mortal graces as I have already engrossed the dolorous life of the Princess Briana, so will I be also the register

---

[361] The moralizing commentary 'Thus may we . . . foreknowledge of God' is absent from the source.
[362] An extensive appraisal of the palace's beauty is deleted.

of your acts, to enrol your memory in the records of fame that it shall be maintainable against all counterpleas and forged evidences. This will I do for you, besides the perpetuity of my service in other matters. And for your brother Donzel del Febo, he hath already found a chronicler', meaning this by Lirgandeo, 'such as his worthiness meriteth'.[363]

Rosicleer, tickled at his talk touching his brother Donzel del Febo, bowed himself thankfully and requested him to go on, saying:

'Right honourable sir, seeing you have entered into this discourse, I pray you continue it, for I knew naught as pertaining to this my brother, save that he was lost in the sea being very young. And I have hitherto thought that he had been dead.[364] And since nothing is hidden from your knowledge, I pray you likewise satisfy me in the same manner as concerning the Prince Edward, my father, that I may seek him if there be hope of finding on this earth'.

'Most noble prince', answered the wise man, 'you draw me into a long tale, and in some point nothing pertinent to you. But know for a truth that the Gentleman of the Sun your brother is alive, already knighted, and for his first prizes, he hath achieved such marvellous deeds of arms as that it standeth you in hand to bestir° yourself if you mind to be matchable,° being the only man as yet unparagonized° through the world. He is now in a country where, without knowledge of his estate, he is notwithstanding much praised for his personage, the region so far distant from this our climate, that if you put yourself on the way to seek him, your pain should be infinite, and as I can learn, needless: for ere° that you pass out of this country, he will come to seek you here. Now as to your demand touching the Prince Edward, whom you call your father. I do you to wit° that he was dead before that you were begotten, and that the royal princess your mother, now destitute of an husband, shall in time recover her lawful husband, and you shall know your father for the greatest and mightiest prince christened. Furthermore, because it is forbidden me to discover of the great secrets of God until it be His pleasure that all men shall know it, I may not answer you, but the event shall witness with my prophecy. Now will I make ready for your passage into Britain, for there must be showed the first flower of your manhood'.

Rosicleer was greatly confused in his understanding at the words which the wise man spoke, being yet plain and easy and he able to make English of every word; but the cause was for that he was unable to find out the true sense which this divinity carried, being repugnant to his former belief. So, hacking and guessing about it to make likelihoods of impossibilities, and examining every point by itself, yet could he never be settled nor make good construction of it, for his mother told him that Prince Edward was his father; the wise man delivered the contrary. And if his mother knew° his father, then how could his father be dead ere° he was begotten? And how could his mother recover her lawful husband being dead? And how could his father become such a monarch after his decease? And so forth . . . Now, if he gave credit to the wise man; yet no man better knoweth the child's father than the mother. So that for reverence of the wise man and to reconcile his mother's words with the wise man's rede,° he framed to himself for that time a new article of belief that one thing might be and not be. Yet time found out a better solution of this sophism.[365]

For this time, seeing it was no reason to importunate° the wise man upon this matter, it contented him to know for a truth that Donzel del Febo, his brother, was yet alive, and he gave him hearty thanks for the courtesy he had showed him herein. But for his voyage into England, he left that to his direction, since he perceived his meaning therein. The wise man said it should be so provided for, as best beseemed his honour.

The third day after, when all things were in a readiness, Artimodoro brought out of his armoury a rich armour and gave it to Rosicleer. The armour was framed so cunningly as for

---

[363] These passages describing the chronicling of the heroes' adventures are investigated in the introduction.
[364] The exclamation of his happiness upon discovering that his brother lives is excised.
[365] Tyler expands his pondering and adds the reference to sophisms.

workmanship, cost, and secret virtue, it excelled all that I have seen. It was closely wrought, curiously engraven, enchased with precious stones, and above all, this efficacy that it resisted the edge of all metal, this effect proceeding either from the stones or the examination of the ascendants in the forging thereof.³⁶⁶ The colour of the armour was all white, well fitting for a new knight. Artimodoro gave at the same time to Rosicleer a bay courser strong and wight° of limb, which he had bought for that purpose in the country of Spain where the best breed of such horses were.³⁶⁷

And after all things set in order thus for their journey, taking men with them for their necessary uses, they shipped themselves in a fair bark, sailing with great swiftness, as the wise Artimodoro had by his skill directed it, in which journey the history leaveth them till their sudden approach unto the lists within Great Britain.

CHAPTER 32

The great feasts began in Oliverio's court

In the fresh and pleasant month of May, when the green boughs and sweet smelling flowers renew joy and gladness in the hearts of young folk, the great city of London and wide fields thereabout seemed not less covered with armed knights than if the mighty hosts of Darius and Alexander had thither° assembled.³⁶⁸ For the great feasts and jousts were so diligently published in every region and country, and the prizes which the king had set were of such valour, that there came thither° from diverse far and strange lands so many knights and ladies as that the number of them was infinite. Now that that especially drew young princes and men of great name thither° was this: the King Oliverio had a daughter named Olivia, the only inheritrix° of his kingdom, of the age of fourteen years, a beautiful and delicate damsel, as not her like might be found in all the quarters. For the fame of her singular beauty thither° came many noble princes and worthy knights to win her liking, each of them wearing so rich and quaint devices that their bravery in short time exiled the long mourning which had continued in Great Britain. The mirth which they made much delighted the King Oliverio, and it joyed him much to see his court and country so well stored of knights and princes, to whom he gave honourable entertainment and countenance of good will, as well of his own subjects as strangers, and all were well content with it, highly commending of his court for magnificence and courtesy. The king at this time was a widower, and therefore he sought much the honour of the princess his daughter.³⁶⁹

But to come to our matter: amongst the knights strangers, the two princes, Bargandel and Liriamandro, bore the greatest strokes; next Don Silverio, Prince of Lusitania, a young knight and valiant in arms, already enamoured upon the fair princess Olivia, for whom he had been a long time suitor in the king's palace, presuming upon his birth and livelihood that she should be granted unto him. And as it fell out, the princess understood some part of his desire, but she

---

³⁶⁶ 'or the examination of the ascendants' refers to the discipline of astrology in which the ascendant signifies 'the point of the ecliptic, or degree of the zodiac, which at any moment . . . is just rising above the eastern horizon' (*OED*, ascendant, B.I.1). Rosicleer here suggests that Artimodoro may have consulted the stars to determine the most propitious moment to forge the armour in order to imbue it with great power. The marvellous and ornate construction of the armour is elaborated in *Espejo*.

³⁶⁷ *Espejo* indicates that the horse originates from the Elysian Fields, which the narrator situates in Spain. The Elysian Fields are the classical Land of the Blessed, where the virtuous reside in the afterlife.

³⁶⁸ Darius I (550–486 BCE): known as Darius the Great, a renowned Persian ruler

Alexander III (356–323 BCE): known as Alexander the Great, a renowned Greek conqueror

³⁶⁹ Whereas in *Mirror* his status as a widower explains his desire to honour Olivia, *Espejo* merely explains that the Queen was long dead.

was of a haughty heart and high mind, making no more account of Don Silverio in respect of that demand than of another ordinary knight or the refuse of other.[370] For amongst all which were already come, she thought none merited to be a peer and match for her beauty, being (as my author sayeth), such in her own conceit° as if no prince were worthy of it. But the truth is that the blind boy, shooting at random, had overreached his mark, as appeared in the second shot at the coming in of Rosicleer.[371] In the third place, there came into this triumph the Prince of Ireland, called Argiles, and Don Orgiles, Prince of Scotland, and Allamades, King of Cornwall, all three vassals and subjects to the King Oliverio. The fourth room° was assigned to Don Brinco, Prince of Namibia in Africa, bringing from his country many valiant knights richly armed, and with them Albalaxes, King of Mauritania, a pagan young and lusty.° There came thither° also two giants of an admirable height and fierceness, being such a terror to the poor commonalty inhabiting the villages near to London; the poor men's fear made them the more insolent to commit diverse riots and other trespasses before the feasts began. This was the several countenances of the knights of most account.[372] But to make short, there came besides many other knights, both Christians and pagans, under the king's writ of safe conduct which himself gave out, that never England more flourished of knights, nor never nation was like to England.[373]

But now the first day of the jousts, before they should ride to the tilt, the King Oliverio invited all the kings and princes to dinner in his palace, where they were feasted royally and with great melody. After the tables taken up, the knights went to arm themselves, and the king, conducted by the ancient lords and barons of his court, took up his seat in a window over the tiltyard. And upon a scaffold before him, reared for that purpose, he commanded the prizes to be put, which were diverse: for unto the crown before spoken off, he added a collar° of like valure° and many other jewels able — for the honour of attaining them and the worthiness thereof — to animate a bastard knight to such an enterprise.[374]

After this, the Princess Olivia, coming forth of the great palace with a hundred ladies and gentlewomen, mounted upon a stately scaffold very richly hanged. Among these ladies, there was the Princess Silverina, daughter to the king of Scotland, and Rodasilva, Princess of Lusitania, sister to Don Silverio, and many other ladies, daughters to the great lords of Britain. But in the middest° of these, the fair Princess Olivia showed not less majesty than the fresh and fragrant rose doth among the briers and stinking nettles, which notwithstanding have their commendation for their green and lively verdure.[375]

But the scaffold being filled with ladies and gentlewomen, there came the knights in place, most of them young and shining in their bright armour. The first that pricked himself forward to joust was Allamades, King of Cornwall, a very good and tried knight, against whom there came to encounter another abled° knight, an Almaine set upon a strong courser.[376] In their shock, their spears flew in shivers° and the King Allamades, somewhat staggering in his saddle, unhorsed the Almaine. After him there came ten other knights strangers, more bold than skilful in feats of arms, all which the valiant Allamades overthrew, with great pleasure to the king and all his court.

Then, the king called for his knights with this Allamades to give them place. [They] voided the lists, and there entered Argiles, Prince of Ireland, which with eight several courses broke eight spears and overthrew eight knights. After him, Don Orgiles, Prince of Scotland came, whom when Argiles espied, not minding to disturb him, he rode unto the list's end. Orgiles,

---

[370] Her haughtiness is added by Tyler.
[371] This sentence, with the allusion to Cupid, is added.
[372] 'This was . . . most account' is an addition.
[373] The sense of patriotism is absent from the source.
[374] The luxuriousness of the scaffold is described in *Espejo*.
    Instead of mentioning these high princes and knights, Tyler strangely introduces the concept of the 'bastard' knight.
[375] Further evocations of her beauty are excised.
[376] Almaine: German

without being moved in his saddle, cast down twelve knights and then followed his fellow Argiles. By and by, Don Silverio came in with a gilt armour, gorgeous to behold, and his horse barbed with cloth of gold cut upon silver imagery, being a lusty° and valiant knight. And as the thoughts of the Princess Olivia emboldened his courage, so besides the haughtiness of his stomach contemned° all other knights in respect of himself. In his journey, he dismounted twenty knights within less than half an hour, so that many thought he would win the honour of that day.

But straightway° there pressed forward the two princes, Bargandel and Liriamandro, having in their company more than 200 knights, with their heralds crying before them: 'Bohemia, Bohemia! Hungaria, Hungaria!' The two princes rode upon fair and strong coursers, richly armed as became their estates, their lustiness being enflamed by their loves, for since their coming to the English court, they were esprised° with love: Bargandel of the Princess Silverina, and Liriamandro of the Princess Rodasilva. And having obtained the good favours of their ladies, they pained themselves to be as bold as the bravest.[377] So finding the tilt empty by Silverio's departing, they pranced forward till other knights came against them. And either of them in their turns, before they left the lists, overthrew at the least thirty knights a piece. So blazing their prowess, by the force they showed that the king and other beholders changed their opinion as touching Don Silverio. Upon this, the two princes, glad of that day's travail° and vaunting themselves before their mistresses, made room for others to do their endeavours. After these, the valiant and hardy knights of the English court came in against the strangers of other countries, where the Englishmen so behaved themselves as that day's honour was theirs.

Now, as the king was in talk with his lords about the glory which his men had gotten, and every man was attentive to that which was before him, suddenly there was heard a great cry amongst the people on the back side of the lists, no man knowing what it meant. By and by there came forth a tall giant with a train of more than twenty knights upon a stone-horse,° which groaned in a manner under his weight. The giant, commanding his knights to stand aside, went alone to the window where the king was, there raising up his beveare° and forcing out a terrible look. Without other reverence, he spoke on this wise:°

'King Oliverio, I am Brandagedeon, Lord of the Islands Baleance, and am hither come because of the prizes which thou has appointed for the best doers. I am well known in all the heathen country, for by the power which my gods have imparted with me there is no mortal man that may gainstand° my puissance, and for that, this day thou shall have some trial of this truth.[378] Behold before the night be shut in there shall no knight of all these which are here keep his saddle unless he keep himself from me'.

And so, in great pride, as you may presume by the course of his speech, he uttered this and pulled down his visor. Then, with a great spear in his hand, he took the one end of the pale.°[379] This his coming was nothing pleasant to the king, for since his arrival in that kingdom he had done many outrages to the poor subjects of the land. And the king feared, lest the knights of his court should not be able to maintain their honour against him. Now this monstrous giant had not stayed there long, but that a valiant knight, a Britain called Brandaristes made a sign unto him.

These two ran together, and in their shock Brandaristes with his horse fell to ground. But the giant, nothing diseased,° held on his way toward another knight by name Brandidarte, a Britain too, a brave knight and as bold as Gawain.[380] But the giant welcomed him like as the other, and thus in short time, the giant, proving himself upon more than a hundred knights of the hardiest,

---

[377] *Espejo* clarifies that Silverio left the field because he did not want to fight the great heroes.
[378] Brandagedeon's boasts are greatly diminished by Tyler.
Islands Baleance: Balearic Islands, an archipelago in the western Mediterranean Sea, east of the Spanish mainland
[379] The spectators' fear is highlighted in *Espejo*.
[380] Gawain: in Arthurian romance, Gawain is Arthur's nephew and an excellent warrior.

both strangers and Englishmen, he made them all to descend from their horses, that the King Oliverio was much disquieted hereat° and would have bought out the giant's presence if he might for more than London is worth, even for the pity which he had upon his knights, not possibly able to withstand this giant.[81]

    The King Allamades, beholding the king's countenance sad and guessing the cause, would needs adventure the honour which he before gained upon the vanquish of such a giant. And taking a fresh horse with a choice spear from the rattler,° he rode to Brandagedeon, whom the giant met so forcibly that Allamades lay on the ground and Brandagedeon, dressing himself in his saddle, passed on.

    By and by, Orgiles, Prince of Ireland set upon the giant, which somewhat estonished° him, but nevertheless Orgiles's hap° for himself was in no other manner than his fellows. Then came in Don Argiles to take Orgiles's part, and fiercely encountered the giant, but to the same purpose.

    Now was Don Silverio ashamed before the Princess Olivia to have tarried behind so many good knights, and therefore forcing his courage to please his lady, upon a light courser he ran against Brandagedeon. And his fortune was so good that he made Brandagedeon to lose one of his stirrups and the reigns of his bridle. But Brandagedeon quitted this with more than a tolerable usury, for he carried him beyond the crupper almost a spear's length, which disgrace before his Lady Olivia made him wood° angry, and willingly would he have challenged the combat if both leisure and place had been convenient.

    Not long after the Prince Bargandel, gathering his forces at the beholding of the Princess Silverina, went to encounter the giant, either of them being well heated, but diversely, as arising of diverse causes. But their strengths, increased by their heats, made their shocks so terrible as neither part had great advantage. The giant fell upon the crupper of his horse and rode the length of a career° ere° he might arise again. Bargandel fell to the ground with his horse under him. This made him hang his head, and stirred up his friend Liriamandro for his succours, who caused Brandagedeon to embrace the saddle bow, himself being clean lifted out of the saddle by Brandagedeon the giant. And Liriamandro lay on the ground to complain him of his mishap before his mistress Rodasilva.

    After these, there was none left so hardy as to dare encounter Brandagedeon, which caused the king and other princes to look ruefully, and the giant to bear himself as insolently. For when there was none left, he lifted up his voice in these terms:

    'Come forth! Come forth, ye knights of the Great Britain! And either know what the force of Brandagedeon is, or if you dare not appear, send me the prizes presently, for to none of the world they do so rightly appertain as to me!'

    And this saying, he galloped up and down in the place, expecting either some knight or the prizes. The king, seeing none come to answer his challenge, was very angry and would have given his best town to have had a knight which could have quailed° the giant's courage. And for very grief he turned himself from the window, till the sudden shout of the people caused him to look out again.

    Then he espied the people flocking together towards one corner of the list, and in the midst of them an aged man with a long white beard riding softly on a mule and bearing the countenance of a very wise man. After him he saw a knight well harnessed in white armour, richly beset with precious stones so that no man in the place had the like: his helmet had a fine plume° and his horse the like; the pommel° of his saddle of goldsmith's carving, and the seat all embroidered with gold and silver. Everything belonging to the knight so brave and lusty,° that none now but gazed on the stranger. After him a good distance, there rode a gentlewoman an easy pace upon a palfrey, driving before her a sumptuous horse.

    The gentlewoman, coming near unto the palace, alighted, and unlacing her mail,° spread a

---

[81] The allusion to London's great worth is added.

fair tent in the plain made all of cloth of gold with such strange devices that neither king nor kaiser° in the world but might have vouchsafed it for himself. But that which was most commendable was the most excellent and brave conceits° with needlework, which could never have been wrought but by an exquisite seamster:° as indeed the wise Artimodoro was the workman.

Now to make short work, when the pavilion was pitched, Artimodoro, leading Rosicleer with him unto the king, spoke on this wise:°

'God increase thy royal estate, King of the Great Britain, and advance the credit of thy whole court! Wit° you, most puissant prince, that from mine° island I am hither come with this young gentleman that he may be knighted by your own hands. And albeit that so great a courtesy neither he nor I have merited of your majesty, yet understand, worthy king, that for his lineage he is such a one as not without reason he may crave to be dubbed knight of so mighty a prince as you are. And I dare warrant, moreover, that it shall not be ill bestowed on him, as yourself shall testify in short time. Although you shall not thoroughly enter into the consideration of his valour till that his death be published by report of his drowning, and that much blood shall be spilled to the greater praise of his prowess, to the contentation° of your person and to the profit of your royal estate. And be it my tale seem incredible, yet I beseech you to remember it well, for I will avouch° the event as I have told you. Retain him, therefore, Sir King, in your court, and believe that the time shall come wherein you would lose the best part of your kingdom to have him near you. But to the end this story now averred by me may carry more authority with your worthy person, know that this reporter is Artimodoro, of whose knowledge you have heard before, for with my skill I have done service to such great lords as you are'.

Artimodoro, here making a reasonable pause, began again on this wise:°

'Sir King, with your majesty's leave, we have here pitched a tent in the name of the gentleman as a challenge against all comers. After you have made him knight, the first which shall unhorse him shall enjoy this tent, the value whereof may content him for his journey'.

And here staying, he said:

'Sir King, I have done'.

King Oliverio, all this while not lending his ears idly as to a fable in a winter night but weighing every point, looked upon Rosicleer, and well thought that his personage might agree with Artimodoro's commendation.[382] But yet, as half in a doubt as touching himself, he made the wise man this answer:

'Assuredly, Artimodoro, with this demand or any other which you shall require, I am very glad that you take occasion of coming to my court, for by the bruit° of your fame I have long time wished to see you. But to send for you indeed, I was never minded because, as I hear, against your will no man may speak with you. And to make you answer, I am in purpose to satisfy you, as well for your own sake as for this gentleman's, whose behaviour seemeth to be such as without your report he cometh sufficiently commended unto me. I promise you here to make him knight with mine° own hands, and I beseech God he prove no worse than you foreshow me'.

Rosicleer and the wise man both bowed humbly on their horsebacks. The king bade Rosicleer to alight, which dismounting from his horse, ascended by a pair of stairs to a little scaffold before the king's window, where kneeling down in the sight of the whole multitude, he received the order of knighthood at the king's hands. The king demanded where the young knight should receive the sword, and the wise man answered that he should stay for that till he could conquer it. Then, after his duty done to the king, Rosicleer returned to horseback, and with a lively grace so demeaned himself upon his horse as that it well pleased the beholders. Now for that which

---

[382] A winter's tale is an old, lengthy story told to idle away a long winter's night. Cf. 'a merry winters tale would drive away the time trimly' and 'drive away the time with an old wives winter tale' from George Peele, *The Old Wives, Tale 1595*, ed. W. W. Greg (London: Oxford UP for the Malone Society, 1908) 104, 119.

A passage in which the king considers Artimodoro's discourse is omitted.

followeth, you must intend° that the wise man uttered his speeches to the king in the audience of the whole multitude, many knights and other compassing him about to hear his errand° so that few or none but were partakers° of it.

    Amongst them was Brandagedeon, bearing himself within the lists as proudly as the cock of the game doth in the cockpit when the craven° is chased.[383] Then, hearing that the tent was put for a reward to him which could unhorse the young knight, when he saw time, he cried aloud to Rosicleer, saying:[384]

    'In good sooth,° new knight, thou bewray° thy folly and lack of experience when thou saw me stand in this place with my spear in my hand to make that challenge, which shall not be in thy power to maintain so surely, but that I will be the master of thy pavilion. And yet God's blessing on thy heart for bringing so fair a jewel, being indeed fitter for me than for thee'.[385]

    Rosicleer, whose courage never tainted, answered as shortly:

    'It shall be thine, giant, if thou win it. And there shall no man forbid thee the possession of it if thou overthrow me'.

    And without more words, he took a great spear from the rattler,° and turning his horse head, he rode softly to the place where the jousts were kept. In his way thither,° Rosicleer, lifting up his eyes to the scaffold of the gentlewomen, he saw the beautiful Olivia standing directly against his face, exceeding no less the other gentlewomen in brightness than the moon excelleth the stars in a frosty night.[386] Oh, poor Rosicleer, what a look was that which locked thee from thy rest! For with her beauty thou was wounded at the heart, that albeit in time the skin overgrew it and the flesh healed, yet the scar remained, and never knight in the world loved more loyally than thou did. For though the sight was short and the blow quick, yet the wound was deep and the smart cureless. Oh, full many a bold enterprise did thou achieve ere° thou gained a reasonable guerdon° for thy great good will![387] And thou, fair princess, being within the hearing of the wise man's speech, did not spare to lend thine ears to another man's tale and thine eyes to another man's bravery, that thy succours being far from thee, thy heart had not the power to repulse thy adversary, love being the only occasion of thy unrest. But Lord, what alteration both of you felt by the interchange of your looks, which served likewise for messengers to tell your tales betwixt° you! And yet I cannot deem but that this love so enraged his courage against Brandagedeon, as otherwise I may think he had not done so well.[388]

    But coming into the place, he addressed himself towards Brandagedeon, both of them now being in a readiness.[389] The king, at this time very sorrowful to see the new knight in his first battle to endanger himself upon a giant and would have talked with Artimodoro about this matter, but the wise man gave no answer. And to the end, not to discover more than was behoveful,° he conveyed himself out of the king's sight. So the king held still his opinion of the young knight's weakness till the issue disproved his thought.

    For in the career,° when the two knights met in the middest° of the tiltyard, the giant's spear burst upon Rosicleer's headpiece, no more moving him with the blow than if he had struck against a wall. But Rosicleer, hurling at the breast of Brandagedeon, overthrew him and his horse to the ground; the horse, in the fall, bruising the giant's shoulder that his knights were fain to carry him out of the press. Whereat all the standers-by° with great admiration beheld Rosicleer, every man being a prophet: as his heart gave him that Rosicleer would prove the best

---

[383] The comparison to the cock is added. The rooster's pride was legendary, as developed in folktales and animal fables.
[384] Rather than finding a timely moment, in *Espejo*, the giant is overjoyed by the prospect of fighting Rosicleer.
[385] God's blessing is absent from the source.
[386] This sentence is discussed in the introduction in relation to the excision of the reference to the goddess Diana.
[387] Tyler addresses the narrator's words to Rosicleer and then to Olivia; the audience is the implied audience in *Espejo*.
[388] 'But Lord . . . done so well' replaces a Spanish sentence that describes Rosicleer's extreme emotion when he notices Olivia looking at him.
[389] Details of the preparations for the battle are omitted.

250 knight in the world, seeing that at his first encounter in tilt, having never had to-do° with any knight before, he had overthrown so mighty a giant.

The king now thought that Rosicleer had well amended the great corsie° which he had taken at his knights' disgrace, and the other knights were glad to have that huge monster rid away, bolder and willinger° valiantly to adventure themselves against Rosicleer than against a giant. And their courage was the more for the richness of the tent which had inveigled their covetous minds to venture the purchase.

But as the knights entered to joust with him, he overthrew them all, being more than a hundred knights, without that any man was able to sit the second journey. Then the king's knights entered, by name Brandaristes, Brandidarte, Allamades, the Princes Argiles and Orgiles,
260 Don Brunio, Prince of Numidia, and other, all which he threw down so lightly° as that they might not turn one course more that day.[390] Some held more tack with him, as you shall hear hereafter but by the way.[391]

The king, turning to his lords, spoke on this wise:°

'Truly, my lords, if I had not myself seen the valorous deeds of this knight, I should hardly have credited another, so incredible the truth is that one should work such masteries. I would the jousts were ended that I might see this knight unarmed to know him and honour him as is reason'.

'True it is', answered his nobles, 'and for his valour there is not so puissant a prince in the world, but that he shall have cause to be glad of his service'.

270 This was a breathing time for Rosicleer, but yet I am persuaded that it was no playing time although no enemy appeared. For he had a greater conflict within his bones than he professed outwardly, and therefore, his heart, neither fully assured nor yet in danger, gazed upon the beauty of Olivia. Whereby the fire, entering closely by the veins, wasted and consumed his flesh sooner than he felt the flame or could think of remedy. But better considering that he was within the compass of Love's seigniory,° and that his matter was to be tried at the great assize° in Love's dominion, he took better advisement to alter it to an action upon the case of covenant against his mistress, the matter arising upon exchange of looks, as you have heard. And for this cause he entertained Sergeant Hope to be his lawyer and feed diverse others to assist him. But Master Despair, an old stager, had won the day of him had not the whole bench, and especially the
280 Chief Justice Desert, stayed° upon a demur,° which relieved much Rosicleer's courage and made him look more freshly upon Hope to find out better evidence for recovery of his suit. But as Rosicleer thus pled° his cause at the bar, so gentle Cupid attended upon his mistress, faithfully serving him and beating into her head the remembrance of his acts and the beauty of his personage that, the windows of her desire being set wide open, she viewed her fill, wishing yet to see his face, thereby to comfort herself if his visage were answerable to his virtue.

Now, Don Silverio, with an envious eye minding to interrupt this medley, provoked Rosicleer to the lists, which Rosicleer refused not.[392] Rosicleer shook somewhat in his saddle, but yet without danger of falling. And Don Silverio, with his courser, tumbled to the ground, so evil entreated as that he was fain to forsake the lists.[393] The Princess Olivia, remembering his former
290 importunity, was nothing aggrieved, thinking thereby his suit to have slaked, the rather to delight in her new champion.

By this time, the greater part of the afternoon was spent, and very few remained in that place which durst° ride a course with Rosicleer, albeit the number of knights were more than 3000. But last of all, Bargandel and Liriamandro, willing to prove themselves upon the new knight with great courage, which the sight of their mistresses caused in them, rode both against

---

[390] Prince Argiles is added to the company by Tyler.
[391] 'Some held . . . the way' is added.
[392] Don Silverio's actions are amplified in *Espejo*, which detracts attention from Rosicleer.
[393] Descriptions of the knights' appearances are omitted throughout the chapter.

Rosicleer. And in their way, as they two strove who should be first, Bargandel, giving the spurs to his horse, ran against Rosicleer. Bargandel, in his race, hit so strongly that his spear flew in pieces, but Rosicleer, knowing Bargandel by a device that he had and mindful of his former courtesy, when he came near him, raised up the end of his spear and rode by without touching of Bargandel. Bargandel, not feeling his adversary, thought that he had missed his rest, and therefore, taking another spear for the re-encounter, he rode again towards Rosicleer. But Rosicleer did as he did before, whereby he clearly perceived the knight's intent to be for to spare him. And waxing mad angry, he avoided the place. Presently stepped in the Prince Liriamandro, to whom likewise Rosicleer so behaved himself as unto Bargandel, albeit himself was well stirred with these shocks.

Liriamandro, as mad as Bargandel to find a friend without occasion, and not knowing his meaning, rode after Bargandel, where both of them departed to disguise themselves, thinking to beguile the knight if peradventure° he had had some knowledge of them. Not long after the trumpets blew the retreat and the jousts should have ended, when these two knights entered with yellow plumes° and gilded armour, their horse trappings all of yellow. And parting company, the one of them ran against Rosicleer, whom he met so strongly that their spears flew in pieces, neither of them being unhorsed. Whereat all the people were dismayed, for no knight that day but was overthrown of as many as Rosicleer had encountered. But these two knights rode again the second time, and as with more choler, so with fiercer stomachs they met. But Rosicleer turned with his horse more than four paces backwards, having much ado to bring him forward. And the strange knight lost his stirrups and fell to the ground with his horse over him. His companion took his room° and ran twice against Rosicleer, neither of them losing their seats. But at the third encountry,° he fell to the ground as his fellow did. Rosicleer, a little diseased° in his saddle, recovered lightly.°

The yellow knights, thus overthrown, mounted on their horses to return the way which they had come, sore displeasant° at the little harm they had done unto Rosicleer. But they beshrewed° themselves for the further attempting of his acquaintance, and musing who it should be, they remembered themselves of the young gentleman Rosicleer and of his great prowess whereto themselves were privy,° thinking that perhaps it might be he; but yet because of his young years they removed this thought again, and could not well judge who he was.

Then, the king commanded every knight to leave off, at which the noise of the instruments were heard so loud that the whole place rang of the sound thereof.[394] Olivia now minded to descend with the other ladies, wherefore the knights and other princes flocked together to give their attendance, among whom Rosicleer, as forward as the best in good will, presented himself unto his mistress, which pleased her not a little.[395]

Entering into the great court of the palace, they there alighted, where the king welcomed them, making several tokens of courtesy to every one. And coming to Rosicleer, he desired him to be at his appointment for that night, for that he had great desire to see him unarmed. All the rest gladly obeyed, but Rosicleer, with his beaver° shut, requested his majesty of pardon for that it behoved him to disarm himself in his tent till the wise man had permitted the contrary. And so saying, he took his leave of the king, entering into his tent where he found the wise Artimodoro, which with two pages abided his coming. When Rosicleer was within, they drew the curtains so close that Rosicleer was not seen of any, and then helped to unarm him. After the tables were covered, and the board° was furnished of all delicacies which Artimodoro had thought on, the wise man himself being both cook and cater°. Rosicleer, sitting down, gave him hearty thanks for his good provision, but indeed his stomach was full with the Princess Olivia, which had so possessed his entrails that the dainty dishes did a not whit° delight his appetite.[396]

---

[394] The publication of the events throughout the city of London is excised.
[395] The degree to which Olivia is impressed by him is not recounted in *Mirror*.
[396] The metaphorical language of love and appetite is added by Tyler.

During this time, the princes and the knights which supped with the king highly extolled Rosicleer's worthiness, each of them being desirous to know him, for they all judged him to be of high parentage. Thus was this night bestowed till the day came, wherein they were to expect fresh matter of discourse and table talk.

CHAPTER 33

An adventure which chanced in King Oliverio's court

The next day, after divine service finished, the king invited to breakfast all the knights. And that done, took his place in that order as you have heard before, looking that some strange knight should joust with the new knight. Now, when the place was peopled with both gentle and ungentle, and that the Princess Olivia was placed on her scaffold, in came Rosicleer, mounted upon his courser, and vaunted himself as joyously before his mistress as if he had not feared the skirmish with ten giants. But that which liked the princess best was a conceit° devised in the pencel° of his spear, being a burning torch, the wax dropping from it, signifying thereby the misery of lovers, with this posy underneath in Roman letters: '*Extinguo* and *Extinguor*'.[397]

After Rosicleer was thus entered, many strong and valiant knights such as had not jousted the day before desired to try themselves upon the new knight, especially Albalaxes, King of Mauritania, who upon hope to be lord of the rich tent, took a great spear and with all his force ran against Rosicleer.[398] But Rosicleer was not taken so tardy in the receipt, but that he met the valiant pagan with such strength as horse and man tumbled to the ground. Rosicleer rode on, somewhat troubled with this encountry°.

And ere° he was well set in his saddle, there ran against him another pagan, Lord of Busia, but Rosicleer finely unhorsed him, and in the same course overthrew four others that there was not a knight left to dare him. At this time, he tarried sometime, awaiting for new comers° in, but there was none.[399] Only at a corner of the lists, he saw a huge giant in white armour upon a great courser with a hoarse and disdainful voice, commanding the people to make him room. And not far from this giant, a gentlewoman upon a palfrey in strange attire much different from ours. Her face was all bedewed with tears as if the giant had used violence towards her.

The giant, approaching to the place where the king stood, made no reverence, but the gentlewoman kneeled down, saying:

'Know, most excellent prince, that the renown of this court hath brought me from far countries hither chiefly for one cause, which the wickedness of this giant hath now made two, the original of them both you shall here now under one. In the farther part of the East near unto the great Cataya, there governeth a princess named Julia, as yet but young of years, but not young for handsomeness, being now, as it were, in the pride of all her beauty.[400] Her father was a right cunning magician, instructing her so perfectly in his skill as now therein there are few comparable. For since his death, she herself divined by her knowledge that she should be prisoner to two giants, and should be enlarged° by one knight which should fight with them both. For the case should stand thus: that if her knight were vanquished, she should as perpetually captivate° be at their command; otherwise to be at liberty if they were yielded.

---

[397] The sentence describing the device, '*Extinguo* and *Extinguor*' (quench and extinguish), is added to the English.
[398] In *Espejo*, Rosicleer parades before the assembled, as many marvel at his appearance and wonder about his identity.
[399] 'new comers in', signifies new people to come in.
[400] Cataya: Cathay, a name for China

   In subsequent books of the romance, it is revealed that Julia is from Gran Tartaria (*Espejo*, II.249) and that she is a lady in waiting of Lindabrides, Princess of Tartary (*Espejo*, VI.158).

Herself foreseeing this, and not finding who he might be, hath provided by her knowledge not to be beguiled. For by her art, she hath made this sword, which no knight may ever unsheathe, but only he which must fight with the two giants for her liberty. And besides, the sword is such as without it, it were a hard adventure; but with it, the knight may boldly venture on his foes.[401] The sword she made and kept close, till time these two giants, by night assailing her, got the lordship of her person, after which time by a trusty servant she caused this sword to be conveyed unto me with this command: to travel for her sake in all princes' courts and to seek out the knight which could and should maintain her quarrel. Three years are passed since I undertook this enterprise, and within this three months, landing in an island towards the west, after a long journey to no purpose, it was my fortune to meet this giant, Candramarte.[402] There, making him partaker° of my suit, he requested to prove the adventure, which I granted. But when he could not draw it out, being covetous of the sword, he denied it me again, saying:

"For so much as you go to the King of England's court, there to seek some knight which will do his devoir° in your mistress's behalf, no man shall attempt the adventure of the sword but he shall first try his forces upon me. And if by him I be vanquished or slain, let him take the sword. Otherwise, I will withhold it from all men".

'With this, he promised to bear me company, and I of two evils determined to choose the less. Albeit at this instant, I am in greater extremity by reason of this giant's wrong done to me and my mistress's thraldom.[403] This is the necessity which drove me hither, and I am humbly to beseech your majesty discreetly to weigh my cause and to give remedy by your subjects as you best may'.

Candramarte, all this time standing by, in the end averred her tale to be true, and further intimated to the knights and princes that seeing he could not draw out the sword, there should no man be master of it but by the mastery of him. But sayeth he:

'I will defend it against any knight which shall demand it'.

All the knights beheld the sword with the rich hangers° as the fairest which they had seen, but the king, somewhat angry at the giant's rudeness towards the gentlewoman, said to him in this manner:

'Candramarte, thou have done ill to take this sword from the gentlewoman, for as it seems Julia made it not for thee. And thy pride is over-great to suppose that none in the world will demand it of thee'.

The giant, angrily looking upon the king as though his eyes would have flown out of his visage, said to the king:

'Demand it then thyself, Sir King, or set any of thy knights to ask it, and I will then make answer unto thee how rashly thou have taken upon thee to correct me'.

These speeches were delivered with so high a voice by the giant that all the knights which were in the compass heard it, but no man spoke a word, so that the king's choler increased both against the giant and his own subjects. And I must bear with them, for the giant was great and tall and as hardy as a lion, and no man living very near matchable° for so good fortune. But yet, there was within the lists both a hardier and more fortunate knight; even then, good Rosicleer, which overhearing his indiscreet talk unto the king, coming near unto the giant, took him up in this sort:

'Candramarte, content thyself and learn to know unto whom thou speak, for I tell thee that King Oliverio hath such knights in his court as can make thee amend thy rusticity, though thou were more untaught than thou are. And for that thou shall not mistrust me, behold I am the last and the least of them yet as one which desires to serve him with the most. In his name and in behalf of the gentlewoman, I charge thee surrender the sword unto the gentlewoman. Or if

---

[401] 'And besides . . . his foes' is added.
[402] The specifics of her journey and the knights she encountered are omitted.
[403] The giant's battle to win the sword is not described.

thou will not that, do thou take that part of the field which shall best like thee, for in this quarrel I will either kill or be killed'.

With a terrible countenance Candramarte stared upon Rosicleer, as who should say: 'Dares thou speak so boldly?'

And perceiving him to be but a young knight, which he noted by his white armour, in great scorn he answered thus:

'I see well, foolish knight, thou have not been long acquainted with the burden of armour, for if thou were in thy kind and had well weighed the success of combatants thou would shake every joint of thee to behold me. But thy ignorance makes thee leap beyond thy lash,° and thrusteth thee forward to thine own decay. But seeing thou have made choice thyself of thy deathsman,° let us go to the battle, for I would not but that thou should repent thee of thy foolishness'.[404]

So Candramarte broached° his horse with the spurs, and Rosicleer did the like, which appeased the king's displeasure that he knew not how to recompense his forwardness in doing him pleasure. Albeit it may be if he loved Rosicleer, that he somewhat mistrusted the event because the giant was big and Rosicleer unexercised in arms, and that which was chiefest,° without a sword.[405] But for remedy thereto, he caused a sword of his own to be fetched, wherewith he charged a knight to deliver it to Rosicleer with this commandment: that seeing in his name he hath so well fitted Candramarte for his answer, and for that cause was to take the battle upon him, now he prayed him to wear this sword likewise for his sake, which he would warrant to be good. The knight did his message accordingly, but Rosicleer, making his excuse gently, returned the sword with this answer:

'I humbly thank the king's majesty for so high a present, the not receiving whereof cometh not of any refusal, but by a promise which I have made, as his majesty can testify, never to wear sword but if I win it. And therefore, I crave pardon at his majesty's hands for this discourtesy, otherwise I were greatly to blame if I thought not myself honoured by being girt in a king's weapon'.

The messenger delivered Rosicleer's answer in the same words as Rosicleer had given it out. So the king — somewhat lamenting the knight's wilfulness, as he thought weaponless to wage battle with so abled° a warrior — mused upon this and for the rest commended him to God. All the standers-by° were sorry to see the new knight so courageous as to fight with a giant without a weapon. And especially the beautiful Princess Olivia could not but be angered at the new knight's jeopardous adventure, as if she had had no small title or claim to his person.[406]

CHAPTER 34

A dangerous battle between Candramarte and Rosicleer

As they prepared themselves to the career,° the people gathered together to see this dangerous fight between the new knight and the giant Candramarte.[407] And they, as glad to see the issue upon their light coursers, with their spears in their rests, so violently hurled against the other that the ground yielded under their feet. The force of their strong arms joined with the fury of their horse in such wise° that the giant made small shivers° of his great spear and constrained Rosicleer to take his pillow on his horseback.[408] But the new knight gave the giant so mighty a

---

[404] 'But thy . . . deathsman' is added.
[405] The king prays for Rosicleer's victory in the source.
[406] In the Spanish text, they marvel at this behaviour, while here they express sorrow and Olivia mistrusts his ability.
[407] *Espejo* attributes the qualities of Spanish architecture to the English court, recounting how they gather in the great plaza of the city of London.
[408] 'to take his pillow' signifies that he made Rosicleer lie down as though on a pillow in his bed

blow that he made his stirrups fall from him, and quickly closing with the giant, he drew him by force from the saddle and threw him to the ground, so that he somewhat bruised the giant's shoulder bone, and presently would have turned again upon Candramarte to have made a dispatch of all, but that the giant, being of great courage and enforcing himself to endure the remnant, got on his legs, and addressing his shield before him with his falchion° in his hand, awaited Rosicleer. For so soon as Candramarte was down, Rosicleer then alighted and sent his horse to his tent. Rosicleer, now being on foot, made towards Candramarte.

Candramarte first assailed Rosicleer with these words:

'What knight thinks thou to fight with me without a sword? What if thou had a better than this, which I wear of the Queen Julia's making, were all the gods able thereby to warrant thee out of my hands? No. And thou shall dearly repay me the pain which thou have put me to in this fall'.

Rosicleer, coming near, answered:

'Candramarte, spare not to do thy uttermost, but cease thy reviling.° For God, which gave me might to overthrow thee, will also give me power and strength without other weapon to subdue thee. And although I bring no sword with me, yet I hope in the living God that thine shall profit me and serve my turn'.

Then the giant was in such a rage that the fury of his choler with the blustering of his breath issued through the sightes° of his equimas,° in like sort as the smoke issueth out of a furnace.[409] And his second assault was with his falchion,° with both his hands fetched compass-wise° against Rosicleer, which seeing the blow coming with such force forward, lifted up his shield, therein to receive the stroke. But the blow was so mighty that it hewed the shield asunder,° and descending upon the headpiece, made Rosicleer abate° his looks and bow his knees for safeguard to his fall. The giant doubled upon him but Rosicleer never yet daunted, and recovering his courage almost against the hare,° stepped aside that the giant's blow was all in vain. And being somewhat out of charity with the first, he determined no more to receive any such counterbuffs,° so that a half hour after the combat had lasted, the giant might never hit him one blow for all that he could do. For Rosicleer was so deliver° and quick that he lightly° avoided them. Candramarte, seeing that Rosicleer would not abide by it, chased him up and down, and Rosicleer led the giant a course likewise; but so that the king and all the lookers-on judged that if the battle should endure long, that the new knight might never escape the death. Rosicleer assayed° many times to couple with the giant and to pull the falchion° out of his hands, but Candramarte was so wily and so well advised of the words which Rosicleer spoke in the beginning of their battle, that he either kept himself aloof off, or in his pursuit bore the point of his falchion° before him.

But by this means the battle continued to the no little discontentment of Rosicleer. For although his armour was such that no weapon might wound him on his body, yet was he sore bruised with travail,° and his bones were in a manner softened with the weariness he had felt for the length of the battle. As the one gave lightly,° so the other pursued as eagerly, but, as I say, never fastening a right down blow, but as he might overthwart° and endlong slipping his blows, and in his pride boasting out these and such like speeches:

'O, knight, how costly shall the challenge of Queen Julia's sword be unto thee, if for it thou must exchange thy life? Had thou not been better never to have been at this marte?° But now know what valour Candramarte is of, for not all the world are of that credit with me as to bail thee out of my hands'.

For the fitting of his action whereunto, he would shake his heavy falchion° so gallantly and roar so terribly that every man took Candramarte rather for a tyrant in a tragedy than a jester

---

[409] Although the *OED* defines 'sightes' as 'a visor' (IV.13.b.), the context here suggests the sides of the equimas, which would support the idea that the equimas is either a helmet, or more specifically the part of the helmet which covers the mouth, hence the allusion to a furnace.

in a comedy.[410] And Rosicleer's friends with their pitiful looks bemoaned the poor Rosicleer as if he had already tasted of most cruel and bitter death in his green youth.[411]

Amongst them, the fair and beautiful Princess Olivia, although as yet altogether unacquainted with Rosicleer, was a spectator neither careless° nor curious, but as one without hope, she only wished well to Rosicleer, whose bruises were as deep-set in her sides as they were imprinted in Rosicleer's flesh.[412] And every wagging of the most huge and monstrous Candramarte's weapon struck a salt tear from her fair eyes. So was she estranged from herself and altogether become another man's.[413] The new knight, eyeing his mistress, became so desperate that he fully resolved either to close with Candramarte and wring the weapon from him, or to die upon him. And watching the opportunity, when the falchion° was over the giant's head, bending his body, [he] stepped within the giant that the giant had no other resistance but to fell him to the ground with his elbows. This was no great misfortune to Rosicleer, for albeit he was fain to bow his knees by the thrust of the giant's elbow, yet, couching his body closely, his chance was so good as to fasten upon the hilts of Queen Julia's sword, which he drew out, the scabbard remaining at the giant's side. Rosicleer, now being seized of the sword, stepped from Candramarte and called upon him on this wise:°

'Candramarte, now thou shall see who shall have the worst bargain of Queen Julia's sword, since on even hands we shall try this combat'.

And with this, remembering the giant's former pride, he laid at the giant so thick and so sure that in short space the blood ran from the giant in more than ten places, for the sword was exceeding sharp, and Rosicleer as fell° and venomous.[414]

Now may you think that the maiden, seeing the sword borne by the knight, was the gladdest woman in the earth, and that the king with other princes and knights thanked God heartily for providing Rosicleer of a weapon the sooner to put end to the battle. But the giant, assaulted so sore by Rosicleer and wounded so dangerously, began wholly to mistrust the prophecy of the sword and to despair of the victory.[415] And as in such cases wanhope° is adventurous — so his armour being rent, the habergeon° unmailed,° and all the riveting out of order — for that cause, the giant would needs put the trial of the challenge upon one blow.[416] When this blow was reached, as far as the giant might to have descended with more violence upon Rosicleer's headpiece, Rosicleer, being more quick then he, met the blow crossways that he cut off both the giant's arms hard by the elbows. The giant thus maimed,° yelling out a loathsome cry, reviled and railed on Rosicleer as a man distraught. And that which most increased his pain was not the torment of his disfigured arms, but either the shame of the victory or the envy at Rosicleer. But Rosicleer, making little account of him, took the scabbard from his side and so left him. Candramarte still followed, blaspheming and cursing both God and man. And when he could neither be his own executioner nor procure another to take the pains, swore, that for sparing his death, he would devise all the mischief he might against Rosicleer, and that he would practise his death also if possibly he could invent the means. But truly, if I had been in Rosicleer's case, I should not have been so strange,° seeing that both it should have been the giant's last request and so little encumbrance towards me.

But the king, princes, and knights were so joyous of the victory against the giant as they bore countenance of more joy outwardly than they had erst° received, everyone openly desiring to

---

[410] The theatrical imagery is added.
[411] The substitution of 'friends' for 'the king and all the high princes and knights who were watching the battle' makes no sense since Rosicleer is an unknown knight and has no friends amongst the spectators.
[412] The medical metaphors are added to the English text.
[413] 'And every .... another man's' replaces an exposition of Candramarte's strength.
[414] The recollection of the giant's pride as an impetus to battle is added by Tyler. She also neglects to describe his fear and self-doubt, which result from Rosicleer's renewed attack.
[415] His mistrust of the prophecy is not mentioned in *Espejo*.
[416] The sense of hopelessness is added.

see him unarmed, but chiefly Bargandel and Liriamandro, being in some jealousy of the knight, whom they had found a friend ere° they looked for, supposing that peradventure° he was Rosicleer, of whom the sudden adventure in the sea had bereft them.[417]

And Queen Julia's gentlewoman, seeing the combat tried and the adventure of the sword achieved, concluding thereby that this was he for whom she had made so long a journey, saluted him courteously with this ambassade:°

'Now that it is evident, noble knight, that you are the person for whose help this sword was framed° by my mistress, I am to certify that my Lady greeteth you by me and giveth you warning that for her sake you must maintain the fight with two brave giants, jointly combatant against you only. For this she hath sent you this sword, the commendation whereof, albeit not unknown, lieth in the continual proof, which she requesteth you never to forsake, for it will much further you in your enterprises. Whereto, I beseech you, give credit and deal effectually as she hath hope in you. But now give me the sword that I may bear it to the king and the other princes that they may justify the truth of my former avouch°'.

So Rosicleer delivered the sword into her hands with the sheath, which the gentlewoman brought before the king and the knights then present, which all attempted the pulling out, but could not do it, as if the scabbard had been a piece of the same metal whereof the sword was and not severed by edge or tool, which made them all confess that to the new knight it was proposed, and to him appertained the fight with the two giants for the franchising° of Queen Julia.[418]

The king redelivered the sword into the gentlewoman's hands and bade her yield it again to Rosicleer, which she did. And taking her leave of him, received this for answer: that he recommended himself unto her good grace, heartily thanking her for so great care over him as to provide a sword, whereof he had need as herself can witness. And for the rest, he promised not to fail her, as he was true knight to God and the world. The gentlewoman, with this recommend,° galloped away as fast as her palfrey might carry her.[419]

The whilst, Candramarte's knights removed their lord out of that place into his tent, whence afterward, with great grief for his sore maim,° they conveyed him into his island, wherein having settled himself, as mindful of his oath, he never left from imagining of crafty means and coining new policies to bring Rosicleer to his death.

When Candramarte was carried into his tent, Rosicleer, mounting upon his horse, took a great spear in his hand and stood at the list's end, thinking that some knight would come against him. But they were all so schooled with the sight of this last victory, that never a knight showed himself.[420] Wherefore the king commanded to sound the trumpet to proceed unto the disposing of the rewards for their travail.°[421] A herald demanding aloud who had done best, they all referred the prizes to Rosicleer.

The king would not contend with them, but sayeth he:[422]

'I will that my daughter have the bestowing of them where she best liketh as touching this tourney'.

She, with much shamefastness° (which her coloured cheeks bewrayed°), accepted the charge, and taking the crown with the collar in her hand, she caused the new knight to be called before

---

[417] Their jealousy is added, as analyzed in the introduction.
[418] Rosicleer's unique ability to free the sword links him to great romance heroes such as King Arthur, who was identified as the true king because he was the only person who could remove the sword from the stone.
[419] 'received this . . . this recommend' is added.
[420] Whereas in *Espejo* they are fearful, *Mirror* places the emphasis on the lessons learned from watching Rosicleer fight.
[421] In *Espejo*, the noise created by the great multitude of musical instruments causes the ground of the plaza to tremble.
[422] The source specifies that the king's decision is motivated by a desire to see the jewels attributed with greater honour.

her, who, burning in love towards her no less than she was servant in liking towards him, dismounted at the first call. And between the two Princes Bargandel and Liriamandro mounted up the scaffold where the beautiful princess was, before whom he appeared with greater fear arising of his conceit° concerning his indignity than erst° attached him in the fight with Candramarte without a weapon.

The two princes, coming before Olivia, made their humble obeisance, and Rosicleer kneeled down. The princess, with a good grace bending to every one of them, spoke to Rosicleer:

'You know, new knight, what charge the king, my father, hath laid upon me. Although far more honourable than I am able to sustain, yet by me assumed neither to resist his will nor yet against my desire, for it is commendable of itself to be a commender° of virtue and never too much may I commend it. The charge is that with mine° own hands I should distribute these prizes according as my own fancy° leadeth me to deem of every man's travail° and valiancy.° The delivery of these jewels were nothing hard nor doubtful, but the disposing is more than hard, because it pertaineth to judgement in deeds of arms, whereunto my sex is not sufficiently abled.°[423] Nevertheless, Sir Knight, as your pains have been greatest (thereto witnesseth this whole multitude), so your prowess in my judgement so much assureth on your part that without doing wrong to any of these princes and knights, I may with good reason confer them upon you. For this, if I know to do right unto whom I ought, it is meet that you do away your helmet. And since your deeds discover who you are, it is no reason that you cover yourself any longer'.

When the princess had thus said, Rosicleer, not having power to excuse himself, unlaced this helmet, which being put off, his face seemed so beautiful by the heat and travail° of the armour, which raised a fresh red in his cheeks that it struck them all in a maze.° And none of those which saw him, considering his fairness with his age, but rather judged him an angel of heaven than a mortal knight.

When the Princess Olivia saw him so fair, as already Love had made a wrack° in the most secret part of her heart by the view of his knighthood, so now the same breach being made wider by the second assault in his beautiful looks, Love entered with banner displayed and finding no resistance, took possession wholly of her heart, and swore all that he found to be his true prisoners.[424] Thus lost she her liberty. And yet, with the best courage that a woman might, she framed out a countenance of great freedom in this manner:

'You needed not by your favour, Sir Knight, to have been ashamed of your face. And yet such as it is, it is far inferior to your manhood; but this is beyond the compass of my commission. Now, come you near and receive at my hands the glory of your worthiness, which your good fortune yeildeth you'.[425]

Rosicleer, approaching very near, kneeled down and the princess put the collar about his neck and the crown upon his head. When the princess had so done, with a little stay° between, Rosicleer took the crown from his own head.[426] And as he was on his knees, said unto the princess:

'Most excellent princess, for the sovereign grace you have showed me, I will remain yours, henceforth to serve you loyally as a poor recompense for so rich a benefit.[427] And as I do receive

---

[423] The additions of 'Although far ... I commend it', above, and 'The delivery ... sufficiently abled' increase Olivia's role in the award ceremony. Significantly, her gendered modesty topos parallels Tyler's comments in the preface, as investigated in the introduction.
[424] The added allegory recalls Petrarch's *Rime* 140, translated by Thomas Wyatt ('The long love that in my thought doth harbor') and Henry Howard ('Love, that doth reign and live within my thought').
[425] Her speech is greatly amplified; in the source she commands him to come closer to allow the assembled to take pleasure his glory provided by his greatness.
[426] In *Espejo*, his feelings for Olivia are alluded to as the narrator explains that he could not determine whether he was on earth or heaven.
[427] In the source, he professes himself to be the most fortunate knight living due to her favour.

this collar as the prize of knighthood in your opinion, so I beseech you to take of me this crown as a testimony of your surpassing beauty in my eye'.

With this, he set the rich crown upon the golden hairs of the Princess Olivia, she being glad of this gift, although somewhat blushing at the words he spoke.

The two princes, Bargandel and Liriamandro, standing by and knowing him to be Rosicleer, whom they had lost in the main° sea, when the ceremonies were finished, went to him, embracing him as goodly as if he had been their own brother, yet courteously challenging him for his unkindness in not making himself known unto them.[428] The King Oliverio, abashed at so great bounty in a knight of so young years, began to think more advisedly of that which the wise Artimodoro had said; from that time he esteemed more highly of the new knight, as you shall hear after this.

But now the noise was so great which the viols made and other instruments that one might not hear another speak, at which time the fair Princess Olivia, with the rich crown upon her head and in her company the knight Rosicleer with the two princes, descended from the scaffold and in great pomp went to the king's palace, the princess leaving them there to take her own lodging. And they all entering the chamber of presence where the king stayed° for them, and after a general welcome, by name taking Rosicleer aside, he said unto him:[429]

'Sir Knight, hither you are very welcome, for I have had great desire to know you. And I would to God, by your stay I might as well be acquainted with you, for by you the honour of my court hath been well upheld'.[430]

'Mighty king', answered Rosicleer, 'I am rather to be born withal if I desire to be your servant, since for the same cause and for to see your court I am come hither'.

The king kissed the knight upon the cheek as tenderly as if he had been his own son, saying:

'Rosicleer, I account more of these words than of the worth of my best city and advise thee well of these speeches, for I am to demand them of thee if thou will not otherwise perform thy promise'.

So, Rosicleer was retained for the king's knight, and all the old courtiers, both princes and knights of great name, ran to embrace Rosicleer with great pleasure unto them to have his company, except only Don Silverio, Prince of Lusitania, whom a jealous thought vexed as towards Rosicleer for that he had unhorsed him in the presence of his lady.[431] But after this order, Rosicleer remained in the English court, where he rested himself till this sudden adventure called him forth, as shall be told you.[432]

CHAPTER 35

A gentlewoman came to the court from the Princess Briana, which made him follow Brandagedeon

The story recounteth that Rosicleer abode many days in King Oliverio's court, well liked and loved of both king and nobles. In which time Rosicleer gave the king the rich tent which the wise Artimodoro had wrought for him, wherein the king took great delight. For although he had many other, both curious° for making and costly for matter, yet had he not seen in his life any either so rich or of so cunning workmanship. So that the king's good will towards Rosicleer

---

[428] Their happiness at discovering him is contrasted with their pain at having lost him in the Spanish romance.

[429] A 'chamber of presence' or 'presence chamber' is the room in which a monarch or other distinguished person receives visitors.

[430] In the source, he desires Rosicleer to remain at court always.

[431] Rosicleer's and the king's great friendship is noted in the Spanish text, effectively opposing Don Silverio's jealousy.

[432] Whereas *Espejo* refers to the contents of the subsequent chapter, *Mirror* addresses the audience directly. The effect is less bookish, more intimate.

increased by Rosicleer's presence, and in that also for his company many other great princes and strange knights remained with the king so long time after that these jousts were ended, which beginning of friendship betwixt° Rosicleer and some of these knights grew in the end to such perfection by his gracious and familiar behaviour, that neither favour of friends nor dread of danger might with their wills sunder° them from this amity.

And if Rosicleer had such power over knights strangers, what had he over the Princess Olivia, being surprised with his love and having engraven° his image so deeply in her imagination that he never departed from her thought but evermore there renewed in her remembrance his knightly deeds and great valour, whereby she made an evident demonstration of his lineage as if naught else had been enemy to her purpose. But this fair princess now so languished with the torment of this amorous thought and pleasant liking of her love Rosicleer, that now the conversation of her gentlewomen was irksome, and to be solitary did most content her, forbearing withal both her rest in sleep and her sustenance in feeding. In which melancholy she was so far gone without the feeling of her own disease,° as that nothing might ease her highness but Rosicleer's presence, which bred her greater bale° in his absence, by the grief galling her most to think that seeing he was a stranger in the land, he would ere° long return to his own country.

One day, casting herself upon her bed and tossing such like things in her fancy,° she sent out many a sorrowful sigh as the forerunners of this which followeth:

'Oh, Love, Love! How well it eased me before times to hear lovers mourn, to read their strange fits, to see figured before me the variable success of their attempts with the fearful frights of thy subjects and captives! Oh, how well at ease was I, when, being far from the fire and out of danger, I might laugh and look on and warm me by their flame![433] But now, not so free nor clean devoid of thought, I rue the little pity I took upon their pain and am therefore scorched not without desert. O, Love! Love, by whom not the feeblest only, but the sturdiest also and stoutest° are unable to quench this fire, if it please thee to kindle it! Alas, do not the wise men seem fools and the hardy cowards, if it be thy pleasure? And dare any man confess the truth in this his passion? And are not all like sick men beguiled, call sour sweet, pain pleasure, bale° bliss, grief gladness, and the losing of their late liberty the enlarging of their new franchise to content their fancies?° And thou, unfortunate Olivia, are thou princess of Great Britain, the daughter of King Oliverio, the woman sued° unto by so pliant petitioners, both princes and knights of great courage, whom thou have all refused? No, assuredly. But thou are some base and mean gentlewoman if the sight of one only knight not known unto thee hath so dimmed thy understanding that reason is become no more defensible. Where is thy late pride, Olivia? Where is thy ancient pleasure? Where are thy haughty looks?[434] Where lies the charter of thy liberty? Where is the estimation of thy beauty? Where is the excellency of thy estate? Oh, the miserable and ever changeable state of man, like unto the herbs or flowers which the morning's dew refresheth, the noon's heat opresseth, and the night shade encloseth in as the grave doth our bodies, being a lively moral of our mortality![435] Alas, Rosicleer, my father thinks he hath made a great purchase by thy being here, but I would to God I might be as sure heir to this purchase, as I am otherwise certain to repent thy coming hither! And yet, whatsoever the event be, my love commands in me the contrary. For is it not better for me to see Rosicleer and to acknowledge the goodness of God towards man in enabling of him to the achievement of such wonders, where by and by the enjoying of his sight I receive such pleasure than never to have seen him, though I lose the hope of augmenting my state? And truly befall what may, in spite of Fortune's rancour, I will stay° myself upon this choice and will not exchange it'.[436]

---

[433] The fire imagery is added.
[434] In the source, she muses on the absence of her elevated thoughts, not her 'haughty looks'.
[435] 'as the grave . . . our mortality' is added.
[436] The allusion to Fortune replaces her five-line lament of pain and hopelessness.

Very wise was the Princess Olivia, and as the times afforded, very well learned; but yet these speeches proceeded rather of her passion than of advised reason or good reading.[437] And the like combat to this of contrary thoughts Rosicleer endured, entertaining in his heart the counterfeit° of the princess in that secret contemplation whereof he was diligently occupied, imagining thereof the bravery of her beauty and the great desert in her to be best beloved. But as again to the princess, in all this subjection to Love and his laws, her honesty is chiefly to be noted, which for all that both the remedy was above her capacity and the pain likely to overcome her patience, yet bore out the brunts thereof in such modesty, rather by sufferance than striving withal, that neither could Rosicleer ever assure himself of her liking, nor any of her servants wring it out by the manner of her disease°.

Rosicleer was as close,° which in him was the occasion of farther trouble, for coveting to be alone the better to rejoice himself and to enter more narrowly into the search of his own ability with the likelihood of his suit, he stumbled as in a blind way upon two blocks so placed as that if he avoided the one, he must needs hit his shin against the other. For this was one: if he revealed not his grief, or not made her privy° to his estate, there was naught to prefer him before another knight. Again, the other was, if he laid open his race, his supplication would lack succour. Now, how could he with candlelight not hazard a fall upon the one or the other?[438] For he was persuaded that Prince Edward, brother to the Princess Olivia, was his father, wherefore the near kindred was to be concealed if he looked for help, and yet the concealment was the only debarring of his hope. In this conflict he did nothing but afflict himself, neither daring to discover his malady nor minded to dissemble it altogether.

By so much the more in worse case than the princess was, as the infirmity of her sex did lessen her pain by yielding at the first. And the magnanimity of his courage to have the mastery did in the end make the deeper impression in his flesh, like as in nature the hardest fight is between the hardiest, and sooner shall the cannon shot deface the high towers than break through a rampire° of wool or flax: and so the issue proved in him.[439]

But being one day with the king and the other noble princes in the great palace to beguile his solemn conceits° which overcame his night's rest, he saw entering a gentlewoman well apparelled, which when she came near, bowing humbly to the king, said as followeth:

'God preserve your majesty, most noble King of the Great Britain. The Princess Briana, my mistress and wife unto the Prince Edward your son, with the remembrance of her duty, craveth to be certified by your good grace what you have heard of her lord and husband, for she never saw him since his first arrival into Hungary. My Lady also by me greeteth the Princess Olivia, your daughter, unto whom she commanded me to deliver a coffer of jewels. But coming to land on the English coast, I was set upon by a great giant named Brandagedeon, as I hear, who taking the coffer from me, bade me come to this court, here to tell a new knight which once unhorsed him that he would make answer to none but to him as concerning the coffer, and that for him he would stay° at the shore, there to make satisfaction according as he was charged.[440] I beseech your good highness, therefore, to send that new knight in your daughter's quarrel against this giant'.

Rosicleer, having known this gentlewoman amongst those which attended upon the Princess Briana, his mother, in the Monastery of the River and that she had to name Arinda, was glad to have the opportunity offered to serve the Princesses Olivia and Briana, and therefore rising from where he sat, he came before the king, to whom he said:

'Sir, seeing it is Rosicleer whom this gentlewoman seeketh, and that Brandagedeon hath sent for me, I beseech your majesty to give me licence to go in these affairs, for it is out of reason to forslack° such worthy service to two so noble princesses'.[441]

---

[437] The comment on women's education, 'Very wise . . . good reading', is added.
[438] 'Now, how . . . the other?' is added.
[439] Tyler adds this paragraph, which contemplates female love.
[440] A sentence is omitted in which she explains that she was obliged to leave the coffer with the giant.
[441] In the Spanish, he does not name himself, thereby temporarily keeping his identity hidden from Arinda.

The king, loath of any occasion at all, ministered whereby he should forsake the court, for fear lest his return would not be over-hasty, for he knew well that he was nothing addict to idleness. Yet, seeing his importunity both to answer the challenge and to employ his travail° in the name of these two princesses would not gainsay his purpose, but wished him not to go alone, for that the giant was well manned with above thirty knights. For this cause, Bargandel and Liriamandro, and other princes and knights offered to go in his company, but they could not prevail, for he excused himself with this: that it should redound° to his disworship° if he should take more company than the giant looked for. And by and by he craved pardon to depart to his chamber there to arm himself.

110   The gentlewoman Arinda, well knowing him but for that time suppressing it, while Rosicleer buckled on his armour, went to deliver her message unto the Princess Olivia, unto whom she told that the coffer with jewels was intercepted by a false barrater,° a giant named Brandagedeon, and that the new knight had taken upon him to fetch them again.[442] Which when the princess heard, although she was glad to understand ought from the Princess Briana, yet was she sorrowful when she heard that Rosicleer would leave the city and would go alone thither° where the giant abode° him, for her mind gave her that she should not see Rosicleer in haste. But turning from this, she demanded of the gentlewoman many things in particular touching her lady, so that the gentlewoman stayed with her till Rosicleer, being armed, called upon her.

Then the princess sayeth:

120   'If there be no other remedy, you may go with him.[443] Albeit, tell the knight from me that I had rather the jewels were lost than he should put himself in so great a jeopardy'.

Arinda said she would do her command, and went down to Rosicleer, being already on horseback with his esquire° Telio. She likewise took her palfrey, and they three rode through the city of London, much gazed after by the king and all the knights and ladies which stood in the windows and battlements of the palace, and with great sorrow pitied him to see him go alone, persuading themselves that if Brandagedeon were slain or in danger that his men would rescue him.

CHAPTER 36

A cruel battle between Rosicleer and Brandagedeon with his knights

Rosicleer, being thus accompanied with Arinda and Telio his squire, willed the gentlewoman to guide him on the way to the place where Brandagedeon was. Arinda, knowing him well enough, said:

'Noble Rosicleer, I dare not so do. The giant is fierce and strong and hath with him many knights, which if he have need shall help him, and then shall I see you in peril of your life. Better were it, Rosicleer, that you should leave this enterprise and take the way towards Hungary, there to comfort the sorrowful Princess Briana, which since your departure from the monastery
10   hath never been merry'.

Rosicleer, perceiving well that the gentlewoman knew him, casting his arms about her neck, said unto her:

'Why, how now, Arinda?[444] How is it that you know me and I have not known myself since my coming into this land? But tell me, gentle sister, how the Princess Briana doth, my good Lady, for whose sorrow I am much aggrieved. Albeit, to remedy it, there were no reason in forsaking this enterprise which I have taken in hand to do her service therein. Besides that, I am

---

[442] A description of Arinda's happiness at Rosicleer's willingness to assist her is omitted.
[443] 'If there . . . with him' is added, emphasizing Olivia's reluctant support of the adventure.
[444] The English formulaic greeting is added.

determined not to return into Hungary before I can hear some news of the Prince Edward, whether he be dead or alive'.

'No', sayeth the gentlewoman, 'but let this matter alone, for it were less loss that the two princesses should want the coffer of jewels than that you should hazard your life in winning of it. And more acceptable service shall you do my lady in going to visit her, than in seeking out the giant to fight with him'.

The gentlewoman withal took hold of the bridle reins to have led Rosicleer's horse out of the way, whereat Rosicleer, laughing a good, answered her thus:

'Arinda, I should get a good report in the court of King Oliverio if, for fear of a battle with this giant, I should turn aside from this journey, which for the same cause I have undertaken. If I were certain of more than a thousand deaths, I would not follow thy advice herein, Arinda'.

And so spurring his horse he kept on his way.

The gentlewoman would not importune him further, but led him towards the giant, where not far off they met another gentlewoman on foot weeping very piteously. At her Rosicleer demanded the cause of her grief, which she uttered straightways in these words:

'Oh, Sir Knight, Fortune, Fortune hath frowned on me, so that better welcome should be the death than the daylight!'

Rosicleer yet requested her to speak more plainly and to tell wherein Fortune had wrought her such despite.

'I will gladly', sayeth she. 'And for truth, Sir Knight, I am a gentlewoman belonging to the Queen of Lusitania, which sent me with a brother of mine, a very valiant knight, hither to bring certain jewels for the Princess Olivia, daughter to the King Oliverio, and for the Princess Rodasilva, her own daughter. Now our mishap was such that entering the shore, we hit upon a great and devilish giant, who examining us whither° we went and what we carried in our fardel,° because my brother made no answer, slew him, and putting me from my palfrey, took from me my horse with the fardel,° over and besides with this command to go unto the King Oliverio and to the knights of his court, there to record my complaint against him. Thus have I, my lord, satisfied your request. Now God be with you, for I will on to crave some remedy'.

With this, the gentlewoman parted from them, but Rosicleer, calling to her, said:

'Gentlewoman, so it is that my errand is for the same purpose: to fight with the giant, for the like trespass by him committed against this gentlewoman here with me. If you will return with us, we shall be very glad thereof, and by God's help I shall well quell° that giant's insolency°'.

'What?' said the gentlewoman. 'Do you purpose alone to fight with the giant?'

'Aye, indeed', answered Rosicleer. 'And have hope to revenge this gentlewoman and your brother'.

'God may well give you power so to do, if it please Him', said the gentlewoman, 'but in respect of the giant's strength, it will not sink into my breast that a hundred such knights as you are can chastise him'.

'Well', said Rosicleer, 'if you will go with me you may at leisure, when you see the event, deliberate what to do if ye will not fare you well, for less shall be your hope of remedy in keeping your way as you now do'.

Rosicleer held on, and the gentlewoman, viewing his goodly personage, thereby persuading herself that it were but little loss to turn back with him, determined to prove his good fortune. And as she was not fully assured in her thought, she spoke on this wise:°

'Be not displeased with me but for the love of God, fair knight, have some greater regard of your own safety not to cast yourself away for the recovery of my damage. It is no great matter for me to take some pains in going with you, but it will be some grief to return again laden with a fresh complaint of a new murder. And therefore, for God's sake, let the giant alone'.

Rosicleer said:

'I may not. But seeing you have promised your company, get up behind my squire and cast your care upon God, which will purvey for your ease, as best shall like Him'.

So they four travelled towards the place where the giant's abiding was. And coming near unto the shore, they saw him hard by the water where he sat upon a great horse, and more than thirty knights in a crayer° not far off, as if they purposed to board a tall ship, which was on float in the sea half a mile. Brandagedeon, by and by, knew Rosicleer to be the new knight by the rich armour he bore, the self same being worn by him in the jousts wherein he was hurled to ground, for which cause, preventing Rosicleer's salutation, with a loud and hollow voice, he cried unto him:[445]

'Now, Sir Knight, may I magnify my gods for that I have thee in such a place where I may be avenged of thee at my pleasure for the despite thou have done me. And all the world shall not ransom thee from my hands'.

'God of heaven shall be my borrow°', answered Rosicleer, 'which also shall correct thy wickedness and tread underfoot thy intolerable pride and arrogancy.° But to tell thee my message, I challenge thee for to make satisfaction unto these gentlewomen of the wrong thou has done them, or to prepare thyself to maintain thy mischief'.

Brandagedeon spoke no word, but signified his meaning by his demeanour, for he turned his horse head in great rage and took a heavy spear with him; the other, understanding his sign, did as much. This first journey broke their staffs° and made them try the rest of the battle on foot. The giant, being clean unhorsed, and Rosicleer's horse giving back so that he rushed against the ground; but the success was diverse and unequal in the riders themselves. For Rosicleer, keeping his saddle, felt no harm in his body, and the giant, thrown violently to the earth, was well shaken with the fall.

But the combat is not yet ended, for Brandagedeon, being strong and mighty, held Rosicleer very hard, as indeed it could not be otherwise. For betwixt them alone the fight continued for two hours, all the meantime neither part giving over nor making any semblance of discomfiture. In the end, the knight, having treble advantage over the giant — first, in Queen Julia's sword, which hit sore; secondly, in Artimodoro's harness, which held out the force of the giant's weapon; and thirdly, the nimbleness of his body, ready both to assail strongly and to decline as lightly° from the other's blow — by which means, having made a wide hole in the giant's armour, he wounded the giant at his pleasure.

The execution of this challenge to so little displeasure on Rosicleer's part made Arinda think it long till she should blaze it at home in the Monastery of the River, but her pleasure was soon overcast, for there was ministered unto her a cup of cold water instead of better liking to allay her thirst.[446] All this happening beyond her expectation, by that giant's knights, which seeing their master at such an exigent,° although in no evident appearance of his end, in great fury came to land, and at once all of them with their swords fell upon Rosicleer. This was no even match: thirty knights and a giant to set upon one silly° knight, before almost tired with two hours' battle against the giant. But what thing may resist God's ordinance?[447] The giant's knights laid on with such courages that it revived the giant, for they were all chosen knights. But I doubt not but that Rosicleer bestirred himself, for so many as he met, he either maimed,° wounded, slew, or threw to ground. And being over-awed by number and fresh onsets, he was fain for defence to his back to withdraw himself into the sea, there to stand in the water and receive their blows before him.

Now, Telio, his squire, and Arinda, the Hungarian, seeing him forced to this extremity were very woe-begone,° but the gentlewoman Lusitanian, as desperate° of all succours by his means, galloped from thence upon her palfrey, which stood by the shore, no less complaining the danger wherein she left this good knight than recureless° lamenting the unjust death of her brother.

As she had ridden some part of her way towards Oliverio's court, there were two knights in

---
[445] 'preventing Rosicleer's salutation' replaces a statement of the giant's happiness at seeing Rosicleer.
[446] The imagery of consuming is unique to the English text.
[447] 'This was no ... God's ordinance?' is added.

her judgement very lusty° and armed at all points which made all the haste they might to get near her. This gentlewoman, coming within the hearing of them and minding to prevent other questions, cried unto them a far off:

'For the passion of God, my good lords, if all nobleness and virtue be not clean buried in you, make haste to succour a knight, the best in the world, which is now environed with his enemies being about thirty knights besides a giant!'

The two knights with these news posted° amain,° and by the same way which the gentlewoman came in short time got a sight of Rosicleer, which at that time stood in the water against eleven or twelve of them, for so many were left alive of thirty persons. Those also which then lived, being well nurtured by Rosicleer['s] discipline, that they would press upon him without good warranties.°

Now by that time that the two knights came, Rosicleer had killed more than twenty, leaving a passage so well trodden as they might easily trace out his footsteps.[448] At their first breaking in among the giant's knights, they burst their staffs° upon two of them, overthrowing them. And then drawing their swords, struck so lustily that the assailants were glad to leave Rosicleer and to defend themselves against the two knights. Rosicleer, having so good help at hand, although he was stirred with the continual heat of the foot-battle, would needs be a party player in the last act of this tragedy,[449] and therefore, chose out Brandagedeon to deal withal, and with his sharp sword gave him so fierce a stoccado° that the bowels trailed after the weapon and the giant fell down. Now, being thus put in possession of his desire, he came to the two knights, uttering these or such like speeches:

'I beseech you, noble knights, to let me know at whose hands I have received so good maintenance that I may the better give you thanks according to the state of your degree and your demerits° towards me'.

One of the knights answered:

'You are not to thank us, for your own hand had wrought your escape before our coming. But nevertheless, at your request we are content to discover ourselves'.

And straightways° they unlaced their helmets, whereby Rosicleer knew them: the one to be Bargandel, and the other Liriamandro, his dear friends.[450] Rosicleer, after his presupposed thanks so happily stumbling on his friends' help, fell to other matters, and first asked of them for what cause they came thither.°[451] They made answer that the only fear they had, lest the giant's knights should at once enclose him, moved them to abandon the court for his rescues.

And as this talk was interrupted by the coming of the two gentlewomen and Telio, Rosicleer's squire, to demand leave of search in the giant's boat for the coffer and fardel,° which had been taken from them. So after the gentlewomen, with leave obtained, departed for to search, these three knights began a deep consultation of their own affairs and what they ought to do. Bargandel spoke first in this wise:°

'We have this month and more loitered very idly in King Oliverio's court without exercise of arms or amour, therefore it were not misbeseeming° us knights if we should for a time forbear our return to practice deeds of arms, that our good name and honour may enlarge our credit in this kingdom and be a means of the sure settling of our memories in this land. And the rather thereto am I led, for that I will not fear any disworship° or vanquish in your company'.

'I am content', sayeth the new knight, 'with this or any other thing which you shall devise. But what shall we do with these gentlewomen?'

'Marry'°, sayeth Liriamandro, 'they shall return to the court with the dead body of the giant, there to present his carcass before the Princess Olivia as a token from thee, Rosicleer, and in

---

[448] The image of the passage of corpses is absent from *Espejo*.
[449] Tyler adds the theatre imagery.
[450] In *Espejo*, they embrace and Rosicleer expresses gratitude and obligation to them.
[451] 'after his *presupposed* thanks' signifies 'after giving thanks'.

part of payment for the great dishonour which the giant hath proffered her in withholding her jewels. They may likewise, when they be there, make all our excuses unto the king for our so sudden departure'.

By this time the gentlewomen returned with their own carriage, and what with the length of the battle and other accidents, the day was so far shut in that, being very dark, they were constrained altogether to turn into a keeper's house near at hand, where they were welcome at such warning, for he knew the three knights at the great feasts.[452] Wherefore he entertained them as honourably as he might. That night, not having wherewith otherwise to busy themselves and the opportunity of the bearers putting them in mind of their mistresses, they gave themselves to inditing° every man of several letters unto his love and lady.[453] Bargandel and Liriamandro delivered theirs unto the gentlewoman of Lusitania, but the other, not willing to make manifest his choice for that time, took Arinda a letter closely to carry unto the Princess Briana, his good lady.[454] And afterwards, amongst other talk, he required to see the coffer of jewels which the Princess Briana sent to Olivia as if it had been only to have seen the riches thereof. Arinda gave him the coffer, which he opened, and tossing° up and down as if to see all the jewels, he secretly conveyed his letter to Olivia under all the papers and redelivered the coffer without being suspect.

Well to make an end, the talk had an end. And when the rest went to their rest, Rosicleer fell into his ordinary humour, driving in his thought the whole order of the delivery and her receipt, with her manner of turning over the papers to view every jewel.[455] This being but the first assay of the humour. But when his fancy° brought him to the finding of the letter, Lord what a f[r]ight he sustained! For the better understanding whereof, you must imagine a young scholar but lately entered into school points overseeing of his theme before he bring it to the review of his schoolmaster. And believe me, in far greater doubt hung Rosicleer of his lady's liking than the boy doth of his master's. For in his reading of the blotted copy, as distinctly as if he were to guess Olivia's conjecture upon every syllable — good God unto what a hard censure was the poor paper subject, as if every sentence had been then arraigned before him! For almost at every line's end, he would say: either this was too much, either this was too little, or this is maimed,° or this too rude and unlearned, or this was not well and finely penned, or that was not plain enough, or this is faulty, or this should be amended. And to draw all into a sum, in every piece he would blame either the little wit in invention or the lack of eloquence in the delivery of the matter, but chiefly his own overboldness° in presuming upon so high a princess with so rude a discourse. And yet, I dare say, it did him good to beguile the princess with this letter in the colour of a jewel, which she must receive and read through ere° she could learn the contents thereof or know the penman. And beginning to reckon afresh after this comfort, he stayed° himself upon these two points: first, that since he was diseased,° his remedy must begin by making his grief known; second, that his conscience told him there was nothing in the letter, the truth whereof he durst° not avouch° as concerning either his own person or the princess's.[456] And this was his night's rest, as I suppose.

---

[452] 'By this time... other accidents' is added.
[453] The explanation, 'not having... their mistresses', is provided by Tyler.
[454] In *Espejo*, he writes to both his mother and Olivia and ponders how best to secretly deliver the letter to Olivia.
[455] The humoural language is added.
[456] This paragraph, in which Rosicleer's emotional dilemma is explored, is greatly expanded in *Mirror* and the tone is much more passionate and intense.

CHAPTER 37

Rosicleer and the two princes seek adventures in the land of Britain, and the two gentlewomen carry the giant's body to Oliverio's court

Not much out of the same manner was the other knights' sleep, dreaming of their delights and other such toys.[457] But the next day, they arose and armed themselves, taking leave of their host and the gentlewomen. But Rosicleer tarried behind to conduct the women a little on their way and to have more secret conference with Arinda about the Princess Briana, the remorse of his conscience stinging him for stealing away so privily° from the princess. In the course of this talk he would sometimes name the princess his lady, sometimes his foundress,° by which name he requested Arinda to make offer of his humble service with the best excuse she might for his long absence, in that he had already entered the quest of seeking the Prince Edward or Donzel del Febo, his brother. And in such speeches he brought them on their way.[458]

Afterward, taking his leave with a friendly embrace, he posted° after his company, whom he overtook in short time.[459] Six days these three knights rode together without happening upon anything worthy the recital. The seventh day in their way, they saw a far off a knight very tall and big made, upon a fair steed: by seeming, a knight of great account. There followed him two squires, the one bearing his lance, the other his helmet, for the heat of the day had made him vayle° his headpiece, to put on a light hat of taffeta. And coming near, they saw that he was of a good countenance, somewhat of colour dusky and black, but in making both manlike and of good proportion, his joints well knit and somewhat large withal, which foreshowed° great likelihood of strength and courage.

This knight stranger, first saluting these three knights riding by, spoke unto them thus:

'Tell me, my lords, I pray you, whether you be of King Oliverio's court or no'.

Bargandel answered him:

'Truly, we are if we list,° and so long as our liking lasteth.[460] But wherefore demand you this?'

'I will tell you', said the knight. 'Sooth° it is that I am a Tartarian, born in that part of Tartary which bordereth upon Europe, and travelling to seek adventures I was cast by tempest of the sea upon the country of Zeeland, where I heard that many knights should assemble in this realm at a great feast and jousts proclaimed by the king, with a safe conduct warranted out under his own signet for all knights Christians and pagans, or of all nations else besides whatsoever, thither° to come and prove their valour.[461] I am, as I say, a wandering knight and have no other errant° but to see such good knights and to try myself amongst them. Upon the report hereof, as soon as my ship was rigged and trimmed and that the wind served for my purpose, I entered in my ship to arrive in this land.[462] Now whether that the way long and dangerous (by the ignorance of my pilot°) shut me from my hope, or that the reporters mistook the day, or rather knew it not, since my coming to land I have in many places been ascertained that the feasts are long ago ended and that the most part of the knights have taken shipping° and departed into their countries, notwithstanding leaving behind them such a good memory in the mouths of

---

[457] 'their delights and other such toys' replaces 'their loves'.

[458] His maternal relationship to Briana is unstated here, unlike in the source.

[459] Technicalities regarding the transportation of the giant's body are omitted.

[460] The alliterative phrase, 'if we list, and so long as our liking lasteth', which configures the relationship as highly flexible, is an addition.

[461] Zeeland: a province of the Netherlands

Tartarian: Tartar. Of the two Tartaries the smaller one (modern Crimea) was closer to Europe. The larger Tartary extended across most of central Asia. In the Spanish text, he says he is from the greater Tartary: 'Tartaria, aquella mayor que cae más hazia la Europa' (*Espejo* II.75). By omitting this detail, Tyler corrects the flawed geographical reference.

[462] This sentence is unique to *Mirror*: 'Upon the . . . this land'.

every man. As much it grieveth me to have lost my labour, for this cause last remembered, I am in purpose for one month's space to ride through this land and to deal with all knights-comers° to prove whether their credit be not above their deserts,° whereunto I have set this condition: that if any of them dismount me or make me yield, that then I must faithfully accomplish all that which the vanquisher shall will me; but if I unhorse any of them or take any of them prisoners, then the vanquished shall commend me to the King Oliverio and make offer of his or their lives and goods at his courtesy as a simple token of my great good will towards him. Since this determination, three days have I journeyed in this land, and I have encountered ten knights whom I have sent accordingly to King Oliverio. And my lords, whether are you retaining to the English court or no? For if you be, I may not break my vow although by your semblance and riding you show to me as the best knights which I have seen in my life'.

This said the knight stranger, and the other three knights were easily brought to the allowing of the conditions. Wherefore Bargandel, which had undertaken to answer, said:

'Sir Knight, we thank you for the large recount you have made unto us of your hither coming, and as to your overlate° arrival and the conditions set to the tilt. Albeit I may not mislike° them, being so equal, yet for my part I answer, and for these knights, that we would not gladly deal with you upon so light occasion, for rather will we honour strange knights than in any wise° be an encumbrance unto them. But since it is your earnest suit, and that therein we shall do you service, we will not refuse you. And by the leave of these, my lords and fellows, myself will be the foremost. But by God, Sir Knight, there is the Lady Silverina in the English court, and if I fail not of my purpose, I will make you kiss her white hands ere° you be many days elder'.[463]

But Bargandel failed indeed of his purpose. For though he was a very valiant knight, yet was he but young and the Tartarian was both mighty and well exercised.[464]

After the Tartarian had buckled on his helm and Bargandel had obtained leave of his fellows to be the first in this adventure, either of them clapped their spurs to the horse sides. And their encountry° was such that Bargandel broke his spear in small shivers° in the shield of his enemy, causing the Tartarian to lose the reins and to writhe somewhat in his saddle. But the Tartarian overthrew Bargandel, horse and man, to the ground. And with the turn to recover the reins, dressed himself in his saddle, passing forth gallantly, while Bargandel lay on the ground, very angry and desirous to have had the combat with the sword. Rosicleer and Liriamandro much wondered at their shocks.

Liriamandro then took the next turn. And Rosicleer, because the stranger wanted a spear, sent his own staff° unto him, which peradventure° if he could have foreseen the event, he would not have done, for by it, Liramandro was hurled to ground and the Tartarian almost unhorsed, his stirrups being broken and himself cast upon the arson° of his saddle. The Tartarian knight was much abashed° at the great force of these two knights, for he had not thought to have met two so strong knights in all this land.

And when there remained none but one knight, and he likewise without a staff° to joust withal, he came to this one and bid the base° to the sword play in these terms:

'Sir Knight, since both of us want spears to joust withal, it shall be well to make up this lack with our swords, that you may either revenge the shame of your companions or else go with them for company, and all three present you[r]selves prisoners to the king, your lord, whose court notwithstanding I shall highly commend off for the great virtue whereof myself hath had proof sufficiently in your fellows'.

'Assuredly, Sir Knight', said this odd° man which was Rosicleer, 'were it not for the duty which I owe to my companions, and for that you should ill acquit their courtesies if you should leave me scot-free to scorn at their mishaps, I would that this combat with swords should be excused, for that I am not accustomed to fight for so small a cause. But since that both my

---

[463] The request to honour his lady is an English addition.
[464] This summary of the future action is an addition.

companions challenge this at my hands, and that it is a point of cowardliness to leave the combat, and also that you will not have us to break companies, I condescend to your device° with this proviso, that if by good Fortune I overcome you, my companions shall be freed from your charge and you shall go in their rooms° to kiss the King of England's hand, as I am sure it will do you good to have acquaintance with his grace'.

'I am well pleased herewith', answered the Tartarian.

And so saying, he drew out a fine sword, Rosicleer likewise drawing his. Thus began the brave combat in which they continued a long time, no advantage being espied on either part by the beholders. What was within them, themselves best knew, but Rosicleer, rather delighted than afraid at his enemy's courage, devised by himself how to win that valiant knight for a friend and to leave the combat, for upon so slender a quarrel he thought the hazard would be too great. Marry,° for all that he did his best, for when he felt the strong buffets he could not but yield the like. The Tartarian knight, burning in rage rather to have the mastery over so valiant knights rather than for any ill will he bore to Rosicleer, compassed how by main° force to subdue his adversary. And in this thought, he struck so furiously that with his charge and the other's answer, the noise was so confused and great withal that it was heard upon the top of hills as the shot of artillery. When the Tartarian knight was so well heated as you have heard, he drove a blow with both his hands full at Rosicleer's head, which lighting upon the fine and enchanted helmet, notwithstanding deprived Rosicleer of his eyesight and enfeebled his hearing at this time. But Rosicleer could not so soon forget it, and therefore, while it was fresh in his remembrance, he restored the like blow, which in the descending missed the Tartarian's crest, otherwise it had put him in danger.[465] But sliding upon his shoulder, it was so heavy that it made the Tartarian stoop to his horse back. The next dangerous blow which the Tartarian gave made Rosicleer bow unto his saddle, both the sword and the reins falling from him. Bargandel and Liriamandro, standing by, fell therewith into a strange admiration of the Tartarian in that he not only kept Rosicleer play, but put him to his trumps. And by this time, I think their desire to fight with him was well abated, seeing they knew now how well he could handle his weapon. And Rosicleer, having got greater courage through the grief of his wound, kept no more his seat, but rising in his stirrups and recovering his sword, which was fastened with a little chain unto his saddle bow, he hit the strong Tartarian so great a blow that the blood gushed out both at his ears and nostrils and he lay for dead upon the crupper, the horse carrying him about the field till he revived.

After not without some abashment as one come out of another world, the Tartarian, when he felt the blood issuing in such measure, lifted up his hand, and calling for help on his gods, saying:

'Assist me, oh, my gods, against this fell° knight, for if I tarry° more of these blows my life shall soon be ended!'

And when he had so said, as purposed to make an end of the fray, he took his sword with both his hands, and with all his force following the blow, he smote Rosicleer upon the helmet to no great harm on his body, but the weight thereof astonished him as much as if a tower had fallen upon him.[466] Whereat Rosicleer waxed mad angry, and not remembering that which before he had premeditated — as to end the battle in quietness — he repaid the trespass with treble damage to the Tartarian. For albeit the Tartarian might well be reckoned among the most famous knights of elder time, being covered with a helmet so well tempered as any prince might have, yet living in that age and encountering such knights, his room was but next the best. And when he saw that terrible blow over his head, he could have wished a whole mountain between him and it.

But there needed no such impossible means to avoid this misfortune, for it was provided by the divine majesty of God that this noble knight should die a Christian and that great friendship

---

[465] *Espejo* specifies that he fights using Julia's sword.
[466] Tyler indicates Zoilo's (the Tartarian's) intense desire to conclude the battle.

should grow between these three knights; and therefore God so directed Rosicleer's hand that it fell not right, but glancing down upon the shoulder, it notwithstanding turned the Tartarian from his horse with so great pain on his right shoulder that he might not rise himself up again.[467] With this fall, his buckles broke and the nailings° rent, and being then half unarmed, he threw his sword from him, putting his knee to the ground to give thanks to his imagined gods for their delivery from so furious a blow.

And then turning toward Rosicleer, he said:

'Noble and valiant knight, the strongest and mightiest which I have ever known or would have believed ever to have been in this court or others, pardon me my rashness, for I have been misadvised. When my will first put me forth to contend with you, only your greatness of body and comeliness might have sufficed to teach me that you were more valiant and stronger than I am. And since I am now vanquished, and rather by great miracle escaped with life from your hands than by mine° own cunning, say on what you command, for I am pressed to accomplish all that which was agreed upon before our combat. And my duty shall not be slacked in any point, but I would rather fulfil more than all that for to gain the society of your worthy person and your companions, for I never met with more nobler knights for valour and bounteousness'.

And so saying, he yielded himself.[468]

By this speech, the fury and choler of Rosicleer was well slacked. And being glad to see the knight so humbled before him, he answered:

'Good knight, I accept in good part that which you have said and it grieveth me much to have had the battle with you, for unto a knight stranger and valorous, I had rather be a means for procuring honour and ease than their trouble and encumbrance. And as to the articles of the covenant which you remember° me of, believe me, I would not have exacted them at your hands, and it shall be yet in your choice whether you will fulfil them or no. And yet I fear not but that you shall well like of your service to the King Oliverio himself, being a good knight and a great honourer of strangers. Likewise, we three shall take it as sign of your good liking toward us if you make us privy° to your name, that hereafter we may know you and do unto you that honour which so good a knight meriteth'.

'Sir Knight', answered the Tartarian, 'I have great desire to go and kiss the hand of King Oliverio, as well to know him as to satisfy that which I owe unto you, and will not fail to depart and take my way toward the king. But to your last demand, I am, as told you before, a Tartarian and my name is Zoilo, prince and heir of that kingdom, which I would with good will forbear for some time, if you and these knights would vouchsafe your acquaintance and company, for I have more desire to travel in these parts than in that country from whence I came, because there is no continual afford° of knights and fresh accidents° as I find in this kingdom. And I should more highly esteem of the friendship and society of such noble and worthy knights than of any riches in the world. And now, for that I have declared who I am, I shall think myself farther in your debt if you make yourselves farther known unto me'.

Rosicleer and his companions gladly heard of his birth and lineage, but much gladder of the friendship whereto he requested them, so they gave him many thanks and told him who they were, diverse speeches of great courtesy passing between them, whereby their amity was so sure confirmed that it remained unto the death, every one labouring to be found most friendly. And this done, they appointed that Prince Zoilo should go to the court only to have a sight of the king, and that Rosicleer with his companions should abide him thereabout, then they four to travel together whither° Fortune would carry them.[469] This being concluded, the Prince of Tartary took his way toward the court of King Oliverio, thinking long to find the time for his return. They took the way towards a forest, where the history leaveth them to entreat of the

---

[467] Tyler adds God's direct intervention.
[468] 'And my duty . . . yielded himself' is added.
[469] Fortune's agency is added.

gentlewomen in the mean time, which brought the body of the great Brandagedeon unto the court of King Oliverio.[470]

CHAPTER 38

The gentlewomen brought the body of Brandagedeon to the court, and the princesses received the letters of their knights

Great was the grief which the Princess Olivia felt by the absence of Rosicleer that neither her high estate nor the courtly disports° sufficed to make her forget her care or help her to cover her liking. But in her lodging she would be without company in the day and in the night without sleep, ever wishing to see him again, whom she loved more than herself, for her mind prophesied to her that she should not see him very quickly.[471] And as it is natural for the patient to communicate his grief with the physician, judging this some ease where the principal remedy wanteth, so the fair princess as unacquainted and to begin in such passions, not being able at the first to counsel herself otherwise, thought it best to discover her grief to one of her gentlewomen named Fidelia, the faithfullest° and most secret of her household, the which many times had importuned her to know the cause of her sorrow.[472]

And one night, as she was alone with her, the princess said to her:

'Thou know, my Fidelia, how among all the ladies and gentlewomen which I have, I have chosen thee only for the faithful treasurer of my secrets. And I have not done nor thought the thing which I have not imparted with thee, which hath come to pass only by the loyal and good service wherein I have always found thee pliant and diligent. With the like confidence unto that which I always have reposed in thee, I will unfold unto thee a secret, which none in the world myself except and thyself shall learn at my hand, in the concealing whereof, unto this day, I have a thousand times endured little less than death. And the matter is such that it is unfitting for anyone to be a dealer therein but myself and thyself, whom I account as myself. At a word, my Fidelia, that tyrant Love, which spareth neither high nor low, hath taken possession of me by the great prowess and beauty of the new knight, and I am sure that but my death, nothing can set me free. Although I have studied all possible means of my liberty, and thereto have set the defence of my honesty and great estate to withstand this conceit,° yet for all that I can do, as long as this knight's race is unknown, I cannot ease myself: my former remedies serving me only against the temptation of the flesh and not to drive out the remembrance of his personage, whence my desire springeth. And truly, I cannot persuade myself other than that this knight's offspring° is right noble. He being of so court-like behaviour and knightly prowess, the truth hereof being somewhat more incredible than the lying fables of our ancient poets. Now if he be a prince born, the only hope to have him for husband — my father and he being therewith pleased — may yield one some comfort in the meantime, while opportunity serveth for the final accomplishment. Wherefore, mine° own Fidelia, seeing that I have fully laid open the bottom of my heart, that which remaineth on thy part is to travail° with his squire or some other to wit° of what parentage Rosicleer is'.

Fidelia had listened very attentively to that which her lady had said, and as she was very wise, so perceiving by the drift of the speech that neither her mistress's malady could be removed by counsel nor that she would accept of it if it were bestowed, besides that, that her desire was lawful to match with Rosicleer if there were no disparage in his stock. She could not gainsay her mistress in flat terms, but made answer that since her grace had laid that charge upon her,

---

[470] Their happy reaction at having met Zoilo is omitted.
[471] 'whom she loved . . . very quickly' is added.
[472] The name Fidelia signifies 'faithful', which is her dominant personality trait.

she was content to receive as also ready to offer her service in any other thing for this matter which she now moved. She said that since her grace's purpose was so good, she should not need to remember her farther in it, for that so soon as Rosicleer should return, she would be in hand with his squire to boult° out the truth of everything.

'And yet', sayeth she, 'I cannot believe by reason of his magnanimity but that he is descended from some noble progeny, which if it so be I like very well that your grace is so affectioned° towards him, otherwise I dare not advise you. But yet, I will tell you my fancy:° it were better for you to abide some pain than to make your head of your underlying°'.[473]

50 The beautiful princess was well apaid° at this counsel, so jumping° with her former determination. And it greatly assuaged the malice° of her passion, in that she had bewrayed° it to her trusty servant.

The next day, the gentlewomen entered into the palace, driving a horse before them loaded with the giant's body. At their entrance the hurly-burly° in the court was so great, every man running to see the wonder, that the king with all those which were with him and the Princess Olivia with her gentlewomen ran to their windows to see what the matter was. And when they saw the giant, they knew him. And as newly abashed° at Rosicleer's virtues, they began to commend of him as of the best knight in the world.

The gentlewomen presently were brought before the king, which received them courteously.
60 And they, in order, declared unto him and the rest that which had chanced to Rosicleer since his departure from the city. The king liked very well of all, save that when they told him that the knights could not return presently, as minding to pursue adventures. For the king feared lest by being so much inclined to knightly deeds, their good success would carry them farther off than should be for his pleasure.

But the gentlewomen departed from the king to do their message unto the Princess Olivia, whom they found in her chamber with the two other princesses in her company. Coming before her, they delivered their message with commendations from Rosicleer and the two princes, which had sent her that giant so dead as a satisfaction in some part for the detaining of her jewels. The princess, pleasantly laughing at that present, caused the gentlewomen to go on in that story and
70 to make report of all occurrents° in their journey, which they did so faithfully that the princess, in the telling, was not able to colour° her affection towards Rosicleer.

This tale ended, Arinda gave into her hands the packet, which the princess opened, and turning over the jewels found a letter, which she put in her bosom, taking it to be Briana's. And in like sort the gentlewoman of Lusitania made delivery of Bargandel and Liriamandro's letters unto their ladies, with the coffer unto Rodasilva. The two princesses, Silverina and Rodasilva, being great friends, went both together in a closet° to read without interruption their loves' letters, so eloquent and so fraught with amorous speeches, which much rejoiced the young ladies to be beloved of so good knights.[474]

And not to break off their several commendations of their knights and lords, we will speak
80 of the Princess Olivia, who, being left alone for the company of the two princesses, dispatched her other gentlewomen into diverse parts of the chamber to have a more secret survey of Briana's letters. When she had read one through (that which was delivered with the packet), she took that other out of her bosom, which she had found in ransacking the packet. And opening it, she saw in capital letters 'ROSICLEER' subscribed, whereby she knew it to be his.[475] And somewhat troubled, she folded it up quickly again, minding to learn by what means that letter was hidden among the jewels. And therefore, calling Arinda, she asked if that anyone had unlocked the

---

[473] 'otherwise I . . . your underlying' is added.
[474] Their hope of marrying their lovers is omitted by Tyler.
[475] The added superscription is discussed in the introduction in the context of Tyler's interest in correct dictaminal form.

coffer after that her lady had delivered it unto her. Arinda, supposing that the princess had wanted something, answered:

'No truly, madam, for I have always kept the keys, and nobody ever had them at my hands but Rosicleer, which requested to see the jewels when we were in the keeper's lodge. And in my presence he shut it, restoring me the keys and not taking out ought whereof I can accuse him'.

The princess, smelling out Rosicleer's shift and somewhat smiling withal to hear whereunto Arinda had construed her meaning, replied merrily thus:

'I asked it not, gentle friend, for that I thought there wanted anything in the coffer, for it was wholly lost when it was in Brandagedeon's power, but I asked it for that I marvelled it fell out so well when Brandagedeon was the keeper'.

Arinda waxing bold, hereat:°

'Nay, marry°', sayeth she, 'with your favour, noble princess, Brandagedeon, misgiving in his mind how little time he should enjoy it, took little care for the opening'.

So this question who opened it was concluded in a laughter, and little talk° continued after. The princess, thinking it long till she might alone read Rosicleer's letter, and therefore somewhat earlier then she was wont, she withdrew herself into her bedchamber with only Fidelia in her company to see her in bed. When the door was fastened, she drew out Rosicleer's letter, and not having power herself to read it, she gave it unto Fidelia. The tenor of the loving letter was this, which hereafter followeth:

Unto the most excellent princess, the Princess Olivia,[476]

That which is appointed by God, mighty princess, may not by man's power be altered or perverted. As in myself I prove it, for since that mine° eyes first told me of your beauty and my judgement gave consent thereto, and that my will hath procured liking thereof in my affection, I have felt an alteration in me so incurable that, striving with it both by art and nature, I have not hitherto found my remedy, which thing, good madam, I trust cannot seem more unlikely to you than it hath been to me in the feeling terrible. The clap of the thunder is the greater when it meeteth with the thicket, able to make more resistance. Longer lasts the kindled fire in the builded oak° than in the parched straw. And more vehement is the fight between two enemies than when the one yieldeth. What force Love hath, as I could well wish your ladyship to consider in me or to feel in yourself. So at least I beseech you to weigh by others and to believe report how that with light assaults he beateth down the stoutest° courages, and with gentle cords bindeth the biggest arms; that his force, neither the wisest nor the mightiest were able to resist; that from his subjection not Julius Caesar, the great monarch of the world, could free himself; that he quelled the pride of the mighty Carthagenian in the delights of Capua, and fettered Mars and Jupiter, two gods of the gentiles in chains of iron; that he transformeth men into sundry shapes and, as it were, by sudden enchantment framed the arm-strong Hercules to the distaff and spindle, Aristotle to be bridled and saddled; that he climeth the highest towers and stretcheth to the lowest valley; that he divideth the hard rocks and bloweth through the easy passages.[477] To conclude, nothing so strong and invincible but that Love can overthrow and doth what him listeth. So that if I confessed myself yielded unto so mighty a conqueror, I should yet be

---

[476] The added salutation is discussed in the introduction in the context of Tyler's interest in correct dictaminal form.
[477] Julius Caesar (100–44 BCE): Roman general and statesman. He was ordered to divorce his wife Cornelia, but he refused. As a result, her wealth was lost and he suffered proscription.

The Carthagenian: someone from Carthage. This is likely a reference to Hannibal, who is named here in the Spanish. He was based in Capua from 216 BCE. Livy describes Capua under Hannibal as immoral and luxurious. He fell in love with a prostitute.

Mars: he transformed himself into a boar to kill Adonis because he was jealous of Adonis's love for Aphrodite.
Jupiter: he transformed himself into a bull to abduct Europa.
Hercules: he fought Achelous for love of Deianira. She unintentionally killed him with the shirt of Nessus.
Aristotle (384–322 BCE): Greek philosopher. In the Middle Ages, a legend circulated, recounting how Aristotle became enamoured of Phyllis and how she refused to requite him unless he gave her a piggy-back ride.

blameless for my cowardice. Yet what have I not attempted? If either counsel of friends or mine° own wit, either physic's° cure or mirth of company might have warranted my quietness. So God, good madam, speed my writing, as I meant not to trouble you with my letters. But the weak complain and the diseased seek remedy, as what grief is so great or wound so wide but it hath some redress or other provided in nature. To you, therefore, good madam, thus boldly have I discovered my unrest, that by your means, whence only I may hope for it, I may receive comfort. And so attending your highness's answer, either of life or death, I humbly kiss your princely° hand.[478]

    Thine resolved to love or not to live,
    Poor Rosicleer[479]

Rosicleer penned this letter either not well in his wits or else greatly perplexed in his thought, so hard it is to find an issue. But I believe, rather, that it came from heart to hand and was so set down without farther advice.[480] Yet, in the meantime that Fidelia read the letter, the fair princess broad awake to hear those amorous words, and feeling them in her heart with the like love wherein Rosicleer wrote them. When it was ended, heaping out abundance of sighs upon the argument of the letter, she said unto Fidelia:

'Ah Fidelia, what force may a tender gentlewoman as I am have to resist the tyranny of Love, when so many famous and so mighty princes could never conquer him? How may I overcome him, which hath had the mastery of so many? Tell me, Fidelia, and counsel me what I have to do in this matter, for I mistrust my own wisdom, and very seld° is the passionate's judgment very sure and requisite'.

Fidelia, nothing wondering at that effect which love had wrought in the princess her lady, for she rather wished herself worthy of so glorious pain, answered her thus:

'Madam, to counsel you aright° were to will you to defy love and to abandon Rosicleer's company. And yet the words of this letter leaveth in me a doubt thereof if the matter be as true as the words importeth. Next were to desire you to have an eye unto your high estate, which yet me thinks is not necessary, for I know you to be so wise as that you will hazard death rather than commit a thing so prejudicial to your honour. Now there remaineth only to learn out Rosicleer's lineage, that if he be such a one as may marry you without disworship,° you may then begin the redress of both your wrongs. Otherwise, if he fail in that point, the first counsel will be most convenient to eschew his presence, which shall in time do away this affection, as in time all things are forgotten'.

Here, the princess, interrupting Fidelia's speech, replied in this manner:

'Ah Fidelia, you think me not such a one but that although the love which I bear unto Rosicleer be such that it procureth me to will his presence, if he fail in gentry, I will rather chastise his boldness with perpetual exile out of this land than give him comfort to the impair° of my credit. And sooner will I die a hundred times than bestow a countenance upon such a one. But this I judge of Rosicleer by the pure and loyal love which he meaneth towards me, that it is likely he may merit me for wife, otherwise it is to be thought that in a knight so virtuous there cannot lie hidden such impudency as to move a lady unto her dishonour'.

In such like talk after the letter read, the princess and Fidelia passed the most part of the night till Fidelia took her leave, the princess, notwithstanding, still canvassing over the letter of Rosicleer and every sweet word which he had written. And she prayed to God with all her heart that he might prove such a one as was not unfitting for a queen's marriage.

---

[478] An entire page of his letter is replaced by the phrase 'So that . . . or death'.
[479] The signature is added; see the discussion of dictaminal form in the introduction.
[480] 'Rosicleer . . . advice' is added.

CHAPTER 39

Arinda, the gentlewoman belonging unto the Princess Briana, told the bringing up of Rosicleer unto the Princess Olivia

Arinda remained a long time in the court, tarrying for such things as the Princess Olivia made ready to send unto the Princess Briana, upon which occasion, as it happened one day, the Princess Olivia, Arinda, and Fidelia to be together, then Arinda not so well advised as she ought to have been in the secret affairs of her mistress, unbri[d]led her tongue and declared to the Princess Olivia all the life and doings of her mistress, the Princess Briana, as far as she had any knowledge.[481] And it may be that she added sometime more than truth. Amongst other things in this tale, she told of the little boys which had been brought up with the Princess Briana, reciting the marvellous tokens which they brought from their birth, and how that the sorrow of her lady was somewhat comforted by them, till Fortune brought one of them into a bark° near a great and deep river running into the main° sea, as you have heard before, and that the other of fourteen years, the princess unwitting° of it, stole away. After entering farther, she told that the same Rosicleer which killed Brandagedeon was the same which departed without leave when he was fourteen years old, whom she knew at the first sight and had entreated to return into Hungary.

When the princess heard this, driving to the conclusion, she demanded where the princess had those little boys.

'Madam', said Arinda, 'in this shall you see the works of God, how marvellous they be, which from so base a stock can raise so worthy imps, and you shall understand that they be sons to a knight named Leonardo, not of the most noble but of the meanest° knights of the city, and for that their father hath to wife a woman, sister to a gentlewoman of my lady's named Clandestria. For her long service in great favour with her grace, for her sake the princess made the parents of these children to nurse° them up in the monastery at her charges until they were all lost, as I made mention'.

When the princess had heard Arinda in this sort blazing the offspring of Rosicleer, what sorrow may be compared unto hers? For in that instant she could well have yielded to death. And why? For that the only hope of all her remedy was in the conceit° of Rosicleer's high estate, thereby meriting to be her mate, which when she saw to be clean contrary, she was in such a case° as if her soul had been taking his leave of her body. When Fidelia saw her colour so soon changed, as understanding from whence this effect proceeded, she rose up and desired Arinda with the other gentlewomen to void the chamber, for that her lady was newly entered into her fit, which oftentimes hath taken her, and she hath no remedy so present as to be alone.

Arinda and the other gentlewomen, not mistrusting her speech, conveyed themselves into another chamber. Now Fidelia, being left alone with her mistress, shut the door, but Olivia sank down in a sound,° whom Fidelia fetched again. Afterwards being well recovered and seeing herself without other witness, she sent out a deep sigh with the company of many tears, as seldom is a stormy wind without a shower of rain, ruefully withal making her moan unto Fidelia on this wise:°[482]

'Ah, my Fidelia! Did thou not hear what the gentlewoman of Hungary hath said as touching Rosicleer? If thou did hear it, why does thou not take part with me in my insupportable grief? Were it any marvel at all if my life should take end with her report? For since the hope which hitherto hath maintained my rest is now ended, I would to God my life would end withal, and rather would I die not to hear such news whereby my hope decays than to be privy° to such a truth and live without my comfort. Oh, my Fidelia, come! Come and help me now either to set

---

[481] Tyler omits the stereotype of female loquacity.
[482] The storm imagery is added.

forward my mishap with some desperate shift, or to lend me thy faithful counsel and advise thee better to assuage my grief and to forget the same misfortune which now assaileth me. Alas, I see that it is not for my quietness to banish Rosicleer! And if by the excellency of my estate I am forced to chastise his overboldness,° in so doing I shall both bar him from the sight and light of [my] eyes and make the stripe° redound° upon mine° own head. For who shall receive greater smart by his absence than I shall? What a wicked world is this wherein men of force° must neglect other men's virtues and magnify their own nobility without desert! Were it not more reason to raise this man to the top of honour, that in him his posterity may glory, than for lack of ancestors famous for like qualities to suppress his virtue and keep under the magnanimity of his courage? When began my fathers and grandfathers to be nobles, but when with the wings of virtue they soared above the vulgar sort? And if by their means only I am advanced to be a princess, what thank is there to me of my highness? And thou, Rosicleer, if by those rare and sovereign virtues, which flower and flourish in thee, thou do mount in credit, not only above the baser sort from whom thou were taken, but also above princes and lords, whereunto thou are to make thy assent? Are not thou worthy of greater renown then we others, which climbing by virtue in like sort, never yet came to the possibility of like worthiness? Is not this a forgery of the world and a plain juggling with nobility when we must make more account of one which perhaps by disorder of life defaceth the honour of his race than of one which reacheth up the ignobility of his stock? Wherein consisteth nobility, in the opinion of men or in virtue indeed? And do men inherit virtue as the child entereth upon the father's land being lawful heir? No, here we receive naught but what ourselves sow, and he that reapeth not may be a lout for all his lordship, as in time appeareth, which judgeth freely and without affection. And for me, if the eyes of my understanding were not dimmed, I should soon confess less merit in me to deserve Rosicleer than wanteth in him to be worthy of me. I am a princess by my father, and my glory resteth in the reckoning up of a bead-roll° of princes, some of them dead a thousand year ago, which nothing pertaineth to this present age. But he may be a prince by his own virtue, and his nobility ariseth not by keeping a tally of names, but by making just proof of his manhood in defence of justice every day. In such sort, likewise, that not any of my ancestors' virtues, whereby they became noble, dare approach to be tried with his in an even balance. And is there not many gentlewomen in the world of as high a calling as I am? And is there any prince or knight of so high renown for virtue and knighthood as Rosicleer is? Have not the best knights of both Christendom and Pagansie° joined with him either at tilt or tourney, and doth he not obscure them all, as when the sun appeareth, no stars dare come in presence? And I, silly° woman, having not so much as the refuse in me of my predecessors' virtue, am notwithstanding by the injury of the times bound to so great folly as that I must not think him worthy to equal me, which is much my better. But since of force° I must yield to the time and rather die than acknowledge the contrary, since my fortune is such that I must live by the imagination of other men, and since my estate may not be yoked with his baseness, have at it: I will forever shut him from my presence for the safeguard of my honour. But withal, seeing without his presence I cannot find ease for this torment, I will make him amends by giving over my life unto the enduring of everlasting sorrow. And if it be best so to do, tell me, my Fidleia, thy mind, for I perhaps am beguiled by my passion, neither indeed have I either judgement or feeling of ought but of grief and sorrow'.

    Fidelia heard the words of the princess, and taking part with the princess, she made up this woeful lamenting with her sorrowful speech, in this sort:

    'Alas, madam, how much better had it been that never the knightly deeds of Rosicleer had been manifested in Britain, for then, without the sight of him you had never received this wound, which now festering in you for lack of looking to, will be very hard to be cured. But the wisest say that in such matters as are hard and difficult, a man must especially employ his travail,° and that the success is not so unlikely but that labour may reach unto it. As for this grief which now distempereth° you, it is not so great but that you may be soon whole, yourself being thereunto willing. For in this, neither nature worketh, neither Fortune, nor the stars, nor the celestial signs, nor any supernatural influence, as you suppose, but only the fancy° and liking of man, the selfsame in effect with that which in the sick is to desire to be whole and in the thirsty to drink. And whosoever with the consent of his own will attempteth the breaking of these snares which his fancy° layeth to entrap him in, may escape scot-free and help others in like necessity. Otherwise, if this love were natural to all men, as all men then should love by nature, so should they not forebear it either for shame or friends' displeasure. And if it proceeded from Fortune, or by grace inspired, whereof the cause is not known but the event is evident, then were our liberty herein irrecuperable.° And in that the principal suit was without us, it might excuse the infirmity of the patient, whereas both experience proveth that love hath been removed by reason, and we daily chide their impotency which are not able to resist the darts of Cupid. It is, therefore, requisite, madam, that yourself put to your hand and frame your will to the obeying of that which may bring remedy, not only for the love which you presently feel, but for that which you fear will hereafter happen by your ill breaking of his absence. And truly, I am persuaded that seeing you have with yourself resolved to exclude him from your company, that the best is to put it in practice faithfully and effectually, lest by forbearing of this correction he take more courage to disturb your rest. And yet am I not against that which you have confirmed with good reason: that we ought to reverence virtue rather than riches. And in my judgement, that gentlewoman which shall match with Rosicleer may think herself happy, for his rare and marvellous deeds of arms make him to glister° more gloriously than all other princes and knights whosoever. And in times past, when all things went not so overthwart° as they now do, he was the best of lineage whose prowess was best known, and he best esteemed, which won his estimation by his manhood. And to this purpose, behold the builder of Rome, by name Romulus, taken from his foster father a shepherd and in a manner edified for the erection.[483] Although there were many builders in the world both before and after, but the difference of their buildings lieth in the excellency of the workmanship. Again, was there ever one in such credit for honesty and wisdom as Socrates, the son of a base midwife.[484] Euripides, one of the rarest men that ever were in tragical° poems, was born of mean° parentage.[485] Demosthenes, the flower of Greek eloquence, was a cutler's° son.[486] Horatius, the poet, born of a bondwoman, which had been taken prisoner.[487] And yet all these preferred for their virtuous qualities before kings and princes. Cicero could not dissemble his progeny, and yet was he lifted unto the consulship in Rome and never proved other consul so commodious for the commonwealth.[488] Serramus and Cnimatus, wise men and thoroughly exercised in their enemies' land, were consuls in Rome and delivered their countries from spoil and pillage.[489] And if for a matter pertaining to a kingdom we had rather take example of kings, let us see if mean° estate hath been any let° for men to aspire unto mighty kingdoms. And by name, let us take a more particular survey of the third, fourth, fifth, and sixth King of Rome.[490] First, Tullus Hostilius had his cradle in a shepherd's cottage and his

---

[483] Romulus: legendary founder of Rome
[484] His father is alluded to in *Espejo*.
 Socrates (*c.* 469–399 BCE): classical Athenian philosopher, who was born to a midwife and a stonemason
[485] Euripides (*c.* 480–406 BCE): classical Greek tragedian, whose mother was a vegetable merchant
[486] Demosthenes (384–322 BCE): Athenian statesman, renowned for his oratory. His father was a sword maker who died when Demosthenes was still a child.
[487] Horatius (65–8 BCE): Quintus Horatius Flaccus, aka Horace, Latin lyric poet, the son of a freed slave who was a herald
[488] Marcus Tullius Cicero (106–43 BCE): Roman orator, statesman, and writer of humble parentage
[489] Serramus: Aulus Atilius Serranus, a Roman consul in 170 BCE
 Cnimatus (520–430 BCE): Lucius Quinctius Cincinnatus, Roman consul and dictator. He is recognized as an exemplary leader.
[490] 'fourth' is added.

bringing up in the wide field.⁴⁹¹ Then, the two Tarquins were sons to a merchant and exiled their country.⁴⁹² Seruius Tullius was son to a bondwoman, as his name importeth.⁴⁹³ All which notwithstanding, in their times were kings of Rome. And if from thence we take our way to other nations round about, what a flock of shepherds, surgeons, labouring men, founders, and such like servile occupations shall we meet, which aspired to the highest place of government in their countries? Alexander, a crowned king, was a gardener's son; Pertinax, Emperor of Rome, born of a slave which lived by thrashing of grain and selling of wood; Severus, the seventh Emperor of Rome, was bred and brought up amongst surgeons, and these of the meanest° sort; Agathocles King of Sicily, son to a potter; Maximianus and Maximus, chief men of the empire, the one of base birth, the other doubtful whether a smith or a carpenter, and yet neither barrel better herring; Vespasianus, which was called the Good Emperor, rose from low degree, and by his virtue blotted out the infamy of his progeny.⁴⁹⁴ And to have more notable testimonies, who was father unto the great Caesar Augustus, the ruler of the world? Virgil, in a jest, made him a baker's son, but his own mind misgave him otherwise.⁴⁹⁵ As for a truth, far worse be they which rise to glory from the misliking° of their parents, like as Hercules, Perseus, and Jugurtha the King of Numidia, all begotten in adultery.⁴⁹⁶ And likewise, mighty Alexander King of Macedon,

---

⁴⁹¹ Tullus Hostilius: the legendary third king of Rome, reigning 672–641 BCE. He was raised on a farm, where he cared for livestock.

⁴⁹² Tarquin I (fl. 6th century BCE): Lucius Tarquinius Priscus, traditionally the fifth king of Rome, accepted by some scholars as an historical figure and usually said to have reigned from 616–578 BCE. His father was a businessman and a refugee. Tarquin was Etruscan and born in Corinth, and so he had to overcome his foreign nationality as well as his social class in order to rise to prominence.

Tarquin II: Lucius Tarquinius Superbus, traditionally the seventh and last king of Rome, accepted by some scholars as an historical figure. His reign is dated 534–509 BCE. His father was a Roman king and his mother was renowned for her skill at weaving and spinning; both were born in Etruria. His grandfather was from Cornith.

⁴⁹³ The addition of 'as his name importeth' indicates a basic understanding of Latin: 'servio' is Latin for 'to serve'.

Servius Tullius: legendary sixth king of ancient Rome, reigning 578–535 BCE. His mother was a noblewoman from Corniculum, captured by the Romans. She was a slave in King Tarquin's household. Servius may be her legitimate son, or he may have been fathered by her second husband, a Roman nobleman, or by Vulcan.

⁴⁹⁴ Alexander (336–323 BCE): Alexander the Great, Alexander III, King of Macedonia, son of Philip II and Olympias, King and Queen of Macedonia. He was not born of a gardener, but rather crowned Abdalonymus, a gardener, King of Sidon. The confusion arises from Petrarch's *Remedies for Fortune Fair and Foul*, which declares: 'Alexander of Macedonia made a gardener king in Asia, which was not the least among his praiseworthy deeds' (2.1.25).

Pertinax: Publius Helvius Pertinax Augustus, Roman emperor from January to March 193, was the son of a freed slave.

Severus: Flavius Valerius Severus, Roman emperor (306–307 BCE), of humble birth

Agathocles (361–289 BCE): tyrant of Syracuse (317–289 BCE) and King of Sicily (304–289 BCE). His father was a potter. He learned his father's craft before joining the army, where he rose to fame.

Maximian: Marcus Aurelius Valerius Maximianus, Roman emperor with Diocletian 286–305 AD. Born of humble parents, Maximian attained political power on the basis of his military skill.

Maximus: Marcus Clodius Pupienus Maximus, Roman emperor with Balbinus for three months in 238 AD. The *Historia Augusta* states that his father was a blacksmith, but he was most likely a senator.

Vespasianus: Caesar Vespasianus Augustus, aka Titus Flavius Vespasianus, Roman emperor (69–79 AD), his parents were of the Roman equestrian order, but he rose in social status and founded the Flavian dynasty. He was known to be a good ruler.

barrel better herring: proverbial phrase signifying never one better than another, nothing to choose between them (Tilley B94)

⁴⁹⁵ Caesar Augustus: Gaius Julius Caesar Augustus (63 BCE-14 AD); first emperor of the Roman Empire (27 BCE-14 AD). His father was of the Roman Equestrian Order and once governor of Macedonia. In Aelius Donatus's *Life of Virgil*, the character of Virgil states that Caesar Augustius's father was a baker (7).

⁴⁹⁶ A reference to incest is excised.

Hercules: Roman name of the Greek legendary hero, Heracles, son of Alcmene and Zeus

Perseus: from Greek mythology, son of Danaë and Zeus

Jugurtha: King of Numidia 118–105 BCE, he was the son of Mastanabal, one of the three sons of King Massinissa, and his concubine.

as concerning whom, his father Philip on his deathbed denied him to be his son by the report of his mother Olympia, for which cause, after his father's death, he would needs be called the son of Jupiter Ammon.⁴⁹⁷ Constantine the Emperor was born of a young maid before lawful espousals, and Jephthah in the Scriptures was son to a harlot.⁴⁹⁸ Or, if you will, madam, that for like examples we run over the histories, whereunto my wit can not carry me in so sudden speech, yet I remember that few years since there died in Spain a stout° king of the Goths called Bamba, which as I have heard was a labouring man.⁴⁹⁹ And at that time, when he was to be crowned king, was faine° to stick his spade in the ground to receive the sceptre, being neither less feared than his predecessors. And not reserved by me to the last place, as one of least credit among others, remember yourself of the great King Arthur, your progenitor, of whom, with your grace's leave, I do not think that men of malice doubted whose son he was.⁵⁰⁰ And we may boldly speak of these and other things so long ago passed without suspect of misliked affection. But why marvel we at these things? Doth not the wise man say that if our life were long, we should see many kings become bondmen and of many bondmen crowned kings? The reason being the same as I have rehearsed: that in elder age the only herald to pronounce a man either noble or unnoble° was his own good deeds, which advanced his good name and renown above the inferior deeds of kings and princes. But to paint out the pride of our times, let us cast down our eyes to the first root, from whence we all take our beginning. Shall we not find it all one for all men? Marry,° in the body of this tree there are many branches, some higher and some only water-boughs° from whom the top boughs keep of the comfort both of sun and showers, yet no man, I trow,° will be so envious as to hinder the growth of the inferior if they be more faithful than the superior, as not always the tallest men do the best service, and the best born for wealth or might prove not the best always for manners and worship. Witness hereto the sons of Scipio and Marcus Aurelius, of which two descended two perverse imps, far more infamous than their parents were famous.⁵⁰¹ And there are infinite more likewise to improve the succession of virtue in the succession of inheritance. And yet for all this long discourse, I cannot choose but reserve my former purpose towards you, for I am afraid that the most part will not be of my judgement. In a word, therefore, to make an end in that wherewith we first began, you must consider both by what means and for what causes the times are altered, and thereupon take advice according to the time. And since that for our sins God hath given us over to a wrong judgement in matters of high estate, rather to prefer wealth than virtue, and since you are now fallen unto that time wherein this error generally hath overgrown the truth and is strengthened by consent of men, I would counsel you to yield unto the time: that is, to take it as you find it and to make the best of your chance. For it were great folly for you — and no less danger — to resist a multitude,

---

⁴⁹⁷ Jupiter Ammon: Jupiter, the Roman king of the gods, came to be associated with the Egyptian deity Amun, following the Roman conquest of Egypt. Plutarch's *The Life of Alexander* reports that Alexander was thought to be the son of Jupiter because his mother, Olympia, had lain with a serpent by her side; it was thought that the serpent was the god in disguise (Book II.iv). Upon visiting the oracle of Jupiter Ammon, Alexander was greeted as the deity's son, and he subsequently commanded that he be called the son of Jupiter Ammon (Quintius Curtius Rufus, *Historiae Alexandri Magni*, Book IV.vii.5–30).

⁴⁹⁸ Constantine: Flavius Claudius Constantinus, Roman emperor (306–337). His parents were Flavius Constantius and Helena; whether or not they were married remains uncertain.

Jephthah: a judge of Israel in the *Old Testament* Book of Judges. He was the son of Gilead and a prostitute (Judges 11.1).

⁴⁹⁹ Bamba: Wamba (d. 687), Visigoth king of Hispania, Septimania and Galicia (672–680). His humble origins were legendary rather than historical (*Espejo*, II.106).

⁵⁰⁰ King Arthur: legendary king of England. On the eve of Gorlois's death, Uther Pendragon impregnated Igraine with Arthur while disguised as Gorlois.

⁵⁰¹ sons of Scipio and Marcus Aurelius: Lucius Cornelius Scipio the Younger (210/209–174/170 BCE), son of Cornelius Scipio (the Elder), was accused and found guilty by the Roman Senate of receiving bribes from King Antiochus III (190 BCE). Commodus, Roman Emperor 180–192 BCE, son of Emperor Marcus Aurelius Antonius, one of the most dissolute and debauched tyrants of the Roman Empire.

and you know your friends will never be brought to esteem so highly of virtue in a base personage, although a precious stone can never be but precious whether set in lead or copper. You must forsake him then, and that is the only remedy. For according as I have read and have heard, the first remedy against a fit of love is to exempt ourselves from the company of the beloved and to shun and eschew the things which may bring it again to our remembrance.⁵⁰² The next is to drive in our thoughts the things which be contrary thereunto, as to think with how many breaches of sleep and with what continual care we desire a thing, either filthy (if unlawfully coveted), or at the least wise° transitory (though never so honest), withal to set before our eyes what harms, what robberies, what murders, what madness, it hath caused in the world, whereof there be too many histories.⁵⁰³ But yet, from all this, you may well acquit yourself, if you will separate from you your former conceit. And if none of these will suffice, there is another remedy behind, which is to bestow your liking upon such a one as may be matchable° to your estate.⁵⁰⁴ For as one nail driveth out another, so men say that the new love dispossesseth the old, which remedy as I have read was put in practice by Assirous and the King of Persia.⁵⁰⁵ And this is my opinion, which it may be your grace would not mislike° were it not somewhat troublous.° But if you have an eye to your benefit thereby, I doubt not but that you will well overcome the trouble.⁵⁰⁶ And I pray you speedily take some way or other, but the best, I say, still is the former for to allay the flame. The next is to take away the wood. And so to forget love is to remove from [the] beloved, for otherwise that which you quench in a month will be kindled in an hour. Now the means to achieve your purpose is by writing yourself to Rosicleer to this effect: that he abandon your presence forever. Myself will be the carrier, although I have some compassion on his pain'.

The princess, knowing the wholesome counsel which her Fidelia as a faithful friend had given her, answered lovingly, but yet with some conscience for her own smart, in these words:

'Those which are whole can easily give good counsel to the sick, and every remedy seems to them easy and possible, as in like sort, thou Fidelia, not yet attainted° with love, tell me of many remedies, which not only seem convenient unto thee but also so easy that thou say it lyeth in my hands to make myself free from the passion which tormenteth me. I tell thee truly that I know both that I am not worthy of Rosicleer and that besides it behoveth me to banish him from my presence. This I know, my Fidelia. But alas, shall this be easy for me? Perhaps I may make him avoid the court and country by the means thou have prescribed. But what then? I have a greater adversary within myself, which makes this match so not even as thou ween.°⁵⁰⁷ I know that when Rosicleer shall have departed the land, that my life will well near depart my body and I shall not easily forget mine° own choice. But yet, as thou will me, I will adventure to put him from his hope, though I bear part of the smart. And I had rather my body should pay for it than the honour of the Princess Olivia should be blemished, nor never shall the force of love be able to disparage her'.

In this heat, she called for pen, ink, and paper, which being brought, she wrote to Rosicleer as you shall hear hereafter. I cannot think that for all her great stomach° to maintain her honour

---

⁵⁰² Cf. Burton, *The Anatomy of Melancholy*, 3.2.5.2.

⁵⁰³ The omission discussed in the introduction, which points to Tyler's use of the 1555 edition of *Espejo* as her source text, occurs here.
   Cf. Burton, *The Anatomy of Melancholy*, 3.2.5.3.

⁵⁰⁴ Another reference to marriage is excised by Tyler.
   Cf. Burton, *The Anatomy of Melancholy*, 3.2.5.5.

⁵⁰⁵ 'For as one nail . . .': proverbial, Tilley N17.
   Assirous and the King of Persia: Artaxerexes, King of Persia, also known as Asuero, Ahasuerus, or Xerxes. In the 'Book of Esther' he divorces Vashti and falls in love with Esther (Esther 2.17–18). Tyler erroneously believes Assirous and the King of Persia to be two distinct individual.

⁵⁰⁶ Further justifications for banishing Rosicleer are omitted.

⁵⁰⁷ 'Perhaps I . . . thou ween' is unique to *Mirror*.

against Rosicleer's baseness, that she could draw those cruel lines with dry eyes. But when she had made an end and closed up the letter, as if she had got some memorable conquest, sayeth she:

'Now dare I compare with the Roman matrons, which for the preservation of their honesty, sacrificed themselves unto their gods.[508] For what have I done else, but in a manner sacrificed myself to God, when for my honour sake I have bound and linked myself to such a continual martyrdom and perpetual imprisonment as the absence of Rosicleer will breed in me, and never more will live as a princess, but rather like a vowess.° But hold! Fidelia, take it!'

At which word, she sent out such a sigh, and wept so bitterly as if her heart had rent° asunder. Fidelia promised to do the message. And after she had comforted her lady, departed speedily, I think fearing lest the princess should reclaim her opinion.[509]

CHAPTER 40

Fidelia, being on her way to carry the letter to Rosicleer, was taken by six knights, and from them delivered by Rosicleer

Fidelia, having already taken leave of the princess to execute the cruel sentence pronounced upon poor Rosicleer, was upon better advice called back by her lady and made stay till the morrow.° The next day, coming before her lady to give her warning of her departure, scarce might she obtain leave to go or tarry. And when she urged the necessity of her going, still the princess would stay° her with some such speeches:

'Sweet Fidelia, tarry yet a little longer. Sweet Fidelia, tarry till my life leave this careful body. It will not be long; my sorrow prognosticates of my end.[510] If thou tarry till I have ended this, my weary life, go in God's name then to Rosicleer. It will be to some purpose to let him understand that though my body be dead, yet I meant mine° honour should remain sure for him'.

Fidelia pained herself to comfort her lady, and thinking it not best to enter any long talk, as if she had gone of some other errant,° she stole privily° from her mistress in the company of other gentlewomen, the less to be suspected. And mounting upon her palfrey, she rode through the city of London, all disguised, to seek Rosicleer.

Ere° long she came to the keeper's house where the three princes had lodged, at whom she learned that they were not far from thence. So with great diligence, she hasted° after them. And as their knightly prowess left behind them the memory of their being there, so wheresoever° she came, she still heard of them. And within eight days after that she had left the keeper's lodge, she came within less than one day's journey of the place where their abode was.

That day, passing alone through the thickest of a forest, there came out against her six knights, which took her horse by the bridle, saying that she should go with them, which when she denied and began to plead for her delivery with words of courtesy, one of them drew out his sword and said he would slay her unless she prepared herself for their company. But whether she would or no, they made her palfrey go by force with them toward the forest.

Then Fidelia, fearing that they meant herein some dishonour to her personage, leapt from her palfrey. And one of the knights perceiving it, alighted to fetch her up again, but she, getting from him, ran thence as fast as she might. And by her good fortune, it came to pass that when the knight had overtaken her and held her in his arms to put her up upon her horse, that

---

[508] She is recalling figures such as Lucretia, Portia, Arria, and Sophonisba who were notable for their choice of suicide over behaviour deemed unchaste or dishonourable.
[509] Her extreme sorrow is recounted at much greater length in *Espejo*.
[510] The concept of prognostication is added.

Rosicleer and the two princes, Bargandel and Liriamandro, then passed through the forest to seek the selfsame knights and to be avenged upon all the evils in which they had wronged that country. These three, hearing the screeches and outcries which Fidelia made, got near the sound to know the matter. In the end, they saw that the knights would carry a gentlewoman away against her will. At which, albeit Fidelia was so well muffled that none of them knew her, they were all displeased. And Rosicleer, more angry than the rest, said:[511]

'Sir Knights, what is the cause that you force this gentlewoman to go with you against her will?'

One of them, in great scorn, said:

'If you will needs be of counsel with us, I will prick you the cause upon my spear's point!'

But Fidelia cried:

'Ah, my lord, deliver me from these false thieves, which will lead me away prisoner I know not wherefore!'

Rosicleer, hearing them both, without more to-do° gave one of them such a blow upon the breast with his lance that it pierced him through, and he fell dead to the ground. The two valiant princes ran against two and, within short time, slew them. The three which remained set upon Rosicleer, but he cleft one with his sword and made the other two to gallop away. The two princes, loath to let any of them escape, followed them in such sort that they four were now entered into the thickest of the wood, Rosicleer being alone with the gentlewoman.

Fidelia, now at liberty and only [in] the company of Rosicleer, stood in a doubt whether after so great courtesy she might in her mistress's name declare so uncourteous a message. But remembering herself to be at another's command, unto whom she had promised her faith in this matter, the time also so fit for the accomplishing of her lady's charge, she discovered herself to Rosicleer, who presently knew her, and much abashed° to see her in that plight, alighted from his horse to embrace her.[512] And as it hath been recounted, his speech was on this manner:

'What misfortune, fair gentlewoman, hath brought you from that heavenly court, wherein you were once acquainted, to seek harbour among such uncivil hosts as these knights are?'

Fidelia's answer was short, in these terms:

'Oh noble Rosicleer, the anguish which Fidelia feels is indeed great, but yet it only ariseth through the remembrance of that message which she hath in charge unto Rosicleer'.

And with that, she wept bitterly. Then, somewhat amazed, he said unto her:

'Tell on, fair gentlewoman! And if your sorrow be for my sake, let me bear part with you. And thanked be God, I am not altogether a stranger to mishaps'.[513]

Yet, wist° he not whereabouts her message was. But he being very earnest to have the message told him, she drew out the letter out of a little box and put it into his hand with so much pain that she could not speak a word withal. Rosicleer, having the letter and desirous to know what was in it, opened it presently, wherein he soon espied the set determination of the princess as touching his exile. But before he had well weighed of the contents, espying only Olivia's name in the inscription — as we say that men's minds misgive° them against a mischief — so his heart throbbed, all his body trembled, and he had much ado to force himself to endure the uttermost. The letter said as followeth:

'The high and mighty princess, the Princess Olivia, Princess of Great Britain, unto the most arrogant Rosicleer, sendeth perpetual disgrace for thy lewd attempt.[514]

Being no less injured by thy presumption than minding the punishment of thy folly, I have written unto thee. And know thou that thy letter hath come not to me in daylight nor delivered

---

[511] Tyler classifies Rosicleer as the most angry, thereby affirming his exemplarity.
[512] 'But remembering ... to Rosicleer' is an addition.
[513] 'And thanked ... to mishaps' is original to the English translation.
[514] The *salutatio* is added. This is noted in the introduction in the context of Tyler's interest in correct dictaminal form.

in thy name, lest I might justly have refused it, but in the night time and that closely° and by stealth conveyed in my coffer that I might first be beguiled ere° I might forethink° me of the deceit.[515] The receiving whereof, albeit so at unawares, hath somewhat blemished my honour, and the shame thereof, if I thought possible to be rubbed out, I would not spare, for Thames water being so near my father's palace. But to make amends for my fault, and lest thou take some pride in thy impudency,° I am driven now to another inconvenience: that is, to answer thee, whom otherwise I would not have vouchsafed in this respect the courtesy of a good look.

In thy letter, the first point of thy pride I find to be in bending thy liking towards me.[516] The second, and greater, in daring to manifest it unto me. The third and especial,° in forcing me by copy of words and an old tale of love's power to give some relief to thy heaviness, which thy intolerable pride as it seemed rare and strange unto me, so it made me more narrowly to sift. And examining myself thoroughly and in every point, if either the lightness of my looks, or my unchaste demeanour, or the lack of foresight in my speech, or the familiarity of acquaintance, might give occasion to so base a knight as to attempt a princess. Wherein if I could have called to mind any little oversight whereby thou might have courage of impeaching my honour, I would first have punished it in myself as I am now purposed to amend it in thee. Only I remember I bestowed upon thee largely; and what then? Thou, therefore, as Lucifer, having more graces than thy fellow angels, will pull God out of his throne? Note that the stay° of true virtue is humility, and there is no glory so clear but pride may darken it. Because I humbled myself so much as to think of thy mean virtues, would thou venture this? Did my beauty cause thee to love me? And could not my estate withhold thy pen, but thou must challenge me for it? I was above thy reach. And why did thou not fear thy overstraining, if thou meant to compass me? God never punisheth the desire of things allowed by nature, but thou shall find occasion of smart in thy disordered affection. What if love be so great as thou pain thyself to prove unto me? Did not other princes see me, from whom yet the honest regard of my greatness shielded me, which thought never entered into so abject a breast as thine is? Yet Caesar, forsooth, and Hannibal, and Mars, and Jupiter were overcome with like passions.[517] What ever good liking I might have had to them, I tell thee I list° not to hear poor Rosicleer's tale. Thou will have me so to use clemency towards thee as I shall thereby to be cruel to myself, otherwise thou bid my loss. Then must I have regard and forever cease thou to trouble me in like manner; or, if because thou love me, I must deal with thee accordingly. I am content. But to thy greater grief: for mark, the greater love deserveth the greater chastisement, and greater is the fault done upon presumption than by ignorance or infirmity, as much less sufferable is the disgrace wrought by a friend than by a foe, and the lover's unkindness is less excusable than the stranger's.[518] Thou profess thyself my friend and lover, and I protest and proclaim myself now to be wronged at thy hand. Judge thyself how I can bear it. For this injury which thus spiteth me, I charge thee avoid this court! Forsake the land! And if thou mean good to me, get thee thither° from whence never news of thy name may be brought to England. This way shall thou prove thy love, and else not. And so she leaveth thee till doomsday,

Thy mortal enemy,

Olivia[519]

When Rosicleer had read the words of the letter, the contents thereof so galled him at the quick that for very grief his senses forsook him and he fell upon the ground, the[re] remaining

---

[515] 'nor delivered in thy name', is added by Tyler to balance the parallelism.

[516] The structure of the letter is clarified in *Mirror* through the numbering of Olivia's points.

[517] The 'bad women' with whom these men sin are invoked in *Espejo*.

[518] The addition of 'as much less sufferable ... than the stranger's' extends the parallelism.

[519] The *conclusio* is appended to *Mirror*. This is noted in the introduction in the context of Tyler's interest in correct dictaminal form.

a whole hour without moving foot or hand. And Fidelia departed.[520] So soon as Fidelia was gone, Telio, Rosicleer's squire, came that way to seek his lord, for he had departed from him before to fetch fresh water at a fountain hard by.° Now when Telio approached and saw Rosicleer stretched in that manner upon the ground as if he had been dead, he made the greatest dole that ever poor creature made. And alighting from his horse, he plucked off Rosicleer's helmet, casting water in his face if perhaps he might revive. In the end, Rosicleer yielding forth a groan as if his heart-strings had burst withal, came wholly to himself, and stretching his joints upon the green grass, began to speak in this manner:

'Oh, fell° Fortune and ever spiteful, why have thou not made an end of my life with the end of my joy?[521] And why live I, since that thereby my life is bereft me? Leave me alone, I pray thee, and my grief shall not grieve me without thy company! Above all, welcome death, the undoer° of my care! Welcome my death, in what manner I care not! Suffer not a knight so unfortunate to appear amongst men, nor to receive common sepulchre! Cato, not to behold the conqueror's face, slew himself with his sword, and Sophonisba poisoned herself to be free from bondage.[522] Now, what reason was there in them by death to fly° common and ordinary mishaps, if I maintain my life to the abiding of far greater torments than are in death? And whence commeth this mischance unto me? From Love. Oh, Love! Love, far more outrageous than fire and water, and far more dangerous to deal withal than chance or Fortune! Thou are strange in all thy purposes, stranger in the execution of them, and in the end thereof, strangest of all.[523] How commonly do thy practices exceed the working of Fortune, for she never giveth pain but in pleasure, never grief but in gladness, and she never overthroweth but at the top and pitch,° so that there is yet some comfort to have been high. But I, which in true love towards Olivia had never countenance of comfort nor pleasure of any height, am now so disgraced and have fallen so low as no adversity of Fortune can match it. Artimodoro told me my kindred should not let° our marriage.[524] But now, farewell my friends, by name Oliverio, King of the Great Britain, my loving lord; Bargandel and Liriamandro, princes inheritors and my loving companions. And farewell Zoilo, Prince of Tartary, as my last acquaintance. Fortune did but show us to each other when we hoped of great acquaintance. And farewell all my comforts, for I will hence to some dark and cloudy country, that not so much as the light of the sun may bring tidings of my smart'.

This saying, Rosicleer rose up and mounting on his horse, rode toward the forest, which leadeth unto the sea, with full determination to leave the country. Presently, his squire, Telio, which both saw and heard his complaint, with great grief followed him, not yet daring to speak a word for fear of disquieting him. Rosicleer, in this journey made great haste, and before night got to a huge and hollow rock about ten miles from the place where he received the letter. Thereon he cast himself, turning his horse loose upon the cliffs. Now being alone, as his manner was, he renewed his complaints with many a sicker sigh.

In the morning when the sun cast his beams upon the large sea, Rosicleer rose from the ground to look if he might see any ship wherein he might put himself. When he espied none, he commanded Telio to ride unto the next haven about two miles off, there to provide° a ship. Himself promised in the meanwhile under that covert° to abide his coming.[525] Telio presently

---

[520] Her sorrow is recounted in *Espejo*.
[521] The allusion to Fortune is unique to *Mirror*.
[522] Cato (95–46 BCE): Roman statesman and politician. Strongly opposed to Caesar's policies, he committed suicide in order to prevent Caesar from judging him.
 Sophonisba (fl. 203 BCE, during the Second Punic War): a Carthaginian. At the urging of her husband, she committed suicide in order to avoid being humiliated in a Roman triumph.
[523] The passionate *exclamatio*, 'Oh love . . . of all', is added.
[524] A lengthy section from *Espejo* is omitted in which his friends are addressed in great detail.
[525] His desire to keep his actions secret from Bargandel and Liriamandro is specifically described in the source.

did as his lord commanded him and made as much speed as he might, not to leave his master comfortless.

But ere° Telio had got to the town, it chanced that Rosicleer, having great desire to be solitary, mounted upon his horse and rode a contrary way, in which way he saw a little ship making towards the land. And out of this ship, from underneath the hatches, there appeared a gentlewoman very high and big of body, but of a good complexion and strangely attired, as was her country guise. This gentlewoman, as soon as the anchors were cast, caused the cock-boat° to be let down, wherein she entered. And coming to land, she took her palfrey to gallop up the sands. But espying a knight alone, whom by all semblance she took to be Rosicleer, she framed a sorrowful countenance and in great ruth° saluted him, to whom he rendered the like salutations, demanding what her grief was.[526]

The gentlewoman, still counterfeiting a show of great sorrow, stayed a time as not able to speak any thing, till being importuned by him with much ado, she, as it were, forced out these speeches:

'Alas, sir, tell me if you can, some news of a new knight, which hath won the prizes at the great feasts in London'.

'Wherefore seek you him?' said Rosicleer.

'I seek him', answered the gentlewoman, 'for that I hear so much of his glory as that I am persuaded that he only is like to give remedy to my travail°'.

Rosicleer — to make haste away, for fear lest his squire should find them — opened himself unto the gentlewoman, saying that he was the new knight. The gentlewoman, seeming to be very glad for to have found him, kneeled down. But he lifted her up and desired her to say on presently what her sorrow was, for he would willingly undertake her demand. The gentlewoman said on this wise°:

'Sir Knight, not far hence there is an island where my father dwelled, a plentiful land and ancient inheritance to our line. This land my father governed a great time in peace and ease, till that Fortune, loath to preserve things in one estate, changed her copy.° And that which grieveth me most of all, found means by me to work the discontentment of my friends. For being young and marriageable and my father's only child, it happened that I had many suitors. But to be short, my father, thinking it safest for the continuance of his line and the peaceable government of his people, which had rather have been subject to their natural country man than an alien, matched me with a lusty° knight both best beloved for his worthiness and of greatest possessions in all that country.[527] Now, amongst my other suitors, there was one of great livelihood, worthy for his wealth to have been preferred before all the rest, if himself had been as worthy; but this lord was refused by me. And taking it as some part of disgrace, he kindled his choler and wrath against my parents and me, and at a time convenient, which was not many nights past, and when we least imagined it, he burst in upon my parents, where he found but weak resistance. But I myself, in the meanwhile, stealing by the shore side, recovered this little boat, wherein I was scarcely entered when I saw a far off my parents and my husband led away prisoners. I think they cannot justly guess whither° I am gone. But after that I was in the boat I met with many which came from the jousts at London. They, seeing my heavy cheer, demanded the cause. And when they understood it, they directed me to enquire after a new knight in the land, for he alone, say they, is able to undo this injury. You hear, sir, both the cause of my care and the occasion of coming into this country to you, sir. Now Sir Knight, if my ruth° may work any compassion, or that you think I have case to complain, do your best to amend my harm. You shall do double justice in restoring the wronged and in punishing the wicked doer'.

---

[526] The woman and her actions are described in much greater detail in *Mirror* than in the Spanish source.
[527] The extensive addition, 'And that ... that country', fully describes her circumstances.

Rosicleer, feeling a yearning in his mind against so unlawful a practice if her tale were true, bade her take her boat again, for he would hazard his person in her quarrel. The gentlewoman, desiring presently no other thing, gave him many thanks. So they entered the boat, and the water being calm, they passed without any danger. But still, Rosicleer — haunted with his ancient° thoughts, now seeing himself far distant from the princess and without hope to return — began afresh to consider of his exile, which thought so overcame him that he wished his soul to depart from his body.

But the history leaveth him on the sea, to recount in the meantime of his squire, which finding a ship in the haven returned to his master. But not meeting him, he was sore abashed° and, in great sorrow, coasted over the country to find him out. After long travel by land to no purpose, he put himself to the sea in a ship prepared towards Almaine, where after continual weariness and not hearing any news of his master, he turned towards [his] own country in the Valley of the Mountains, where he was well welcomed by his brothers.[528] There let us leave him, till time carry him from his father's home to meet with his master.

Now telleth the history of Zoilo, Prince of Tartary, which had travelled towards the court of King Oliverio, as hath been recited. When he came to the court, he found in the palace hall the Princess Olivia with the king, her father, and diverse noble princes, devising and sporting of diverse matters and especially of Rosicleer's worthiness, which not a little tickled° the Princess Olivia for all that cruel sentence which she had given of him.

The Tartarian Zoilo, entering the hall in goodly manner to the great amaze° of the knights and nobles which beheld him, after he had made his humble obeisance to the king, he spoke as followeth:

'It may be, noble and worthy King, that the greatness of my estate forbiddeth me to be so humble, but the great virtue which I have found in the knights of your majesty's court hath enforced° me above my wont to do you that honour, which I would deny else to any king or emperor in the world. Now, I beseech your majesty to accept of my service and to receive me into the number of your knights, for I have great desire to belong unto your court, if it so like you'.

The king — very well liking of the majesty which the knight bore, albeit he knew him not [nor] whence he was — of courtesy embraced him gladly, and raising him from ground, answered thus:

'Sir Knight, you are very welcome. For as your personage and good behaviour is above the credit of a mean° man, so have I great opinion of your high estate. And as to your request to be entertained of my court, I receive you willingly and promise you therein my royal favour, for I would live no longer than to make of your likes.[529] And I pray you, Sir Knight, tell me who you are, lest peradventure° I should fault in not honouring you according to your calling'.

Zoilo answered:

'Most puissant king, the report of your courtesy assured me your good favour before I demanded it. And now, sir, understand you that I am named Zoilo, son to the King of Tartaria, in that part which bordereth upon Christendom, and that I have spent many winters both on sea and land, till that Fortune cast me on the English shore, then coming out of Duchland.[530] After here in your country, minding as my usage was to try myself upon knights errants, it chanced that I met with three of your knights in a forest. Their names were, as I learned of them, Rosicleer, Bargandel, and Liriamandro. With these I jousted. And after that I had cast down the two last at the tilt, I fought with Rosicleer at the sword's point, but in the end I was vanquished. Rosicleer, when I was yielded, having some liking of me, desired me to come and be acquainted with your majesty and to kiss your royal hand in his name. All which I have done

---

[528] Almaine: Germany
[529] 'to make of your likes': to be of your liking
[530] Duchland: Germany

as well for to offer my service to so mighty a prince as for to accomplish the charge of so valiant a knight. Neither think I it any disgrace to be vanquished by him; for besides that his bounty and courtesy meriteth to be beloved rather than envied, his valour and knighthood promiseth the conquest over the whole world. He hath received me for a perpetual friend, and his acquaintance do I more set by than the whole kingdom of Tartary, my lawful inheritance. Therefore, because I hope the longer to enjoy this new friendship in your service, I have been bold to crave the name of your court, which shall be as well welcome unto me as the title which you have unto your kingdom'.

The king was glad to hear some news of Rosicleer at that time and much praised his own good Fortune to have lighted upon him, for that by him his court had daily increased in worship. And so, turning towards the Tartarian, he said on this manner:

'Pardon me, mighty prince, in that I have not done you that honour which appertaineth to a king's son, but the little acquaintance I have had with you and the ignorance of your estate shall excuse me henceforwards. If I amend not, let me be without excuse'.

And with these same words, the king led Zoilo to the princess, willing her to welcome the knight stranger. Zoilo, coming before the beautiful Princess Olivia, kneeled down before her to kiss her hand, which she refused. But gentle kissing him, she bade him welcome. Farther talk had she not, for the often naming of Rosicleer brought to her remembrance the wrong which she had done to him. And her heart was so great that she had no power to speak a word, but craving pardon she departed to her chamber. This seemed strange to her father, but because her colour was so pale it was thought to be by reason of sickness.

When she was within her chamber doors, she let her tears flow at liberty, which before she restrained for fear of being espied. And thinking in what manner her father's court was honoured by Rosicleer, and in what estimation he was held among those princes and knights, how glad they were of his friendship and how loath her father was to lose him, she burst out into abundance of tears.[531] And with the repentance of her former fact, she began in this sort to repent her rashness:

'Thou hasty and over-credulous Olivia! What thing did the poor Rosicleer crave of thee but the acceptation of his service and that thou would become his lady?[532] Why did thou not receive him offered? Especially when so many puissant princes and worthy knights require to have and are refused, why would thou not be lady over him, whom the best in the world would be servant unto? Where was my judgement and the eyes of my understanding, that I forethought me not of these things? Now do I too much repent that which I hastily willed, as touching the banishment of Rosicleer'.

Here, she stayed° her speech and, in great disease° of mind, shut herself in her closet. Here now wanted° the faithful counsel of her servant Fidelia, for had she been at hand she might have slaked her mistress's sorrow, which in the end grew so far, as besides the loss of speech and her often sounding,° she fell into a hot, burning ague,° which left her not of a great while, till more comfort came by means of another letter, which she read, of her love's to his mother Briana. Till that time, we will help the two knights, Bargandel and Liriamandro, out of the wood and bring them from the search of Rosicleer to the court of King Oliverio.[533]

---

[531] An extensive description of her thoughts and feelings is omitted.
[532] Olivia chastises herself as 'hasty and over-credulous' in *Mirror*. These stereotypical slights, usually uttered against women by scorned men, are surprising in this context since they are spoken by a female character in a translation that tends to omit the negative portrayals of women from its source.
[533] The description of her sorrow is shortened.

CHAPTER 41

The Princes Bargandel and Liriamandro, returning from the forest, miss Rosicleer

The great desire which led Bargandel and Liriamandro to pursue the knights of the forest made them to follow on so long till they joined at a great and well-towered castle, standing at the one end of the said forest. There, before these two knights could enter to save themselves, the two princes had overtaken them. And getting between the castle and them, they put them to so great scathe° that the knights, unable to resist, cried 'Amain!°' to those which were within the castle for succour. Yet ere° they could come, they were overthrown sore wounded.

And as the princes lighted down to make dispatch of them, ten men issued out of the castle well armed. And coming near, laid at the princes in great rage, for they weaned their lords to have been slain. But this skirmish lasted not long between them, for the two princes were valiant. And putting themselves in press° amongst the thickest, in short time made riddance of the greater part. And those which remained besought the princes of pardon, which being easily granted, the two princes returned to the two knights, which had been felled but late before. These two knights, seeing in what case they were and pitying the destruction of their people, yielded themselves to the will of the conqueror, promising that if they might enjoy their life and liberty, they would amend their folly and make satisfaction to all gentlewomen, whereof the princes were glad.

And taking their oaths for the performance, departed in haste toward Rosicleer as they thought; but he was not where they left him, wherefore they sought him out in all parts. This day, till night they never descended from their horses. At night, they took their bed under a tree until the coming of the next day. And they were very pensive, for that they knew not the cause why he absented himself. Yet, with some hope that the next day they should hear some news of him, they drove out that night, and on the morrow° mounted up their horses again to find him out. But it was no boot:° for eight whole days, they travelled through the country and heard no news of him. In the end, thinking they should meet with him at the court, they rode thither° in the company of many knights, whither° let them go, while we in the meantime bear the gentlewoman company, which had carried Olivia's letter unto Rosicleer.

This gentlewoman, Fidelia, as I told you, perceiving as well by the witness which his eyes gave of his outward grief as also by the sound° wherein she left him as an argument of his inward sorrow that he needed comfort, and yet not daring to show him hope contrary to her majesty's commandment, struck her palfrey, and without more stay, galloped on her way towards London, whither° in short time she came. But when she had entered the palace, she would not presently° make her coming known unto the princess, lest her sudden return should work some alteration, whereby the other gentlewomen might misdeem° of her errand. But when she had learned of the gentlewomen that her lady was sick, she well wist° whence her disease sprung. And therefore, wisely coming before her mistress, she yet spared to name Rosicleer till she understood how well she would take his heaviness.

The princess, now uncertain in judgement whether to commend of Fidelia's faithfulness in executing of her device if the letter were delivered, or to like of her good Fortune if some occasion had hindered the delivery, being now alone, stayed° yet to hear either 'yea' or 'nay' as touching the dispatch of her message. But Fidelia, as well for her own compassion over Rosicleer as for sorrow to see her mistress in that plight by her own conceit, uttered never a word, but burst out into weeping, whereby the princess, more troubled than at the first, with a feeble voice spoke unto her:

'Tell me, Fidelia, what thou have done in thy message. And doubt not but thy travail° shall well please me, for although the love I bear him feareth to hear thine answer, yet shall mine° honour countervail° the dread, in which quarrel I will, as I told thee erst,° venture my life rather than yield my body to any opprobry°'.

50   This saying, she lent her ear unto Fidelia's answer and fastened her eyes upon Fidelia's looks, as if no word should have escaped unmarked or unadvised of her. Fidelia's answer was short in these terms:

'For a truth, madam, I had sought Rosicleer no little time ere° I could find him. And as it fell out, I found him when myself was not without danger, as it were to participate of that cruelty towards him wherein I was partly a dealer. But that which maketh me especially to repent my pains herein was that my delivery was wrought by him. For at the same time I met him, six knights outlaws set upon me in a forest and had led me captive away, there to be spoiled of my honour. But that by my outcries, Rosicleer, with two other knights, came thither,° none of them having any knowledge of me, [or] who I was. There, in my presence, he killed three of them, the other flying° away were followed by the two knights in Rosicleer's company, by which means being alone with him, I there delivered your letters. But I believe that he had rather have received his death's wound than that letter. Ere° he opened it, his colour changed and all his body shook for fear. But after he had read the superscription, his eyes were filled with tears, and never man was so woebegone as he; yet he read it out. And as I remember, with the last words, he gave a great groan and sank to the earth. Whether he ever recovered or no, I wot° not, for I durst° not stay with him, therein to fulfil your grace's charge, which was not to receive answer from him'.

This understanding the princess, and that Fidelia had obeyed every jot of her will so well, although she would that her servant had failed in some small point of diligence in this matter. Yet, thinking to learn more at her hands, she demanded what thing he did when she parted from him and what words he spoke, moreover what she thought the event would be. To all which questions, Fidelia answered at once that she left him for dead upon the ground and to divine was not in her skill. With this, the princess waxed angry and blamed her very sore for not abiding the time of his recovery. Whereto Fidelia excused herself by her commandment. But yet because the princess would have it so, needs must Fidelia be thought in a great fault and crime for not doing so. Now may you guess that Fidelia's trustiness was like a cup of cold water to her burning ague, the more to enrage it, or like drink to a dropsy man, whereby his malady the rather increaseth. For in like manner, as Rosicleer's heaviness came by reading her letter, so hers grew by Fidelia's report of his heaviness. And albeit that we hear seldom time of man or woman dead for love, yet it is natural for overmuch grief to abridge man's days. As now it was not love which so much afflicted the princess, but the injury which she had offered Rosicleer, and the grief which she conceived by the despair of ever seeing him; and this grief had almost wrought her utter bane.

CHAPTER 4[2]

Rosicleer's departure is published in the court of King Oliverio; Olivia, after knowledge whose son he was, reverseth judgement passed by a countermand in another letter, whereof Fidelia likewise is the bearer

The princes Bargandel and Liriamandro, in the quest of Rosicleer, rode far and near and could not understand anything as touching him, till that having travelled over a great part of that country, they met with people strangers, which certified that themselves had seen a knight in that suit of armour embarking himself with a gentlewoman, and after that a squire sore weeping entering into a ship to follow them, for the which news Bargandel and Liriamandro were very sorrowful. And for now they were sure that he had forsaken the kingdom, whereupon they agreed to return unto the court.

And one day, as the King Oliverio with the Prince Zoilo and other worthy princes and knights were gone out of the city to solace themselves in the fields, these two princes came toward the place where the king abode, which had beheld them before very heedfully, for they seemed unto him to be two comely and noble knights and, therefore, he desired to have a more perfect view. But valiant Zoilo knew them by their devices upon their armour, and said to the king and to the other then in presence that he greatly marvelled why Rosicleer came not with them, for sayeth he:

'When I parted from them, they were all three together'.

When the king knew them to be the two princes, he caused his train to stay° till the two princes came against him. Those he embraced with great love and thanks for their return, demanding withal for Rosicleer. They which, I dare not say, knew the right cause, but conjectured some likely cause by the strangeness it wrought in him, with great grief made a narration of each particular as far as they knew, both what befell him within the realm and in what manner he avoided the realm, as they had heard of others, only in the company of a gentlewoman. And they added, moreover, perhaps of their own heads, perhaps, as I said before, upon some farther knowledge, that it could not otherwise be but that he had some great wrong offered unto him by some person within the realm.

The king, excusing himself to the princes for his own dealing towards Rosicleer, became very sad and heavy for him, as also those which were near, with him not being able to guess of his return. And indeed, if they had been certain of his long absence, it would much more have been grievous unto them, so rare was the love they all bore to him. But with some little hope of Rosicleer's speedy return, the king with those princes his friends tarried some days in the palace, till that, because he was from them so long, the three princes — Bargandel, Liriamandro, and the Tartarian Zoilo — together took upon them to seek him, in which time they adventured many strange exploits as shall be specified hereafter in this history.

But in the end, as the greatest part of these nobles and princes stayed in England for the love of Rosicleer, so his presence wanting, that court diminished so fast that in short time there was not behind remaining in the court any knight of great account but the Prince Don Silverio, unto whom the loss and absence of Rosicleer bred no small contentation,° as it wrought in the King Oliverio to the contrary no lesser displeasure and disquiet as if the loss of Prince Edward had again renewed. For there was no one in his kingdom which could and would advance his private credit and the honour of his country by worthy prowess and by valiant deeds of arms.

But when all the kingdom began to bewail the loss of Rosicleer, what did that fair Olivia, which had abandoned him the country and loved him more than anyone in the world? Might she forget him one instant? No, but when she weighed well that for the accomplishing of her charge he had forsaken the land, her good will increased towards him, and instead of the daily view of his personage, in his absence she gazed at will upon the counterfeit° and portraiture which she had imprinted in her fancy.° This did she the oftener because she found not in her solitary contemplation any other thing to present itself. For amorous thoughts are ever enemies to company, and being alone, as commonly she was by reason of sickness, what was there to remove this solitary thought and conversant companion from her? This companion she still entertained, which by use and continuance of time grew to a settled sentence. And her love waxed greater than it was before, and then increased the flame which burned more earnestly than ever before it had been.

But as it chanced, tossing of these things in her remembrance withal, she remembered that Arinda had told her how that Rosicleer had written unto the Princess Briana. And as the amorous are accustomed to build themselves castles of hope, albeit sometime without foundation or sure ground whereon they may surely stand, so her love waxed jealous over him and she began to cast° with herself why Rosicleer should write to the Princess Briana, being to her no kith nor kin° to her, and so mean° born. Out of which, in the end, she picked out this hope that out of doubt his birth was as good as his bringing up.[534] In this matter, therefore, she laboured Fidelia secretly to steal that letter from the gentlewoman Arinda, her bedfellow.

---

[534] This addition is essential since it clarifies her motive: 'Out of which ... bringing up'.

And talking about this matter one certain time with Fidelia, among other things, she said:

'Oh, my Fidelia, as I had the power to banish Rosicleer the land, so would I that I could banish him from my memory! How profitable had thy counsel been then unto me! But what shall I do, for that remedy is no more available since his absence wounds me more than his presence? I grant thee, the sight of the beloved to some encreaseth love, still offering itself to be seen; and yet to other some again, the thing daily seen bringeth little delight, but rather the loathsomeness, as contrariwise,° sometimes love is moved by discontinuance, and sometimes men's desire increaseth the flame, albeit the beloved appear not in presence. But this thou take to be impossible, for thou are not touched with the like passions, and none knows the bitterness thereof but the experienced, as appeareth by thee which has ministered a medicine not of force against my disease.° But make me amends, and once again venture for my sake. I remember that Arinda hath a letter of Rosicleer's to the Princess Briana, to what purpose I know not, but I would gladly see it. This steal from her, and bring it me that I may read it. I cannot say what good news my mind foretells me by it, but sure I long to read, as if there were some great secret contained therein. And quiet shall I not be till I have had it'.

Hereto Fidelia replied briefly that this matter should be left unto her to watch her opportunity. And indeed, when Fidelia and Arinda slept together one night, Fidelia espying Arinda fast asleep, rose as softly as she might and taking one of the keys which Arinda had tied to her girdle,° therewith she opened the casket and pulled out Rosicleer's letter, which she brought to her mistress['s] lodging, whom she found waiting for some glad news. The princess herself would not open the letter, but gave it to Fidelia, which unsealed it and read as followeth:

'To his good mother, the high and mighty Princess Briana,[535]

If my departure from your presence procureth your just displeasure, believe me, madam and my good mother, your son, Rosicleer, can not be well pleased therewith, foreseeing the great solitariness wherein you remained.[536] And yet, because this my journey hath so prospered with me, I am the better contended and I beseech your grace to quiet yourself upon God's ordinance, from whom I am persuaded this motion in me proceeded. Besides the story of mine° own good fortune, which Arinda may safely report, I have heard news as touching yourself, the redelivery of my father, and the safety of my brother. For, since my departure, I have got acquaintance with Artimodoro, a great wise man of Greece — perhaps he is not unknown unto you — of whom I have learned that your husband, my father, shall ere° long return unto you; that the Gentleman of the Sun, my brother, is alive and already knighted, and for prowess so greatly approved as not the knights of elder time are thought matchable;° that he and I shall know our father to be the most valiant and worthiest prince on the earth; that we shall have a pleasant end of our sorrowful beginnings, which God grant. As touching mine° own estate, I have been brought by this Artimodoro to the court of King Oliverio, where by his own hands I have been dubbed knight and have received such honour as if I had been his known nephew. And had it not been that your grace had commanded the contrary, not suffering our progeny to be known, I should for this favour have bewrayed° the truth at least to have given him some comfort for the supposed loss of Prince Edward; but I will obey your command. And these news I thought to make you privy° unto, as not being ignorant of your heaviness, which I pray God lessen to your comfort. Further as touching these matters, Arinda may tell you of the specialities. The Almighty send you speedily your desired husband. I take my leave, kissing your royal hands.

Your obedient son,
Rosicleer'

When Fidelia had ended the letter and the princess had well understood the secrets thereof, what tongue may express the great joy that entered into her sorrowful mind, as if she had but

---

[535] The *salutatio* and *conclusion* are original to *Mirror*; Tyler's interest in correct dictaminal form is discussed in the introduction.

[536] The salutation and the addition 'and my good mother' highlight the maternal relationship from the outset.

now recovered her lost hope? And had she not now counterpoised her ancient sorrow with this late-sprung joy, her life had been in danger; for in no other thing, excessive joy may do so much harm as in the hearts of true lovers, amongst whom I can compare these two princes, Rosicleer and the beautiful Olivia, as the chiefest.° This princess, now rid of some part of her fear, and as it were brought into a new world, thought to make amends by punishing herself for her cruel letter. Thus sayeth she:

'Oh, how well am I worthy of the pains, which I now sustain in the repentance of my former fact, not only for that which against Rosicleer I have committed, but also for the little credit that I have had of his valorous personage! Where were mine° eyes and judgement when I did not prove his nobility by his virtue? How great was my pride in that I would in such sort despise so worthy a knight and banish him, not only my presence but this kingdom also? Oh, inconstant and frail womankind, for just cause lightly regarded among wise men since we are light in belief, light in judgement, and over-hasty in showing the effect of our conceit! What occasion had Rosicleer given me that I should make exchange for the great good will which I bore unto him with so cruel a sentence as to dispatch him from my presence? What had he in his letter any dishonest word, any unlawful demand? Or did he move me to the thing prejudicial to my great estate? This he desired: that I should know he loved me. Why should I be ashamed that my inferiors love me, and that he should like of me was the thing I desired?

Tell me, Fidelia, what is thy counsel for to amend this fault? Me thinks we are in worse case than before. Rosicleer is already departed the country, and if I send to call him back he will not regard me. Or will it not be thought lightness, after that I had in such earnestness refused him as it were yesterday, this day suddenly to alter my purpose? Besides that, when he returneth into this court, his glory may increase to my disworship.° And again, if to bear out my former fact, I let the matter pass as it hath done, what shall then become of me? I know not how to live, he being banished from my presence, whom I love better than myself. But, Fidelia, as thy part was in the first counsel to banish Rosicleer, so now put to thy help that Rosicleer may return again without the blemish of mine° honour'.

Very joyful was Fidelia to hear the letter, and being well content that her mistress had kept her former conclusion in this matter, as touching the marriage of Rosicleer if his parentage were not so far inferior, soberly answered:

'Madam, leave off your complaints and be more glad than ever you were, since God hath been so favourable unto you as to make Rosicleer of so high estate that he may merit you. For in good sooth,° I stood in doubt whither° of your pains were the greater, and I knew no means how to slack them. But since now this secret is disclosed, the remedy is in our hands and not so difficult as you make it. For be it that you shall send unto Rosicleer to demand pardon of him for the offence which you have committed against him, shall you think you do yourself any wrong therein in respect of your princely estate? No, for assuredly he loveth you loyally. And because he is of nigh° parentage with you, you may therein beguile suspicious eyes. And after his return, you may bolt it out of him, whether he love you, yea or no. If he do, without peradventure° you may acquit him, and love of all things would be rewarded. I dare warrant that your love shall detain him with us, and to this purpose: madam, your hand and my head, which jointly committed the former fact, shall now together make the recantation and cry 'Peccavi!'° The effect may be only to will him to return to your presence. And myself will be the messenger, and I promise never to return into this country till such time as I find him and have delivered your letter to his hands. Withal', sayeth she, 'this ought presently to be put in practice, for by the grief Rosicleer took at the sight of your letter, I guess that he is either departed this life or avoided the country'.

The princess was very well content with her haste as the thing which she most desired, and so embraced she Fidelia gladly and spoke unto her:

'Fidelia, now I know the good will which thou have to serve me. And I confess that I have not made thee privy° to my heaviness without great hope of comfort at thy hands. Therefore, I beseech God once to reward thee as I wish. But bring me pen, ink, and paper, for I will straightway° follow thy counsel herein'.

Fidelia brought unto her pen, ink, and paper, wherewith the princess wrought her reclaim° with as many sugared words as the other letter had sharp and sour. This letter the sequel will show unto you, when we come to the meeting of Fidelia and Rosicleer. But before that time, the letter written after this manner was delivered unto Fidelia, and it was agreed upon between themselves that upon the next day she should go to seek him. This night they took their rest, the one for the better enduring of her long travail,° which she should sustain; the other, to make satisfaction for her broken sleeps.

Ere° broad morning Fidelia was up, and having conveyed Rosicleer's letter where she found it, she went unto the princess to take her leave of her. When, as they were departing:

'Oh my good Fidelia!' said the princess, 'Do as much as thou may to return again speedily, for if thou stay long I shall live but a small while; there is nothing that may so soon shorten and cut off my days as to hope without success and to dread the worst. I tell thee that till thy coming again, my nights will be turned to watchings° and I shall reckon the clock hourly awaiting thy presence. Oh, God! Fidelia, when the day cometh I will look for the night, then when as the night is overpassed,° I will make account of the day to come, and I will never leave casting° of perils till that I shall hear thee bring some tidings of that good knight'.

Fidelia was very sorry to think of the cares which her lady was like to receive, and principally for that she should leave her alone wanting with whom to communicate her pain. Wherewith being somewhat troubled, and also foreseeing the long time of her absence, so she departed weeping in this manner:

'Madam, it is needless for you to charge me farther in these affairs: the pains wherein I leave you are sufficient to hasten my journey. I would to God my Fortune were answerable to the desire which I have to serve you in this matter. But be of good courage, and hope for the coming of your knight, or else look not for me'.

With these, they broke off, and Fidelia went to her fellows, unto whom she told that she would sojourn with her parents in the country for a season. After going to the seaside, she entered into a ship prepared towards Almaine, wherein the history leaveth her sailing, to recount of other things which chanced in the meantime.[537]

CHAPTER 43

Rosicleer was betrayed into the island of Candramarte, that giant whose hands had been cut off before by Rosicleer

You have heard how Rosicleer departed from the Great Britain in the company of the strange gentlewoman, never hoping to return again into that land, only for the accomplishing of the exile whereunto he was bound by his lady's appointment. Now the history sayeth that the gentlewoman with whom he was in the boat was sent by Candramarte, whose hands Rosicleer had cut off before the King Oliverio for Queen Julia's rich sword, and that she was sent under colour° of a distressed gentlewoman to bring him to her father's island, there to be avenged of the hurt and shame which her father had received. This device was thought fittest, both for that Rosicleer, as a noble knight, pitied such oppressed gentlewomen, and that for other cause than to show himself Rosicleer could not be brought out of England.

In this island, Candramarte had two young giants to his sons, whom for that purpose he had knighted, being in making no less than himself. Besides these, Candramarte had forty chosen knights, all which he armed to assault Rosicleer lest he should escape them. By this guile, the

---

[537] Almaine: Germany

lady giantess, daughter unto Candramarte, carried him to her father['s] island, wherein, without any farther advice, he adventured himself for very grief of heart which he conceived to see himself abandoned his lady's presence. But now six days have they been on the sea, at the end whereof the wind was so favourable that they came within kenning° of the island, to his judgement very strong and to the show very pleasurable. This being discovered by the governor,° the gentlewoman said that that was the place wherein her parents and husband were taken, crying and tearing of her hair as if the sight of the place had redoubled her sorrow. This made Rosicleer to be more earnest in her quarrel and to think it long till he were landed.

Which his desire being accomplished, the gentlewoman led him up upon the shore where Rosicleer viewed at ease the whole sight of the island. In the first entry upon the land, there were two strong castles as two bulwarks, situated upon a steep rock as it were a bowshot° distance over against the other. Before the castles there was a great broad plain, shadowed with great oaks.

And when they had come near unto these great castles, the gentlewoman, pointing to the one castle, said to Rosicleer on this manner:

'If that, Sir Knight, you will avenge my quarrel, you must go to that castle which is on the right hand, for that is the traitor knight's castle, which hath taken my parents and husband as prisoners. And until your coming, I will stay here in this little boat: we women are weak-hearted and fearful, and above all, I would not come into his power, for then would he for a surety murder my parents and my husband, whom now perhaps he entertaineth more gently upon hope to win me'.

'If you will, be it so', answered Rosicleer, 'for your long gowns are not fit to fight withal, and your sex shall well answer the challenge of your cowardice'.[538]

With this speech, Rosicleer departed, and taking his horse, mounted thereon to come to that castle on the right hand. The gentlewoman took her ship again, and drove from land amaine.°[539] By and by, Rosicleer heard the winding° of a horn at the one castle, and presently he heard an answer at the other castle, whereby suspecting that this token was given of his coming, he turned his head to see the gentlewoman whom he had left on the shore. The gentlewoman, hovering about the bank (now sure of his escape) and straining her voice, cried:

'Come forth! Come forth, sons of Candramarte, for here is the new knight which cut off our father's arms!'

Now wist° Rosicleer by this horn and the gentlewoman's outcries that he had been betrayed. But as one careless° of his life, as quietly as he could, he prepared himself, which he certainly looked for. His prayer was this:

'Lord Jesus, have mercy upon me whom Thou so dearly has bought with Thy bloodshed. Pardon my sins, and receive me into Thy kingdom. As for my carcass, be it as Thou have appointed me, for death cannot betide me in a better time'.

After this, he stayed not as dismayed, but passing farther to see in what manner this treason was compassed, he saw the gates of the one castle set wide open, and thence issuing a huge giant upon a mighty courser with more than twenty knights well armed at his tail. At their first coming, they made a great shout as if they had got some great victory. And the giant amongst the rest said unto him:

'Thou miserable and wretched knight, well shall thou abye° the shame which thou did to my father Candramarte when thou did cut off his arms at London!'[540]

Rosicleer, as desperate,° made answer:

'I doubt not but for all your threats you will give me leave to die. But ere° that happen, it may be you shall be disappointed of your purpose'.

---

[538] In *Espejo*, Rosicleer exclaims that women ought to be fearful rather than daring, especially in cases such as this, where fear is justified.
[539] *Mirror* adds the gentlewoman's departure into her boat.
[540] His Spanish counterpart threatens that all the power of his gods will not let Rosicleer escape his hands.

And with that, he drew out Queen Julia's sword, with the which he encountered the tall giant which came against him with a great spear. The spear hit Rosicleer on the breast, and indeed, were it not for the finesse° of the armour, it had pierced him. But the metal being such as it was, the Greek made no more for the blow than if he had been hit with some delicate young knight. And before that the giant could recover his horse['s] rein to fetch the second course, Rosicleer gave him such a blow with his sword that he cleft him to the bowels. The great giant fell dead to the ground, the blood issuing in great abundance. Here the great brag was quailed,° when he which came to avenge another man's quarrel could not warrant his own safety.

70 But truth it is that those which immeasurably do seek revenge, do oftentimes heap on themselves the greater mischief.[541] And what did this tyrannous Candramarte else, which placing himself at his window to behold the battle and to make more solace at Rosicleer's harm, as if the only report had not been sufficient? Now instead of his former wrong, he found a greater by the death of his son[ ]. But yet this is the beginning only of his misery, for the valiant knight, not fearing death at all, in great choler rushed among the other knights, which likewise assailed him courageously, and had within a while with their battle axes hewn his horse in pieces.

When he was on foot, he laid about him manfully that, in short space, the scantling° of ground in which they fought was covered with breastplates and targets.° And as their number lessened and that he had more room, so his courage increased and he did them more scathe.° But well 80 fare[d] his enchanted armour, which had served to more purpose in defending than his sword in offending, or else his courage had tired before the end of so dangerous a fray. Now are there few alive — and those either striving for life upon the grass or in weak case upon foot —readier to fly° than to fight.

But presently, there came fresh succours from the other castle, for the other son of Candramarte with more than thirty knights, in great haste came against this good knight, not being idly occupied among the other knights. The giant, for other good-morrow,° gave the good knight so strong a blow with his battle axe upon the headpiece that had it not been rather in the headpiece to withstand the blow than in himself to resist the giant, Rosicleer had lain brainless on the ground. But all this grieved him not, saving that the weight of the blow made him kiss the earth, 90 whence yet he start[ed] up lightly.° And minding to requite courtesy for courtesy, as he was purposed at the giant, there stepped in a knight between them, whom Rosicleer divided to the breastbone, whereat the giant and those which beheld him were much abashed. Notwithstanding this, they being many and he wearied, he might not defend himself long from them, especially from the giant which only watched opportunity of advantages, yet lengthened he the fight by his noble courage a long time, until for very faintness he was fain to give back and to get his shoulders against a wall, from which afterward he was driven by main° force. And being pursued, he withdrew himself to the sea, ever as he warded one blow, bestowing another. After he had got the sea at his back, he waxed bolder, and above all watched Candramarte's son, which had hurt him most especially. Him he hit so sure that the blood gushed out in three or four places.

100 In the meanwhile, Candramarte, viewing the battle to no great liking, blasphemed heaven and earth. And leaving the window, ran to the seaside, where the battle was continued. And with a loud voice, he called on his knights, reviling them as cowards and bastards if one knight might resist them so long. And above all, to his son he spoke thus:

'Thou vile and dastard° sheep! How like thou are to thy miserable mother! I swear by heaven and earth, if thou escapeth out of this battle alive, my cause and thy brother's death unrevenged, that I will starve thee in the same place where I starved thy mother'.[542]

The giant and his knights, thus railed on for shame and fear, gave a fresh assault upon the good knight, so that as he dispatched some, there stepped in new in their rooms. And ever the battle was, as it were, new to begin to poor Rosicleer, which drove him to seek farther succour

---

[541] The diatribe against vengeance is shortened in *Mirror*.
[542] In the Spanish text, the punishment invoked is burning.

in the water and to stand up to the navel. Thinking his death to be very nigh, he prayed to God with all his heart for his soul's health, as one that altogether detested his life, and determined no longer to defend himself than the water would give him leave. Then taketh he his sword with both his hands and layeth on so thick that there are slain more than ten knights ere° he leaveth, as the sea gave witness, which made the bank seem as all bedewed with blood.

Now, behold and see how God never forsaketh His, and especially those which abide His pleasure, as He did unto this knight, which now standing equally betwixt° life and death, though neither fearing the one, nor hoping the other, and sure of neither, yet hath he remedy besides his hope and is comforted of his own brother, unknown to both. So may Fortune sometime vex and annoy° us, yet at the length she returneth back and relenteth again. But for this matter which we entreat of, we are to remember° ourselves of that valiant Grecian,° son to the Emperor Trebatio, left in the little boat sailing through the ocean seas, with the which he had passed the bounds of Africa, and coasting by the Mediterraneum Seas, was driven along the Spanish shore, and from thence, at length sailed by the island of Candramarte at such time as Rosicleer now enforced° himself to abide the uttermost of the skirmish with resolute mind, presently to receive the death or to be conqueror.[543]

But this boat, guided by a wise man as you heard before, took landing almost against Donzel del Febo's will, about a bird-bolt° shot from Rosicleer, where he espied a cruel fight. But that which most amazed him was that one knight, though strong-timbered and valiant, yet had set himself against so many, and with their bodies had made so great a slaughter. So with a great admiration, rather amorous then jealous, he said unto himself:

'Who would believe that in our days there might be found a knight furnished with such excellency of manhood? Assuredly, his fame is as worthy to be spoken of as that Greek's[544] which had killed the famous Trojan, Hector. Thanks be to the gods, which have brought me hither. For although I should lose my life, I will not leave him unsuccoured°'.

Thus saying, he waded in the water to come near him. And seeing the giant to oppress him so much, and without a shield, for he had lost it in battle with the first giant, he took his sword with both his hands and let drive with all his force at the giant's head, that he cleaved in unto the brain, and afterward rushed among the rest, killing many of them.

When Rosicleer saw with one blow the giant struck down and such unhoped° for succours,° the great wonder that he received may not be told. And as if the enterprise had been achieved or his life saved, with a fresh courage he went out of the water and valiantly thrust himself among his enemies, where he well gave them to understand that he was desirous the battle should end. Here two brothers, albeit unknown each to others, gave brotherly help in time of need. And there was never a one left, which either cried not pardon or fled his way. The suppliants were pardoned.

But let us think of Candramarte, which now saw his other and only son slain at one blow. In what plight do you judge him to be? But the worst is good enough. Whereas if he had held in his hungry desire of revenge with a long delay or had dissimuled° his choler, he might have lived quietly with his sons by him, able sufficiently to defend foreign invasion and maintain his. But now childless, knightless, and armless, besides at the mercy of his enemy, he was far out of charity with all the world, that cursing heaven and earth and what was in them, he ran headlong into the sea, there drowning himself among the waves and bequeathing his soul to the devil, who long ere° that expected to be his executor.[545] Tell me, I pray you, gentle readers, how often you have seen the immeasurable desire of revenge have a lucky end, or not rather to procure a farther harm when as that which might be pardoned or dissimuled° with honour afterward is bewailed with sorrow and grief? It is written that he that seeketh revenge, vengeance will light

---

[543] Mediterraneum: Latin for Mediterranean
[544] 'that Greek' who killed Hector was Achilles.
[545] A lengthy description of the giant's grief is excised.

on him. For why, the same God sayeth: 'To me, vengeance belongeth, and I will reward it'.⁵⁴⁶ Oh, ye malicious and wicked men, which with infinite travail° beat your heads to ordain mischief for the least displeasure! Take this lesson for your amendment, and make Candramarte your example.⁵⁴⁷

But let us continue our history of the two brothers, the Knight of the Sun and Rosicleer, which now the battle being ended and the misdoers pardoned, had little leisure to learn of each other who he was. Rosicleer pulled off his visor and spoke to the Knight of the Sun, saying:

'Knight, the most valiant that ever I met withal, I know not how to reward you for the great friendship you have showed to me. But tell me your name, I pray you, and I shall account myself the happiest man this day living. And while I live, will I remember your valour'.

The Knight of the Sun, noting the great slaughter of knights with the mangling of armour in that place where the first battle had been fought, besides the monstrous blow wherewith the first giant had been slain, and after viewing his personage, his beard but now burgeoning, he pulled off his helmet and after the manifesting of his beautiful looks, such as passed all the knights of his time, he answered gently:

'Right valiant knight, I am to thank my gods for that they have brought me hither in so good a time as to know so valiant a knight and to see with mine° eyes the knighthood, which I would scarce have credited with mine° ears. But whereas you demand of me who I am, know you that I am called the Knight of the Sun for the device which I bear in my armour. And, for my birth, I can show you no farther, neither know I more of my estate. But the adventure which brought me hither hath been by occasion of a storm which drove me on this shore. And this is the first land whereon I set foot since this tempest took my ship. And courtesy commanded me to lend mine° aid when I saw you overmatched with number. And thus much for answer to your demand, but now again that I have told you that which you required, so I pray you tell me your name and for what cause this cruel battle hath been fought between these giants and you'.

While the Knight of the Sun spoke thus, Rosicleer beheld him very sadly, and hearing him say that he was the Knight of the Sun and that he knew no more of his estate, he thought that peradventure° this same might be his brother, of whom Artimodoro had told him such marvels.⁵⁴⁸ But leaving this suspicion till he might question of it more at large, he satisfied the Knight of the Sun as to his question in short speech after this manner:

'Your friendship was great and so I make reckoning of it, otherwise I should not have happened on so good a time to tell you my name, in which because you would learn of me, you shall understand that my name is Rosicleer, and that I was of good report in the court of King Oliverio, the King of Great Britain, although my mishap causing it, I doubt me so much that my name is once mentioned amongst them. But that matter I will leave off as not pertinent. This which you require about our fight, sprung upon this occasion'.

And so he showed the whole order, both of the receiving of his 'avant, chevalier' at the king's hands; the first day's jousting; the second day's combat with Candramarte; the honour of the jousts; the envy of Candramarte; and point by point, the whole story as you heard before.⁵⁴⁹

Which tale Rosicleer had scarcely finished, when the gentlewoman which all this while remained in the ship cried out, whereat they turning their heads, saw in what manner she outraged, saying:

'Oh, spiteful Fortune! Do what thou can, for the succour which I have wanted on land, I hope

---

⁵⁴⁶ This is from Hebrews 10.30.
⁵⁴⁷ The discussion of vengeance is again shortened.
⁵⁴⁸ Since Rosicleer knows his brother's name to be the Gentleman / Knight of the Sun, his musing on the subject seems strange.
⁵⁴⁹ The Spanish text here recounts 'the whole order' that we 'heard before'.
'avant, chevalier': promise of knighthood

to find in the bottom of the seas! And the god Neptune, which hath power over the swelling waves shall keep me from farther vengeance'.⁵⁵⁰

Wherewith she leaped into the sea, but being clad in large garments, she could not drown presently. The Knight of the Sun and Rosicleer, seeing her in that estate,° pitied her greatly. But she was too far off for them to wade near, so the Knight of the Sun took his boat hastily to help the gentlewoman, where otherwise than he looked for, the boat was carried by violence another way. And albeit he strove to bring it towards her, yet prevailed he nothing, for it sailed in the sea as swiftly as sometimes the clouds rack in the air, being driven by the winds.

Presently Rosicleer, with great grief, lost the sight of the boat, wherefore fetching a deep sigh as for that his former hope was clean dashed to have found his brother, he said as followeth:

'Fortune, the thing which I most detest, therein thou show thyself most favourable unto me: this is my life, which now twice thou have restored me without my wish. But that which my heart most desired and with which my life should find most ease, therein thou show thyself an adversary to me, so that whatsoever good happeneth unto me, thou make me think that it happeneth for the worst; for the longer I live, the more are my pains increased'.

Now, by that time that he had lamented a while for this sudden loss of the strange knight, he saw the gentlewoman cast upon the sands not yet dead, whom he caused those knights which were escaped in the battle to carry unto the castle and there to find some remedy for her. Thus the knights did, with whom he went to one of the castles, where for this time we will leave him to follow the Knight of the Sun on his journey by sea.

CHAPTER 44

The Knight of the Sun was carried to the island of Lindaraza, where he achieved many strange and fearful adventures

With great swiftness and incredible haste, the boat whereas the knight sailed was carried, passing in short time the deep Atlantic and West Ocean, near the uttermost Cape of the Ponent, till from thence it drove upon the Pillars of Hercules, where his mighty arm and steeled fork made place for the ocean to enter and water the earth.⁵⁵¹ This Sea is called Mediterraneum Sea, and into this sea the Knight of the Sun shoved his boat, where he found well-peopled towns and greater delight than appeared in the wide and West Ocean. And he began to receive some joy of his hither° arrival, as if not without cause he were carried in such haste and that some great thing was thereby hoped for. But as sorry for his sudden acquaintance with Rosicleer, he beseeched his gods with all his heart that they might once meet again, and at more leisure recount each to other of their adventures. Well on all griefs, whether for his friends, Brandizel and Clavergudo; of this unacquainted Rosicleer; or the unskilfulness of his way, were extinguished by that his learned governor° guided their bark whither° it was convenient.

So still hoping for the port and haven wherein his little boat should ride, he sailed, as I said, in the Middle Earth Sea, where on the left hand he saw Spain, Portugal, and those countries where he could gladly have bestowed himself, but that he was not to command the steersman. But in good time came he thither,° as shall be recited in the history hereafter.⁵⁵² Although by shore on the right hand he left Africa, Carthage, and Tures, and forward as he sailed he

---

⁵⁵⁰ Neptune: the Roman god of the sea. His Greek equivalent is Poseidon.
⁵⁵¹ Pillars of Hercules: the entrance to the Strait of Gibraltar
  Cape of the Ponent: Cape of the west, most likely Cape Finisterre (on the North-West of the Iberian Peninsula, in the region known as 'Galicia'). 'Ponent' signifies west and the name 'Finisterre' means the End of the Earth, i.e. 'Finis Terrae'; in the Middle Ages this was thought to be the westernmost point of the world, hence the name.
⁵⁵² Middle Earth Sea: Mediterranean, from Latin 'medius' (middle) and 'terra' (earth)

discovered the Islands Belears and Sardinia, with the warlike Italy and the fertile Sicily, where the flames of Aetna Hill a while stayed° him.⁵⁵³ There might he see the ruinous relics of old Syracuse and many perilous mermaids haunting those shores, much feared by all the mariners.⁵⁵⁴ Then saw he the fresh water of the River Nile, which entereth the sea by seven mouths. From thence, on the other hand, might he see Greece, wherewith he would more willingly have fed his eyes if he had then known the right which he had thereto. But from thence he launched into the broad Euxino, where the wide sea conveyed all things out of sight that nought appeared but clouds above and waves beneath.⁵⁵⁵ Long thus he sailed, marvelling when his navigation should take end.

30   After this, as it were a fair calm following a stormy tempest, there appeared above the water a fair island unto the which his boat drove, whereat he was merry and pleasant, thinking that there abode him some adventure wherein he might try his manly prowess. And full fain he was to leave the sea. Here, I say, at this island his bark stayed,° whereby he knew that his journey was thitherward.°

Then, the knight leaped to land, upon the entry whereof there was a bank cast of hard stone. And somewhat farther, he saw a fresh and pleasant soil full of the sweetest herbs that ever he had seen. There was a fence or closure made of tall, high trees, some of them with so lofty tops that it wearied him for to look upwards. Beneath this, there was a meadow plat,° whereon grew many flowers and herbs of all sorts. And it was compassed with a still water, gently rolling upon
40   the pumice stones; the water was as clear as any crystal.⁵⁵⁶ Among the thick trees, he might have seen the swift hart and the fair unicorn with the little beaverette° and the small cony° banking the green boughs, beside the light squirrel climbing the tall oak, with the sweet chirping lays° which the birds made, recording so pleasantly among the tender sprays that it would have made a man utterly forlorn to receive comfort, and he that was surprised with Love or Love's darts might have found a more present remedy than the harts of Crete do when they are wounded by the hunter.⁵⁵⁷ This pleasure to have enjoyed, you would have thought yourself to have been transported into another world or into a celestial paradise.

When the Knight of the Sun had both beheld and heard all those things, he imagined presently that the island was well stored with people, thither° resorting for the delight there to be found.
50   But yet he marvelled why their paths were no more trodden. And gazing on every part, which way to take best, he took the way which was most beaten. Therein he walked, heavily laden with his armour. But his desire to know the end of this adventure, and the sweet melody of the birds continually accompanying him, made him think his journey shorter.

About a mile or more out of this meadow, he entered into a plain pasture, so beset with flowers as the meadows were. In the middle of this pasture, as it were a bowshot° from him, he saw the fairest castle which ever eye had seen, as well for the height and largeness as for cost and workmanship. The matter was all of jasper, which when the sun began to cast his beams thereon, shined so bright that it dazzled the eyes of the beholder. The form was quadrangle: after an even proportion as broad as long. In every of the corners there were ten fair turrets, which reached
60   by man's seeming to the clouds. The outward wall of the castle was hard marble, hewed out of

---

⁵⁵³ Islands Belears: Balearic Islands
   Tures: Tunis
   Aetna Hill: Mount Etna, a volcano in eastern Sicily
⁵⁵⁴ Syracuse: city on the east coast of Sicily
   'mermaids' is a mistranslation of 'Sirtes', probably due to a confusion of the place name with the Sirens; the Sirtes are two gulfs on either side of Tripoli, Libya. Tyler later refers to the Sirens as mermaids.
⁵⁵⁵ Euxino: The Black Sea
⁵⁵⁶ 'pumice stones' is a mistranslation of 'pequeños arroyos' (small streams).
⁵⁵⁷ Harts of Crete: The remedy alluded to here is the herb 'dittany', popularly known as 'hind heal', since it was credited with the property of ejecting arrows from the body. In Virgil's *Aeneid*, Venus heals Aeneas' arrow wound with dittany from Cretan Ida.

the Island Paros.⁵⁵⁸ Round about the castle there was a deep ditch with a device: that albeit there was no spring in it to nourish it, yet was it maintained with a fresh flow, partly by the fall of waters from the mountains, partly by the rivers we named amongst the meadows, which at every spring cleared the channel.⁵⁵⁹ Upon this water there stood a bridge with three strong turrets: one in the beginning, the other in the middest,° the other in the end towards the castle. Through them a man cannot enter but by plain force, for the keepers open not but constrained, and they need to be right valiant for the porters are fell.°⁵⁶⁰

The Knight of the Sun gazed upon this very attentively, so amazed at the strangeness of the work that he could not think it to have been built by man's hand. And having as then no other skill of God but the gentile's law, he thought that peradventure° this might be the house of his gods, when they descended from heaven to sojourn amongst us. So, very desirous to know the end thereof, he came unto the bridge where he stayed a while ere° he proceeded farther, for he judged that according to the great strength of the arches, the depth of the water, and the height of the wall, that no man might enter without leave asked. And as he there wanted not matter of marvel for the wonder of the castle, so marvelled he that near so rare and magnificent buildings he met no person of whom he might demand to whom the fair castle did belong.

Amid these thoughts, it seemed best in his fancy° to call to them within, if perhaps any would answer him. And therefore, coming to the gates of the first turret, which was then nearest to him, he found a porch opened and right before a fair stately court enclosed with walls of jasper. And in the midst before him, a pair° of stairs of a ten or twelve degrees,° which led up to a fair pillar, whereunto was fastened with a chain of gold, a fair horn and a rich baldric to it.⁵⁶¹ The horn was tipped all with gold, and in the end were set many precious stones, the riches thereof might have contended a right covetous eye. Underneath the horn, upon the same pillar, there were engraven letters, which the Knight of the Sun perceiving and hoping there to learn some more news, he mounted up the stairs and read as hereafter followeth:

'This castle belongeth to the beautiful Lindaraza. The gates may not be opened to any, save to him which windeth the horn. But let him take heed withal, for when they are open, there shall not fail him cruel and fierce porters to give him the death if it be possible'.

When he had read the letters and gathered by them that there were porters to answer him, he feared not a whit° for all the threats of the writing, but with an heroical° heart, he untied the horn and winded° it so shrill that all the castle echoed with the noise. At the sound hereof the inner gates of steel flew open as if they had been shaken with a tempest. And presently there appeared a fierce giant, bearing in the one hand a bar of iron and in the other a chain, wherein he led tied a dragon, the most hideous that ever man looked on. This beast was from the breast downward as high as any man on horseback, and the tail thereof was ten paces in length, wherewith he sweeped the ground.

Now the strong giant, coming out of the gates, let loose the dragon and took the bar of iron in his hands, pacing towards the knight which was now in descending from the pillar. Ere° the knight could easily come to the ground, the giant met him with a counterbuff° on the shield that he missed two or three steps in coming down.⁵⁶² The monstrous dragon beneath was ready to receive him. But the nephew of Alicante lightly esteemed all this and rather took courage in this that there was something worthy his pains behind when the castle was kept by such ugly porters.

---

⁵⁵⁸ Tyler adds the allusion to Parian marble, which is a high quality, flawless white marble quarried on the Greek island of Paros.
⁵⁵⁹ The description of the marvel, 'Round about . . . the channel', is added. This, and the subsequent addition, are investigated in the introduction.
⁵⁶⁰ The marvel, 'Through them . . . are fell', is also added to *Mirror*.
⁵⁶¹ 'fair' renders 'marfil' (ivory), which is likely to be a mistranslation. Perhaps Tyler confused 'marfil' with 'marvel' and, in keeping with her tendency to alter 'marvel', changed it to 'fair'.
⁵⁶² Rather than miss some steps, in *Espejo* the giant stands with one foot on the steps and the other on the ground.

And drawing out his sword, he struck at the serpent a blow on the top of the head, but it did him no more harm than if it had lighted upon a smith's anvil, but it a little benumbed his senses and beguiled him of his fore-hoped° grip. This little harm which he had done to the serpent did much amaze him, and the better to save himself from the serpent, he got under the pillar. And then he bestowed another blow upon the serpent's head with all his force. The serpent, so sore struck, waxed wood° and brayed out so loud that all the court rang of the noise. And fain would it have got between the Knight of the Sun and the place under the pillar where he stood to have raught° him in his paws, but the good knight defended himself lightly° from him and laid at the dragon still with the sword.

The giant abode still at the stairs' foot to wait for the knight's tumbling on the stairs.[563] At length, he came down headlong, where the strong giant let drive at him so great a blow with his bar, that the bar burst, and the good knight thought his head had been bruised. With this, as well as he might, he rose up, and driving at the giant he cut his legs clean from his body, the giant falling to ground.

The serpent, raising his tail, grasped at the Knight of the Sun, but I can not tell how the knight escaped it. And withal he took up the greatest piece of the bar of iron which the giant had, and hasting toward the serpent, he gave him such a blow therewith upon the head that he fell down. And before he could rise, the knight gave him such another that his skull, as hard as flint, burst into two pieces. Yet for all this, the great serpent was not thoroughly dead, but bounded up into the air and swept the ground with his tail, seeming to be more fierce than at the beginning. The Knight of the Sun purposed to strike no more, but quickly got up higher on the stairs to be out of danger. In the end, the dragon stirred no more, whereby he judged that he was dead.

And marvelling what besides this there might be found in the castle, he hung the fair horn about his neck, and with the bar in his hands, he entered the first tower, and from thence through the first arch of the bridge till he came to the second tower, which was in the midst of the bridge, the gates whereof were of steel and shut as fast as the gates of the first arch were.[564]

Chevaliero del Febo winded° his horn, and presently the gates were opened and there came issuing out a giant no less strong than the first, having in the one hand a club and in the other a chain wherein he led a lion, the wightyest° of limb and biggest of bone that ever man saw: the body as big as a bull, and every of his claws was a handful long; his eyes shined like lamps.

This lion, the giant untied straight and set upon the knight, which with no little courage —as he had a greater quest in hand — awaited him. And at the first blow he struck him so fell° upon the head that the brains started out, and the monstrous lion fell stark dead without more stirring. When he had this done, he encountered the giant. And the giant let drive at him; but the knight, not minded at that time to assay° or put his trust to the fine metal of his enchanted helmet, started aside, that the club fell upon the bridge. But before the giant could rear his club, the son of Trebatio hit him so strongly beneath the knees that his shin bones were burst withal, and the giant, with great clamours, fell down.

The Knight of the Sun, leaving him sure enough for making resistance, took up his heavy club to go farther and to see what was within. Thus passed he through the second tower, till he came to the third and last tower of the bridge, whereof finding the gates shut as the others, he winded° his horn. And with the shrillness thereof, the gates burst open, making as great a noise as if the bridge had rent° in two. Presently stepped forth a huge giant, nine foot in height, all his body covered with a tough hide, so hard and strong that no sword could enter. At his waist he had a sword, and in his hand, a chain of iron, whereto were fastened two tigers of wonderful greatness, by the fierceness of their looks able for to have affrayed° any man.

---

[563] In the source, he waits for the dragon to knock him down the stairs.
[564] The term 'marvelling' appears here, while 'marfil' (ivory) is omitted from the sentence; this supports the earlier hypothesis that Tyler misconstrued the word 'marfil' for its near-homonym 'marvel'.

150 For all this, the hardy Grecian° was nothing appalled, for he lifted up the heavy club so strong, as if the great Hercules should have come to fight with him, only with the show it might have made him to tremble. Those fierce beasts, so soon as the giant had unloosed them, opening their horrible mouths, ran with such swiftness upon him that it seemed their feet touched not the ground. At such time as they came both upon him, he gave one of them such a blow upon the shoulder that he burst all his bones in pieces, wherewith the tiger fell to the ground. Then came the other and caught hold of him in the shoulder, so gripping him that he could not stir his arm, neither one way nor other. And grasping almost all the headpiece within his sharp teeth, he thought to have crushed it in pieces, but the helmet defended the head and the magic armour kept of[f] the tearing of his nails. Now the good knight, seeing neither purpose of his club nor

160 use of his sword while he was thus entertained by the tiger, throwing away his club, he struggled and wrestled so long with the tiger that in the end he cast the beast upon the hard flint stones with such a fall that the brains flew out of the head.

The wild giant, when he saw the tiger thus slain, with a hellish fury, he went toward the Knight of the Sun. And taking his long sword, he gave him such a blow upon the top of the helmet that there sparkled° out great flakes° of fire, and the knight fell upon his hands and knees. But as soon as he could, the knight recovering his sword, requited him so courageously. The giant being unarmed, that had not the strong hide stood him instead of complete armour, the sword had entered the flesh, whereof at this time it missed. Hereat° the wild giant, taking up again the heavy sword, struck the Knight of the Sun upon the top of his headpiece. But he avoided the blow

170 lightly,° in such sort that the heavy sword fell upon the ground and broke in pieces, the hilts only remaining in his hands. Now before the giant could raise up his sword, the Knight of the Sun ran him through.

When the Knight of the Sun had accomplished thus much of his purpose, he thought there had been no more to be done save now to know the secrets which abode behind, and wherefore this straight° warding was ordained. Therefore, he went through all the bridge until he came to a pathway, which led between the outward wall and the great castle. When he had walked this path, about a bowshot° off he saw a little door all engraven° with sundry kind of portraiture, the strangeness whereof, with the variety of the story therein portrayed, might have held a good carver a long time: the imagery was so drawn that it would have troubled the wit of Praxites to

180 have matched it.⁵⁶⁵ The gates were not great, but the chief part was of steel, as surely closed as the first.

The Knight of the Sun, thinking that percase° they would open at the first push, rushed against them with all his force; but his labour was lost and he prevailed no more than if he would have broken down the walls with his feet. Therefore he winded° his horn, whereat the gates burst open, but no man appeared without, save that when he was about to enter, he saw two giants, the one on the one side, and the other armed from top [to] toe, with headpieces of fine steel and their armour a finger deep in thickness. They held in their hands two battle axes raised up aloft, ready to discharge their blows upon the comer in. The fierceness of their semblance was so strange that it is hard to believe that any man had the courage to enter against his will, but if it

190 had been the dog Cerberus, he could not have defended him the passage.⁵⁶⁶

This valiant knight, seeing them in such sort prepared for the fight, albeit he wanted not courage to assay° that fearful entry, yet he stayed in doubt how he might enter without danger and ward the two first blows; for to receive both their blows at once was not possible without great hazard, and otherwise enter he could not. But after long pausing, he came nearer. And as if he would have passed through, he showed himself, whereat the giants, as if he had entered indeed, let drive their blows, the whilst the knight stepped in between them. And taking the next

---

⁵⁶⁵ Praxites: Praxiteles, famed Greek sculptor in 4th century BCE. The original refers to Pyrgoteles, a renowned gem-engraver, also from the 4th century BCE.
⁵⁶⁶ Cerberus: in Greek mythology, the three-headed watchdog of the underworld

to hand, he hit the one giant overthwart° the paunch, but his sword entered not. The giants, which at their first blows had broken their heavy clubs, drew out their broad arming-swords° and laid at the Knight of the Sun. The one he received on the sword; the other he avoid[ed] lightly° by stepping aside. And willing to see the end of the adventure, he struck one of them full upon the visor, wherewith he had thought to have hewed his face; but he was deceived, for it did the giant no more harm than if he had been smitten with a hazel wand. The giants now laid on load, but he disappointed them by the deliverness° of his body.

And now, consider what thought this good knight was in, to feel himself assailed° by two fierce enemies and not able to hurt again. Neither was it possible to master one of them by wrestling, for both the weaker of the two was too strong for him; and perhaps while he should deal with the one, the other might displease him, so that neither of these ways were convenient. Without some present help the danger [was] certain; yet, in the end, he began to rebuke himself, ever saying:

'Stick to it, thou coward! And albeit as yet it seems impossible for to escape this perilous skirmish, yet stir not thy foot. Wither° shall thou soon overcome or soon lose the victory, but never shall thou lose thy infamy if thou die flying°. Many times such hard adventures have been occasion of greater glory, and if anybody but myself achieve it, I shall not like myself as long as I live'.

So gazing about to seek advantages, he marked the wicket standing open somewhat beneath the porch, where through he might well pass by little bowing himself, but neither of the giants might, except they fell on all four, for they were higher than he by the breast downward.[567] When he saw this door, he bethought himself how to be out from the danger of blows, which fell into his brain at a time of need. Thus, it was as the giants were desirous to hit him, he ever stooped under, and watching one of them, as he was lifting up his arms, before the blow could descend, he ran and closed with him. And taking him by the girdle,° carried him by strong hand, and with all his force ran against the wicket, that the giant not being able to pass through burst both head and shoulders against the wall. The giant there died in his armour.

This done, the strong knight passed farther, and letting the body fall, with so much speed as he might, he ran to meet with the other giant, which then approached with his sword in both his hands to have smitten him. But these giants little acquainted with feats of arms, and the Knight of the Sun, by the dexterity of his body, defended himself lightly° from them and obtained victory. For when the giant had let his sword fall out of his hands, he embraced the giant with both his hands, and turning himself twice about, at the third time, he let him fall that through the weight of his body his gall° burst in his body and he died presently.

This marvellous combat being ended, the good knight was now weary and therefore took his ease upon a seat of stone, which was in the porch. There to occupy himself, he beheld the strong buildings of the castle. After roaming about to find some other way to depart thence, he found at one end another gate all of iron and the gates shut as all the first, whereby he saw that he had yet farther trial to abide. And therefore he rested himself where he sat.

After which done, he arose and passing through the first wall to the second, he found the gates shut, and therefore he winded° his horn. Presently, the steel gates opened and there came out thereof a flame of fire accompanied with great smoke as if it had been some place of hell. Until the smoke vanished away, he could see nothing. After, he saw before the gate a beast in form like a crocodile but somewhat more hideous, as it were a misshapen monster purposed by nature to show the loathsomeness of deformity. Out of his mouth, he sent great flakes° of fire in the fangs. There sat a tusk without the mouth about a half a yard, very sharp and cutting.

The good knight, abashed now to see so many fierce keepers in that castle as if it had been

---

[567] A description of his height coupled with a reminder that his father was 8 feet tall is excised.

nothing but a lodge of warders, as he supposed, to keep in durance° the sons of Titan, which once rebelled against Jupiter, the which tale he had often heard in his gentile's law.[568] And yet, the travail° of conquering grieved him not alike to the long looking for of the end. But not minding to debate the matter at this time, he took his sword in his hand, assaying the entry. But the ugly beast cast out such a flash of fire that the Knight of the Sun little liked of it. And not being able to endure it, he gave back till the heat should slack.

This may a man say that it troubled the knight more than all that had passed: one cause was for the extremity of heat; and other for that he saw no way to come near the beast, for before he might approach it, the beast would be all on a light fire. But remembering himself of the club which he had left in the first entry, and thinking that it should be the best weapon he might have, he ran to fetch it. And returning speedily, he found the monster, as you heard before, spitting out his fire. The Knight of the Sun, with his long reach in his hand, gave the beast upon the forehead such a blow that the head rent° into two, and the terrible beast fell to ground, beating his feet against the ground so hard that it seemed the castle shook withal. And the smoke which it sent forth, as at the quenching of a great fire, so blinded the Knight of the Sun till it was stark dead, that he might not enter.

From thence after, he came to a fair court, the sumptuous building whereof amazed him much that in comparison the golden statues which Nero the Emperor of Rome erected might not more delight him, no, nor yet the wonders of the world — the stately pyramids of Egypt, wherein only their kings are buried, and wherein they wasted the most part of their substance — might like delight them. In beholding the strangeness of these buildings, I cannot tell precisely his thought for every circumstance, but if his thought were as my thought, or if the report be true which first came from him, surely there was matter enough to gaze upon.[569] But what think you he noted especially? Nothing but a marble stone. But as it fell out, to some good purpose.

In the marble stone were engraven° the valiant acts of all knights alive or dead, in such order of time as they lived: first the ancienter,° then the later, till he came to the nearest, very few or none omitted. A rare piece of work, and must needs have been done by other cunning than story or carving. For the one, the pains were infinite; for the other, no man's reading stretcheth so far as to know every story. But herein he took great pleasure, and from the first to the last he ran them over.[570] He stayed° at his own picture, whereunto joined next above was Trebatio, and the next beneath was Rosicleer. These three pictures were fresher to his fancy° than the others, as if they had been new made. Remembering by the picture of Rosicleer the countenance of that knight whom he had found in the island of Candramarte, he yielded forth a great sigh. And blessing the picture from the bottom of his heart, he spoke these words unto like purpose:

'Thou are a right good knight and worthily placed among the most famous knights of the world, for I believe not that among so many as are here painted there is one so valiant as thou are. For albeit commonly we make much of our elders' virtues, it is but as commonly many things show fairer a far off, whereas when they come to trial they are but as ordinary'.[571]

After this, he mused in himself who that Trebatio might be, for he never heard of such a man. But by the draft of the picture, he took him to be a comely personage, of a mild and sad countenance. And it did him good to behold him. So looking farther, he saw the whole story of the Emperor Trebatio drawn underneath: from his first landing in Hungary till the hour of his

---

[568] The Titans formed the first pantheon of Greco-Roman divinities. They were overthrown by the Olympians, led by Jupiter/Zeus in the Titan War (Titanomachia). The Knight of the Sun recalls one of the battles which formed the great war.
[569] The addition, 'I cannot . . . gaze upon', gives the impression that the narrator spoke to him directly. The narrator's authority and the relationship of complicity created with the readers through such additions is analysed in the introduction.
[570] The engraving is imbued with greater importance in *Mirror* through added descriptions.
[571] The proverbial tone is created through slight expansions of the source.

enchantment in that castle — how he was in the company of Lindaraza, without knowledge of himself or witting° of his friends. Now did he at length learn the purpose of the strong wards, which was to hold in the Emperor Trebatio, there bewitched for the company of Lindaraza, whom before he could restore to the knowledge of himself, he must bring from that piece° of the castle, which was enchanted to that only effect. This, when he understood it, pitied him much that so good an emperor should there be in hold by false means to the great sorrow of his subjects and principally of his wife the Princess Briana, whom he saw likewise all clad in black like a widow.

And to work some means of his delivery, he looked about him which way was best to take. And liking best one of the galleries, the which was nearest to the paved court, that he followed mounting up a pair of stairs all made of jasper, in the midst whereof he met coming down a big knight armed with rich and glistering° armour, his face bare and of a fresh colour, which approaching to him, drew out his sword. And without saying [n]ought, laid at the Knight of the Sun as fiercely as he could. The Knight of the Sun would rather have talked with him to have learned some news, but it could not be. So it behoved him to draw his sword and to defend himself. There began a hot skirmish, that the clattering of their armour and the flashing° of their swords rang throughout the palace. This fury, notwithstanding, lasted not long, for the Knight of the Sun, in a choleric rage, hit his adversary so sure upon the top of his helmet that the big knight fell down and lay for dead.

The Knight of the Sun stayed not to make dispatch of him, but rather having compassion on him, for he seemed a noble knight, he unlaced the knight's helmet to give him air. But not being able then to recover him, he passed farther. And coming to the gallery, he then went up another pair of stairs, so wide and broad that if two were going up near the two ends, scarcely the one might know the other. Now in this his way, albeit many things were which might have stayed° either an idle gazer or a curious eye, and many things beside to have invited a wearied man to take his rest, yet the desire of finding the emperor carried his feet. And overcoming the pains of the way, he came to a portal curiously wrought, to the entry whereof there led three steps of beaten silver. By them he entered into the great chamber, where first the Emperor Trebatio had a sight of the fair and beautiful Lindaraza and was bereaved of his wits.

In this chamber, he was greatly abashed at the cost and workmanship of rich tapestry and other ornaments, and ever though the stuff were of the costliest, yet the workmanship bettered the matter. Hence must he, as I told you, convey the emperor if he means to make himself known. Now, for your farther instruction, know that among other things which the wise Lirgandeo gave unto the Knight of the Sun at his departure from Babylon, he gave him a little stone set in a ring of excellent, fine gold, the same being of so strange virtue that no enchantment might prevail against it. By this he was bold to enter the chamber, and being within, was free from the charm.[572]

Out of this chamber, he came to the orchard whereunto this chamber looked, so fresh and delectable that if ever pleasure might ravish the senses of man, a man might affirm it of that place. In the arbour near the entry, he saw a number of fair gentlewomen clothed with silk, their breasts bare and white as snow. Some played on instruments, and other sang sweetly to them. Such kind of mermaids would have beguiled a well-stayed° Ulysses; [f]or such musicians, as well for their cunning song as their company, would have brought a watchful Argos to a sleepyhead.[573] A good way off, he saw the Emperor Trebatio and the fair Lindaraza alone, set in several chairs, all unmindful of other things but of their love and wish to other. The Emperor Trebatio leaned his head upon the white and delicate breasts of Lindaraza with such show of pleasure therein that the young Greek, feeling thereby in himself that which all men have, could

---

[572] 'and being within, was free from the charm' is added to clarify his immunity from the enchantment.
[573] Recalling the earlier mistranslation of 'Sirtes' as 'mermaids', Tyler here also refers to the Sirens as mermaids.
   Argos: Argus, a hundred-eyed giant who was killed by Hermes while he guarded Io for Hera

have been content with the other's room.° And for very love, he made an invective against nature, which had ordained that kind to have such sovereignty over valiant knights, with many words to the same matter. But this was yet the wantonness of his imagination; his neck had not felt the yoke. Ere° after, perhaps he will speak more earnestly when you shall believe him.[574]

Now when the gentlewomen espied him, as all abashed, they laid aside their music, with the sudden stay° whereof Trebatio and Lindaraza lifted up their heads. And seeing a knight so strongly made to come towards them, they were overtaken with fear, especially Lindaraza, which guessing at the truth of the matter that her long love should now take end, for very sorrow fell to ground. Trebatio comforted her in as much as yet no violence was offered, but she replied with tears, saying:

'Alas, my lord, I shall die unless you do justice on this knight, which hath here entered without my leave and which hath interrupted our joys by the destroying of my keepers!'[575]

Herewith the emperor, very angry, spoke to the knight, saying:

'Sir Knight, why have you come within this place without the licence of this lady, it being hers and kept by strong keepers for her use?'

The Knight of the Sun gently answered:

'Noble emperor, I confess I demanded no leave, and till now I met with none which would ask wherefore I came. But my errand is for yourself, which here live unknown and have forgotten your wife and empire'.

The emperor angrily replied:

'Neither thou nor the whole world may bring me hence! And for thy good zeal to put me from my joy, stay a while and I will acquit thee thy fee'.

So hastily he flung to a chamber where he armed himself, the while that Lindaraza, whom it touched as in especial,° reviled the Knight of the Sun for his thither° coming.[576]

'Oh', sayeth she, 'thou saucy and unmannerly knight! How have thou had the face to enter my castle in despite of my porters? Either depart hence quickly or tarry to abide the emperor's puissance. And if my mind deceive me not, I shall soon be satisfied for this disgrace'.

The Knight of the Sun, knowing how grievous it would be unto her that the emperor should leave her, said contrariwise° with fair words to persuade her to give consent to his departure, saying:

'Worthy lady, may you not content yourself with so many years in which you have detained this noble and famous emperor both from wife and kindred, from land and subject, but will you also for your pleasure, neither lasting nor honest, undo a whole country and take a man from his wife which hath mourned for him twenty years?[577] I beseech you, madam, content yourself with that which is past, and let him not wade farther in this error, which if it may please you to remove to your great honour at my entreaty'.

Hereat Lindaraza, all fiery, could not abide the end of his suit, but with great outcries to incense the poor emperor, she put him off. The emperor being armed, in great choler, ran upon the Knight of the Sun, and without saying anything, laid at him with all his force. The Knight of the Sun, knowing that what the emperor did was but as done in a dream, would not strike him to do him harm, but only to save himself and to find the means whereby to bring Trebatio from that enchantment. Thereupon by little and little he gave back, that the emperor following him, he might in the end bring him from the enchanted chamber. This came to pass accordingly, for as he made show of lack of resistance, so the emperor, thinking to follow the advantage, pursued him to the great chamber where the enchantment first took effect. In short, by this

---

[574] *Espejo*'s misogyny is omitted from the narrative.
[575] The English translation is more emotive as Lindaraza exclaims against the loss of their joys rather than laments the destruction of her castle.
[576] In the Spanish text, he is accompanied by several ladies who help with his armour.
[577] His loss of wit and memory, his subjects' troubles, and Briana's anguish are all invoked in *Espejo*.

foresaid means, there also this emperor was brought to the point of avoiding the chamber. Whereat Lindaraza, fearing least he might be led, cried with a loud voice:

'Stay! Stay, my lord, for this knight is full of falsehood, and if you go out of this chamber both you and I shall die!'

Hereat° the Emperor, who was not desirous of anything but to please her, returned back. The Knight of the Sun would not follow him, but still kept at the pitch° of the entry, and the emperor would not come to him for fear of Lindaraza.

Well, this device not succeeding, the Knight of the Sun thought now to try if he might carry him by main° force. This he knew would be a dangerous matter, for the courage which he knew in the emperor, but all was well employed if he might set him at liberty. So towards the emperor he goeth, whom not prepared to fight, he suddenly catcheth in his arms, and with a lusty° courage raiseth him from ground to have carried him away.[578] But before the knight might get to the door, the emperor catching hold likewise, held the knight so short that for a while they tumbled in the hall, neither part gaining any great scantling° of ground. But the odds was the knight's, and in the end, he quickly lifting up the emperor (would he or not), he brought him without the chamber. The emperor struggled to recover the door, but in their struggling they both tumbled down the stairs. Now hath the Knight of the Sun played the man, for ere° they came fully to the ground, the doors of the enchanted chamber clapped together, wherewith and with the noise thereof a great part of the edifices sank withal.

The emperor, returned to his former wits, presently saw that he thought he had not stayed there past a day, and that which passed between him and Lindaraza had been but a short and pleasant dream. After calling to mind his wife the fair Princess Briana and the great host which he had left before Belgrade, he became so sorrowful that the tears trickled down his cheeks in great measure.

But of this manner and condition are we mortal men, that for our pleasures we sometimes forget our spouses, the one half of ourselves; sometimes neglect our children, the more half to ourselves, as in whom the hope of posterity resteth; and lastly, sometimes we overturn our country, which ought to be dearer to us than ourselves, neither mindful to what use we are created, namely to the benefit of others, neither careful what loss ensueth, as in especial° our own discommodity.[579] But that which is more than careless is the little thought of change, and the loathing to depart from it, that when we are at our way's end, we seem but as it were now to begin afresh. It is like a sweet sleep. But let us shake off this drowsy humour and let us open our sleepy eyes. Let us use ourselves so that sometimes we have recourse to matters of more importance, and to think of heaven, to despise the vain temporal things of this world, to separate ourselves from the man of flesh and willingly to leave him least he leaveth us against our wills. Little shall remain thereof after scores of years, and that which remaineth shall be shame and grief for the life passed, besides desperate repentance which is a double torment.

And much after this same manner was this valiant emperor for his long delights with Lindaraza. Now twenty years was but a summer's day, and yet there left him not shame of his fact to fret his conscience, albeit he advised himself the best remedy which I have read off, which is amendment of life, the safest haven for a weather-beaten penitent.[580] First, therefore, knowing that this knight was he which had, as it were, awaked° him from this dream, he pulled off his helmet and embraced him, giving hearty thanks for his deliverance. Withal, professing that he thought himself unable to requite that great courtesy, yea, even with the bestowing of his empire, so assuredly he meant not to forget it, if peradventure° God would show him the occasion of doing him service.[581]

---

[578] Trebatio's gigantic size is omitted.
[579] Children and country are not listed in the source.
[580] The concept of repentance is added.
[581] Again, the idea of repentance is added to his discourse.

'For', sayeth he, 'you have not saved my life, here might I have lived without danger of sword, but you have saved my soul', and et cetera, extolling the greatness of the benefit.

And in the end, he prayed him of courtesy to tell him his name and country, with the cause of his coming to that island. The Knight of the Sun answered him gently:

'Valiant emperor, the thing which I have done in your service is not like to that which I wish for. As your valour forceth my will, so my will sueth° a desert on your part, more unto you than to all the knights of the world. But wit you, I am called the Knight of the Sun. My country I know not, but my bringing up hath been in Babylon, where I was told that I was found upon the sea, being a very child. My coming to this castle was by chance. My boat being driven by tempest upon the shore, where seeing it so fresh and fair, I had desire to know the owners. And fortune being favourable, I passed through all, killing the keepers till I came within this court, where I saw engraven your whole history from the time that you were married with the Princess Briana till the time you were brought hither. There knew I the manner of your bewitching, and albeit yourself were unknown to me, yet, I thought I would set you free if that I might, from whence this hath proceeded, which you have seen'.

When he had ended, the emperor embraced him many times with great pleasure, as well wondering at his great prowess, for he could not be ignorant of Lindaraza's power, as also at his boldness for a matter not touching him in any respect by all appearance, for he neither knew country nor parents.[582]

But as the remembrance of his wife and empire caused in the emperor much grief, so he besought the Knight of the Sun that they might depart from thence to go into Greece, where he might better thank him than he had erst° done. The Knight of the Sun, with a good affection to bear him company, condescended easily, rather yet upon desire to know the country wherein he had heard to be right [full of] valiant knights than of any hope of reward. So when they came near the outward court they found that knight, whom the Knight of the Sun had left in a trance, now returned to himself and upon his feet safe and sound.

The knight, when he saw the emperor and the Knight of the Sun coming down, giving great sighs and weeping bitterly, began to say:

'Oh, what a dismal day is this for me! Now my sister Lindaraza is dead, and I have lost a sweet companion. I would rather that I had been killed by this stranger, which hath destroyed all our good, than that I should live and sustain such anguish. Little have the monstrous keepers prevailed, whom we put in our castle to defend her life and to defend the death which so suddenly hath taken her away'.

The emperor, hearing him and knowing him, ran to embrace him, saying:

'My dear friend, Flamides, how chanceth this heaviness in your countenance? Why do you fetch such deep sighs and spill so many tears with so great sobs? If it be for my departure and for the liberty which I have received by this knight, you know how long time I have here remained out of my remembrance, and forgetful of my empire and kingdom. And shall I not go to comfort her, which long time by my absence hath been comfortless?'

'My lord', said Flamides, 'I cannot deny but your reason is good and that the injury hath been great in detaining you so long from thence. But as your excellency knoweth, there is no love more natural than between brother and sister. Oh, the death of my sister Lindaraza pierceth me to the heart! And I had rather than my life have accompanied her in death, than thus to bewail her lack after death. For so soon as you came out of the enchanted room, my sister died presently.° So was it appointed by the destinies, that no longer than she should enjoy your presence, she should live'.

'Blessed man', said the emperor, 'and is Lindaraza dead?'

'Yea, assuredly', quoth° he.[583]

---

[582] He likewise marvels at the Knight of the Sun's chivalric feats in *Espejo*.
[583] Flamides's reply is added to *Mirror*.

'Now, on my honour', said the emperor, 'her death grieveth me, and during my life shall I be sad as oft° as I shall call her to remembrance. And although my case is such as in more need of comfort than likely to comfort others, yet me thinks I may tell you that you ought not to bewail her death so much, for belike° a long time have you known that her life should not last after my departure. Now wherefore do you lament her so sore as if it were but now thought on and not before foreseen? Again your overmuch carefulness in fortifying your castle was but needless, for it is given to man to have the mastery over beasts, which either by art or nature become tractable. And be it your castle had been inexpugnable° for all men in the world, yet what fence had you to shut out death? A man in no place can warrant himself such safety as that at every step he draweth himself nearer unto death. Whether we be free or bond, on foot or horseback, sleeping or waking, whole or sick, we daily draw near unto our end. Or, if you will speak more truly to our perfection, for then man beginneth to live indeed when he goeth out of this miserable world. Lindaraza is dead and weeping may not recall her. If you bear unto her any love, you may show it now, after her death, in receiving to her place her daughter Lindaraza. For her provide that she may depart from hence, and I will carry her to my kingdom, where she shall be in that estate as is due to the daughter of such parents'.

When the emperor had thus said, Flamides forced himself so much as he might for to speak, and thus answered him:

'Your reason satisfieth my understanding, and I confess it true that we ought not to weep when death assaileth us, neither ought we to make strange of it, for in the end we must leave this world, and then is there nothing more certain. But my conceit° builded° upon outward sense, being contrary to reason, troubleth again that part where affections are and maketh it rebellious. And howsoever men be provided for death by continual thought that they must die, ordinarily, notwithstanding, we think ourselves immortal till death attacheth° us. And what old man only for age is so feeble that he hopeth not for a day to live? But as to Lindaraza, my sister, I believe that although you had stayed here many days, the secret of this adventure had never been disclosed unto you, neither do you know the cause why you were brought and put here.[584] But I will tell you plainly. My sister Lindaraza and I had both one father named Palisteo, being the second son to the King of Phrygia. My father, not being born to the kingdom, fell rather to seek his own delight without envy than to trouble himself with the care of governing. Above all, he studied the [the] art [of] magic, where by his pains, at length came to the most absolute perfection of all in Asia. He was matched with a lady of high parentage, by whom he had two children: my sister Lindaraza and me. We were of young years when our mother died in labour of the third child, so there remained none else but our father alive. And loving to be solitary, came and dwelled in this island, bringing with him my sister and those waiting women which you have seen. By his great skill he builded° this castle. Here he lived until my sister and I were of some discretion to guide ourselves. Here he drew many histories of things passed in the world, and among other, the pictures of many valiant knights which were then alive. With the rest, you were so lively drawn that it happening my sister to enter one day where the imagery was, by the sight of your picture she was surprised with your love. Our father Palisteo, knowing her disease,° devised you should be brought by following your own wife carried from you. For this cause was this enchantment made in that quarter of the castle wherein you abode, without making yourself privy° to your own estate that if your knights came to seek you they might not persuade you hence. Neither could ever persuasion have served, only force, which this man hath used. When the wise man our father had done all this, he declared unto us the secrets of these things and

---

[584] The phrasing in *Espejo* is confusing: Flamides speaks of 'Lindaraza, your daughter and my sister', which only makes sense if the reader remembers that Trebatio and Lindaraza had a daughter also named Lindaraza. Since their daughter only was mentioned in passing much earlier in the romance (in Chapter 9), the phrase may cause readers to presume an incestuous relationship between Trebatio and Lindaraza, who appears to be both his daughter and lover. Tyler's clarification is very warranted.

farther told us by his art that the time should come when you should be delivered from the enchantment, although he knew not when nor in what manner. He told us that at such time as you should be at large, my sister Lindaraza should die, either for the grief that she should conceive or for that the fates had so appointed. Moreover, that you should have a daughter by her, which might not hence depart till there should come a knight which should win the entries once again and after marry her. Of this knight, he said that there should spring the race whence issueth the two noble families much spoken off throughout the world: the one house to be called Mongrana, the other Claramonte.[585] Me, he charged not to leave the castle till my niece, Lindaraza, should be acquitted. After this, our father Palisteo, being sore sick, died. Since his death, hitherto everything hath fallen out accordingly. And thus you have heard the whole process of my tale, and the cause why your daughter Lindaraza can not go from hence at this time'.[586]

The emperor and the Knight of the Sun had very attentively listened to all that which Flamides had spoken. And albeit the emperor was desirous to carry his daughter Lindaraza with him, he could not yet refuse to leave her when he could not otherwise choose. And he besought Flamides that at such time as they came both out, that they should take the way to Greece, there to rejoice with him.

After they had thus argued a little, Flamides brought them through that part of the castle which was not enchanted, showing them many things: as well of halls, of cloisters, as of pictures and paintry,° whereat the emperor and the Knight of the Sun were greatly amazed. And for that that day the Knight of the Sun had not eaten, Flamides made them sit in a fair parlour, where they had plenty of dainty° viands.° When they had eaten, the emperor, being desirous to depart, desired Flamides to convey him through the gates.[587] So, by the way, this piece of the story, as I have heard, was afterward penned and portrayed in the court hall of the emperor's palace at Constantinople.

But they went through all the gates of the castle and of the bridge till they came where the pillars stood. There, Flamides took his leave of the emperor and of the Knight of the Sun.[588] When Flamides had departed from them and they had passed through the bridges, presently the gates of the towers clapped together with great noise, being as surely° shut as ever they were.

The emperor and the Knight of the Sun were amazed at the strange things which had happened in that castle, and took the way towards the sea by the same path in which they had come, rejoicing at the sweet harmony which the birds made in those pleasant trees, so that although they went afoot, yet it seemed no pain unto them. And the love that they bore to each other was so great that it could not have had been more if they had known each other, especially the emperor, who so often as he saw his face thought upon the Princess Briana, whom he much resembled.

In this manner, the father and the son travelled, running over in their discourse strange things of the enchanted castle, till that they approached the main° sea, whereas yet the little boat stood in which the Knight of the Sun had come thither.° Now for that along the shore there were no more boats, the emperor was somewhat sorrowful, seeming to him that he was ill furnished to go whither° he purposed. And telling it to the Knight of the Sun, the Knight of the Sun answered:

'My lord, I pray you be not aggrieved with this, for the boat is guided by a wise man, a friend of mine, one as I believe so careful° to carry me hence as he hath friendly sent me to work your

---

[585] Mongrana and Claramonte: families of some of the major Carolingian heroes
[586] The story of Palisteo is often cited in the context of *The Tempest*, as a source, analogue, or as part of the 'broad intertextual framework that underlies Shakespeare's play' (Virginia Mason Vaughan and Alden T. Vaughan, eds., *The Tempest*, pp. 54–56; Geoffrey Bullough, *Narrative and Dramatic Sources of Shakespeare*, 245–47).
[587] In *Espejo*, they see the guards who the Knight of the Sun previously defeated and killed and they marvel at his strength.
[588] Their leave-taking is emotional in *Espejo*, due to the great love between Flamides and Trebatio.

deliverance. Besides, this boat will hold us both, and if it be so you will vouchsafe my ship, you shall never sail more safe, neither better provided for victuals'.

The emperor was greatly amazed at it, that all things were so plentiful with the Knight of the Sun.[589] But both very merry, they entered into the boat, which being driven from shore, so soon as it took the shore sailed amain.° Neither missed they ought which was then thought necessary. Quickly they hasted° over the Sea Euxinus, where we will leave them until another time, to write of other things which chanced before this time.

CHAPTER 45

The three princes, which went in the quest of Rosicleer were transported into the Empire of Trabisond, where chanced to them a fair adventure

As the valiant deeds of Rosicleer, while he was there, caused great joy in the court of King Oliverio, so no less was the grief there for his sudden departure amongst his friends. Yet all these sorrows joined in one might not be equal to that which the fair Olivia felt, for she, seeing she had been the cause thereof, took thereat such inward grief that she became both weak and pale, and her father with the whole court greatly lamented for her. In this general sorrow for the loss of Rosicleer, you must think that the Princesses Rodasilva and Silverina were not free, for the loss of Rosicleer procured the absence of their loves; so, as the history recounteth that they two, together with the valiant Prince Zoilo, took upon them the search of him. And therefore, let us leave the court of King Oliverio to tell you of them.

Thus, it is that after they were all embarked in the haven which was nearest to London, they sailed forwards a month's sailing, not desiring to bend either this way or that way. At the end of the month, rather upon chance than their purpose, they were driven upon the coast of Trabisond, where yet glad they were when the country was discried° to see it and to abide there. Coming to land, armed with their rich armour and their esquires accompanying them, they took their horse.

And riding through a beaten path at the side of a pleasant wood, they heard a noise, whereat being moved, they turned back to see what it might be. Out of the thickest of the wood, they saw a wild boar, driving so fast as possibly it might, and in the pursuit thereof, a young gentlewoman upon a mighty courser and a boar spear in her right hand; her hunter's weed° was all of green velvet; her tresses hanging down, in colour like the gold of Araby; in her left hand, a wand of gold; and two rich pearls hanging at her ears.[590] She came spurring her horse in such wise° and with such courage to overtake the boar, that she much delighted them. And at such time as the boar crossed the way between them and her, she struck the boar on the flank that her spear appeared at the other side of the boar. The game was got.

And the lady not taking heed of the other knights, perhaps shadowed by the trees, returned with soft paces to her company. But the knights overtook her and, as I may say, abashed at that which they had seen, at her graces and beauty, they only gazed one upon the other, not once making offer to salute her. Whereat, the lady, more bold than the men, as it were, to awake them out of their dreams, took and winded° a fair horn, which hung at her neck, so loud and shrill that all the forest and valleys rang thereof. And when she had thus done, she came to the three princes, in her seeming the properest° knights that ever she set eye on, whom she friendly welcomed on this wise:°

---

[589] His great desire to return to Hungary to honour the Knight of the Sun according to his merits is omitted.
[590] Araby: the Arabian Peninsula

'God save you, gentle knights, and send you the comfort of your loves. For by your sad and demure looks, it seems you are either strangers or others' thrall.⁵⁹¹

The knights, turning towards her, made their courteous obeisance.° And for them, the valiant Tartarian spoke in this manner:

'Madam, we have stood astonished neither for strangeness nor for ill success in love, which some of us have not yet tried, but only for the thought of your beauty, being a lady huntress as if you were Diana, which in like attire was wont to hunt the forests.⁵⁹² But as you say, we are strangers indeed, and because we would carry somewhat worth the telling, we crave your name and the fashions of the country'.

The lady delighted in the good behaviour of the three knights, and tickled with the words of the Tartarian, in great majesty answered him:

'Assuredly, Sir Knight, I know no cause you have to marvel at me, but rather I at you. For if I seem to you like to Diana, the goddess of the Gentiles, you likewise seem to me the three sons of Priamus — Hector, Paris, and Troilus — not far inferior in renown to the gods themselves. Whereas you desire me to make you know who I am, I will do it gladly, but yet conditionally that afterwards you tell me your name and country. This shall be one for one, and by just exchange we shall hereafter find peace. Wit° you now that I am called Claridiana, the daughter of Theodoro, lord of this empire, and to the Empress Diana, Queen of the Amazons, which two, having been mortal enemies as by long wars appeareth, continued hotly on either part, they were after great friends, meeting in a pitched field, either being then young and unmarried. I am their only child, which since my young years have been brought up in hunting. And I am promised to be made knight, for my mother, being but young, achieved such enterprises that in her time there was no knight more famous. And I am desirous to be somewhat like unto her, especially in that point. And now, Sir Knights, tell me who you are, for I would well accompany such lusty° knights'.⁵⁹³

The Tartarian, who had first taken in hand to speak, answered:

'Noble princess, we were sure enough that there wanted not in you the divinity we spoke of, but yet we failed in the name, for so many graces which accompany you could not be in a lady of less estate. As my religion, being Pagansive,° would rather have induced me to take you for the daughter of Jupiter than of the Emperor Theodoro.⁵⁹⁴ And now since your excellency hath showed us such undeserved favour as to tell us who you are, it is reason that we obey in telling who we are and where we were born'.

This knight, pointing to Bargandel, sayeth:

'He is the Prince Bargandel, the King's son of Bohemia. This', by Liriamandro sayeth he, 'is the Prince of Hungary, called Liriamandro, and I am called Zoilo, son to the King of Tartary. We have joined for adventure beginning in the Great Britain to find a new knight, a friend of ours taken from us we wot° not how. Him, we are determined to look [for] in the world. And we have already sailed a month since we left England. So this morning we landed here, very glad to have found your highness'.

'God be praised', said the princess, 'for the names of so high princes ought not to be concealed, especially here where the emperor, my father, would be glad of such knights for the honour which his court should receive thereby. And I, for my part, would think it a great courtesy in

---

⁵⁹¹ By adding the phrases, 'and send you the comfort of your loves', 'For by your sad and demure looks', and 'or other's thrall', Claridiana configures the knights as lovers and imbues the scene with the mysteriousness of a romantic interlude.
⁵⁹² The additions related to the theme of love reinforce the amorous tone created by the additions to Claridiana's previous speech.
⁵⁹³ While she claims Amazonian ancestry to explain the mingling of the feminine and the chivalric in her character, neither Claridiana nor her mother exhibit the separatism or anti-male attitudes typically associated with the Amazons.
  Female knights, like Claridiana and Britomart from *The Faerie Queene*, form part of the romance marvellous.
⁵⁹⁴ Diana was Jupiter's daughter.

you, if you would stay here till I were knighted, for by such noble princes might I be honoured. In the meanwhile, the courtesy which our court can afford shall be accomplished to the full, and after that you may turn you to your purposed journey'.

When the princess had thus said, straightways there came from the forest thirty gentlewomen on rich palfreys and in long weeds° of green taffeta, among them also a troop of more than thirty knights, all surely° armed with their spears in their hands, coming to seek the princess, which being better horsed than they, had killed the boar long before their approach. The princess, when she saw them, said to the three princes:

'My good lords, if you thought it not amiss, I would see what my knights would do in my defence'.

Bargandel answered:

'Noble lady, the thing cannot displease us which contenteth you. We will endanger our persons to serve you'.

The princess then called her knights and said unto them:

'In good time, my friends, are you come. These three knights, whom you see here, would have carried me away against my will, but I prayed them not to offer such wrong to a gentlewoman. And if they would therewith satisfy themselves, I offered them that of my knights, so many as they should hurl down or unhorse, they should have so many of my gentlewomen for reward. And themselves or any of them were overthrown, that then the party faulting should forfeit horse and harness. Hereto they have agreed. Now do the best you can to defend the gentlewomen, which are in your company'.

Here the Prince Zoilo, which knew the princess's meaning, said unto her:

'Nay, madam, let us first know whether the gentlewomen will yield to our covenant or no, and let their knights speak for them'.

'Marry°', answered the knights, 'we are content'.

'Yea, but so are not we', said the gentlewomen. 'Shall we say they venture imprisonment upon our knights, and they lose nothing? They may betray us if they will, but we fear rather that it will not be in their power'.[595]

'Yea, marry°', answered the knights, 'you are now wise. But if you be so fearful, we pray you alter the jousts to the trial of the sword, and you shall see presently these knights both ashamed and unhorsed'.

'Nay, but yet', quoth the gentlewomen, 'we had need of better warrants than your words. But if you will deal with our knights as we would have you, you must wager your horse and armour to be given them with us if you fail. And hereto we request these knights strangers otherwise to discharge the princess of her promise'.

The three princes feigned to mislike° the gentlewoman's device, and the knights of the country were angry to see how little hope their gentlewomen had in them. So coming unto the three princes, they said unto them:

'Sir Knights, you may behold here that our gentlewomen are not content with the first match, therefore we will unbind it and lose as much as you should. Therefore, take to yourselves so much of the field as you shall think good and let us to the joust, for we will deceive the women of the little hope they have in our virtue'.

Three of the knights, at this alarm,° prepared themselves to joust. And the three princes did as much, glad to show there their manhood. The three first knights were borne down, horse and man, to the great discomfit of the ladies, whereof one mocked her knight for his courage, crying:

'Marry,° it seems, Sir Knight, that I might have been safe between your arms, when you know not how to sit sure within your saddle'.

---

[595] 'They may . . . their power' is added.

Which words caused as great laughter in the princess as shame and confusion to the knights, which were on ground.

Then came three other, which doing as much as the other, were in like manner welcomed, so that to make short tale, from three to three, the princes unhorsed whole thirty, and no man offered a second course. But yet the shame of their falls so egged them on that they demanded the combat with the swords.

Hereat° the knights which knew well enough the princess's purpose, made a great stay,° as it were to consult with their power, being strangers and but three. In the end, sai[d] they:

'You know that the prize which was ordained at these jousts were your horse and armour, the which you have lost. If you will, therefore, needs urge us to the combat with the swords, lay away your horse and armour, which are ours, and come your ways. Otherwise, you must beg the use of them at these gentlewomen, to whom we surrender our whole title'.

'Marry°', said one of the gentlewomen, 'my lords, we accept of your courtesy, and here we else stay° the combat, for we will not give them leave the second time to lose both themselves and us'.

The knights were so ashamed as well for the princes' words, as for the gentlewoman's rebuke, that altogether, with their swords drawn, they would have rushed upon the strangers if the princess coming between had not stayed° them, speaking to the strangers that this was sufficient and it greatly liked her that they had thus showed their valour. Whereto Prince Zoilo answered:

'Madam, we have besides to demand our prizes, which we will not otherwise remit but to yourself', whereat smiling, they all unbuckled their helmets.

Bargandel and Liriamandro, being then of the age of twenty years, seeming so beautiful that as well the gentlewomen as the knights were amazed at them. After them, the Tartarian showed himself, who, although he was a Morian° born and somewhat of colour tawny, yet had he a manly countenance and therewithal pleasant, that he pleased them as well as his companions with this.

'There are no more foes to be feared, as it appeareth', said the princess, 'if you challengers unarm yourselves. But if it be no grief to you, let us go together to the city of Trabisond, not being far off, for at your instance I may the sooner receive the order'.[596]

The princes, thanking the lady for that favour, prepared themselves to obey her command. So rode they on with the princess towards Trabisond, where they stayed about fifteen days, much increasing their honour at the feasts proclaimed for the knighting of the inheritress,° they being made known to none but to the princess. Here likewise, the great prowess which the Princess Claridiana showed were such that every man was amazed at them, albeit the three princes never jousted against her. But hereafter you shall hear sufficiently of her and them. Now to the two princes, Brandizel and Clavergudo, whom we left in the Kingdom of Persia, very sad for the loss of their dear friend, the worthy Knight of the Sun.

CHAPTER 46

The two princes, Brandizel and Clavergudo, stole secretly out of the Kingdom of Persia to find the Knight of the Sun

Now you are to remember° yourselves of the two valiant princes, Brandizel and Clavergudo, which remained in the Kingdom of Persia, very pensive for the loss of their friend, touching whom, the history sayeth, that after these two princes were in Persia some days, having great desire to find out the Knight of the Sun and to seek strange adventures, one day as they were

---

[596] Trabisond: Trabzon, a city in north-east Turkey, on the coast of the Black Sea
Claridiana employs the term 'order' as shorthand for 'the order of knighthood'.

with Armineo, uncle to Clavergudo, they determined between themselves for to depart closely° from them and to go by sea whithersoever° Fortune would transport them. Whereto, although Clavergudo and Armineo would have made the King Florion privy,° yet the Prince Brandizel would in no case consent, believing that if his parents knew of it, they would not give him leave to go from them. So, to pleasure° him, they kept that counsel as privy° as they could.

And when all things were in readiness, one night secretly they conveyed themselves out of the city and so straight to the seaside, where they entered into a ship provided for that purpose. And hoisting up sails, they were carried they neither knew nor cared whither.° For the courages of these two princes, resolved to the search of worthy adventures, would not let them be quiet, so that anything might better content their ease at home.

But as soon as they were gone, the wise Lirgandeo knew of it, and weighing the great commodity which might ensue thereof to themselves and others, he would not hinder it, nor yet make as if he knew it; yet had he great care to guide their ship wherein they sailed. And they reached thither° in fifteen days, which to other is an ordinary month's sailing. That the mariners were abashed to see the swiftness of the ship being more than usual, which when they had discovered to their lords, the princes knew presently by whose means it so happened.[597] Wherefore yet they were the better apaid,° for now they were sure thither° to be carried which fitted best for their avail.°

Well, shortly after the princes' departure and before it was either so noised° or suspected, Lirgandeo declared the truth to the King Florion and the Queen Balisea, willing them withal not to afflict them, for that they thereby should gain much honour and should return safely with the Knight of the Sun in their company. With this, the king and queen were indifferently° appeased.

Now all matters quieted in Persia for the princes' absence, we may the freelier° bear the knights company, which are yet sailing on the sea. So that the fifteenth day after they were departed from Persia, they landed in a haven of Polonia, where their ship stood still. And taking land to learn some news and know the country, ere° they had long travelled, they saw before them a little town, to their judgement pleasant, and round about great flocks of men and women scattered, and making great cries as if some great mischance had happened to them.[598]

Armineo demanded of them the cause of their sorrow, whereto an ancient man among them answered that a fierce giant with more than fifty knights had come in this morning upon them to steal away the Princess Clarinea, daughter to the King of Polonia, their liege lord, that he had killed the greater number and spoiled the residue, and, as he thought, was ere° this time on his way with the princess in his carriage, from whom if it so be not, all the world may recover her.

'Why so?' said Armineo. 'And where is the king? Or where are his knights, that they do not defend their lady?'

The old man answered:

'They are in a town four mile off, not mindful of any such matter. And it hath not been past eight days since the princess came to this town, and now this which you have heard hath happened to her'.

When the three knights heard this of the old man's relation, without staying longer, they galloped with their horses so fast as they might. And coming near to the town, they saw issuing out of the gates a great troop of knights, the one part driving the other before it. For so it was that the giant having the princess in his power was carrying her away and the townsmen fought with him, but their power little prevailed: the giant was strong, his knights many, and so they murdered all that came, in such sort that the town dwellers fled.

---

[597] *Espejo* renders this more explicit, recounting how Brandizel detected Lirgandeo's agency and informed his companions, who were pleased with the knowledge.
[598] Polonia: Poland

Then came the other knights, which slew many of them. Twenty of the giant's knights at once fell upon them, laying at them with all their forces. The meanwhile, the giant held in his arms the Princess Clarinea, and thinking that his knights would make riddance of these three, he took no more keep but rode away softly with the princess. The princess cried out so loud that it was great pity to hear her. And those which heard her of her own knights came pitifully, crying to the knights strangers that for the honour of God they should go help her.

When this was spoken, Brandizel besought his companions to stay there in the battle and to give him leave to follow the giant, which when they granted him, he, putting the spurs to his horse, followed the trace, the whiles the knights of France thoroughly galded° their enemies. For the one of them matchable,° I dare avouch,° with the ancient Franconio, the Trojan's son, of whom he descended.⁵⁹⁹ For he putting himself in press among them, to some he clave their heads, to other some their shields, murdering many and felling many that at length there was none so hardy which durst° stand him a blow. But every [one] of them did his best to save one. His uncle Armineo in the broil helped not a little, for he was a valiant knight and much esteemed of in France.

But let us leave them and speak of the Prince Brandizel, who pursued the giant. He rode so fast that ere° the giant came within a flight-shot° of the sea, he overtook in a large plain, and crying aloud bade him redeliver the princess, false faitour° as he was. The giant looked back to see what he was, and seeing but one, though riding in haste, he cared not for him, save that not to be found unprovided, he loosed the princess from between his arms and set her on ground.

The prince, coming to him, spoke never a word, but drawing his sword hit him so great a blow upon the helmet that he made him bow his head to his breast, wherewith the giant increased in choler and gave him the like.

This began the skirmish between them, wherein the noise was so great that the Princess Clarinea, before in a sound,° returned to herself, and seeing the battle with so little hope as that one only knight should adventure her deliverance, fell into a sound° again, wherein she had died for sorrow had not God provided her the means she looked not for and the comfort she hoped not. And she was the rest of the battle a joyful beholder. When they had thus fought an hour, it was a wonder to see their bruised armour with their hacked shields, but ever the steel coat defended the biting of their swords, especially Brandizel's, which made by [the] art [of] magic had this virtue that no metal might pierce it.⁶⁰⁰ The giant was hurt in many places, whereat as at the force of his adversary, he was greatly astonished and blasphemed his gods in desperate° manner, which had made him stay° that good knight's coming.

The Princess Clarinea, seeing the giant's blood thus cover the ground, was very glad. And her colour became fresh, which much increased her beauty, whereto also Fortune willing to be favourable, it was so that the Prince Brandizel beholding her was enamoured of her beauty and entirely loved her.⁶⁰¹ For his heart now set on fire augmented his courage, and he buffeted the giant so that in short time he unarmed him in many places. In the end, the prince, desirous to give end to the battle, raised in his stirrups, stroke a full blow at the giant upon the shoulder that his sword entered a handful and the giant fell dead.

The prince, seeing him fall, presently leaped from his horse, and pulling off his helmet, went to the princess to recomfort° her, saying:

'Madam, I beseech you accept in good part this little service at his hands, which desireth to do you much more'.

The princess, very joyful to see her enemy on [the] ground and more glad to see her friend so goodly a man, courteously answered:

'Noble knight, you have done so much for me that with all that which my father hath I shall

---

⁵⁹⁹ Franconio is a fictional creation.
⁶⁰⁰ In the source text, Clarinea does not faint again, but rejoices upon seeing Brandizel.
⁶⁰¹ He thinks she is the most beautiful woman in the world, in the Spanish text.

not be able to requite it you. But if you will that this good which you have done me do like me indeed, show me so much favour as to carry me to the king, my father, for hither° will come the residue of the giant's knights. And then my liberty is to begin again'.[602]

The prince, gently taking both her hands in his, kissed them and said unto her:

'Madam, if it please you we may return to the town from whence we came, for I believe that these knights of whom you speak are but few alive to put us in danger. I left my companions fighting with them, who I am sure have done their parts; and yet they shall do us no wrong though they be many. But in far greater jeopardy am I of my life by you, if you vouchsafe me not your service'.[603]

Wherewith the princess was nothing offended, for she liked very well his comely personage, but she answered nothing.[604] The prince, seeing the princess without a palfrey, took her up behind him and with easy paces rode towards the town. In which way the prince, with many amorous words, feasted the princess and manifested to her his love. And after disclosing himself, also he beseeched her to keep it secret, which she did, resolving, notwithstanding, if her father were so content not to match otherwise.

Well, near the town they came where they saw a great troop of knights hasting so fast as they might. And indeed, they were the king and his knights, more than 500 in number, who, by the report, exited to succour their princess.[605] [They] came to the town, and finding almost all the giant's knights taken or slain by the Prince Clavergudo and Armineo with such aid as the town afforded, they altogether follow[ed] on in the pursuit of the giant, which had led her away.

Now there were of the company which a far off ascried° the princess behind Brandizel, and learning that it was the knight which rode to follow the giant, they told it to the king, whereat he was very glad. And making much of the three strangers, especially of Brandizel, he spoke on this wise:°

'Sir Knight, how shall I be able to requite this friendship, which you and your companions have showed to me? Assuredly, I know not, though I should give you my kingdom, for were it not for you I should have lost this day my daughter Clarinea, and with her my joy and pleasure, which being lost what joy should I have found in ruling?[606] But tell me, I pray you, how you dealt with the giant, for he was strong and great?'

'Sir', sayeth Brandizel, offering to kiss his hands, which the king gently refused. 'Sir', sayeth he, 'mighty prince, my companions and I think our fortune to be very good in that we are thither° arrived where we may do service to so courteous a prince, and it is reward sufficient your acceptation. As touching the giant, his ill purpose was his own decay, for he is already dead, not far from hence'.

The king wondered to hear tell that the giant was dead, for by the report of his bigness, he thought it impossible that one only knight should cope with him. And then much more making of the princes, he embraced them often times and desired them to tell him their names, which at length they did. And the king, understanding of their births, carried them with himself towards the town, where in the way he told them who that giant was and what the cause was why he had come thither° in such sort, saying:

'My lords, this giant was called Lambardo, Lord of the Island of Perda, not far hence. He hath, since the time he was first knighted, never employed his time to other advantage but to robbing and spoiling, and for this he hath an island exceeding strong, but very little and scarce well peopled. In this he may defend him from any enemy. And bestowing his espies° in every

---

[602] 'liberty' replaces 'peligro' (danger) in *Espejo*; the alteration makes little sense since her problems, rather than her freedom, will be renewed.

[603] His declaration of love is omitted.

[604] Following the omission of his declaration of love, the exploration of her feelings is likewise omitted.

[605] The king is accompanied by 100 knights in the source.

[606] The loss of Clarinea is linked to his rulership in *Mirror*, while in the source his status as ruler is not considered.

corner to watch for some such chevisance,° he knew that my daughter Clarinea was in this town with a few knights. So hither he made a voyage and had stolen her away, but that God be blessed, such valiant knights as you came in such a time for her succour'.

While the king told this tale, they were within the town walls. And as they entered through the streets, the whole town gathered together to see the prince which had slain Lambardo. And then through the town they came to the king's palace, where they abode a great while.

CHAPTER 47

Rosicleer departeth from the Island of Candramarte and meeteth with certain adventures on the sea

The history left the valiant Rosicleer very sad in the Island of Candramarte, as well for his lady's letter as for that the Knight of the Sun departed from him so suddenly that he could not know him; for remembering himself of the words which the wise Artimodoro had told him as concerning his brother, his mind gave him that it might be he. Wherefore, as without hope ever to see him and not having to comfort his afflicted spirits, he burst out into tears, saying:

'Oh, Fortune! How have thou been froward° to me above all men? First, before I was born, I lost my father. And when I was born, my mother was in sorrow and care for me. And scarcely began I to know the world, when I was banished from her whom I loved dearer than myself. And now by chance, have I been brought to the company of a noble knight with whom I might have been more friendly acquainted, but the waves rose up against me and have carried him away from me, as if I were unworthy of any good'.[607]

When he had wept his fill, he went to one of the castles, there to set such things in order as were disquieted by the death of their lord and to comfort the woeful giantess, whom he after matched with one of the best knights of all those whom the giant had left, giving them livery and season° in that land, and making others to swear obedience. Short time after, he would needs depart, with full purpose to keep in the sea and not to depart till that he should have sailed so far that no words might be heard of him in those quarters. Therefore, he took his armour, wherein was drawn the god of love, in such sort as our ancestors were wont to paint him: with his eyes out, his bow and arrows in his hand. The picture being so lively drawn that Rosicleer knew it was done by the wise Artimodoro, and thereupon he took his name of that device, from which time he never called himself other than the Knight of Cupid, under which name he achieved many enterprises. And Rosicleer's name came never more to the ears of Olivia.

Having put on his armour, he took his leave of Candriana, for so was called the daughter of Candramarte.[608] And for remembrance only [took] the ship wherein he first saile[d] when he left Great Britain, with two mariners to conduct it, whom he charged not to call [him] by other name than the Knight of Cupid and to guide the ship eastward.

When he had so sailed fifteen days without chancing to him anything worthy of recital, it was so that one morning, by sun rising, he saw a little boat pass by him, out of which he heard many cries, as if it had been the labour of some woman. And thinking that there might be need of some help, he was desirous to know what was in the ship. And thereupon, he commanded to join with them. Presently,° there stepped upon the hatches a sad, ancient man with a white beard, all armed save the head, which demanded what he would. Rosicleer said:

'I would know who is in your ship, for me thinks I have heard some woman complain. And if it be so, I will venture my person to do her good'.

The ancient knight beheld Rosicleer, and taking him to be some knight of great bounty,

---
[607] A second lament to Fortune is omitted.
[608] The emotional reactions of the giantess and her husband are excised from the text.

especially in that he had offered himself so freely, when he had thoroughly beheld, he opened the matter on this sort:

'Assuredly, good knight, I thank you for your great good will. And it is not misbeseeming° your outward beauty to have some inward virtue like thereto. But know you that in this ship there abideth a gentlewoman making towards the Great Britain, there to complain her to the King Oliverio and his knights of the outrage which is done unto her. Now because our stay° is dangerous, I may not tell you farther of this matter: our enemies follow us. And so rest you with God'.

When the old man had said this, Rosicleer, having desire to know more, stayed° him and besought him to discourse more at large, for himself was a knight of that court and could tell him what remedy was to be hoped for there. The old man was loath to stay longer, yet hearing him say that he was of the same court, he told him in few words that this gentlewoman was the Princess Arguirosa, one of the fairest ladies in the world and a Princess of Thessaly, only heir to that kingdom.[609] That her mother being dead, the King Arguidoro, her father, fell in love with a gentlewoman of Thessaly, not so honest nor of so high estate as wanton and of base birth.[610] And loving her affectionately, after married her, to the dispossessing of his own child.[611] Then in the time of her father's life, there was in the court a knight called Rolando, besides his great living,° one of the strongest knights in all those parts,° but proud and little respecting the whole world. That this knight, during the life of the king, was liked of Ipesca, and so soon as the King Arguidoro died of a sudden disease, was promoted to the king's bed by matching with the Queen. And being of great revenues that he now enjoyed the kingdom by force, and excluding the right heir, none of the kingdom daring to gainsay him, for the most able are his nigh kinsmen; the other learn patience perforce.° But that which worst of all was that to undo her rightful claim, he mindeth to marry her with a kinsman of his and to give only some little town to dwell in, reserving the title of the kingdom after his own days to a son, the which he hath begotten on his Queen Ipesca.

'I am kinsman', sayeth he, 'to the princess, being her mother's brother, and therefore I have adventured to relieve my niece. But not knowing any remedy at home because my power is not equal with Rolando's, I have brought her out from thence and I determine to go to the Great Britain, whereas I have heard are there many valiant knights, especially a new knight, of whom I have heard especially since the great feasts there held. If this knight help me not, I know not who may withstand Rolando. Three nights and days have we been upon the sea — only I, the lady, two gentlewomen, and our mariners — and I believe that there come after us Rolando's knights. Now have I told you the whole of your desire, and I beseech you tell us what news you know of that good knight'.

Rosicleer, now having heard the whole state of the Princess Arguirosa's matter, was much troubled. And desirous to help her, he answered the ancient man that for his stay he thanked him.

'And as touching your demand', sayeth he, 'of the new knight, truth it is that in Britain none can tell you news of him, wherefore your labour should be lost if you sought him there. But the princess's affliction so much moveth me, that albeit I was purposed otherwise,° yet would I gladly fight with Rolando in the princess's behalf'.

The ancient knight was very sad to hear that the new knight was not in Britain, but well eyeing this knight, which had so told him and made proffer of help, he stood in doubt whether to take or refuse. By and by, he discovered two ships under sail and by their tops° to be of Thessaly, whereat striking himself on the breast he cried out:

---

[609] Thessaly: a geographical region of Greece, previously named Aeolia. It is on the eastern coast of mainland Greece, extending from the Aegean Sea northwards to Macedonia.
[610] *Espejo* recounts her mother's circumstances.
[611] The Spanish text does not specify that Arguirosa was disinherited; instead, it explains that Ipesca was made queen.

'Oh, most unhappy° that we are! Here cometh Rolando's knights, which will take us. And being brought again to Thessaly, we shall there receive most cruel death'.

And he wept, cursing the hour of his departure. The Princess Arguirosa, hearing the complaints which her uncle made, his great sorrow which he sustained, the extreme danger they were in, and the cause why he did it, took it as heavily, and woefully bewailed their misery.

When Rosicleer saw them in this plight, he much pitied them, especially Arguirosa, which the Princess Olivia not remembered might have well contented him. Therefore, he willed them to get under the hatches again and to let him shift for their safety.[612] The old man, thinking that Rosicleer would defend them by saying that they were his people, did so, not ceasing yet to fear the worst and to pray earnestly for their escape.

Rosicleer leapt into the princess's ship and sat upon the brim thereof to see what would happen, till that the other ship came near and that he which was the captain commanded to grapple. And espying Rosicleer, with a proud voice bade him say both who himself was and what people he had in his ship, and not to fail in any point. Whereto Rosicleer, by and by, answered:

'I am a stranger in these parts, and farther it is no reason that you know who they are that are with me, for we keep our way without molesting thee or thine°'.

The captain, angry for his short speech, said to him:

'I will strike thy head into the water unless thou answer me directly to my question'.

And so saying he held and pulled Rosicleer to have forced him.[613] Rosicleer, thus rudely entreated, rose up and with his gauntlet gave the captain such a blow upon the helmet that his brains flew about his head. And presently he fell into the water, where the weight of his armour kept him down.

Straightaways, more than twenty knights well armed and well angered for the death of their captain, altogether with their swords in their hands, smote at him. Rosicleer, drawing out Queen Julia's blade, struck again with such courage that at three blows three knights were slain. And those which presently knew his great prowess drew back, making no great haste to come near him. Rosicleer, knowing his enemies' fear, leaped into their ship, and there laid so about him that in short space he killed half of them.

The Princess Arguirosa and the ancient knight now began to show themselves above board, and they greatly wondered at his manhood.[614] So shortly after, Rosicleer was alone in his enemies' ship without resistance: either all being slain; or all slain or wounded; or slain, wounded, or by flight escaped, for Rosicleer's own ship was lost in this garboil.° Now returned he to Arguirosa's ship, wherein she with the old man received him.

Rosicleer's salutation to the princess after this exploit was in this wise:°

'Madam, what hath been done yourself hath seen, but for a recompense hereof, I shall think myself thoroughly satisfied if you will venture that into my hands which you dare hazard into the hands of the new knight. For I promise you, I will as willingly jeopard° my person as he shall'.

Now when Rosicleer had so said, the princess and the old man stayed a good while without speaking word, for the consideration of their own danger, past recovery if this man failed, made them the more weary. And so between the examination of Rolando's valour and Rosicleer's hardiness, in the end, Arguirosa herself, rather upon love towards him than of assured confidence, would put her matter to no other trial than Rosicleer's.[615] So she commended her quarrel to him on this sort:

'The courtesy, valiant knight, which you have offered me, though unworthy, hath been so

---

[612] In *Espejo*, he stresses the importance of them remaining unknown.
[613] In a lengthy omission, the narrator addresses the knight, warning him of Rosicleer's strength.
[614] They observe Rosicleer through a little window, refraining from coming above board in the Spanish text.
[615] Her feelings are explored thoroughly in *Espejo*.

great that I want the boldness to accept more. Yet because you erst° defended me from death by the vanquishing of Rolando's knights, and now again you will needs take upon you a further matter, rather not to refuse you than willing to trouble you again, I will return with you to my country and commit wholly to your hands the whole ordering both of myself and my cause'.

Her uncle gave his consent thereto, and Rosicleer thanked them much. So they sailed to Thessaly, where by the way, Rosicleer, casting in his thought how to redress the princess's wrong to the least displeasure of her and her uncle, which were loath to be known, determined as a stranger to enter the land and to demand justice, as it were, against a person not known. To which device, after he had made them privy° and promised that they should not be disclosed till it so served for their avail,° they were better comforted and sailed with so good wind that they took landing in a haven near the place where the king was.

Taking land, he made the princess to put on a muffler° and the old knight to cover his head, besides bidding both to counterfeit for the time some strange behaviour, either in holding down their heads or in disguising their attire.[616] To either of them he gave their horse, and himself mounted upon a courser, the best of all Candramarte's stable. In the cool of the evening, they took their way to the nearest city, where then were many knights and ladies coming out of the city to disport° them in the shadow.° Rosicleer, being of a comely personage and so lustily° mounted, pranced forth to be seen, and was well liked of, and praised amongst, them all. As they followed on their journey towards the gates of the city, the king at that time came out accompanied with his nobility to solace himself in the field, as at other times before he was accustomed. The king rode upon a mighty horse, with trappings and harness most of beaten gold, his horse being so brave and himself so fierce and stern to look to that it would have daunted a right good knight to have but spoken to him. So soon as the princess and her uncle saw him, they counterfeited the best that they could, and for fear their blood sunk down into their bellies.

The valiant Greek, knowing that this was Rolando whom he sought for, as nothing afraid of his terrible looks, but rather glad to have met with him so conveniently and in the company of so many knights, willed the princess and the knight to follow him. So came they all three before the king, Rosicleer speaking to him and saying:

'Mighty King in justice, stay° thy horse to hear a poor lady's complaint and to right the greatest wrong that ever was offered to a gentlewoman.[617] Why she complaineth to thee is for that thou are the king, and should above all men repulse the wrong-doer, so further discovering of the king's duty'.

Now the while Rosicleer spoke thus, Rolando beheld him very well, liking both his courage and personage. And albeit of his own nature, he neither feared God nor kept justice in things which pertained to himself, yet hearing in Rosicleer's discourse himself to be made on now and then as of a right judge, and that he would not consent that other than justice should be executed in his kingdom, he was tickled therewith, and bade Rosicleer tell on, for he would hear his matter willingly. Rosicleer, straining his voice that what he said might be heard and noised° abroad, spoke as followeth:

'Know you, mighty King, that the father of this gentlewoman was lord of great possessions, which marrying with an honourable woman begot on her this lady. Few years after his wife deceasing, this lord married also another woman, by whom he had no child. After that the lord himself died also, the stepdame° remaining alive, and shortly marrying with another man, whom in her husband's days she had a liking to. This man, Sir King, matching with the mother-in-law, hath dispossessed the true heir of her lawful inheritance, insomuch too, as being so

---

[616] In *Espejo*, she wears a mask rather than a muffler.
  Tyler adds the phrase: 'bidding both . . . their attire'.
[617] By adding 'in justice', Rosicleer punningly draws attention to Rolando's greatest fault: his injustice. Rosicleer also thereby foreshadows his attack on Rolando, which is motivated by Rolando's injustice.

disseised° she hath in no wise° been considered of as such a man's daughter. Now seeking her redress abroad, it was my chance to meet with her, to whom, after she had declared her case, I made offer for to fight for her with any which impugned her right. These are, therefore, to require thee, oh, King, so to tender her suit in the honour of justice, either that she may lawfully enjoy her own or that you authorize the lists,° that the conqueror may enter by a lawful mean'.

So Rosicleer ended, expecting the king's answer, who neither warily nor advisedly weighing and understanding the drift and purpose of this parable answered:[618]

'Sir Knight, thy demand is just, and the knight which has done this wrong cannot choose but take the one of the two. Therefore, tell me who thou are and I will send for him to answer thy challenge'.

'Be it as the king hath spoken it![619]' said Rosicleer. 'And know for truth that the knight which hath done this injury is thyself. The gentlewoman which received it is the Princess Arguirosa, which here standeth by me, the lawful inheritor, as thyself knoweth, of this kingdom. Thou, without just title, have intruded upon it; therefore, do that which thy mouth hath witnessed to be just'.

When Rosicleer had said, Rolando, much amazed at his great presumption and not being able to bridle his choler, answered despitefully:

'Thou foolish and unhappy° knight, how hath so great madness entered into thee as to appear before me with such a demand, that were it not for the sentence which I have given, I would ere° this have abated thy pride? But I will not keep long from thee the rod of due correction. I am content to take the battle, and with the conditions which thou have named. Hard enough, I warrant thee, for thyself and that woman, whom I will so cage up that she shall no more seek such knights as thou are'.

When the king had thus said he went on his way, and all those which heard the demand of Rosicleer were much abashed° at his boldness, for though he was big, yet seemed he nothing so strong as to resist Rolando. Presently, it was published throughout the whole city, and the battle was appointed to be on the morrow,° where you should have seen most part of the town pray to God for the right of their natural queen. Many scaffolds were erected to see the lists.° The ancient knight, uncle to the princess, was called Alberto, and he had a nephew, a strong and lusty° knight, dwelling a mile from the city in a castle of his own, whence he seldom departed for fear of the king. Thither° did the uncle of the princess for that night carry them, where they were received gladly and took their rest.

CHAPTER 48

The battle which Rosicleer had with Rolando

Rolando made no account that night of the battle which he was to fight the next day, for he thought no harm could happen him, though there had been ten more such knights as his adversary was. The day being come, he arose and armed himself, where enquiring whether the knight, his adversary, were in field or no, it was told him: 'yea'.[620] Wherefore, he made the more haste, and coming to the lists with a troop of armed knights, for his more honour, he defied the Knight of Cupid, for so was Rosicleer then called of the device which he bore.[621] The king's words were to this effect:

---

[618] The sentence is expanded in order to stress Rolando's lack of deliberation and justice.
[619] This addition, 'Be it as the king hath spoken it!', creates an intense, dramatic moment.
[620] In the Spanish text, the king enquires to see if Rosicleer is armed and ready.
[621] *Espejo* boasts a lengthy description of the preparations and of the knights' and spectators' entry to the field.

10 'Tell me now, foolish knight, do thou not repent thy yesterday's challenge? Would thou not give much not to be here now?'

Whereto Rosicleer:

'No, assuredly I repent me not, for if thou vanquish me I look for naught but death, which I set so light by as in so right a quarrel. I would venture my life twenty times, but thou ought rather to repent thyself and to have remorse of thy ill dealing'.

Rolando heard him say so and began to laugh aloud.

'Are thou', sayeth he, 'become a philosopher, who wanting strength of arms to purchase honour, when they lie striking themselves on their couches can talk gallantly, which they account for as great a glory? Thou trust more I perceive in thy tongue philosophy than in chivalry or manhood. And yet, to be spoken of after thy just punishment, thou will die forsooth° in defence of justice. But if death in such a quarrel be so acceptable, prepare thyself for it, for thou shall stay no longer than the proof of my spear'.

So saying, Rolando turned the reins of his horse to take the carrier, the meanwhile that the judges were placed on their bench, and that the queen, with her ladies, had taken the windows to behold the battle. The Princess Arguirosa sat upon her palfrey all heavy and only accompanied with Alberto, for none else durst° make any countenance of well meaning towards her for fear of the king.

But to our matter, these two knights, putting their spurs to their horses with their spears in their rests, ran together. And with their force, the earth shook and their spears burst in sunder.° The king, in the midst of the carrier being borne upon his crupper, and Rosicleer not moved at all, save that his horse peytrals° burst with the rushing.

And both knights lighted down, where began a fierce battle on foot, either laying at other so thick that their shields were burst in pieces, and themselves so wearied that either followed the other staggering and not certain of his gait.[622]

The beholders of the battle were much amazed at Rosicleer and at the danger wherein he put the king. But if any marvelled, much more did Rolando, which both felt it and could judge what terrible shakes he had borne both on horse and foot. And he thought in himself never to have met with the like knight, one or other, man or giant. Ever Rosicleer's nimbleness helped him much, for he could step easily aside and escape the blow.

40 But Rolando found a want of his horse, for he was so heavy that he could not avoid one blow. At length, stark tired, his bones aching for very pain of travail,° he would have taken breath, but fearing to make his adversary privy° thereto, he forced himself quickly to kill or be killed. And heaping his blows upon Rosicleer, he so galled him that the lookers-on mistrusted Rosicleer's party. But would he or not, Rosicleer enduring the uttermost, Rolando was fain to give over. Whereat Rosicleer, though not having so much need, yet not to take so foul on, did the like.

They two, leaning their breasts upon the pummels of their swords, beheld each other a long while, where Rolando, thinking it not best so to end the matter, but to take it up some other way, spoke to Rosicleer, saying:

50 'I had not thought, knight, that so much courage had been in thee. And yet, ere° the end, it will little further thee against me, but for that I am given to love and like of such knights as thou are, I will use clemency towards thee, which I never determined to do towards one which hath so much offended me. This it is: I will that thou leave of the battle which thou have in hand for the Princess Arguirosa, and from thenceforth that thou abide in my court, where I will do thee that honour which thy person meriteth, and I will bestow a living upon thee wherewith thou shall live contentedly'.

Rosicleer, here well perceiving what he went about, said unto him:

---

[622] In the source, they leap to the ground, each knight amazed at the other's strength.

'I would willingly, Rolando, that as thou have in show offered me great honour, for the which I thank thee, so that thou would indeed perform another thing, which should be less impair° to my present honour than the leaving of the battle. The battle, as thou say, would I gladly end, not only for mine° own danger, which I am like to be in, but for thy sake whom I rather wish to amend thy fault by living and restoring the lady to her own than by dying in a wrong cause to hazard the utter perdition of thy soul. And for truth, take this: that I will choose to die rather than to suffer her cause to be lost by my collusion. Take, therefore, some other means to leave this battle, for this will not succeed. Or let us fight it out, for I hope in God that He will defend the innocent'.

When Rosicleer had said this, Rolando, thinking that his own gentle speech had made his enemy more bold, became mad outright, and forgetting his weariness, took his sword with both his hands and therewith he struck Rosicleer so hard on the headpiece that he made bow both hands and knees upon the ground — the blow being so heavy as if a tower had fallen upon him. Rosicleer, rising up, acquitted it him, that he made him stagger five or six paces backward. And between them the combat was renewed.

Now this especially refreshed the poor Princess Arguirosa, that her knight troubled her enemy more now than at the beginning. And not long after it was apparent that Rosicleer had the better, for Rolando began to be weary and could not move out of his place. Rosicleer, knowing the advantage and willing to end the battle the sooner both for the contentment of the princess and the safety of Rolando's life, whom he judged to be a valiant knight, offered again the conditions before mentioned. But it was not Rolando's good hap,° and true it is that those which live so wickedly, die commonly as desperately,° lest they should repent their faults and find mercy.

But Rolando, more than mad at the courtesy which was offered him, would hear naught, but struck at Rosicleer with all his force. Rosicleer stepped aside and the sword fell upon the ground, sticking up to the hilts. The whiles that Rolando haled° at his sword, Rosicleer discharged his blow with great strength and cut the neck in sunder° from the body. Wherewithal the whole multitude shouted, but in diverse tunes: some for sorrow of the tyrant's death, but most crying, 'Live thou Arguirosa, our queen and lady!' Then albeit some of the king's friends would have avenged his death, they durst° not signify it, the people being so bent after the new queen.

The Knight of Cupid, when the battle was ended, thanked God and demanded of the judges whether ought else were to be performed for the restoring of the Princess Arguirosa to her kingdom. To which all said 'no', and the trumpets sounded.[623] Yet sat the princess upon her palfrey till there came to her of the most principal knights and other citizens, which now all fear set aside, durst° discover their good affection.[624] The princess, therewith, and the Knight of Cupid with her uncle, Alberto, rode in great honour to the palace, where that present day the princess was crowned queen, the chief lords kissing her hand in the name of the gentlemen and commons. After, there was no talk but of the marriage of the queen. Every man, as he wished, naming the Knight of Cupid, which herself more desired than they all, but knowing that the Knight of Cupid had elsewhere bestowed his liking — which she gathered by likelihood of speeches, which she had heard in the ship; by the deep sighs which he hourly fetched; and especially by his device, which did not argue in a new beginner — she ruled her passion the best she might, and for this time moved him not therein.

Afterwards, she sent for Rolando's wife, her mother-in-law, to keep her company, but the report was that for anguish of mind she had slain herself.[625] Well, yet she commanded them both to be interred as belonged to the kings and queens of that land. Rosicleer remained in that kingdom six days at the great entreaty of [the] queen to help all things to good order. After

---

[623] The music of the trumpets is added in *Mirror*.
[624] The princess's great joy at Rolando's death is excised from *Espejo*.
[625] *Mirror* omits the extensive narration of her suicide.

feeling the wound, which sat more deeply imprinted in his heart than the image thereof in his armour, he departed thence. And so, let us leave him to recount of the Emperor Trebatio and the Knight of the Sun, who were left sailing upon the sea.

CHAPTER 49

The Emperor Trebatio and the Knight of the Sun are in their way to the Kingdom of Hungary

The Emperor Trebatio and the Knight of the Sun, departing from the Island of Lindaraza, were left sailing in the Sea Euxino. Now the ship wherein he was, having so good and skilful a governor° as we have told you, was carried so swiftly that, within two days, they entered the mouth of [the] Danube. And being upon the river three days and three nights, the fourth day in the morning they were set on land ere° that they wist.°

The emperor, looking about him, knew the country very well since he had followed the chariot to the selfsame place. And being glad to have arrived to Hungary so safe and so shortly,° he embraced the Knight of the Sun for joy, telling him that this was Hungary, where the Princess Briana lived.[626] So he devised with him in what manner he might best make himself known to the princess and convey her into Greece.

The Knight of the Sun, being so friendly asked his advice, answered as faithfully:

'My lord, it is requisite for us first of all to know where the King Tiberio is, and in what order the princess now abideth, which being done, you may the better compass that which you purpose'.

'You say right well', answered the emperor. 'Let us keep along the shore, that if perhaps we meet with anyone, we may enquire what news there are'.

So on foot they walked through a forest leading° upon the river, wherein they travailed° half a day without meeting anyone. After, somewhat wearied, they sat them down to rest themselves, where they fed on such viands° as they had brought with them from the boat.

A half hour after, when they had rested indifferently,° they saw near at hand a gentlewoman upon a palfrey making as much haste as she could, and after her a knight on foot with a naked sword, threatening her if she stayed not, when he overtook her to run her through. The gentlewoman, seeing the emperor and the Knight of the Sun, leapt from her palfrey, crying out:

'Succour me, good knights, for this traitorous knight will ravish me!'

The emperor rose up, and comforting the gentlewoman, stayed a while till the knight came to lay hands on her. Then he said:

'Sir Knight, either let this gentlewoman alone or tell us why thou will carry her against her will'.

The knight, which was both proud and peevish, answered him:

'I will carry her away maugre° your teeth! And I have no charge to make you other answer. But as to the cause, wit° you well that it is for myself and for no other, whereof you shall be no let° I warrant you'.

'But you carry her not away', said the emperor, 'for sooner shall you die than touch her honour'.

The knight, thus overawed in words, thought to make amends in deeds, and suddenly he hit the emperor under the ribs. The emperor, to yield it him again, struck at his head, which he received in his shield. And not daring to abide another, he fled through the forest as fast as he might.

---

[626] In the source, rather than inform the Knight of the Sun that Briana resides in Hungary, Trebatio expresses an inability to adequately thank and recompense the young knight.

Neither the emperor nor the Knight of the Sun would follow him, but demanded of the gentlewoman why that knight pursued her.

'Alas, my lords', said she, 'my fellow and I came riding through the forest where we were met with four knights, which would have carried us away by force. Myself fled this way, my companion another, and but if you do help her, these wicked knights will do her villainy'.

The emperor, having alone begun the battle, desired the Knight of the Sun to abide there the while he took the gentlewoman's palfrey to succour the other lady. The Knight of the Sun would rather have taken that travail° upon him than to expect the report, but not to importunate° the emperor, he promised to stay his coming or to follow him.

The emperor took up the gentlewoman behind him to conduct on the way, and being brought by her to the midst of the forest about a flight-shot,° they heard the screeching of some gentlewoman. And following that sound they found four knights laying hands upon a gentlewoman, whereat she cried out. The emperor, presently as he saw it, dismounted from his horse and cried to the knights, saying:

'Knights, let this gentlewoman alone, for it is great villainy to force a woman!'

One of them, hearing the emperor, cried again:

'Who made you a justice? Or do you look for an attorney's fee?'[627]

And they all three laid at the emperor. But it had been better for them not to have been so hasty, for ere° long they received just reward for their insolence, for the emperor cleaved one of them to the skull; and one other from the shoulders downward; the third, as he made haste to escape, was taken shorter° by the legs. For the emperor, albeit very inclinable to any reasonable pity, yet was in this point very rigorous, not to spare the dishonourers of virginity. His saying was that it quenched the natural love between father and mother, sister and brother, between kith and kin;° that the bastard born seldom came to good purpose; that it was partly the sin of sodomy', and et cetera. And for his own fault, it was indeed mere ignorance, or rather constraint, and thereby the more pardonable. Or perhaps the detesting of it himself made him more severely exact the keeping of chastity in others.[628]

But forward with our matter. The emperor, beholding this gentlewoman whom he had succoured, knew her presently to be Clandestria, a gentlewoman belonging to the Princess Briana, wherewith he was the gladdest man in the world, as hoping to hear some good news at her hands. Yet, to cover himself, he made the gentlewomen sit down, himself sitting by them, and to tell him whither° they went and wherefore they were in those parts. The gentlewomen, glad and fain° that they might, without danger, tell of what country they were and what their errant° was thitherward,° answered:

'Sir Knight, we are belonging to the Princess Briana, daughter to the king of this land. The cause of our coming is that, long time ago, our lady lost her husband, the Prince Edward, Prince of Britain, and hath never since heard of him. For his sake she hath remained a widow in the Monastery of the River, demeaning° a very sorry life, as pent up in a religious cloister. Her belief was always that he was dead, till within these fifteen days, she dreamed that she saw him alive and that he came by sea to this land, very merry, of the same age which he was of when he first left her, which dream she hath dreamed three nights together. The last night of the three, there appeared to her an ancient man much rebuking her for her distrust, whereat the princess, though hardly persuaded, yet being so admonished, the better hath credited that night's vision and hath sent us to a religious house, dedicated to Our Lady, the Blessed Virgin, with rich offerings and many good devotions for his safe return. Whence after we were returning by this forest, these knights beset us and ravished us, but that we cried so loud that you heard us, and you have,

---

[627] Tyler retains the fiscal language of the villain's reply, 'Wait a bit, for soon we will pay you for your audacity', but alters the response, placing the emphasis on legality and justice.

[628] The discussion of chastity and sexual sin — 'His saying ... in others' — is original to the English text.

thanks be to God, well eased us of them. And for your so great courtesy, if it so please you to ride with us, I doubt not but our mistress will well consider you'.

The emperor, much rejoicing at the great constancy of his wife Briana and desiring to discover himself, asked the gentlewomen if any of them had seen the Prince Edward or no. Whereto Clandestria answered:

'Yea, Sir Knight, very well. And I would that God would once show him me, I should know him by his lovely face, excelling all other knights which I have ever seen'.

'I will see that presently', said the emperor.

And so saying he put off his helmet:

'And how now?' sayeth he. 'Whom take you me for?'

'Oh', say they both, 'yourself are Prince Edward!', and kneeling down before him, would have kissed his hands.

And they earnestly entreated him to go with them to the Monastery of the River.[629] The emperor consented gladly.

'For I have', sayeth he, 'as great desire to see her. But here, not far hence, there is a knight which stayeth° for me. Him must we seek and carry in our company, for he is the man next unto God to whom I am most beholding, for by him have I been delivered from prison and from enchantment. The whole story I will tell you by the way'.

So, the emperor made the gentlewomen to mount upon their palfreys, and himself took one of the horses pertaining to the dead knight[s] for himself, and an other for the Knight of the Sun. And by the way he discoursed, as he promised, of his own estate with Lindaraza till that they met with the Knight of the Sun, with whom the emperor communicated of his good adventure to light upon Briana's maids and what news he had heard of them. Whereat the Knight of the Sun became as joyous. And they made a merry journey towards Belgrade, which held them four days travel from that place.

CHAPTER 50

The emperor and the Knight of the Sun, riding towards the Monastery of the River, are by an adventure separated

The emperor, in the way, declared to the gentlewomen and to the Knight of the Sun who he was: not Prince Edward as they thought, but in his name Briana's bridegroom, and so forth of that matter, which you may conceive by that you heard before. Whereat the gentlewomen were not a little amazed, but nothing sorry. And with the Knight of the Sun, the emperor entered into farther counsel in what order he might make the King Tiberio privy° to his fact and carry the Princess Briana into Greece. Whereto, the Knight of the Sun counselled thus:

'My lord, you know the faith of a prince, a bond very straight° for kings and great lords as touching the preservation of their honour in promise, for which many times many have preferred the trust laid upon them before the safety of their near kindred. This I say for that peradventure° Tiberio will be right glad to have matched his daughter with you, yet, for the Prince Edward's sake, coming under his safe conduct, he may not take it in good part. Or, if he did, had not King Oliverio just cause to be angry, being so abused as under his word to have lost his son and subjects withal? My counsel is, therefore, for the better dispatch of your business and avoiding of being shent° if you venture rashly upon an enemy not reconciled, that you go secretly to the monastery and carry away the princess from thence, scarce letting herself know whither° you shall go. Save that behind you, you may leave a letter which shall signify the whole effect of that

---

[629] Her extremely sorrowful state, bereft of all happiness, is noted in *Espejo*.

which is passed. By this means, if the King of England bewail the death of his son, the King Tiberio may complain of the loss of his daughter. And in time, when these sores are skinned, there may friendship be made on either part'.[630]

The emperor liked well this counsel, and giving him many thanks, told him that he would put it in effect.

So, two days they kept company, nothing in the meantime happening worth the telling. The third day, coming to a cross-way well trodden, they saw a pavilion pitched, and not far off twelve gentlewomen clothed in black and having very sad countenances.[631] At the tent door, they saw three knights, which were their keepers. When the emperor and the Knight of the Sun approached, the gentlewomen cried out, whereat the Knight of the Sun stayed and spoke unto them:

'Gentlewomen, as well by your countenances as by your outcries, we perceive you are distressed. Show us now the cause thereof, and if the thing be such as that we may remedy, it we will do our best to do it'.

One of the chiefest° of them answered:[632]

'Sir, your courteous words makes us the bolder to utter our grief. Therefore, know you that I have a sister called Elisandra, Duchess of Pannonia, and married to a knight, the most wicked man that was ever born, for he hath slandered her with such a misreport as the like hath not been heard of. So it is that my sister and he have been married eight years and have had no children, wherefore, he fearing that after his decease the dukedom should return to her kin — as by right it should, being her only inheritance — and minding to establish the state in his own name, hath suborned a desperate person to challenge her of adultery.[633] By which means, she being executed as false to her husband, all her lands and goods are forfeited to the husband, as it were to make him amends of his wife's wrong.[634] Now this slander is apparent to all men, but because the duke offereth that the combat shall be granted to him which shall gainsay the slander, the matter is made the likelier and is born out, though not by strong hand, yet by policy. And yet, no man dare oppose himself to the challenger.[635] For there is a knight in the land called Aridon, Lord of the Black Wood, by report the strongest knight which ever was in these parts, albeit very like unto the duke in his ill living. Him hath the duke made his friend and accuser of the princess for a plot of ground adjacent to his seigniories.°[636] His accusation lieth thus: that with himself she committed adultery, whereas though he was a long sojourner in her court, yet he neither persuaded her to it, nor would ever move her in it, for he knew his answer. But the matter was thus canvassed, the while the duke kept at the court of the King Tiberio. Thither° word is brought of the false packing° of the duchess and Aridon. The duke presently complaineth to the king, and both parties are sent for in all haste. Aridon, being first asked, confesseth it, and is acquitted by his confession; as, by the way, our law in this case acquiteth the man once confessing it, though otherwise never so great an offender, and only stretcheth to the woman in respect of her faith given at marriage. Now, what could the princess do, standing before the king and accused not of hearsay, but by himself, with whom she is said to have lain? Yet, denyeth she it well. The duke, charging her with it, and she purging herself, she was fain to require respite for providing a sufficient knight to maintain her innocence. Yet was she commanded to prison under sure keeping. And there is a day set for the trial. Aridon being the accuser, against whom

---

[630] Proverbial, Tilley S649.
[631] There are only two gentlewomen in the source.
[632] Their positive assessment of the Knight of the Sun, which encourages them to reply, is excised.
[633] In the source, the gentlewoman herself is the rightful inheritor. By altering the text so that the damage is done to 'her kin', the gentlewoman appears to be acting altruistically on behalf of her family rather than for personal gain.
[634] In *Espejo*, she further explains that as a result of her disinheritance her brother-in-law would remain Duke of Pannonia, with absolute freedom in selecting his wife.
[635] The explanation of the situation is more clearly articulated in *Mirror* than in *Espejo*.
[636] An extensive recounting of how they met, which occupies an entire page of *Espejo*, is omitted.

I do not think that any man in her defence (though the cause be righteous) dare show himself, for we have tarried here these twenty days and have not found any. Now because here are crossways, in which it is likely that many knights should pass, we determine to abide the rest of the prefixed time. And this is the cause, Sir Knight, why we mourn'.

And so she ended, weeping bitterly.

The emperor and the Knight of the Sun pitied them much, marvelling so ungodly dealing could have any place to rest in Hungary:[637]

'But God is wise', say they. 'Yea, and seeth His time'.[638]

So the Knight of the Sun, talking apart with the emperor, said to him:

'My lord, you see good cause binding me to pity the duchess in her extreme need. If you be pleased therewith, I will go answer for her in the court of King Tiberio. In the meantime, it will be best for you to go to the Monastery of the River, the most secretly that you may. And I will not fail to certify° you from the court if I hear ought which might avail you being known.[639] This being done, I will, with God's help, come to Greece, where I look to find you very merry'.

The emperor was loath, but seeing the urgent necessity, he was content and answered that he would not be against his pleasure, although it would grieve him to be so long without his company:

'But at Constantinople shall we meet!'

Thereupon, the Knight of the Sun turned to the gentlewomen, saying:

'Gentlewomen, your mourning hath so much grieved this knight and me that although his affairs lie otherwhere° and that he cannot be present, yet for his sake will I go with you to the court, there to answer for the duchess, if she be so content'.

The gentlewomen willingly accepted of the knight, and not staying longer but to thank him, they pulled down their tent and to horseback they go. By the way, he had much talk with Elisea, for so was the duchess's sister named. He comforting her, and she requesting him to make speed:[640]

'For we lack not many days of our appointed time, when, if we fail, we shall lose a good cause for lack of pity in knights adventurous'.

But let us leave this, and turn we to the emperor in the company of Briana's gentlewomen.

CHAPTER 51

The Emperor Trebatio came to the Monastery of the River, and there was made known to his wife, the princess

The emperor, having good hope to meet with the princess, whom he loved no less than before he had when he hazarded his person for her sake upon Prince Edward, made great haste.[641] And he travelled with the gentlewomen three days and three nights.[642] Now we have told you often that the princess's lodging was in one quarter of the monastery separate from the other, whereto she had a postern gate towards the wood, by which Clandestria had carried Donzel del Febo and Rosicleer to nursing.° And by this gate, no man either entered or went out, but by Clandestria's leave: she was groom-porter° and kept the key herself. And for to cover this matter,

---

[637] In the source, they marvel specifically that a man could act so maliciously against his own wife.
[638] The invocation of divine agency — 'But God . . . . his time' — is added.
[639] He further promises to discover the king's reaction to the marriage in *Espejo*.
[640] Elisea's encouraging speech is omitted.
[641] Trebatio's sadness upon his separation from the Knight of the Sun is omitted.
[642] In the Spanish text they travel for two uneventful days, and on the third night they arrive at the monastery.

which the emperor would in no wise° have known, it was very fit that Clandestria was there in company. For when they approached the monastery, sayeth Clandestria:

'My lord, if you will not be known to the gentlewomen here belonging to our lady, best it were that I should first enter and see what they do, and that I should cause the princess to take her most secret chamber, where as I shall find her, so I will declare of your coming.[643] Otherwise, it may be that your so sudden approach might work some alteration in her body to the danger of her health, she being so sore weakened by continual mourning.[644] But this night shall pass, and the morrow° you shall come unto her'.[645]

The emperor liked well of Clandestria's speech, and so he stayed in a place which she provided for him, the whilst that the gentlewomen went to the princess.[646] Some will think that the emperor should be much changed, this being the twentieth year of his absence, but it was not so, for when he first entered the castle of Lindaraza he was but thirty-five years in age, and no more was he when he came from the enchantment, neither his age increasing, nor his beauty decreasing. When the emperor left the Princess Briana, she was but fourteen years old, and counting the time that she had lived afterward, she was just one year under him, wherein her beauty best appeared, and the great sorrow which she before had taken did not so abate her colour, but that the joy of his return fetched it again more fresh and lively than it was before.

But the story sayeth that the gentlewomen found their mistress alone, praying devoutly upon her knees, and more merry than she was before, whether by inspiration or by imagination, conceiving hope in the dream I told you of. But her gentlewomen were very glad to be witnesses of her mirth.[647] The princess lovingly welcomed the gentlewomen, especially Clandestria, which was her sure friend, demanding of them how they had sped in their journey. Clandestria answered:

'Madam, we were once in danger to lose both our honours and our lives after that we had done as you commanded us'.

'Ah, Blessed Virgin!' said the princess. 'And is it possible that you should ever be in so great danger for my cause?'

'Yea, it is most certain, Madam', answered Clandestria, 'but as after a foul evening comes a fair morning, so after this trouble we had some quietness by the means of our flight, for we met with a good knight, which not only saved us from great shame by killing these wicked knights which would have spoiled us, but after told us such news as you have cause to be the gladdest woman in the world.[648] He said that not many days before, he departed from your husband, which was in good health and of the same age as he was when you first knew him, for since he was with you, he hath been enchanted, and being now set at coming to you'.

'Oh, good Lord! And is it possible', said the princess, 'that Thou are so favourable unto me as to send me my husband alive, or is this some dream, the farther to increase my dolour? Tell me, Clandestria, in good faith, is it true which thou say, for I can hardly believe thee?'

'Yea, assuredly', said Clandestria, 'for the knight which reported it is so credible as that he will not tell other than truth'.

'Ah, Clandestria', said the princess, 'thou have been always diligent, discreet, and liberal in those things which have touched my service hitherto. But in this now, concerning my life especially, thou have been negligent or have wanted discretion. For why did thou not bring him before me that myself might have heard it of his own mouth? Would it not then have been

---

[643] In the source text, Clandestria wisely plans to reveal his identity slowly to avoid shocking Briana.
[644] Tyler adds the observation of Briana's weakness due to her extended period of mourning.
[645] In *Espejo*, Clandestria supposes that Briana shall pass the night believing it all to be a dream.
[646] Trebatio's feelings in response to Clanderstria's words are explored in the source.
[647] The addition — 'But the story . . . her mirth' — narrates Briana's altered state, foreshadowing her joy at Trebatio's return.
[648] Proverbial, cf. Tilley M1178.

pleasant unto me to have seen that knight, which so lately saw my loving husband, and to have known of him in what manner he met with him, and for what cause he commeth not so soon as the other?'

'Madam, be not aggrieved with this', said Clandestria, 'for the knight which told it me is not so far hence but that within a quarter of an hour you may see him if you have desire thereto'.

'Desire?' said the princess. 'I desire nothing so much in the world. Therefore, go and fetch him before me that I may know whether that be true, which my heart thinketh so incredible'.

'I will go my ways', said Clandestria.

And so she went out of the princess's lodging and straight to the emperor, to whom she told all that talk which she had had with her lady. Whereat the emperor was so glad that up the stairs full fain he goeth, and by such privy° ways as none but Clandestria knew, he is brought before Briana. Clandestria first entering, then the emperor, clothed in rich armour and his visor pulled down.

The princess was somewhat afraid to see so big a man all armed, but the emperor, pulling off his helmet, quickly showed his lovely face, the which she had imprinted in her remembrance. And with hasty paces, he made towards the princess, whom he kissed on the mouth so sweetly that their tongues this while were silent, not to interrupt the joy of their first meeting. Anon, after the princess, which indeed had the chiefest° wrong, spoke to the emperor thus:

'My lord and only life, what cruel fortune hath detained you from this land and banished you so long from my presence? In what strange and hidden countries have you been, that we could never hear word of you?'

'Madam', answered the emperor, 'you may call that fortune cruel, for it hath offered you a great wrong by forcing you to endure a far greater penance than Penelope did by Ulysses's absence.[649] But one thing you may assure yourself, of that the fault was not in me; though, I am not to be excused, for if I had had life, and liberty, and judgement, all the world should not have stayed° me from you. Since my freedom, if I have not had as loyal a regard of your constancy and my duty, then blame all mankind for my sake of un-steadfastness and wrong. And for this time, let these things slip with less grief to entertain our present joy'.

So he kissed the princess again, and they both sat down together, kissing and colling° each other, like two young lovers.[650] When they were thoroughly entered this delight and that the emperor was sure of her good liking towards himself, whomsoever he were, he bewrayed° to her the whole matter. First, that he was not the Prince Edward, as she thought, but the Emperor Trebatio. And so in few words, he told her the whole story of his first heat by the prisoner's confession, and from thence, in order, to this deliverance wrought by the Knight of the Sun.

The princess, for a great while, stood hereat° amazed and began to gather more of the words which Rosicleer had written to her. And not being displeased with her former error, in the end she told him that whomsoever he was indeed, yet was he the same to whom she was married, and that vow which she then made, she said she would perform to him alone. The emperor, courteously thanking her, bade her say on what had happened.[651] Whereat she, graciously blushing, told him that she had been delivered of two children at one burthen,° being two goodly boys with strange marks in their bodies. Of them she told him farther, pouring down many a tear, the manner of their loss: the one called Donzel del Febo, at three years of his age; the other named Rosicleer, at seventeen:

'And for Rosicleer', sayeth she, 'he hath proved a right manly knight'.

---

[649] In Homer's *Odyssey*, Penelope waits twenty years for her husband, Ulysses (also known as Odysseus), to return from the Trojan War, devising ingenious ways to preserve her chastity and remain faithful to him.

[650] Tyler adds the simile comparing them to young lovers, which recalls the passage of time and reminds us of the fact that Briana is no longer young.

[651] In *Espejo*, Briana takes great pleasure at being married to such a great emperor; in the translation, however, she focuses on his person rather than on his social status.

And therewith she gave him the letter, which Arinda had brought. The emperor read the letter and was very glad to hear of that hope which Artimodoro had put him in as touching the recovery of his brother. And in good time, while we have occasion to entreat of Trebatio's children, let us hold on with the Knight of the Sun, whom we left in the way travelling to the court of King Tiberio, which shall be declared in the chapter following.

CHAPTER 52

The Knight of the Sun, riding to the court of King Tiberio, jousteth with a knight for passage

The Knight of the Sun and the gentlewomen with their knights rode towards the city of Ratisbona, where the King Tiberio and his court for that time lay.[652] Three days almost they travelled, hearing of naught that might be told you, till towards noon upon the third day, they met with a fair gentlewoman upon a palfrey, which saluted them courteously in this manner:

'God save you, Sir Knights! I pray you tell me whether you are going to the court of King Tiberio or no, for if you go thither° I have certain news to tell you'.[653]

'Marry°', said one of the knights, 'that we do. What do you command us thither,° fair gentlewoman?'

'I will tell you that willingly', sayeth she, 'if the knight which hath the device of the sun will grant me my asking'.

'I grant it you, gentlewoman', answered the Knight of the Sun, 'if it be neither let° to my journey nor prejudicial to my person'.

'I am content with these conditions', sayeth she, 'and so I accept of your promise. Now, Sir Knight, truth it is that riding this way, I must of force° pass over a bridge stretching over Danube, not passing two miles from the great city of Ratisbona, over which you must also pass if you would go to the city. This bridge', sayeth she, 'is kept by a knight called Florinaldes for the love of a lady named Albamira, equally beloved of two knights: the one is this Florinaldes, the other is an earl named Orfeo.[654] And they two have been at long strife for her love. She to be rid of the one, she careth not whither,° hath commanded that in her presence they should severally° keep this passage fifteen days space, promising that he which doth best shall be her knight. Florinaldes hath been the first and hath kept this bridge twelve days in Albamira's presence, where are many knights and gentlewomen. Now it being so near the court, there come daily many good knights to prove themselves, but he hath the mastery of them all and his praise is spread far abroad. This morning, myself riding towards Ratisbona for certain business I have there, would have passed the bridge, but I could not be suffered except I would have confessed Albamira to be the fairest lady in all Hungary.[655] This if I would not do, they bade me bring some knight that should win the passage for me.[656] When I heard this, I called to see the beauty of Albamira, that I might judge whether it were so or no. Then was I led into a rich tent, wherein Albamira sat accompanied with many gentlewomen, and I beheld her at the full. But truly, if my glass at home lie not, wherein I was wont to see mine° own beauty, hers is nothing equal to mine. So I told them that for ought I had seen I must be fain to return back and to find a knight which would break the passage. Now the gift which I demand of you, Sir Knight, is that

---

[652] Ratisbona: the modern Regensburg, Germany. It is located in Bavaria, where the Danube and Regen rivers meet.
[653] 'God save ... Knights' and 'for if you ... tell you' are added.
[654] Tyler omits the lady's lofty appraisal of Florinaldes: in *Espejo*, his great deeds of knighthood inspire her to esteem him the best knight in the world.
[655] In the source, she must also declare Albamira to be worthy of Florinaldes's love.
[656] This important addition — 'This if ... for me' — provides the motivation for the lady's actions.

hereupon you joust with Florinaldes. And in the maintenance of my beauty against hers, be you assured of the victory'.

When the gentlewoman had said thus, those that were present laughed a good.[657] And the Knight of the Sun, to shift her off, answered:

'Gentlewoman, if your business had been so great to the court as you would have us think, you would not have stayed for so small a matter'.

The gentlewoman, very angry, replied shortly:

'Call you it so small a matter? Mark what I say.[658] You are not so courteous as I took you for, if you so little esteem women's suits. You, being a knight, now know you that a woman esteemeth° her beauty above all, and that there is no injury so great for a woman as to say that another is fairer than she. I tell you that I had rather be called any other name of reproach than not a well-favoured woman. And being as I am, I account myself much fairer than Albamira, or rather would I all my great business undone than to confess that, which the knight of the bridge doth will me to. Now, since you have given me this grant, perform it or otherwise during my life I will complain me of you'.

The Knight of the Sun and those which were with him laughed to see the gentlewoman so hot for the light regarding of her beauty, and they said:

'Since we must pass the bridge, we will see the beauty of Albamira. And if it be less than yours, then will we do our best that you shall pass uncontrolled'.

'Of the one part, be you sure', quoth° the gentlewoman, 'that my beauty is more. And if I had the maintenance which Albamira hath, Florinaldes or the Earl Orfeo would rather quarrel for my beauty than for hers'.

At this and other like things they laughed till they came to the bridge, where they saw a big knight armed and a fair rich tent pitched, with certain knights and gentlewomen walking by the riverside, who so soon as they saw these knights come, gathered unto the tent. The Knight of the Sun and his company offered to ride over the bridge, but there came a gentlewoman out against him, saying:

'Sir Knight, this bridge is defended [against] you by Florinaldes. Over may you not pass unless you joust with him or confess that Albamira is the fairest gentlewoman in this kingdom, and that Florinaldes is the knight which best deserveth her, the which also must these gentlewomen say, which are in your company, or bring knights to answer for them'.

'We could be content', answered the Knight of the Sun, 'to agree to these conditions which you speak of, but the gentlewomen in our company make such account of their beauties, that they will rather return back than confess that which you would. Now that they are in our company, we must answer for them'.

'Determine what to do. And for your choice, it must be one of those two', said the gentlewoman.

And so she departed.

Florinaldes and Albamira heard all this and presently they caused the tent door to be set open, where these strangers saw Albamira amongst the gentlewomen, much excelling them all, which made them take up a fresh laughter at their merry gentlewom[a]n. Florinaldes issued forth of the tent, taking a spear in his hand. And coming towards the knights, he spoke, saying:

'You have known already, knights, that this bridge is kept by me. If you say not that which I demand of you, or otherwise presently joust with me'.

The knights answered:

'We will do what we like best'.[659]

---

[657] The Knight of Sun's reasoning and reaction to her speech are omitted.
[658] The addition — 'Call you . . . I say' — is important in terms of character development and it emphasizes the importance of female beauty in her society.
[659] Florinaldes's preparations for battle are omitted.

And therewith, they required the Knight of the Sun that they might joust first, which he granted them. And so the one, taking a spear in his hand, ran to encounter Florinaldes, but he was unhorsed. And so the second and the third, all of them as easily and with no more ado than I have had in telling you.

The Knight of the Sun, seeing these three knights thus cast down, spoke unto the gentlewoman which had brought them thither:°

'Gentlewoman, this knight is no babe, you see. Were it not better for us to say as he sayeth? Then might we go free. And the rather for that I have seen Albamira, which in my eyes is much fairer than you'.

'Blessed Mary', sayeth the gentlewoman, 'if Albamira be fairer than I, it is for her apparel only. But since you have promised this, you must perform it. And although I gain nothing herein, yet shall it do me good to see you fly from your saddle for the little skill you have in discerning beauties'.

Albamira heard this and the other gentlewomen, and knowing that this was the gentlewoman which had been there before, they laughed much at her, whereat she waxed angry. The Knight of the Sun then took a spear from the rattler° and called for Florinaldes. Then ran they together with such force that they made the bridge to shake. Florinaldes only burst his spear upon the Knight of the Sun, but the Knight of the Sun bore Florinaldes over, and over so strongly that he had a sore bruise and might not rise. His knights took him in their arms into his tent, where he was heavy, and it is uncertain whether more grieved with the sore of his bruise than with the shame of his fall, so to be foiled before his mistress. But if I may meddle in school points, I think he had rather burst an arm than so to have cracked his credit with both lady and friends, such as many resort thither° from Tiberio's court to see him joust.

And the Knight of the Sun, seeing Florinaldes so unhorsed before his Lady, was as sorry for him and presently departed. The gentlewomen and their knights in whose company he travailed° were glad for the hope given them of a farther trial. But above all, the gentlewoman which had required him to these jousts triumphed now, as if rather in her quarrel than by the knight's strength Florinaldes had been overthrown. And she bade them aloud to remember the comparison of Albamira's beauty and hers.

From this time she liked much better of herself, but age coming upon her, her beauty decayed, as there is nothing more uncertain, either impaired by sickness, or withered by age, or by sundry accidents in man's life corrupted and depraved. And what should I talk of the harm that thence issueth? It is at home a breeder of unrest, a robber of ease abroad, a continual care, a cause of many dangers, a sea of travails,° and an everlasting grief, whether coming or going. But what needeth this so long a digression? The rest let us leave to those that are idle, to discourse at leisure. Now more at large of our necessary matter.

The Knight of the Sun with his company rideth to Ratisbona, whither° th[e]y came ere° full sunset, and lodged for that night at a friend's house of Elisea. The story sayeth also that Florinaldes and his company dislodged their tent and came that night to Ratisbona also, all greatly amazed at the Knight of the Sun, to whom Florinaldes bore such an evil will that it had almost cost him his life, as the next book shall tell you hereafter.

CHAPTER 53

The Knight of the Sun answered before the King Tiberio for the Duchess Elisandra, and the battle was appointed between him and Aridon of the Black Wood

The next day being come, the Knight of the Sun armed himself. And being ready, only with Elisea went towards the palace. Whither° when he came, he found the king amongst his nobles, and with them the Duke of Pannonia and Aridon of the Black Wood, either of them not a little puffed up with vainglory that the time prefixed was now spent almost and no man daring to answer for the duchess. Now at the coming in of this knight with the device of the sun, there was suddenly a great silence, belike° by occasion of some in the company which had seen his valour proved upon Florinaldes. And the Knight of the Sun, glad of such convenient time of hearing, after he had humbly bowed to the king, spoke as followeth:

'Mighty king, I am a knight and a stranger neither of your court, country, nor religion.[660] But Fortune casting me upon this coast, it was my chance to meet with this gentlewoman, sister to the Duchess of Pannonia, whom you hold prisoner. This gentlewoman travailed° to seek a knight, which would answer the accusation that the duke, her husband, layeth against her. And lighting upon me, she hath opened to me the whole treachery and packing° of the Duke, her husband, with the perjured Aridon of the Black Wood. In the justifying of which words spoken by the gentlewoman and the improving of Aridon's false and shameless slander, I am hither come to prove that he belieth the duchess upon his body'.[661]

The king, now, and all which were present beheld the Knight of the Sun very earnestly and were abashed to see him being so young to speak so courageously.[662] Aridon, very angry, rose up, and to the Knight of the Sun spoke on this wise:°

'Sir Knight, it appears that thou are both young and a stranger in this country, for if thou were of years or knew Aridon, which now talketh with thee, thou would not be so hardy as to defy him in presence. And were it not for the king, my lord, I would in some wise° tell thee of thy rudeness. But there needeth no such haste. I hope I shall have time enough, since thou cannot detract the battle whereto thyself hath first made offer. But let us go to it presently, and end it in this place'.

Aridon's high disdain sore displeased the Knight of the Sun, as appeared by his look. But he refrained for honour to the king.[663] And for the rest, he desired the king to authorize the lists.° The king answered him gently that [that] day it might not be, both for that it was needful the Duchess of Pannonia should appear openly to put her quarrel into his hands, and for that also judges must be ordained of the field and the lists° erected, which could not be provided in so short warning. The Knight of the Sun yielded to the king's pleasure. And after that had witnessed his forwardness to defend the duchess, he took his leave of the king, and to his host he goeth.

The king, as soon as he was gone, by occasion of this young knight calling to mind his son Liriamandro, whom he had not heard of in long time, wept bitterly and said aloud that diverse heard it:

'If my son Liriamandro be like to this lusty° knight and have a care to be notable, no doubt he will excel all his ancestors'.

Whereat those which were thereby° declared to the king what themselves had seen of this knight and how strongly he had overthrown Florinaldes, which report did in a manner discomfit Aridon, that he would have wished his stake out at that dealing with all his heart. But indeed, a very desperate° contempt, both of God and the world, brought him to his end.

---

[660] In the source, the Knight of the Sun admits that he is from another land and ignorant of the laws of Pannonia.
[661] In *Espejo*, he further discusses how he is motivated by a quest for justice and decries the dishonourableness of the friendship between Aridon and the duke. He concludes his speech with a clear articulation of the duchess's innocence and his willingness to prove it in battle with Aridon.
[662] The source explains that some of the assembled are pleased to hear his words.
[663] Tyler omits a section in which his great desire to respond to the king is vocalized. As a result of this excision, the Knight of the Sun's reasoning is difficult to understand.

CHAPTER 54

The battle between the Knight of the Sun and the strong Aridon

The next day, the king rose earlier than he was wont to do because of the battle which was to be made between Aridon and the knight stranger.⁶⁶⁴ And Aridon likewise made more haste, nor the Knight of the Sun failed for his part.⁶⁶⁵

When all were in the field, the king caused the duchess to be brought, which came thither° in a mourning weed,° and with so sorrowful a countenance that no heart so stony but would have pitied her, for she had been very fair, always accounted as wise and honest. The king demanded of her whether she would refer the trial of her cause to the success of her knight, whether good or bad. Whereto she answered 'yea', and that she had no other help but in God and the innocency° of her cause.⁶⁶⁶ So was she led to a scaffold provided for her and other gentlewomen. The judges next were called for, which were named by the king: the Duke of Austrich and the Duke of Saxony, two ancient knights and then resiant° in the court.⁶⁶⁷

The judges thus placed, Aridon and the Knight of the Sun took their spears in their hands, forcing themselves against each other. Now sounded a trumpet, and a herald cried:

'Go to, knights! And God defend the right!'⁶⁶⁸

With this, they ran together with all the force they could. Their encountry° was such that Aridon burst his spear and diseased° not his enemy. But the Knight of the Sun both burst his spear and unhorsed Aridon, and with the fall he gave him almost burst his back, while he pained himself to keep the saddle. Aridon, thus bruised, lifted up his eyes to heaven, and in despair of conscience murmured to himself some like thing:

'Thou, oh God, as I believe have sent this young man from heaven to revenge my misreport. Otherwise, who is [t]his he in this world which might have sat so quiet in his saddle after so violent a push as I have given him? Or, who might have annoyed Aridon so?'

And with a desperate rage, he drew out his sword to have sheathed it in the knight's horse belly. But the knight descended and, with his sword before him, went toward Aridon that between them the battle beginneth. The king and the princes there present were very glad to see so good a beginning of the duchess's deliverance. And Aridon failed not to do his best, that the Knight of the Sun could not but take him for a strong knight. The battle endured a great while, no man being able to judge who had the better, till that the Knight of the Sun's courage grew as his honour increased, for he was not angered at the first. The end of this battle, for it was not long neither very equal, was in this manner. Aridon hit the Knight of the Sun on the headpiece that he bowed his knees to the ground. Then the Knight of the Sun gave him another, that he staggered with it. The second time, Aridon hit the Knight of the Sun a blow upon the headpiece, whereat the last time, the Knight of the Sun, stretching himself and following his blow with all his might, hit Aridon so sure that Aridon fell upon the ground, moving neither hand nor foot. The Knight of the Sun, thinking it to be but an amaze,° stood still while Aridon might recover again.

The whilst, all the beholders much praised the Knight of the Sun for the best knight living, as

---

⁶⁶⁴ Tyler omits the Catholic ritual of hearing mass. The religious bent of the text is analysed in the introduction.
⁶⁶⁵ The gathering of the crowd to watch the battle creates an anticipatory atmosphere in *Espejo*.
⁶⁶⁶ Her sorrowful, tearful state is described in *Espejo*.
⁶⁶⁷ Tyler excises the reference to their progeny — the beautiful Policena and the strong Ruberto — and the advertisement that their stories will be recounted later in the romance. They appear in Ortúñez's third book.
   Austrich: Austria
   Saxony: an area of Germany
⁶⁶⁸ Tyler adds the herald's cry.

well commending his courage as his activity. The Duchess Elisandra likewise, now having some hope by her knight, got her colour again, and her joy was as much as her husband's sorrow.

But you have not yet heard the worst of the wicked Duke, for Aridon revived, whom when the Knight of the Sun saw raising himself up, he came hastily. And holding the point of his sword against Aridon's throat, he spoke, saying:

'Thou shall die, false Aridon, unless thou confess the treason that thou have devised against the duchess. And if thou do die in this obstinate mind of concealing so great outrage, thou hazard thy soul's health'.

Aridon, as it were half awake and yet not so loath to die as struck with a terror of his own conscience,[669] answered:

'Thy words have abashed me more than the death which thou threat; the fault which I have committed hath bred a greater horror in my flesh. But make the judges come near, and I will declare the whole'.

The Knight of the Sun called the judges. They, coming near, heard these words of his own mouth: the substance of the duke's shifting to wring his wife's inheritance to himself, in such manner as you have heard in Elisea's report. The judges straightaways declared it to the king, who detesting their fact, caused the duke to be apprehended and both to be executed in that place. For albeit many of his nobles entreated for their pardon, yet the king so abhorred the villainy that nought availed. And at this time was the law first enacted in Hungary that the law of punishment for whoredom should stretch as well to the man as to the woman, and that equal penalty should be assigned to like offenders, whereas before the men escaped [and] the women only were in danger.[670]

Now after this execution, the Duchess Elisandra was set at large and the Queen Augusta received her with great honour into her company. The Knight of the Sun was very desirous to leave the city, but the king desired much to know him and to have him abide for some time in his court.[671] In the time of his abode, the Knight of the Sun grew in more familiar acquaintance with the king, and was much liked of him because he seemed to resemble the Princess Briana. But one day, the king importuning the young knight to know his kindred, used such like words:

'Sir Knight, we thank you heartily for the pains that you have taken in the Duchess of Pannonia's behalf and for the maintaining of her honour. Whereby, if she has received some commodity of living and avoiding shame, so have I received some quietness in my realm by the open detecting of such malefactors. And their punishment will be occasion of fear in others. For this cause I have willed you to stay here, as thereto I pray you heartily. But I pray you, let me know your name and where you were born, for I know not how to call you'.

The Knight of the Sun, well nurtured in the sultan's court, after his humble thanks for his majesty's most gracious proffer, and the promise of acceptance being a thing indeed very convenient for the certifying of the emperor, began as followeth:[672]

'For your majesty's favour, I shall most willingly do your highness service. And for the duchess, I am glad that the equity of her cause furthered my attempt. And for my name or country, I can better tell you the story of my life since I came to years than declare that.[673] Yet, am I called the Knight of the Sun by my device. And my education hath been in the sultan's court at Babylon, thither° I being brought by the king's son-in-law, the King of Persia, when I

---

[669] His semi-wakeful state, his fear, and the urging of his conscience are added factors that explain his behaviour in *Mirror*.

[670] The source relates the law's celebration throughout the kingdom and its persistence until the present day.

[671] The process of disarming and his welcome at court are fully recounted in *Espejo*.

[672] The statement, 'well-nurtured . . . the emperor', replaces a Spanish passage which declares that his motivation stems from the fear of being thought ungrateful if he were to refuse the king's favour as well as his desire to remain at court long enough to discover the king's reaction to the marriage of Briana and Trebatio.

[673] Tyler adds the sentence, 'And for . . . declare that'.

was but a child and, as it hath been told me, found in a little boat up[on] the sea. For my life hitherto, it hath been in arms, and that do I mean to pursue'.[674]

The king and those which were with him were greatly amazed that he had come from so far a country and had been found upon the sea, and that he knew no more of his estate. But they thought that yet he was of some noble birth. The king thanked him, and in this order the Knight of the Sun stayed with the King Tiberio for certain days, where he gained many friends and one only enemy, by name Florinaldes, which could not forget the shame received before his mistress, although it had done him no scathe:° for in the end, Albamira preferred him before the Earl Orfeo.

So as I say, yet Florinaldes seeing the honour of the Knight of the Sun daily to increase to the discredit of the born Hungarian, his stomach rose against him. And one day he set upon the Knight of the Sun at unawares, but to his own loss, had not the Knight of the Sun been more merciful. After they were made friends.[675] But let us break off this story to dispatch the Prince of Lusitania out of England.

CHAPTER 55

Don Silverio demanded the Princess Olivia for wife of the King Oliverio

The great sorrow which the loss of Rosicleer caused in the court of King Oliverio hath been ere° this declared to you, for all the good knights his friends went to seek him, leaving the court bare and naked for noble men. And above all, the Princess Olivia was worse wrung, albeit her grief was not so manifest.[676] Now yet, there stayed in the court the Prince Don Silverio, strangely surprised with the love of Olivia and using the help of his sister Rodasilva to the persuading of Olivia. One day, the last I take it, he unfolded his grief unto her, telling her that unless she found the means, he should here leave his life in a far country:

'The matter is mine° old suit that you wot° off. My desire is that at least I may be assured of her good will. Sure I am if I move the king in it, that I shall obtain it'.

The Princess Rodasilva, moved indeed with her brother's affliction, promised the uttermost of her pains. And within a while after, she had some talk with the princess about that matter, her words tending to like effect:

'Madam, you know right well the great love, which since I came to this court, I have borne unto you, and how I have done you service in all that I was able. That which more is, in what manner I have absented myself from my parents only to be in your company, which if you know and confess to be true, you must likewise believe that that which I shall say now rather proceedeth of good zeal towards your honour than of any purpose to work mine° own contentment. Though, I cannot deny but that if I obtain, it will content me highly.[677] But I do not desire the thing which standeth not with your honour. And for my pains, reward seek I none, but that I may be heard. If I err in ought wherein I shall counsel you, then may you blame me. And yet I doubt not but when you shall have thoroughly examined the whole, you shall rather impute the fault to lack of skill than to any lack of good meaning. And as I am certain that you have this same opinion of me without any further suspect, so will I tell you my mind flatly. You know that you are the only inheritrix° of this kingdom, that your father, the king,

---

[674] 'For my ... to pursue' is added.
[675] The movement from jealousy to friendship and the conflict between Florinaldes and the Knight of the Sun — 'So as I ... made friends' — is an English addition.
[676] *Espejo* specifies that her grief is due to her recognition that her behaviour has caused the situation.
[677] Whereas here Rodasilva claims that her own happiness will ensue if Olivia follows her advice, in the source Rodasilva only seeks and desires Olivia's honour.

my lord, must needs marry you with such a one as may equal your estate, both for the natural care which he hath over you in respect that you are his daughter, and for the profit which shall thereby redound° to his subjects, which cannot be well governed, the seat wanting a rightful heir. You are, withal, at this time, marriageable. My suit, therefore, is that herein you will have a more regard of the Prince Don Silverio, my brother, a worthy knight of personage and valour, of a high birth, a king's son and heir, besides loving you so entirely as he can nothing more. Long hath he endured this torment and never would bewray° it to any but to me. And I have hitherto suppressed it not to molest you now for compassion towards him, whom I must love and honour: mine° own brother. I require this, that at least you show him some good countenance, whereby he may be encouraged to demand you of the king your father, which suit shall not be impossible if only your liking may be won'.

The princess, angry at the heart with this speech, for it was the thing most contrary to her wish, replied shortly:

'Madame Rodasilva, if I had thought that the zeal and love which you have professed (and I do confess) had tended to this issue, I should less have liked your company. And I cannot think well of it, that either you should break with me of such matters or should have communication thereabouts with your brother, who, as you say, lacketh boldness to discover his affection, which cannot be. Doth he love so earnestly, when he vouchsafeth° not to speak unto me but by a messenger? I suspect your words. Perhaps if I had heard the man speak, I might have judged in his countenance whether he had lied, yea or no. But for truth, you know I am of young years at this instant, neither have I will to marriage. I pray you, therefore, name it no more unto me. And yet when I am of years, I may not choose my husband; and I am at the king's commandment, which I must obey'.

The Princess Rodasilva, so sharply rebuked by the Princess Olivia and thereby gathering the little good will she bare unto her brother, demanded pardon of her speech and returned to her lodging, whither° she sent for the Prince Don Silverio. And to him she told the whole talk with the princess's answer, willing him notwithstanding not to give over but to make a better show as if her answer misliked° him not, and covertly to labour the king for his consent:

'This can he not deny you. And after you may win the princess, for as yet her excuse is but of years'.

The prince, liking her counsel, departed from the princess, his sister. And the next day, finding the king at leisure, he required his majesty of a secret matter. The king commanded those in presence to avoid and took him to a window, where the prince, after his duty done, began on this sort:

'With your grace's favour, I trust I have this long time been a well-willer to your daughter, the Princess Olivia, and to have her to wife, whereto if it might please your highness to condescend, I know my parents would well agree thereto for the great love which they bear to your majesty and to me their son. And thereby should I take myself to be the best rewarded for my long tarrying that ever prince was. I humbly beseech your highness to let me know your mind herein'.

This demand of the prince was nothing strange to the King Oliverio, for he suspected this matter long before. And therefore, his answer was short: that he was content to accept him for son-in-law, as well for his own worthiness as for his birth and for the friendship betwixt° their people.

'Yet', sayeth he, 'you shall give me leave to think thereon and you shall have a more resolute answer'.

The prince hop[ed] that his desire would take effect.

Now the king, to know the princess's mind therein, went himself to the princess's lodging, where finding her alone, he counselled her in this sort:[678]

---

[678] The king's deliberation on the matter is presented in *Espejo*.

'It hath pleased God that the Prince Edward thy brother should be lost in the realm of Hungary. I, having none other child but thee, think it convenient both for mine° own liking and the common profit of my subjects to have thee married with some prince of like estate.[679] This have I thought on a long time, and now upon mature deliberation had with some special of my council, I have found one: a prince which both for his power may, and for his courage will, and for his nobility is worthy to bear sway in so great an estate as this is. Him am I content to take for son-in-law, and to commend my title unto you. This prince is Don Silverio, Prince of Lusitania, whom you know right well: a comely knight of personage; valiant in arms; of a courageous spirit; above all virtuous; and in his dealings circumspect, courteous of speech, and of high estate, as I know few like. There are besides to commend this match, the intercourse of traffic between our subjects and the friendship between his parents and me.[680] Herein, therefore, say your own fancy,° for so far as reason will, I am content to hear you'.[681]

Thus said the king. But the princess, whom these words more galled than sword or spear, not knowing how to shift off the king, her father, and not to answer his demand, stood in amaze° for fear.[682] The king, seeing her so silent, asked the cause why. She answered nothing yet a while. In the end, forced to say somewhat, she rather excused her silence than re-resolved° the doubt.

'My lord and father', sayeth she, 'I have not answered you hitherto because I know not how to do, neither may you now look for a full answer. The matter is so strange unto me, as that I never thought of it before. And your highness knoweth that I am of young years, and as yet I have no desire to marry. The time groweth on when I shall be of more age, and then perhaps shall I have more desire, which whensoever° it falls out shall be of your choice more than of mine° own'.

The king, thinking that she had spoke as she meant, and that her young age had been her only stay,° took in good part this excuse, willing her notwithstanding to remember what he had said.[683] So, the king departed and the princess remained somewhat better apaid° by the king's liking of her answer. But her hope was that Rosicleer would come and that he being present, the king's mind might be altered as touching Don Silverio. And for this cause she made many a secret vow for his speedy return, but above all she looked for Fidelia.[684]

The king, at his return, caused Don Silverio to be called, to whom he declared his talk with his daughter and her answer, adding moreover that hereafter he thought the matter possible enough for her good liking beside his, whereof he might be assured. Don Silverio was the gladdest man alive, and thanking the king for so high favour, for that time he departed from the king. But the princess grew to be more melancholic than before, for she espied what courage he had taken by the comfort which the king had given him. After, Don Silverio, thinking the matter sure enough, departed the realm with his sister, Rodasilva, where let us leave him and turn to the Emperor Trebatio.

---

[679] In the Spanish text, the king explains that she needs to marry so that her husband can inherit and defend the kingdom. As England was being ruled by an unmarried queen at the time, this statement is in direct contrast with English policy, and so understandably, it is omitted. The alterations involved in the discussion of female consent to marriage in the king's speech are discussed in the introduction.
[680] In the Spanish romance, he also claims indebtedness to Silverio and Rodasilva because of their long period of residence in his court.
[681] The primary importance of her happiness in the match is omitted.
[682] An extended description of her feelings is excised.
[683] He urges her to further consider the proposal in *Espejo*.
[684] *Espejo* clarifies that she awaits the return of an amorous letter from Rosicleer.

CHAPTER 56

The Emperor Trebatio carried away the Princess Briana from the Monastery of the River

In great pleasure and contentation° did the Emperor Trebatio remain with the Princess Briana at the Monastery of the River, where by their continuance together, their loves increased so towards each other that either of them delighted in the other, and either of them thought themselves happy when they were in the other's company.[685] This love between them was in other manner than that which ariseth by a blast of beauty, and it endured so long between them that neither years, nor sickness, nor death scarcely could once impair it. And for this love's sake could the Emperor Trebatio willingly have forborne both kith and kindred° and acquaintance in his own country. And for his love durst° the princess adventure to fly° her father's realm, and to abandon herself to unknown passages, and to travel with Trebatio into Greece.

As the Emperor Trebatio, finding opportunity, told her that he had counselled with the Knight of the Sun as touching their departure, by whom he understood that both for themselves and for the King Tiberio it was meetest° to depart, otherwise, sayeth he:

'May the king, your father, be blamed for the death of the Prince Edward, and our joy might find end if I were discovered'.

But for the dispatch of this whole matter, he said that he would leave a letter in her chamber wherein should be showed both how and in what manner all things had been done, which you have heard of.[686] The princess yielded thereto gladly, and between themselves they provided things necessary for their departure, none being privy° thereto but Clandestria and the other gentlewomen.[687] The day before the princess should depart, she told her gentlewomen that she had vowed nine days fast in her lodging, charging that for that time none should trouble her, save that she would have Clandestria as she was wont, and this gentlewoman for necessary occasion.[688] The princess was thus wont to do very often, which made it probable.

The next day, when all were ready and had voided° the princess's lodging, the emperor threw in his letter and Clandestria shut the door. So by the secret postern° they all departed. This was a good while before day.[689] And they took such horse as had been provided by the princess. By the opening of the morning they had ridden a pretty way, and the princess, being weary, turned out of the way to rest herself in a shade, as everything made her afraid and weary,[690] till that Clandestria hastened her on by saying that she thought their business would be suspected in that she fetched not the broths as she was wont. So up to horse they go.[691]

And here breaketh off the first book. What happened by the way, the second book declareth. Now let us remember by the way where we left our worthy princes, that when we have need of them we may there find them. The emperor is in his way to Greece. The Knight of the Sun abideth in Tiberio's court. Don Silverio is upon the sea towards Lusitania. Rosicleer now

---

[685] The extent of their love is fully explored in the source.
[686] He asks the king's pardon in *Espejo*.
[687] The narrator declares that Clandestria and the other gentlewomen were privy to the plan and then contradicts herself in the next sentence, informing us that Clanderstria is Briana's sole confidante. The confusion derives from an inconsistency in translation. In *Espejo*, the emperor is accompanied by another gentlewoman, who knows the details of the adventure. Tyler omits this character, but a trace of her remains in the phrase 'and the other gentlewomen'.
[688] The nine-day fast, or the novena, is a Roman Catholic form of devotion. The religious allusion is lessened by omitting the Catholic terminology ('novena') used in *Espejo*.
[689] The description of Trebatio writing the letter is omitted.
[690] The addition, 'as everything made her afraid and weary', heightens Briana's vulnerability, contrasting her with her servant and the male heroes.
[691] Clandestria's encouragement replaces a passage in which they dismount, eat, rest, re-mount their horses, and cover their faces so as to avoid recognition.

departeth from Thessaly, after the establishing of the kingdom to the Queen Arguirosa. Brandizel and Clavergudo stay in the King of Polonia's court, where the Prince Brandizel maketh love° to the Princess Clarinea. Zoilo, Prince of Tartary, Bargandel, Prince of Bohemia, and Liriamandro, Prince of Hungary, all three together sojourn at the emperor's court at Trabisond, with the Princess Claridiana, a woman knight, of whom this whole story specially entreateth, but more at large hereafter. And thus endeth the first book.[692]

 Finis.[693]

---

[692] This first part of *Espejo* ends by declaring that 'thus they travelled eight days, in which nothing worth recounting happened, nor was the princess missed at the monestary because everyone thought that she would be locked in her room, performing the novena, as she had said. And so the emperor managed to exit Hungary with the princess without any impediment, and following their route we leave them, and what happens to them will be recounted in the next book'. Tyler alters the conclusion, providing a summary of the different plot strands. By reminding her readers of all that is left unresolved — not just the story of Trebatio and Briana — she heightens the suspense and piques the readers' interest to discover the ensuing action in the romance's sequels.

[693] 'Finis' is Latin for 'the end'.

TEXTUAL NOTES

Title page. 1 The] The *1578*; The First Part of the *1580? 1599?*
Title page. 3 and excellent] and excellent *1578*; *omitted 1580? 1599?*
Dedication. 10 insufficiency] insufficiency *1578*; sufficiencie *1580?*; insufficiencie *1599?*
Dedication. 15 their] their *1578*; *omitted 1580? 1599?*
Dedication. 16 reserving] reseruing *1578*; referring *1580?*; referuing *1599?*
Dedication. 16 to] to *1578*; for *1580? 1599?*
To reader. 3 story] storie *1578*; historie *1580? 1599?*
To reader. 9 all] all *1578, 1580?*; *omitted 1599?*
To reader. 9 warlike] warlike *1578*; worldly *1580?*; worldlye *1599?*
To reader.14 findeth] findeth *1578, 1580?*; finde *1599?*
To reader. 18 wages] wage *1578*; wages *1580? 1599?*
To reader. 55 the] *the 1578*; *omitted 1580? 1599?*
To reader. 73 so] so *1578, 1580?*; to *1599?*
To reader. 87 thy] thy *1578, 1580?*; the *1599?*
To reader. 88 as] as *1578*; *omitted 1580? 1599?*
1.1 The] The *1578*; The first part of the *1580? 1599?*
2.30] the *1578*; *omitted 1580? 1599?*
2.52 unto] vnto *1578*; into *1580? 1599?*
2.56 which] which *1578*; that *1580? 1599?*
3.27 to] to *1578*; *omitted 1580? 1599?*
3.28 you] you *1578*; *omitted 1580? 1599?*
3.39 time] times *1578*; time *1580? 1599?*
4.6 this] these *1578*; this *1580? 1599?*
4.9 his] his *1578*; this *1580? 1599?*
4.10 easily] easely *1578*; easie *1580? 1599?*
4.17] *omitted 1578*; was *1580? 1599?*
4.23 these] these *1578*; those *1580? 1599?*
4.35 the] *the 1578*; my *1580? 1599?*
4.39 and] & *1578*; with *1580? 1599?*
4.39 the] the *1578*; *omitted 1580? 1599?*
4.45 should] should *1578*; would *1580? 1599?*
5.31 of] for *1578, 1580?*; of *1599?*
5.39 in] on *1578*; in *1580? 1599?*
5.48 cunning] running *1578*; cunning *1580? 1599?*
5.51 others] others *1578*; other *1580? 1599?*
5.52 then] then *1578*; now *1580? 1599?*
5.60 you] you *1578*; *omitted 1580? 1599?*
5.102 arm] arme *1578, 1580?*; arms*1599?*
5.119 when] when *1578*; which *1580? 1599?*
5.146 to] with *1578*; to *1580? 1599?*
5.151 mean] meane *1578*; means *1580? 1599?*
6.39 unto] vnto *1578*; *omitted* 1580 *1599?*
6.53 prince's] princesse *1578*; Princes *1580? 1599?*
8.27 to] in *1578*; to *1580? 1599?*
8.76 This] This *1578*; Thus *1580? 1599?*
8.92 Saying] Saying *1578*; Sailing *1580? 1599?*

8.103 forwarder] forewarder *1578*; forward *1580? 1599?*
9.4] a *1578, 1580?*; omitted *1599?*
9.22 goodly] goodly *1578*; good *1580? 1599?*
9.48 little] little *1578*; omitted *1580? 1599?*
9.69 closing] closed *1578*; closing *1580? 1599?*
9.70 to] to *1578*; *1580? 1599?* into
9.84 and] omitted *1578*; & *1580? 1599?*
9.86 he] he *1578 1580?*; shee *1599?*
9.131 unto] vnto *1578*; into *1580? 1599?*
9.140 enchased] enchaffed *1578*; enchafed *1580?*; enchased *1599?*
9.142 wherein] where *1578*; wherein *1580? 1599?*
10.12 had] had *1578*; omitted *1580? 1599?*
12.21 of] for *1578*; of *1580? 1599?*
12.65 one] one *1578*; a *1580? 1599?*
13.25 meinie] mainye *1578*; mainie *1580?*; Nauie *1599?*
14.17 these] these *1578*; those *1580? 1599?*
14.18 And] that *1578*; And *1580? 1599?*
14.19 thereby] thereby *1578*; whereby *1580? 1599?*
14.20 gentlewomen] gentlewomen *1578, 1580?*; gentlewoman *1599?*
14.31 gentlewomen] gentlewomen *1578, 1580?*; gentlewoman *1599?*
14.46 they] they *1578*; it *1580? 1599?*
14.78 looks] lockes *1578*; lookes *1580? 1599?*
14.97 but] put *1578, 1580?*; but *1599?*
15.15 so] so *1578*; omitted *1580? 1599?*
15.56 not] no *1578*; not *1580? 1599?*
15.71 he] he *1578, 1599?*; she *1580?*
15.73 promission] promisison *1578*; permission *1580? 1599?*
15.108 care] rare *1578*; care *1580? 1599?*
15.147 those] these *1578*; those *1580? 1599?*
16.14 twenty] xx *1578*; 40 *1580? 1599?*
16.22 celebrated] celebrate *1578*; celebrated *1580? 1599?*
16.49 knew] wotte *1578*; knew *1580? 1599?*
16.51 of] in *1578*; of *1580? 1599?*
16.88 his] his *1578*; the *1580? 1599?*
16.101 hoisted] hoysed *1578*; hoised *1580?*; hosed *1599?*
17.7 they had ever] they had euer *1578*; euer they had *1580? 1599?*
17.32 so] so *1578*; as *1580? 1599?*
17.32 as] as *1578*; so *1580? 1599?*
17.45 the] the *1578*; omitted *1580? 1599?*
17.68 which] which *1578*; that *1580? 1599?*
17.93 would] would *1578*; omitted *1580? 1599?*
17.93 But] but *1578, 1580?*; omitted *1599?*
17.107 time] time *1578*; omitted *1580? 1599?*
17.113 and] omitted *1578*; and *1580? 1599?*
17.114 recomforted] recomfort *1578*; recomforted *1580? 1599?*
17.127 here] here *1578*; there *1580? 1599?*
18.72 these] this *1578, 1580? 1599?*
19.36 and] and *1578*; with *1580? 1599?*
19.61 his] the *1578*; his *1580? 1599?*
19.120 giant's] Gyant *1578*; Gyants *1580? 1599?*
19.122 prisoners] prisones *1578*; prisoners *1580? 1599?*

TEXTUAL NOTES

19.129] so *1578, 1580? 1599?*
19.133 this] this *1578*; the *1580? 1599?*
19.142 mischief] himselfe *1578, 1580?*; mischiefe *1599?*
19.178 benefits] benefites *1578, 1599?*; benefiter *1580?*
19.187 to] to *1578*; the *1580? 1599?*
20.38 the] the *1578, 1580?*; *omitted 1599?*
20.60 these] these *1578, 1580?*; the *1599?*
20.83 into] *omitted 1578*; into *1580? 1599?*
20.84 thou not] thou not *1578*; not thou *1580? 1599?*
20.89 there] ther *1578*; *omitted 1580? 1599?*
20.107 bear] beare *1578*; heare *1580? 1599?*
20.131 night] knight *1578*; night *1580? 1599?*
20.139 more] *1578, 1580?*; most *1599?*
20.140 sire] sier *1578, 1580?*; sir *1599?*
20.143 as] as *1578*; so *1580? 1599?*
20.166 battle] battell *1578*; matter *1580? 1599?*
20.172 to] in *1578*; to *1580? 1599?*
20.176 of] in *1578*; of *1580? 1599?*
20.182 you] you *1578*; *omitted 1580? 1599?*
20.183 as] as *1578*; and *1580? 1599?*
20.197 stones] stone *1578*; stones *1580? 1599?*
20.202 this] *1599?* his
20.203 his] hys *1578*; the *1580? 1599?*
20.203 for] for *1578, 1580?*; of *1599?*
21.1 is] is *1578, 1580?*; *omitted 1599?*
21.14 with] with *1578*; of *1580? 1599?*
21.31 at] at *1578*; of *1580? 1599?*
21.32 proud] proude *1578*; lowde *1580? 1599?*
21.33 give now] giue now *1578*; now giue me *1580? 1599?*
21.48 had he] had he *1578*; he had *1580? 1599?*
21.61 would] would *1578*; could *1580? 1599?*
21.64 now] now *1578*; not *1580? 1599?*
21.72 her] his *1578*; hir *1580? 1599?*
21.91 in] in *1578*; to *1580? 1599?*
21.96 the] the *1578*; this *1580? 1599?*
21.98 cuirass] curasse *1578*; carcasse *1580? 1599?*
21.110 of] of *1578*; in *1580? 1599?*
21.114 helm] helme *1578 1580?*; helmet *1599?*
21.115 scarce] scare *1578*; scarce *1580? 1599?*
21.117 hath] hath *1578 1580?*; had *1599?*
21.151 gory] gore *1578 1580? 1599?*
21.164] *omitted 1578*; had *1580? 1599?*
22.14 to] *omitted 1578*; to *1580? 1599?*
22.35 be] the *1578*; be *1580? 1599?*
22.45 thy] thy *1578 1580?*; the *1599?*
22.53 of] of *1578 1580?*; in *1599?*
22.90] *omitted 1578*; the wise *1580? 1599?*
22.95] *omitted 1578*; that *1580? 1599?*
23.51 was] was *1578*; were *1580? 1599?*
23.54 his] his *1578*; this *1580? 1599?*
23.59 one] to *1578, 1580?*; one *1599?*

23.61 uprisen] uprisen *1578, 1580?*; uprising *1599?*
23.101 set] set *1578*; sat *1580? 1599?*
23.160 confidence] confidency *1578, 1580?*; confidence *1599?*
23.179 This] This *1578*; The *1580? 1599?*
24.11 were] were *1578*; are *1580? 1599?*
24.19 to] with *1578*; to *1580? 1599?*
24.44 looking] looked *1578*; looking *1580? 1599?*
24.59 the] the *1578*; *omitted 1580? 1599?*
24.68 of] of *1578*; in all *1580? 1599?*
24.87 clean] cleane *1578*; *omitted 1580? 1599?*
24.120 man's] mans *1578*; man *1580? 1599?*
24.133 not] not *1578*; that *1580? 1599?*
24.137 it was] was it *1578*; it was *1580? 1599?*
24.156 greater] more *1578*; greater *1580? 1599?*
24.172 avail] auailed *1578*; auaile *1580? 1599?*
24.172 beaten] bet *1578*; beaten *1580? 1599?*
24.198 have] haue *1578, 1599?*; gaue
24.204 to] to *1578*; vnto *1580? 1599?*
25.18 of] on *1578, 1580?*; of *1599?*
25.27 that] That *1578*; The *1580? 1599?*
25.29 50,000] fifite thousands *1578*; fifteene thousand *1580? 1599?*
25.59 embracing] embracing *1578, 1580?*; embraced *1599?*
25.85 thanking] thanking *1578, 1580?*; thanked *1599?*
26.60 abided] abid *1578*; bid *1580? 1599?*
26.113 so] so *1578, 1580?*; *omitted 1599?*
26.138 were] were *1578*; was *1580? 1599?*
27.11 had] *omitted 1578*; had *1580? 1599?*
27.22 were] were *1578, 1580?*; was *1599?*
27.31 this] this *1578*; his *1580? 1599?*
27.49 and] *omitted 1578*; and *1580? 1599?*
27.60 this] this *1578*; this it *1580?*; that it *1599?*
28.27 bush] buske *1578*; huske *1580? 1599?*
28.41 that] that *1578*; as *1580? 1599?*
28.46 his] his *1578, 1580?*; the *1599?*
28.49 situated] situate *1578, 1580?*; situated *1599?*
28.55 this] this *1578*; the *1580? 1599?*
28.55 came] came *1578, 1599?*; come *1580?*
28.61 their] their *1578*; the *1580? 1599?*
28.64 rescue] rescewes *1578*; rescewe *1580? 1599?*
28.65 his] his *1578*; the *1580? 1599?*
28.74 their] their *1578*; his *1580? 1599?*
28.79 had] haue *1578*; had *1580? 1599?*
28.106 praising] praying *1578*; praising *1580? 1599?*
29.9 gates] gates *1578, 1580?*; gate *1599?*
29.14 swooned] swounded *1578*; sounded *1580? 1599?*
29.38 wistly] wistly *1578, 1580?*; wishly *1599?*
29.39] *omitted 1578*; for *1580? 1599?*
29.68 ever he had] he had euer *1578*; euer he had *1580? 1599?*
29.72 low] lowe *1578*; lowde *1580? 1599?*
29.83 himself] hir selfe *1578*; him-selfe *1580? 1599?*
29.141 with] vnto *1578*; with *1580? 1599?*

29.141] *omitted 1578*; most *1580? 1599?*
30.12 his] his *1578, 1580?*; this *1599?*
30.15 him] him *1578*; *omitted 1580? 1599?*
30.21 him] *omitted 1578*; him *1580? 1599?*
30.40] in *1578*; *omitted 1580? 1599?*
30.49 other] other *1578*; *omitted 1580? 1599?*
30.52 he] he *1578*; *omitted 1580? 1599?*
30.56] *omitted 1578*; verie *1580? 1599?*
30.64 his] this *1578, 1580?*; his *1599?*
30.87 for] for *1578*; and *1580? 1599?*
30.97 as] *omitted 1578*; as *1580? 1599?*
30.97 the] his *1578, 1580?*; the *1599?*
30.134 so] *omitted 1578*; so *1580? 1599?*
30.164] *omitted 1578*; a *1580? 1599?*
30.170 friends] friende *1578*; friends *1580? 1599?*
30.173 their] their *1578*; his *1580? 1599?*
30.196 the] the *1578, 1580?*; *omitted 1599?*
31.39 solid earth] selide earthe *1578*; selide earth *1580?*; fierme ground *1599?*
31.66 far the] *the* far *1578*; far *the 1580? 1599?*
31.80 from] for *1578, 1580? 1599?*
31.98 so] so *1578*; *omitted 1580? 1599?*
32.22 strokes] stroke *1578, 1580?*; strokes *1599?*
32.34 Namibia] Numidio *1578*; Numidia *1580? 1599?*
32.53 to] unto *1578*; to *1580? 1599?*
32.135 heats] heates *1578*; heartes *1580? 1599?*
32.162 that] that *1578*; as *1580? 1599?*
32.187 may] may *1578*; shall *1580? 1599?*
32.213 aloud] aloude *1578*; aloud *1580?*; *omitted 1599?*
32.235 felt] felte *1578*; felt *1580?*; left *1599?*
32.271 greater] greater *1578, 1580?*; great *1599?*
32.314 But] that *1578, 1580?*; but *1599?*
32.320 they] they *1578*; he *1580? 1599?*
33.37 hath] hath *1578*; *omitted 1580? 1599?*
33.40] *omitted 1578, 1580?*; it *1599?*
34.64 the] his *1578, 1580?*; the *1599?*
34.80 wanhope] wanhoope *1578*; wann hope *1580?*; when hope *1599?*
34.89 man] men *1578*; man *1580? 1599?*
34.93 giant's] gyants *1578, 1580?*; gyant *1599?*
34.104 this] this *1578*; his *1580? 1599?*
34.119 recommended] rec*ommen*ded *1578*; recommended *1580?*; commended *1599?*
34.126 his] the *1578, 1580?*; his *1599?*
34.129 this] this *1578, 1580?*; the *1599?*
34.150 is] is *1578*; *omitted 1580? 1599?*
34.151 of] of *1578, 1599?*; *omitted 1580?*
34.158 his] the *1578, 1580?*; his *1599?*
35.9 his] his *1578, 1580?*; hir *1599?*
35.22 the] the *1578*; *omitted 1580? 1599?*
35.35 his] his *1578*; *omitted 1580? 1599?*
35.58 that] that *1578*; *omitted 1580? 1599?*
35.58 whereof] whereoff *1578*; wherein *1580? 1599?*
35.60 to] to *1578, 1580?*; *omitted 1599?*

35.60 and] & *1578, 1580?*; *omitted 1599?*
35.65 as] as *1578*; so *1580? 1599?*
35.97 where] where *1578, 1580?*; whence *1599?*
35.100 forslack] forslacke *1578*; withslacke *1580? 1599?*
35.121 a] a *1578, 1580?*; *omitted 1599?*
36.38 for] for *1578, 1580?*; of *1599?*
36.42 with the] with the *1578*; and my *1580? 1599?*
36.92 in] in *1578*; *omitted 1580? 1599?*
36.149 gentlewomen] gentlewomen *1578*; gentlewoman *1580? 1599?*
36.165 so] so *1578, 1580?*; *omitted 1599?*
36.168 honourably] honourably *1578, 1580?*; honourable *1599?*
36.190 the] the *1578, 1580?*; *omitted 1599?*
37.1] *omitted 1578, 1580?*; great *1599?*
37.79 either] either *1578*; *omitted 1580? 1599?*
37.81 had] had *1578, 1599?*; hath *1580?*
37.83 this] this *1578, 1580?*; the *1599?*
37.105 this] that *1578, 1580?*; this *1599?*
37.127 premeditated] premeditate *1578*; premeditated *1580? 1599?*
37.142 would] *omitted 1578*; would *1580? 1599?*
37.151 he] *omitted 1578*; hee *1580? 1599?*
37.167 and] and *1578, 1580?*; with *1599?*
38.42 as] as *1578, 1580?*; *omitted 1599?*
38.63 would] would *1578*; should *1580? 1599?*
38.65 gentlewomen] gentlewomen *1578*; gentlewoman *1580? 1599?*
38.67 commendations] commendacions *1578*; commendacion *1580? 1599?*
38.69 gentlewomen] gentlewomen *1578*; gentlewoman *1580? 1599?*
38.76 loves'] loues *1578*; louers *1580? 1599?*
38.87 supposing] supposing *1578, 1580?*; supposed *1599?*
38.101 it] *omitted 1578*; it *1580? 1599?*
38.112 you] *omitted 1578*; you *1580? 1599?*
38.126 unto] vnder *1578*; vnto *1580? 1599?*
38.128 mirth] mirth *1578*; might *1580? 1599?*
38.135 Thine] The *1578*; Thine *1580? 1599?*
38.143] for *1578*; *omitted 1580? 1599?*
38.160 unto] vnto *1578*; to *1580? 1599?*
38.167 the] the *1578*; *omitted 1580? 1599?*
39.16 entreated] entreatie *1578*; intreated *1580? 1599?*
39.22 knights] knightes *1578*; knighte *1580? 1599?*
39.39 is] as *1578*; is *1580? 1599?*
39.51 my] his *1578, 1580? 1599?*
39.59 flower] flower *1578*; flowe *1580? 1599?*
39.61] *omitted 1578*; and *1580? 1599?*
39.73 his] his *1578*; *omitted 1580? 1599?*
39.97 it] *omitted 1578, 1580?*; it *1599?*
39.123 their] their *1578*; the *1580? 1599?*
39.133 of] at *1578*; of *1580? 1599?*
39.162 grace's] grace *1578*; graces *1580? 1599?*
39.168 and] or *1578, 1580?*; and *1599?*
39.169 take] take *1578*; toke *1580? 1599?*
39.179 we] he *1578, 1580?*; we *1599?*

39.190 and] or *1578*; and *1580? 1599?*
39.199] *1578, 1580? 1599?* and
39.203 flame] flame *1578*; heate *1580? 1599?*
39.215 for] for *1578*; to *1580? 1599?*
40.14 long] long *1578, 1580?*; longer *1599?*
40.15 she] shee *1578*; *omitted 1580? 1599?*
40.26 for] to *1578, 1580?*; for *1599?*
40.28 fearing] fering *1578*; seeing *1580? 1599?*
40.29 fetch] fette *1578*; fetch *1580? 1599?*
40.38 her] hir *1578, 1599?*; your *1580?*
40.70 misgive] misguie *1578*; misgiues *1580? 1599?*
40.80 be rubbed] be rubd *1578*; bee rubde *1580?*; rubbe *1599?*
40.81 thou] *illegible text 1578*; thou *1580? 1599?*
40.101 in] in *1578*; by *1580? 1599?*
40.103 a breast] a breast *1578*; an heart *1580? 1599?*
40.103 Caesar] *illegible text 1578*; Caesar *1580? 1599?*
40.129 with] which *1578*; with *1580? 1599?*
40.130 thereby] whereby *1578*; thereby *1580? 1599?*
40.173 stayed a time] stayed a tyme *1578*; *omitted 1580? 1599?*
40.188 her] hyr *1578*; hir *1580?*; his *1599?*
40.189 of all] of all *1578*; *omitted 1580? 1599?*
40.222 his] *omitted 1578*; his *1580? 1599?*
40.292 mistress's] mistresse *1578*; mistresses *1580? 1599?*
40.293] of *1578*; *omitted 1580? 1599?*
41.4 them] *omitted*; them *1580? 1599?*
41.21 horses] horse *1578*; horses *1580? 1599?*
41.24 horses] horse *1578*; horses *1580? 1599?*
41.31 to] *omitted 1578*; to *1580? 1599?*
41.51 answer] answered *1578, 1580? 1599?*
41.70 he] hee *1578*; shee *1580? 1599?*
41.72 for] for *1578*; in *1580? 1599?*
41.74 and] and *1578*; or *1580? 1599?*
41.77 her] hir *1578*; the *1580? 1599?*
41.81 this] this *1578*; his *1580? 1599?*
42.1 42] 41 *1578, 1580? 1599?*
42.3 is] is *1578, 1580?*; was *1599?*
42.6 not] *omitted 1578*; not *1580? 1599?*
42.22 conjectured] connected *1578*; coniectured *1580? 1599?*
42.49 she] he *1578*; she *1580? 1599?*
42.66 my] *omitted 1578*; my *1580? 1599?*
42.97 to be] for *1578*; to be *1580? 1599?*
42.101 suffering] *illegible text 1578*; suffering *1580? 1599?*
42.119 that] that *1578*; *omitted 1580? 1599?*
42.174 a] *omitted 1578*; a *1580? 1599?*
42.184 these] these *1578, 1599?*; the *1580?*
43.27 a] *omitted 1578*; a *1580? 1599?*
43.47 his] his *1578*; *omitted 1580? 1599?*
43.65 he] he *1578*; it *1580? 1599?*
43.97 to] to *1578*; *omitted 1580? 1599?*
43.119 which] which *1578*; and *1580? 1599?*

43.150 he] he *1578, 1599?*; she *1580?*
43.174 ears] eares *1578*; eies *1580? 1599?*
43.219] as *1578*; omitted *1580? 1599?*
44.8 greater] *illegible text 1578*; greater *1580? 1599?*
44.9 wide] wide *1578, 1599?*; winde *1580?*
44.14 his] his *1578, 1580?*; this *1599?*
44.41 banking] bancking *1578*; banking *1580?*; barking *1599?*
44.73 arches] archers *1578*; arches *1580? 1599?*
44.81 with] with *1578, 1580?*; omitted *1599?*
44.90 the] his *1578, 1580?*; the *1599?*
44.101 esteemed] esteemed *1578*; esteeming *1580? 1599?*
44.122 to be] to be *1578*; omitted *1580? 1599?*
44.126 this] this *1578*; omitted *1580? 1599?*
44.132 wightyest] wightyest *1578*; mightiest *1580? 1599?*
44.143 Thus] This *1578*; Thus *1580? 1599?*
44.165 his] omitted *1578*; his *1580? 1599?*
44.168 this] this *1578*; that *1580? 1599?*
44.169 his] hys *1578*; the *1580? 1599?*
44.186 on] of *1578*; on *1580?*; in *1599?*
44.187 deep in thickness] deepe in thickenesse *1578*; thicke in deepnesse *1580? 1599?*
44.246 his] his *1578*; the *1580? 1599?*
44.256 out] out *1578*; omitted *1580? 1599?*
44.265 the] the *1578 1580?*; his *1599?*
44.270 ancienter] auncienter *1578 1580?*; auncient *1599?*
44.275 to] to *1578*; in *1580? 1599?*
44.279 placed] place *1578*; placed *1580? 1599?*
44.286 the] that *1578*; the *1580? 1599?*
44.288 of] to *1578, 1580?*; of *1599?*
44.314 the] the *1578*; a *1580? 1599?*
44.415 a] a *1578, 1580?*; omitted *1599?*
44.416 this] this *1580?*; the *1599?*
44.437 the] omitted *1578, 1580?*; this *1599?*
44.437 you were brought hither] you were brought hether *1578*; you *1580?*; omitted *1599?*
44.461 I] you *1578*; I *1580? 1599?*
44.497 so] so *1578, 1580?*; to *1599?*
44.539 dainty] daynty *1578*; delicate *1580? 1599?*
45.21 possibly] possibly *1578, 1580?*; possible *1599?*
45.54 on] on *1578*; in *1580? 1599?*
45.54 either] either *1578*; euerie *1580? 1599?*
45.81 When] omitted *1578, 1580?*; When *1599?*
45.81] and *1578, 1580?*; omitted *1599?*
45.138 themselves] *illegible text 1578*; themselues *1580? 1599?*
45.140 as well for] *illegible text 1578*; as well for *1580? 1599?*
46.2 find] finde *1578*; seeke *1580? 1599?*
46.19 yet] it *1578*; yet *1580? 1599?*
46.25 avail] auayle *1578*; purpose *1580? 1599?*
46.26 the] these *1578, 1580?*; the *1599?*
46.40 had] had *1578, 1580?*; omitted *1599?*
46.62 the] *1578, 1580?*; his *1599?*
46.63 galded] galded *1578*; galled *1580? 1599?*

TEXTUAL NOTES

46.65 he] *omitted 1578*; he *1580? 1599?*
46.66] *omitted 1578, 1580?*; the *1599?*
46.72 faitour] faytour *1578*; traitour *1580? 1599?*
46.73 he] he *1578*; it *1580? 1599?*
46.81 her the means she looked not for and the comfort she hoped not. And she was the rest of the battle a joyful beholder] hir *the* means she looked not for and the comfort she hoped not: and she was *the* rest of *the* battaile a ioyful beholder *1578*; *omitted 1580? 1599?*
46.107 speak] speak *1578*; spake *1580? 1599?*
46.119 exited] exited *1578*; excited *1580? 1599?*
46.120 aid] ayde *1578*; aide *1580?*; *omitted 1599?*
46.122 of] of *1578 1580?*; in *1599?*
47.1 adventures] aduenturers *1578*; aduentures *1580? 1599?*
47.11 dearer] deerer *1578*; better *1580? 1599?*
47.16 after] after *1578*; afterward *1580? 1599?*
47.33 some] *omitted 1578*; some *1580? 1599?*
47.56 parts] parties *1578*; partes *1580?*; parts *1599?*
47.66 relieve] relieue *1578*; rescew *1580? 1599?*
47.89 heavily] heauily *1578*; heauie *1580? 1599?*
47.98 to] to *1578*; *omitted 1580? 1599?*
47.100 no] no *1578*; not *1580? 1599?*
47.106 about] aboute *1578*; aboue *1580? 1599?*
47.117 this] this *1578*; the *1580? 1599?*
47.120 hereof] hereoff *1578*; *1580? 1599?* thereof
47.125 past] past *1578*; with *1580? 1599?*
47.144 their] their *1578*; his *1580? 1599?*
47.148 As] As *1578*; And *1580? 1599?*
47.149 out] out *1578*; *omitted 1580? 1599?*
47.158 came] come *1578*; came *1580? 1599?*
47.172 years] yeare *1578*; yeares *1580? 1599?*
47.172 his] his *1578, 1580?*; this *1599?*
47.192 his] his *1578, 1580?*; this *1599?*
47.200 which] which *1578*; that *1580? 1599?*
47.206 whence] whence *1578, 1580?*; when *1599?*
48.1 Rosicleer] Rosicleer *1578*; Rolando *1580? 1599?*
48.1 Rolando] Rolando *1578*; Rosicleer *1580? 1599?*
48.5 arose] arose *1578, 1580?*; rose *1599?*
48.14] not *1578*; *omitted 1580? 1599?*
48.19 a] a *1578, 1580?*; *omitted 1599?*
48.38 the] *omitted 1578*; the *1580? 1599?*
48.38 or] of *1578, 1580?*; for *1599?*
48.48 to] to *1578*; *omitted 1580? 1599?*
48.62 thy] his *1578, 1580?*; thy *1599?*
48.63 rather] rather *1578*; *omitted 1580? 1599?*
48.70 upon] vnto *1578, 1580?*; vpon *1599?*
48.103 interred] entered *1578*; interred *1580?*; enterred *1599?*
48.107 left] lost *1578*; lefte *1580? 1599?*
49.33 well] *omitted 1578*; well *1580?*; will *1599?*
49.53 it] *omitted 1578*; it *1580? 1599?*
49.60 one other] one other *1578*; another *1580? 1599?*
49.60 third] thirde *1578*; other *1580? 1599?*

49.61 shorter] shorter *1578, 1580?*; shorte *1599?*
49.64 born] broode *1578*; borne *1580? 1599?*
49.71 her] hir *1578, 1580?*; his *1599?*
49.83 night's] night *1578; 1580? 1599?* nights
50.2 an] an *1578, 1580?*; *omitted 1599?*
50.4 in] in *1578*; by *1580? 1599?*
50.18 you] you *1578*; she *1580?*; shee *1599?*
50.39 his] hir *1578*; his *1580? 1599?*
50.50 her] hir *1578*; his *1580? 1599?*
50.68 rest] rust *1578, 1580?*; rest *1599?*
50.78] *omitted 1578*; so *1580? 1599?*
51.10 cover] couer *1578*; recouer *1580? 1599?*
51.11 no] *omitted 1578*; no *1580? 1599?*
51.13 to] by *1578*; to *1580? 1599?*
51.15 I will] I will *1578*; will I *1580? 1599?*
51.19 she] she *1578, 1580?*; they *1599?*
51.44 and] *1578, 1580*; *omitted 1599?*
51.45] *omitted 1578*; my *1580? 1599?*
51.51 have] haue *1578*; hath *1580? 1599?*
52.7] the *1578*; *omitted 1580? 1599?*
52.70 those] those *1578*; these *1580? 1599?*
52.74 these] these *1578, 1580?*; the *1599?*
52.76 knights] knight *1578, 1580?*; knights *1599?*
52.78 otherwise] otherwyse *1578*; els *1580? 1599?* els
52.100 heavy] heauy *1578*; heauie *1580?*; healed *1599?*
52.100 with] wyth *1578*; *omitted 1580? 1599?*
52.106 for] for *1578*; of *1580? 1599?*
52.117 came] came *1578, 1580?*; come *1599?*
53.8 for] for *1578*; *omitted 1580? 1599?*
53.8 in] in *1578*; *omitted 1580? 1599?*
53.21 to] to *1578*; *omitted 1580? 1599?*
53.27 hath] hath *1578*; hast *1580? 1599?*
53.27 first] first *1578, 1580?*; *omitted 1599?*
54.25 out] *omitted 1578*; out *1580? 1599?*
54.43 raising] raysing *1578*; raising *1580?*; arising *1599?*
54.43 hastely] hastely *1578, 1580?*; lastely *1599?*
54.48 a] a *1578*; *omitted 1580? 1599?*
54.78 or] or *1578*; and *1580? 1599?*
54.86 yet] yet *1578*; *omitted 1580? 1599?*
55.2] *the 1578*; *omitted 1580? 1599?*
55.2 been ere this] bene ere this *1578*; ere this bene *1580?*; ere this beene *1599?*
55.6 yet] yet *1578*; is *1580? 1599?*
55.11 that] that *1578*; *omitted 1580? 1599?*
55.11 it] *omitted 1578*; it *1580? 1599?*
55.28 profit] profit *1578, 1580?*; report *1599?*
55.49 which] whom *1578, 1580?*; which *1599?*
55.67 This] This *1578*; The *1580? 1599?*
55.70 people] people *1578*; parents *1580? 1599?*
55.80 his] his *1578, 1580?*; hir *1599?*
55.87 own] owne *1578*; *omitted 1580? 1599?*
56.17 he would] he would *1578, 1580?*; I should *1599?*

56.18 how] what *1578*; how *1580? 1599?*
56.21 gentlewomen] gentlewoman *1578*; gentlewoman *1580? 1599?*
56.30 their] their *1578*; her *1580?*; hir *1599?*
56.34 is] is *1578*; *omitted 1580? 1599?*
56.34 his] *omitted 1578*; his *1580? 1599?*
56.39 at] at *1578*; of *1580? 1599?*

GLOSSARY

All definitions are based on the *OED*. Where the word or expression to be defined is not included in the *OED*, my definition is based on the context in which the term is found in *Mirror* and verified against *Espejo*. Various inflections of the term to be glossed are provided in parentheses, after the headword, where applicable. If the word is used in distinct senses in different parts of the romance, chapter numbers are provided to direct the reader to the correct definition.

A

abashed	discomfited or disconcerted
abate	lower
abled	capable; vigorous, thriving
abode	dwelled (Chapter 12); waited for (Chapter 35)
abye	pay the penalty
acceptation	the action or fact of receiving something favourably
accidents	unexpected circumstances
adamant	magnetic
advertise	inform
affectioned	favourably disposed
affiance	faith, trust
afford	supply
affray(ed)	frighten
aforehand	in advance
a-good	heartily, a good deal
ague	an acute or high fever
alarm	call to arms, warning of danger
allowed	commended
amain	with full force
amaze	extreme astonishment, wonder
ambassade	the message borne by an ambassador
ancient	long established
ancienter	the more ancient
angerly	angrily
annoy(eth)	injure, be a cause of trouble
apaid	satisfied, contented
aright	rightly
armant	sharp
arming-sword	a sword that forms part of arms or armour
arrogancy	the quality or state of being arrogant.
arson	saddle-bow
ascertained	made certain
ascried	attacked (Chapter 5), discovered (Chapters 26, 46)
assailed	assaulted
assay(ed)	try, test
assize	judicial inquest
astonishing	amazing
attached(eth)	attacked

GLOSSARY

attainted	affected
attent	attentive
avail	advantage
avouch(ed)	vouch for
awaked	to waken

B

bailed	confined
bale	sorrow
barbed	barbered
bark	small ship
barrator	quarrelsome
barred	made fast, confined securely
base	challenge
bases	lower part of a shield
bead-roll	list of names
beautifullest	most beautiful
beaver, beveare	the lower portion of the face-guard of a helmet, when worn with a visor; but occasionally serving the purposes of both
beaverette	small beaver
beforehand	to anticipate something
begored	besmeared with gore
behoveful	necessary
belike	in all likelihood
beshrewed	treated evilly
bestir	to rouse into activity
betwixt	between
bewept	drowned in tears; marked or disfigured by weeping
bewray(ed)(ing)	reveal.
biding	abiding
bird-bolt	blunt-headed arrow used for shooting birds
board	table used for meals
(no) boot	useless
booted	helped
borrow	guarantee, pledge
bo(u)lt out	find out
bounced	knocked loudly
bowshot	distance that an arrow can be shot from a bow
bravery	splendour
broach(ed) (ing)	spur
broken	disclosed
brook	tolerate
brothers	kinsmen
bruit	reputation, renown
bruited	noised, reported
builded	constructed
burthen	birth, responsibility (Chapter 25)
buskle	prepare
butting upon	adjacent to

C

captivate	made captive
career	the space within the barrier at a tournament
careful	full of care
case	state of manners
cast(ing)	arranged, ordered; thinking, exclaiming (Chapter 42)
cater	buyer of provisions or 'cates'
certify	to make a person certain of something
chance	fortune
chape	metal plate or mounting of a scabbard or sheath
chevisance	expedition to gain wealth illicitly or dishonestly
chiefest	most important, principal
childing	child-bearing
claw-backs	sycophants
close	enclosing line, boundary
close(ly)	secret, private
closes	closing passages of an argument
closet	private room
cloyed	burdened
coat-armour	vest of rich material embroidered with heraldic devices, worn as a distinction by knights over their armour
cock-boat	small boat often towed behind a vessel or ship
collar	necklace
collation	light meal
coll(ed) (ing)	embrace
colour	misrepresent
colourable	capable of being presented as true or valid
comers	those who come
commender	one who commends
commonalty	common people
communed	conversed
compass	plan, contrive
compass-wise	in compass
conceit(s)	idea, opinion, conception, device (Chapter 33)
concionated	shared
concluded	agreed
contemn(ed)	disdain
contentation(s)	satisfaction
contraried	opposed
contrariwise	antagonistically
controlment	control
contumely	insolent reproach or abuse
convenient	appropriate
cony	rabbit
copy	copiousness, abundance
copy, changed her	changed her behaviour or character
corsie	source of trouble and grief
counterbuff(s)	blow given in return
counterfeit	likeness, portrait
countermanded	stopped by contrary command

GLOSSARY

counter-peise	counterbalance
countervail	prevail against
couragiousest	most courageous
courser	a swift, powerful horse
covert	shelter
covertliest	most covert
craven	a cock that owns himself beaten or is afraid of his opponent
crayer	small trading vessel
cuirass	piece of armour reaching down to the waist, consisting of a breast-plate and a back-plate, buckled or otherwise fastened together
curious	skilful
cut	pass sharply through
cutler	one who makes, deals in, or repairs knives

D

dainty(ies)	foods that are pleasing to the palate
danger	jurisdiction
dastarde	despicable coward
deathsman	executioner
degree	steps in a flight of steps
deliver (ness)	nimble, agile
demand(ed) (ing)	ask
demean (ing)(ed)	lead a life, behave
demerits	merit, deserving
demur	continuance
desert(s)	deserving
desperate(ly)	despairing
device(s)	contrivance, emblem
devising	deliberating
devoir	that which one ought to do
discomfit	the fact of being discomfited
discomfited	defeated
disease (ed)(ing)	disturb
disheriting	dispossessing
displeasant	displeased
disport	divert (verb); diversion (noun)
disseised	dispossessed
dissimuled	disguised
distempereth	from the notion that attributed the 'humour' or 'temper' to the preponderance of one or other of the bodily humours: to disturb or disorder the humour or temper
disworship	dishonour, disgrace
dole	grief, distress
draw out	evoke, delineate
drumslare	drummer
dullness	gloominess
durance	imprisonment
dure	endure
durst	dared

E

ecstasy	a state of unconsciousness
embased(ing)	lowered
encountry(ies)	encounter
enforce	strengthen, add force to, to force
engraven	engraved
enjoineth	imposes a penalty
enlarged	set free
ensure	engage by a promise of marriage
enterprised	undertake
entreat	treat, deal with
equimas	helmet
ere	ever (Chapter 18); before, here (Chapter 44)
errand	message
erst	before
escried	espied
especial	particular
especial, in	especially
espies	spies
esprised	inflamed with love
esquire	squire
estate	group, state
estonished	astonished
excellency	excellence
exigent	state of pressing need
exquisite	accomplished

F

fain	gladly (adverb); glad (adjective)
faithfullest	most faithful
faitour	impostor
falchion	broad sword more or less curved with the edge on the convex side
fancy (ies)	fantasy, imagination; ideas (Chapters 3, 6); whims (Chapter 35)
fardel	bundle
feared	frightened
fee-farmer	one who owns a fee-farm, one who owns a fee-farm, i.e. 'that kind of tenure by which land is held in fee-simple subject to a perpetual fixed rent, without any other services' (*OED*, n. 1)
fel	very
fell	fierce
finesse	fineness
finger	a unit of measurement corresponding to the breadth of a finger or to ¾ of an inch
flakes	detached portions of flame
flashing	drawing or waving of a sword with a flash
flatlings	prostrate
flight-shot	distance to which a flight-arrow is shot, a bowshot
flour-de-luces	flower-de-luce or fleur de lis
flung	rushed
fly(ing)	flee

GLOSSARY

fly at fowl	in hawking, when the falconer causes a hawk to attack by flying
foam	foaming saliva issuing from the mouth
foison	plenty
forbear	tolerate
force, of	of necessity
foreconceived	previously conceived
fore-end	front
fore-hoped	previously hoped for
fore-passed	previously passed
foreshowed	foreshadowed
for(e)slack	be slack in, neglect
foreslow(ing)	neglect
forespoke	predicted
forethink(ing)(thought)	think out beforehand
fore-wearied	wearied
forsooth	in truth
forwarder	most forward
foundered	stumbled, fell
foundress	female founder
four-square	square
framed	made
franchising	setting free
frayed	frightened
freelier	more free
froward	unfavourable
fume	fit of anger
furniture	armour, weapons; necessities, supplies (Chapter 4)

G

gainsaid	opposed
gainstand	withstand
galded	made sore by chafing or rubbing
gall	gall-bladder
garboil	tumult
germane	first cousin
girdle	belt worn round the waist
girdlesteads	waist
glass	plausible pretext
glister(ing)	glitter
goodly	many; good-looking, well-favoured or proportioned (Chapter 9); favourably and with propriety
good even	good evening
good morrow	good morning
govern	care for a person's health
governor	captain of a vessel
Grecian(s)	Greek
gripe	grasp
groom-porter	officer of the English Royal Household in charge of gaming
guerdon	reward

H

habergeon	sleeveless coat or jacket of mail or scale armour
haled(ing)	pulled, hoisted (Chapter 30)
hammer	the knocker of a door
hangers	loops or straps on a sword-belt from which the sword was hung; often richly ornamented
hap	chance or fortune
happiest	most fortunate
hard by / upon	near by
hare	harassment
hasted	made haste
hereat	as a result of this
heroical	heroic
hest	behest
hither	here
hoised(ing)	raised aloft by means of a rope or pulley and tackle
hostry	hostelry
hue and cry	outcry calling for the pursuit of a felon
hurly-burly	commotion

I

ill-willers	one who wishes evil to another
impair	impairment
imparted with	shared in
imperials	member of the emperor's party
importunate	inopportune (adjective); bother (verb)
impudency	immodesty
incontinently	immediately
increase	the result of an action
indifferent	undetermined
indifferently	equally
inditing	writing, composing
indwellers	inhabitants
inexpugnable	incapable of being overcome
inferred war	waged war
inheretrix	female inheritor
inheritress	female inheritor
innocency	innocence
inquest	chivalric expedition
insolency	the quality of being insolent
insonable	indissoluble
in sunder	into separate parts
intend	endeavour
irrecuperable	that cannot be recovered

J

jessamines	a climbing shrub with fragrant white flowers
jeopard	put in jeopardy
jumping	coinciding

K

kaiser	emperor
keep	heed
kenned(ing)	saw
kirtle	skirt or petticoat
kith and kin(dred)	country and kinsfolk
knew	had sexual intercourse with

L

laid about	struck with vigour
lash	a dashing or sweeping stroke
late	recent
layed	pledged
lay(s)	short lyric or narrative poem
leading	serving as a passage for
learnedest	most learned
let	hindrance (noun); hinder (transitive verb)
lightly	nimbly
lightness	swiftness
list	desire
lists	a place of combat
little talk	small talk
living	income
looked	expected
loud	flagrant
lust	inclination, desire
lustily	pleasurably
lusty(iest)	pleasing, merry, healthy
lying down	being brought to bed of a child

M

mail	bag
mailings	coat of mail
maim(ing)(ed)	lasting wound or bodily injury
maims	grave damages
main	exerted to the full (Chapters 8, 17, 30, 37, 43, 44); high, open (Chapters 15, 30, 34, 39, 44)
mainprize	action of procuring the release of a prisoner on someone's undertaking to stand surety for his or her appearance in court at a specified time
maketh love	pays amorous attention to, courts, woos
malice	harmfulness
mammering	a state of doubt
man-child	male child
mantling	cloth covering
marry	interjection expressing surprise, astonishment, outrage, etc., or used to give emphasis to one's words
marte	battle
massy	solid and weighty

matchable	comparable, equal
maugre	notwithstanding
maze	amazement
mean(est)	of low or inferior status
meetest	most suitable
meinie	attendants, retainers
mess	serving
mewed	confined
middest	situated in the middle
midst	middle point
mine	my
minster	monastery
misbeseeming	unsuitable
miscontent	discontented
misdeem	mistake
misgive	filled with suspicion or foreboding
mislike(ed)	dislike
misliking	unhappiness, trouble
misliving	evil or sinful living
molest	trouble
Morian	Moor
morrow	morning, tomorrow
muffler	a sort of kerchief or scarf worn by women in the 16th and 17th centuries to cover part of the face and the neck

N

neck, in the	immediately upon or afterwards
nigh	near
nigh hand	almost
noised	reported
not	naught
nurse(ing)	person who takes care of, looks after, or advises another (noun); rear, bring up, nurture (verb)
nuzzled	to educate or nurture a person in a particular opinion, habit, custom, etc

O

obeisance	homage or submission to a person in authority
occasioners	one who occasions something
occurrents	occurrences
odd	singular in merit
offspring	ancestry, lineage
oft	often
opened	declared
opprobry	reproach, disgrace
original	origin
otherwhere	elsewhere
out	outlying
outbrayed	to outdo in braying
out-creeks	out-of-the-way corners

GLOSSARY

outpassed	surpassed
outraged	behaved immoderately
overboldness	excessive boldness
overlate	excessively late
overpassed	passed
overshadoweth	shelters with one's influence or power
overslipping	letting slip, letting pass
overthwart	across, perverse (Chapter 39)

P

packing	plotting
pagans	non-Christians
Pagansie, Pagansive	Paganism, non-Christian condition or practice
paintry	painted matter
painture	painting
pair	a set or flight (of steps or stairs)
pale	an ordinary consisting of a broad vertical band in the middle of a shield, extending from top to bottom and usually occupying one third of its breadth
parage	equal
parents	kin, relatives
parley	converse
partaker	one who takes another's part or side
pavises	flat shields, more or less oblong in outline, but sometimes with a convex top edge, with a wide, flat, raised medial band, hollowed out at the back, extending from top to bottom
Peccavi	an interjection used to acknowledge one's guilt or responsibility for an error
pencel	small pennon or streamer
peradventure	maybe
percase	perchance
perforce	by force
periwig	wig
perverst	most perverse
peytrals	a piece of armour to protect the breast of a horse
physic	natural or human science
piece	area, room
pilot	helmsman or navigator
pitch	slope
place, give	give ground, yield to pressure or force
plaining	in the plains
plat	small patch of land
plaudit	audible expression of praise or approval
pleasure	please
pleasured	served, pleased
plume	feather
plyed	applied themselves assiduously (Chapter 21); used their tackle to direct the boat (Chapter 30)
poignant	sharp-pointed
pomell	knob at the end of the hilt of a sword or dagger

pommel	the upper front part of a saddle, saddlebow
portraiture	likeness
possessioners	those who possess something
posted	rode with great speed
postern	back or side entrance, often secondary or private
posy	motto or short inscription
pounced	embossed or chased for decoration
presently	immediately
press	the thick of the fight
prick and price	praise of excellence or success
princely	belonging to a prince
principallest	most principal
privily	privately
privy	acquainted, private (Dedication, Chapters 46, 51)
professions	religious beliefs
profitablest	most profitable
promission	divine promise of future benefit or blessing
properest	most proper
provide	make ready
puissant	powerful

Q

quailed	suppressed
quailing	losing heart
quell	suppress
quick	pregnant
quicken	bring to life
quit	acquit
quoth	said

R

raise	drive an animal or bird from a lair or hiding place.
rampire	rampart
rapine	pillage
rated	berated
rattler	ratelier, a stand for lances or other arms
raught	reached after
receipt	where hunters wait with fresh hounds for driven game
reclaim	recall a person
recomfort(ed)	comfort
recommand	recommendation
reculed	retreated
recureless	without hope of recovery or amendment
rede	counsel
redound	contribute to, or reflect; rebound (Chapter 39)
reines	region of the kidneys
remember	cause a person to have a memory or recollection
rent	tear, pull apart or to pieces
require(ing)	request

GLOSSARY

re-resolved	further resolved
resalutation	greeting made in reply
resiant	resident
revested	reinvested with authority, ownership
revilings	insult or abuse
richesse	riches
rive(n)	tear apart or in pieces
roll	to sway, rock, like a boat
room	post (Chapter 16); place (Chapter 32); opportunity (Chapter 32); territory (Chapter 37)
roseal	resembling a rose
rounded	whispered
rover	pirate
roving	the activities of a pirate
royalest	most royal
rub out	to live or last out
rush, not worth a	of little value or importance
ruth	sorrow

S

scantling	a limited measure of space
scathe	hurt, damage
seamster	seamstress
season	opportunity
seigniory(ies)	territory under the dominion of a lord
seld	seldom
sely	insignificant, foolish
semblable	something that is similar
sequel	ensuing narrative
serving-men	male servants
servitor	male servant
several(ly)	separate, distinct, different
sewers	attendants at a meal who superintended the arrangement of the table, the seating of the guests, and the tasting and serving of the dishes
shadow	shade
shamefast(ness)	bashful, modest, shy
shedding	flowing
sheen	bright, shining
shent	disgraced
shipboard	on board a ship
ship-boat	a boat carried or towed by a ship
shivers	fragments
shorter	cut in half
shortly	speedily
sightes	visor
silly	deserving of pity, compassion; helpless
sine	without
sooth	truly (adverb); true (adjective); truth (noun)
sort	manner

sound(ing)	swoon
souse	heavy blow
space	time
span-fulls	spans; the distance from the tip of the thumb to the tip of the little finger when the hand is fully extended, averaging nine inches
sparkled	sparkles or small particles issued forth
sparkles	small sparks
spilled	ended in death
spin	run quickly
staff(s)	spear, lance, or other weapon
stained	disgraced
stalled	installed
standers-by	bystanders
staring	shining
stay(ed)	stop, remain stationary, wait
stepdame	stepmother
stoccado	a thrust or stab with a pointed weapon
stomach	courage
stone-horse	stallion
stout(est)	proud, brave
straight	strict (Dedication, Chapter 44); honest (Chapter 50)
straightway(s)	immediately
strange	unknown, unfriendly (Chapter 34)
strange, make	to be unwilling
stripe	disgrace, blow
struck	made his way
succours	help
sued(eth)	wooed, courted (Chapter 2); petitioned (Chapter 19)
sufferable	patient
suits	pursuits
sultan	chief ruler of a Muslim country
sunder	separate, divide
surceased(ing)	ended
surely	thoroughly
surplusage	excess
suspect	suspicion

T

tacklings	tackle
tail-back	stern
taken shipping	embarked
targets	light round shields or bucklers
tarry	wait for
temperature	due measure and proportion of temperament
thereby	nearby
thine	your(s)
thither	there
thitherward	towards that place
tickled	vexed, irritated
to-do	ado, business

GLOSSARY

tops	topsails
tossing	turning over and over
towardness	promise, natural aptitude and good disposition
tragical	tragic
trance	swoon
transporting	travelling
travail	labour, work, often also with the connotation of travelling; childbirth (Chapter 11)
troublous	causing trouble or grief
trow	trust

U

umbrere	visor of a helmet
under colour	in the pretext
underlying	subordinating
undoer	destroyer
unhappy	unfortunate
unhoped	unexpected
unmailed	not covered or protected by mail
unmailing	detaching the links of a mail-coat
unnoble	not noble
unparagonized	unmatched
unsuccoured	unassisted
unwitting	unknowing

V

valiance(y)	bravery, valour
valure	material or monetary worth
vayle	take off
venturous	adventurous
viands	victuals
voided	empty, clear
vouchsafeth	condescend to engage
vowess	woman who makes a vow of devotion to a religious life; a nun
vulgar	vernacular

W

wanhope	hopelessness
want	lack
warded	fended off
ware	aware
warrantise	guarantee
watchings	wakefulness
water-boughs	watershoots
weed	article of apparel
ween	think
weighty	heavy
whereafter	after which
wheresoever	wherever

whit	a very small amount
whither	to what place, where; which (Chapters 22, 42, 52); what (Chapter 26)
whithersoever	wherever
wight	mighty
wightyest	strongest
willinger	more willing
winded	blew
wise	way
wist	know
wistly	with close attention
wit(ting)	ascertain, know
wither	whether
woeful	miserable
woe(fully)-begone	beset with woe
wonted	customary
wood	fierce, violent
wot	know, knew
wrack	injury
wreak	avenge
wreathe	twist or coil

Y

ye	you, your(s)
yellow	blond

NEOLOGISMS

This list presents words used by Tyler that do not appear in the *OED* or that predate their first relevant citation in the *OED*. All of these terms are explained in the glossary, with the exception of 'confidency', used in the first two editions, which has been emended to 'confidence', based on the reading of the third edition.

ancienter	hare
armant	inheritress
attached	insonable
bailed	learnedest
beautifullest	main
beaverette	mantling
concionated	mailings
confidency	Pagansie
couragiousest	Pagansive
covertliest	perverst
deathsman	plaining
drumslare	pleasured
equimas	principallest
estonished	profitablest
forwarder	rattler
freelier	re-resolved
hangers	wightyest

BIBLIOGRAPHY

Akbari, Suzanne Conklin, *Idols in the East: European Representations of Islam and the Orient, 1100–1450* (Ithaca: Cornell University Press, 2009)

Alwes, Derek B., 'Robert Greene's Duelling Dedications', *English Literary Renaissance*, 30 (2000), 373–95

Anglo-Spanish Literary Relations (database), <http://www.ems.kcl.ac.uk/content/proj/anglo/pro-anglo.html>

Arber, Edward, *A Transcript of the Registers of the Company of Stationers of London 1554–1640 A.D.*, 5 vols (London, privately printed, 1875–94)

Arcara, Stefania, 'Margaret Tyler's *The Mirrour of Knighthood*', in *TRAlinea* vol. 9 (2007) <http://www.intralinea.it/volumes/eng_more.php?id=529_0_2_0>

Atkinson, David, 'Marriage Under Compulsion in English Renaissance Drama', *English Studies*, 67 (1986), 483–504

Bennett, H. S., *English Books and Readers, 1558–1603* (Cambridge, University Press, 1965)

Bibliotheca Reediana: A Catalogue of the Curious & Extensive Library of the Late Isaac Reed, esq. of Staple Inn, deceased... (London: J. Barker, 1807)

Bly Calkin, Siobhain, *Saracens and the Making of English Identity: The Auchinleck Manuscript* (New York: Routledge, 2005)

Boro, Joyce, 'All for Love: Lord Berners and the Enduring, Evolving Romance', in *The Oxford Handbook to Tudor Literature, 1485–1603*, ed. by Mike Pincombe and Cathy Shrank (Oxford: Oxford University Press, 2009), pp. 87–102

—, 'Multilingualism, Romance, and Language Pedagogy: Or, Why Were So Many Sentimental Romances Printed as Polyglot Texts?' in *Tudor Translation*, ed. by Fred Schurink (Basingstoke: Palgrave Macmillan, 2012), pp. 18–38

—, '"this rude laboure": Lord Berners's Translation Methods and Prose Style in *Castell of Love*', *Translation and Literature*, 13 (2004), 1–23

Boutcher, Warren, 'The Renaissance', in *The Oxford Guide to Literature in English Translation*, ed. by Peter France (Oxford: Oxford University Press, 2000), Oxford Reference Online, <http://www.oxfordreference.com/views/ENTRY.html?subview=Main&entry=t194.e152>

Briones, A. Valbuena, 'La influencia de un libro de caballerías en *El castillo de Lindabridis*', *Revista Canadiense de Estudios Hispánicos*, 5 (1981), 373–83

Briquet, Charles-Moïse, *Les filigranes: Dictionnaire historique des marques du papier des leur apparition vers 1282 jusqu'en 1600, avec 39 figures dans le texte et 16,112 fac-similés de filigranes*, 4 vols (Paris: A. Picard & fils; Geneva: A. Jullien, 1907)

Bullough, Geoffrey, *Narrative and Dramatic Sources of Shakespeare*, vol. 8 (London: Routledge; New York: Columbia University Press, 1975)

Campos García Rojas, Axayácatl, 'El Ciclo de *Espejo de Príncipes y Caballeros* [1555–1580–1587]', *Edad de Oro*, 21 (2002), 389–429

—, *Espejo de príncipes y caballeros (Parte I) de Diego Ortúñez de Calahorra (Zaragoza, Esteban de Nájera, 1555): guía de lectura* (Madrid: Centro de Estudios Cervantinos, 2003)

Catalogue of the famous library of printed books, illuminated manuscripts, autograph letters and engravings collected by Henry Huth, and since maintained and augmented by his son, Alfred H. Huth; the printed books and illuminated manuscripts [. . .] sold by auction by Messrs; Sotheby, Wilkinson & Hodge, auctioneers, 9 vols (London: Dryden Press, J. Davy and Sons, 1911–20)

Chamberlain, Lori, 'Gender and the Metaphorics of Translation', in *Rethinking Translation*, ed. by Lawrence Venuti (London: Routledge, 1992), pp. 57–75

Charlton, K., *Education in Renaissance England* (London: Routledge, 1965)

Coad, Kathryn, intro., *Margaret Tyler*, Early Modern Englishwoman: A Facsimile Library of Essential Works, vol. 8 (Aldershot: Scolar Press, 1997)

Coldiron, Anne E. B., *English Printing, Verse Translation, and the Battle of the Sexes, 1476–1557* (Farnham: Ashgate, 2009)

Cooper, Helen, *The English Romance in Time: Transforming Motifs from Geoffrey of Monmouth to the Death of Shakespeare* (Oxford: Oxford University Press, 2004)

Cruz, Anne. J., ed., *Material and Symbolic Circulation between Spain and England, 1554–1604* (Aldershot: Ashgate, 2008)

Curbet, Joan, 'Repressing the Amazon: Cross-Dressing and Militarism in Edmund Spenser's *The Faerie Queene*', in *Dressing Up for War: Transformations of Gender and Genre in the Discourse and Literature of War*, ed. by A. Usandizaga and A. Monnickendam (Amsterdam & New York: Rodopi Press, 2001), pp. 157–72

del Corro, Antonio, *The Spanish Grammar* (London, 1590)

Dering, Edward, *A briefe and necessarie catechisme or instruction, very needfull to be known of all housholders* (London, 1572)

Drouin, Jennifer, 'Diana's Band: Safe Spaces, Publics, and Early Modern Lesbianism', *Queer Renaissance Historiography*, ed. by Vin Nardizzi, Stephen Guy-Bray, and Will Stockton (Farnham: Ashgate, 2009), pp. 85–110

Eisenberg, Daniel, *An Edition of a Sixteenth-Century Romance of Chivalry: Diego Ortúñez de Calahora's Espejo de Principes y Cavalleros [El Caballero del Febo]* (unpublished doctoral thesis, Brown University, 1971)

—, ed., *Espejo de príncipes y cavalleros: el cavallero del Febo*, by Diego Ortúñez de Calahorra (Madrid: Espasa-Calpe, 1975)

—, *Romances of Chivalry in the Spanish Golden Age* (Newark, N.J.: Juan de la Cuesta, 1982)

Farnsworth, Jane, 'Margaret Tyler, Dedication, *The Mirrour of Princely Deeds and Knighthood* (1578)', in *Reading Early Modern Women: An Anthology of Texts in Manuscript and Print, 1550–1700*, ed. by Helen Ostovich, Elizabeth Sauer and Melissa Smith (New York: Routledge, 2004), pp. 332–33

Ferguson, Moira, ed., *First Feminists: British Women Writers, 1578–1799* (Bloomington: Indiana University Press, 1985)

Fleming, Juliet, 'The Ladies' Man and The Age of Elizabeth', in *Sexuality and Gender in Early Modern Europe*, ed. by James Grantham Turner (Cambridge: Cambridge University Press, 1993), pp. 158–81

Florio, John, trans., *The essayes or morall, politike and millitarie discourses of Lo: Michaell de Montaigne* (London 1603)

—, *Florio his firste fruites* (London, 1578)

Fuchs, Barbara, *Exotic Nation: Maurophilia and the Construction of Early Modern Spain* (Philadelphia: University of Pennsylvania Press, 2009)

Gallagher, Catherine, 'A History of the Precedent: Rhetorics of Legitimation in Women's Writing', *Critical Inquiry*, 26 (2000), 309–27

Gartenberg, Patricia and Nena Thames Whittemore, 'A Checklist of English Women in Print, 1475–1640', *Bulletin of Bibliography and Magazine Notes*, 34 (1977), 1–3

Gregory, Tobias, *From Many Gods to One* (Chicago: University of Chicago Press, 2006)

Hackett, Helen, '"Yet Tell Me Some Such Fiction": Lady Mary Wroth's *Urania* and the "Femininity" of Romance', in *Women, Texts and Histories, 1575–1760*, ed. by Clare Brant and Diane Purkiss (London and New York: Routledge, 1992), pp. 39–68

—, *Women and Romance Fiction in the English Renaissance* (Cambridge: Cambridge University Press, 2000)

Hamilton, Donna B., *Anthony Munday and the Catholics, 1560–1633* (Aldershot: Ashgate, 2005)

Hannay, Margaret P., 'Introduction', in *Silent but for the Word: Tudor Women as Patrons, Translators, and Writers of Religious Works*, ed. by Margaret P. Hannay (Kent, Ohio: Kent State University Press, 1985), pp. 1–14

Harrison, William, *The Description of England*, ed. by George Edelen (Ithaca: Cornell University Press, 1968)

Heng, Geraldine, 'Jews, Saracens, "black men", Tartars: England in a World of Racial

Difference', in *A Companion to Medieval English Literature and Culture c. 1350–c. 1500*, ed. by Peter Brown, (Malden, MA: Blackwell, 2007), pp. 247–69

Holinshed, Raphael, *Chronicles* (London: 1577)

Hosington, Brenda M., *Renaissance Cultural Crossroads: An Analytical and Annotated Catalogue of Translations, 1473–1640*, http://www.hrionline.ac.uk/rcc/

—, 'The Renaissance Cultural Crossroads Catalogue: A Witness to the Importance of Translation in Early Modern Britain', in *The Book Triumphant: Print in Transition in the Sixteenth and Seventeenth Centuries*, ed. by Malcolm Walsby (Leiden: Brill, 2011), pp. 251–69

Hume, Martin, *Spanish Influence on English Literature* (New York: Haskell House, 1964)

Hutson, Lorna, *The Usurer's Daughter: Male Friendship and Fictions of Women in Sixteenth-Century England* (London: Routledge, 1994)

Krontiris, Tina, 'Breaking Barriers of Genre and Gender: Margaret Tyler's Translation of *The Mirrour of Knighthood*', *English Literary Renaissance*, 18 (1988), 19–39

—, *Oppositional Voices: Women as Writers and Translators of Literature in the English Renaissance* (London: Routledge, 1992)

Lamb, Mary Ellen, 'The Cooke Sisters: Attitudes toward Learned Women', in *Silent but for the Word: Tudor Women as Patrons, Translators, and Writers of Religious Works*, ed. by Margaret P. Hannay (Kent, Ohio: Kent State University Press, 1985), pp. 107–25

Lamb, Mary Ellen, *Gender and Authorship in the Sidney Circle* (Madison: University of Wisconsin Press, 1990)

Lawrence, Jason, *'Who the Devil Taught Thee So Much Italian?': Italian Language Learning and Literary Imitation in Early Modern England* (Manchester: Manchester University Press, 2005)

Levin, Carole, *Dreaming the English Renaissance: Politics and Desire in Court and Culture* (New York: Palgrave Macmillan, 2008)

López-Baralt, Luce, *Islam in Spanish Literature: From the Middle Ages to the Present*, trans. by Andrew Hurley (Leiden: Brill; San Juan: Editorial de la Universidad de Puerto Rico, 1992)

Lyly, John, *Euphues: The Anatomy of Wit; Euphues and his England*, ed. by Morris W. Croll and Herbert Clemens (London: Routledge, 1916)

Mackerness, E. D., 'Margaret Tyler: An Elizabethan Feminist', *Notes and Queries*, 190 (1946), 112–13

Martin, Randal, *Women Writers in Renaissance England* (London: Longman, 1997)

Marotti, Arthur, *Manuscript, Print, and the English Renaissance Lyric* (Ithaca, NY: Cornell University Press, 1995)

Matthiesson, F. O., *Translation, an Elizabethan Art* (Cambridge: Harvard University Press, 1931)

McGrath, Lynette, *Subjectivity and Women's Poetry in Early Modern England: 'Why on the ridge should she desire to go?'* (Aldershot, Hampshire: Ashgate, 2002)

Murphy, James J., *Rhetoric in the Middle Ages: A History of Rhetorical Theory from Saint Augustine to the Renaissance* (Berkeley: University of California Press, 1974)

Newcomb, Lori Humphrey, *Reading Popular Romance in Early Modern England* (New York: Columbia University Press, 2002)

O'Connor, John J., *Amadis de Gaule and Its Influence on Elizabethan Literature* (New Brunswick, N.J.: Rutgers University Press, 1970)

Overbury, Sir Thomas, *New and Choise Characters, of seuerall authors: together with that exquisite and unmatcht poeme, The wife* (London, 1615)

Parker, Patricia, *Inescapable Romance: Studies in the Poetics of a Mode* (Princeton: Princeton University Press, 1979)

Patchell, Mary, *The Palmerin Romances in Elizabethan Prose Fiction* (New York: Columbia University Press, 1947)

Perott, Joseph de, '*The Mirrour of Knighthood*', *The Romantic Review*, 4 (1913), 397–402

Petrarch, Francesco, *Remedies for Fortune Fair and Foul: A Modern Translation of* De Remediis Utriusque Fortunae, ed. by Conrad H. Rawki (Bloomington: Indianapolis University Press, 1991)

Phillips, Joshua, 'Chronicles of Wasted Time: Anthony Munday, Tudor Romance, and Literary Labor,' English Literary History, 73 (2006), 781–803

Plomer, Thomas, 'Thomas East, Printer', *The Library*, series 2, 2.7 (1901), 298–310

Prescott, Anne Lake, *Imagining Rabelais in Renaissance England* (New Haven: Yale University Press, 1998)

Radway, Janice A., *Reading the Romance: Women, Patriarchy, and Popular Literature* (Chapel Hill: University of North Carolina Press, 1984)

Robinson, Benedict S., *Islam and Early Modern English Literature: The Politics of Romance from Spenser to Milton* (New York: Palgrave Macmillan 2007)

Robinson, Douglas, 'Theorising Translation in a Woman's Voice', *The Translator*, 1 (1995), 153–75

Scherb, Victor I., 'Assimilating Giants: The Appropriation of Gog and Magog in Medieval and Early Modern England', *Journal of Medieval and Early Modern Studies*, 32 (2002), 59–84

Schleiner, Louise, 'Margaret Tyler, Translator and Waiting Woman', *English Language Notes*, 29 (1992), 1–9

Sieber, Harry, 'The Romance of Chivalry in Spain: From Rodriguez de Montalvo to Cervantes', in *Romance: Generic Transformation from Chrétien de Troyes to Cervantes*, ed. by Kevin Brownlee and Marina Scordilis Brownlee (Hanover: University Press of New England, 1985), pp. 203–19

Simonini, R. C., *Italian Scholarship in Renaissance England* (Chapel Hill: University of North Carolina Press, 1952)

Smith, Jeremy L., *Thomas East and Music Publishing in Renaissance England* (Oxford: Oxford University Press, 2003)

Thomas, Henry, *Spanish and Portuguese Romances of Chivalry: The Revival of the Romance of Chivalry in the Spanish Peninsula, and its Extension and Influence Abroad* (Cambridge: Cambridge University Press, 1920)

Tilley, M. P., *A Dictionary of Proverbs in England in the Sixteenth Seventeenth Centuries* (Ann Arbor: University of Michigan Press, 1950)

Travitsky, Betty, *The Paradise of Women: Writings by Englishwomen of the Renaissance* (Westport, Conn.: Greenwood Press, 1981)

Trill, Suzanne, 'Sixteenth-Century Women's Writing: Mary Sidney's *Psalmes* and the "femininity" of Translation', in *Writing and the English Renaissance*, ed. by William Zunder and Suzanne Trill (London; New York: Longman, 1996), pp. 140–58

Uman, Deborah and Belén Bistué, 'Translation as Collaborative Authorship: Margaret Tyler's *The Mirrour of Princely Deedes and Knighthood*', *Comparative Literature Studies*, 44 (2007), 298–323

Underhill, John Garrett, *Spanish Literature in the England of the Tudors* (London: Macmillan, 1899)

Vaughan, Virginia Mason and Alden T. Vaughan, eds, *The Tempest*, William Shakespeare, The Arden Shakespeare (London: Thomson, 1999)

Vives, Juan Luis, *The Education of a Christian Woman: A Sixteenth-Century Manual*, ed. and trans. by Charles Fantazzi (Chicago: University of Chicago Press, 2000)

Wall, Wendy, *The Imprint of Gender: Authorship and Publication in the English Renaissance* (Ithaca, NY: Cornell University Press, 1993)

Wayne, Valerie, 'Some Sad Sentence: Vives' *Instruction of a Christian Woman*', in *Silent but for the Word: Tudor Women as Patrons, Translators, and Writers of Religious Works*, ed. by Margaret P. Hannay (Kent, Ohio: Kent State University Press, 1985), pp. 15–29

Werth, Tiffany Jo, *The Fabulous Dark Cloister: Romance in England after the Reformation* (Baltimore: Johns Hopkins University Press, 2011)

INDEX OF CHARACTERS

Note: Italicized page numbers refer to critical material in the introduction and notes.

Achilles *33*, 52
Africano:
   attack on Babylon 106–07, 108–13
   battle against Donzel del Febo 113–18
   conquests in Asia 84, 106
   Florion's description of *10*, 108
   wearing of Vulcan's armour *33*, 115
Albalaxes 140, 147
Albamira 227–29
Alberto 213–17, 218
Alceo 56
Alcino 56
Alfonte 56
Alicante *33*, 52
aljamiado literature *14*
Allamades 140, 142, 145
Alpineo 56
Argante 57
Argiles, Don 140, 142, 145
Argion 127–31
Arguidoro 214
Arguirosa *21*, 214–16, 217, 218–19
Aridon 223, 229–33
Arimont 57
Arinda 156–59, 161, 162, 167–68, 170, 185–86
Armaran 79
Armineo:
   discovered with Clavergudo 87–89
   education of Clavergudo 91
   in battle against Africano's men 116–17
   in battle against Lambardo 210–11, 212
   in retaking of Persia 118
   received by Sultan of Babylon 90
   remembers Lirgandeo's prophecy on Donzel del Febo 123
Artdoro 57
Artimodoro:
   arrival at Oliverio's contest 142–43
   as chronicler *33, 52*, 137–38
   gift of armour to Rosicleer 138–39
   magical works *10*
   theme of friendship and *22*
Augusta 55, 62–63, 74, 232
Austrich, Duke of 231

Babylon, Sultan of:
   Africano's attack on 106–07

   Brandafileo's attack on 91–96
   knighting of Donzel del Febo 102
   lineage 83
   Radamira's appeal to 97–99
   reaction to Donzel del Febo's battle against Raiartes 104–05
   resistance against Africano's men 116–17
Balides *22*, 126–29, 130–31
Balisea:
   informed of princes' quest for Donzel del Febo 210
   marriage to Florion 84
   reactions to Donzel del Febo's fight against Raiartes 101, 102, 105
   reception of Donzel del Febo after Africano's defeat 117
   return to Persia 123
   upbringing of Brandizel, Clavergudo and Donzel del Febo 90–91
Bargandel:
   at Oliverio's competition 139, 141, 145–46
   compared to son of Priamus *33*, 207
   defeated by Zoilo 163
   encounter with Claridiana 206–09
   envy of Rosicleer *22*, 152
   love for Silverina 141, 167
   meeting with Rosicleer 133
   recognition of Rosicleer 154
   search for Rosicleer 184–85, 206
   theme of friendship and *22*
   to Rosicleer's aid 160
Belgrade, Archbishop of 61
Bohemia, King of 57, 72, 76
Boristhines 56
Brandafileo *10*, 91–97
Brandagedeon 141–42, 144, 156–57, 159–61, 168
Brandaristes 141, 145
Brandidarte 141, 145
Brandidonio 131, 132
Brandimardo 117
Brandizel:
   as companion to Clavergudo and Donzel del Febo 90–91
   brief reunion with Donzel del Febo 121–22
   defeat of giant *10*
   love for Clarinea 211–12
   search for Donzel del Febo 209–10

INDEX OF CHARACTERS

theme of friendship and *22*
Briana:
  age 225
  as mother *6*
  Catholic references to *9*, *12*, 72, 236
  chasteness *12*
  compared to Helen *33*
  delivery of sons 74–76
  female legitimacy and *30*
  grief at loss of Donzel del Febo 81–82
  literacy *62 n.52*
  marvellous qualities *11*, 62
  message to Oliverio 156
  promised to Prince Edward 54, 55
  quasi-rape by Trebatio *28*, 63–64
  revelation to Rosicleer of their relationship 123–25
  Rosicleer's letter to 186, 226
  theme of friendship and *22*
Brinco, Don 140
Briontes 94
Brunio, Don 145
Busia, Lord of 147

Calinda *22*, 136, 137
Candramarte 148–53, 188–92
Candriana 188, 213
Clandestria:
  aids Trebatio and Briana's secret departure 236
  Briana confides in 73, 77
  bringing of Briana's sons to monastery 77–78
  delivery of Briana's sons 74–76
  prepares Briana to see Trebatio again 224–26
  sister of 78, 80–81, 170
  Trebatio reveals identity to *20*, 220–22
Claridiana:
  association with Diana *16–17*, *33*, 207
  compared to an Amazon *28*, 49
  encounter with Bargandel, Liriamandro and Zoilo 206–09
  in Martínez continuations *3*
  in other English texts *4*
  marvellous qualities *10*
  theme of friendship and *22*
  union with Donzel del Febo *28 n. 85*
Clarinea *22*, 210–13, 237
Clavergudo:
  campaign to retake Persia 118–20
  Christianity 96
  envy of Donzel del Febo *22*, 96, 101, 116
  Florion's discovery of 87–88
  made knight 106
  resistance against Africano's men 116–17
  reunion with Brandizel 120–23
  search for Donzel del Febo 209–10, 212
Constantine *33*, 52
Crimson Island, Lord of, *see* Lirgandeo

Dardante 56
Dardario 107, 110

Edward:
  Briana promised to 54, 55
  death 59–60
  departure to see Briana 57–58
  depiction of *19*, *22–23*, *59 n.46*
  search for 71–72
Elisandra *30*, 223, 230, 232
Elisea 223–24, 229

Febo, Donzel del:
  advice to Trebatio 222–23
  answer to Africano's letter 107–13
  arrival at monastery 78–79
  battle against Africano 113–18
  battle against Aridon 229–33
  battle on behalf of Radamira 99–106
  birth and naming 75
  conception 64
  discovery by Florion 85
  fight with serpent *19*
  in other English texts *4*
  jousts with Florinaldes 227–29
  Lirgandeo's gift of a sword to *10*
  loss at sea as adult 120–23
  loss at sea in childhood 79–83
  made knight 102
  marvellous qualities *10*, *11*, 91, 100
  meets Rosicleer 192–93
  misogyny in *Espejo* *31*
  on Lindaraza's island 193–206
  rescue of Trebatio *11*, 199–206
  slaying of Brandafileo 91–97
  theme of friendship and *22*
  title of romance and 53
  union with Claridiana *28 n.85*
Fidelia:
  advice to Olivia 171–75, 187
  bears Olivia's letters to Rosicleer 176–79, 183–84, 188
  Olivia confides in 166–67
  reads Rosicleer's letter to Olivia 168–69
  steals Rosicleer's letter to Briana 186
  theme of friendship and *22*
Flamides 203–05
Florinaldes *22*, 227–29, 233
Florion:
  as Saracen *14*, *15*
  battle with Mambriniano 86–87

campaign to retake Persia 118–20
description of Africano *10*, 108
discovery of Donzel del Febo 85
informed of princes' quest for Donzel del Febo 210
lineage 83
marriage to Balisea 84
overthrow by Africano 84–85, 106
resistance against Africano's men 116–17
theme of friendship and 22

Helio III *34*, 53
Herbion 107, 109–10

Ipesca 214, 219

Julia 147–48

Knight of the Sun, *see* Febo, Donzel del

Lambardo 210–13
Leonardo 123–24, 170
Liberio 56
Lindabrides *4 n.20*
Lindaraza (daughter) 71, 204–05
Lindaraza (mother) *11–12*, 28, 69–71, *69 n.81*, 201
Lirgandeo:
  advises retaking of Persia 118
  as chronicler *33*, *36*, 138
  education of Donzel del Febo and Brandizel 91, 96
  false religion of 96–97
  gifts to Clavergudo 101
  gifts to Donzel del Febo *10*, 101, 108, 113–14, 200
  informs Florion of princes' departure 210
  prophecies *14*, *20*, 85, 119
  third son of Orixerges 83
Liriamandro:
  at Oliverio's contest 135–36, 139, 141, 145–46
  birth 74
  compared to son of Priamus *33*, 207
  defeated by Zoilo 163
  encounter with Claridiana 206–09
  envy of Rosicleer *22*, 152
  love for Rodasilva 141, 167
  meeting with Rosicleer 133
  recognition of Rosicleer 154
  search for Rosicleer 184–85, 206
  to Rosicleer's aid 160
Liverba 128, 131, 132

Mambriniano 86–88
Melides 57
Molossus *33*, 52

Nicoleonte 57

Oliverio:
  Don Silverio's suit and 234–35
  esteem for Rosicleer 154
  father of Prince Edward 54
  jousting competition 133
  love for daughter Olivia 139
  Olivia's marriage and 24
  Rosicleer's intention to see 126
Olivia:
  arrangement of marriage 24
  beauty *16*, 76–77, 139
  believes Rosicleer is low-born 170–71
  confides in Fidelia 166–67
  haughtiness 139–40
  learning *15*, 156
  letter to Rosicleer 175–76, 177–78
  love for Rosicleer 153, 155, 156, 166, 169, 185
  regret at spurning Rosicleer 182
  response to Rosicleer's prowess 145, 146, 147, 151
  Rosicleer's first sight of 144
  Silverio's attempt to win 233–35
  theme of friendship and 22
  use of modesty *topos* 28
Orfeo 227, 228
Orgiles, Don 140–41, 142, 145
Oristeo 88
Orixerges 83, 94

Palisteo 204–05
Pannonia, Duke of 229–30
Pansanias 52
Persia, King of 83
Polonia, King of *22*, 210
Pyrrhus *33*, 52

Radamira:
  fear on Donzel del Febo's behalf 101, 102, 105
  in Raiartes' power 97–99
  perception of Donzel del Febo's marvellous qualities *11*, 100, 105
  return to Cyprus 106
Raiartes 97–106
Rodasilva 140, 141, 158, 167, 206, 233–34, 235
Rodomarte 56
Rodopheo 56
Rolando *21*, 214, 215–16, 217–20
Rosicleer:
  armour *10*
  arrival at monastery 78–79
  at Oliverio's contest 143–47
  battle against Candramarte 149–52

INDEX OF CHARACTERS

    battle against Zoilo 164–65
    birth and naming 75
    conception 64
    direct/indirect speech *21*
    education by Leonardo 123–24
    escape in search of adventure 125–28
    first sight of Olivia 144
    in other English texts *4*
    learns of true relation to Briana 124–25
    letter to Briana 186, 226
    loss at sea 135
    love for Olivia 156
    meets Donzel del Febo 191–93
    on Artimodoro's island *10*, 136–39
    portrait on Lindaraza's island 199
    reaction to Olivia's letter 178–79
    renaming as Knight of Cupid 213
    rescue of child from bear 126–27
    secret letter to Olivia 161, 167–69
    slaying of Argion 128–31
    theme of friendship and *22*
    title of romance and 53

Saxony, Duke of 231
Silverina 140, 141, 163, 167, 206
Silverio, Don 139–40, 141, 145, 154, 185, 233–35

Telio *20–21*, *22*, 132, 135, 157, 179–80, 181
Theodoro 52, 53, 83
Tiberio 53–54, 57–58, 71–72, 76, 222, 233

Trebatio:
    betrothal to Briana as Prince Edward 61–62
    departure on quest for Briana 56–57
    dream vision 65–66
    election as emperor 52
    lineage *33*, *49 n.7*, 52
    love for Briana 55–56, 60
    marvellous qualities *11*, 52, 91
    on Lindaraza's island *11–12*, 67–71, 72, 225
    quasi-rape of Briana *28*, 63–64
    rescued by Donzel del Febo 199–206
    reunion with Briana 226
    reveals identity to Clandestria *20*, 222
    reveals true identity to Briana 226
    siege of Belgrade 54–55
    slaying of Prince Edward 59–60
    theme of friendship and *22*
    treatment of English knights *23*

Zoilo:
    as Saracen *14*, 209
    at Oliverio's court 181–82
    compared to son of Priamus *33*, 207
    conversion *15*
    encounter with Claridiana 206–09
    first encounter with Rosicleer and company 162–66
    on Claridiana's beauty *10*
    search for Rosicleer 184–85, 206
    theme of friendship and *22*

INDEX TO INTRODUCTION AND NOTES

The Adventures of Master F. J. 31
Aeneid 194 n.553
Albertus Wallenstein 4
The Alchemist 4
Allde, Edward 3
Amadís de Gaula 3–4, 7, 54 n.32, 94 n.195, 97 n.209
Amazons 17, 47 n.2, 207 n.589
An Answer to the First Part of a Certaine Conference 9
Antonio and Mellida 4
Arcadia 11
Arcara, Stefania 29 n.86
Aristotle 11
Arnalte y Lucenda 5, 31
ars dictaminis 17–18
Arthurian legend 64 n.59, 152 n.416
Arthur of Little Britain 1
Atkinson, David 24

Bacon, Anne Gresham 7
Bacon, Nathaniel 7
Barrey, Lodowick 5
Bedford, Francis 39
Belianís de Grecia 3, 4
Bennett, H. S. 9
Berners, John Bourchier, Lord (c.1467–1533) 4 n.14, 5
Bevis of Hampton 1, 9, 13–14
Bible:
 Genesis 11
 Jephthah 16
 the number forty 76 n.120
 parables 29
 Sodomites 16
 trumpets 116 n.294
The Bird in a Cage 4
Bistué, Belén 6, 18, 30
Bly Calkin, Siobhan 13, 14
Brown, Sir Anthony 8
Budapest 55 n.36
Burby, Cuthbert 3
Burghley, William Cecil, Baron (1520–1598) 8
Burton, Robert 5
Byrd, William 9

Calderón de la Barca, Pedro 3
Cárcel de amor 4 n.14, 5, 31
Castell of Love 4 n.14

Cecil, William, *see* Burghley, William Cecil, Baron (1520–1598)
Cervantes Saavedra, Miguel de 3
Charlemont, James Caulfeild, Earl of (1728–1799) 41, 42
chronicle 29, 32–35
Clerc, John 5
Coldiron, Anne 1
Constantine I, Emperor of Rome 33
Corro, Antonio del 8
The Countess of Montgomery's Urania 26
Creede, Thomas 3
Cuarta Parte de Don Florisel de Niquea 97 n.209
Curbet, Joan 17 n.63

Dekker, Thomas 4
Dering, Edward 10
A Discouerie of the Conspiracie of Scottish Papists 9
Don Bellianis of Greece 4
Don Quijote (Cervantes) 3
Don Quixote (Shelton) 7
Dowland, John 9
dreams 65 n.61

East, Edmund 9
East, Thomas 3, 6, 8, 9
Eastward Hoe 5
Eisenberg, Daniel 2
Elizabeth I, Queen of England 8, 17, 24
Emaré 74 n.116
England:
 assimilation of French and English in 15
 Catholics in 7, 9
 knowledge of foreign languages in 8
 national self-construction 7, 11
Espejo de caballerías 32
Espejo de príncipes y cavalleros:
 eroticism 28 n.85
 errors in 16, 24–25
 as Greek-authored chronicle 34, 36
 the marvellous in 10–12
 title 32
 title page 28, 32, 47 n.2
 translations 3
 transmission and influence 2–3
Essex, Robert Devereux, Earl of (1565–1601) 7
Euphues and his England 4, 9
Euphues: The Anatomy of Wit 9

INDEX TO INTRODUCTION AND NOTES

The Faerie Queene 11, 207 n.589
Ferguson, Moira 6
Fernández, Jerónimo 4
Fierabras 11
Fletcher, John 5, 8
Florando de Inglaterra 3, 4
Flores, Juan de 5
Florio, John 8, 25
Floris and Blancheflour 82 n.146
Florisel de Niquea 3
The Four Sons of Aymon 9
friendship 22
Fuchs, Barbara 13

Galen 63 n.55
Gallagher, Catherine 30
The Gamester 4
gender, *see* women
Gerileon of England 7
giants 11
Greene, Robert 32
Gregory, Tobias 13
Grisel y Mirabella 5, 31
The Guardian 5
Guy of Warwick 1, 13, 14

Hackett, Helen 64 n.59
Hamilton, Donna 7, 8, 13, 15
Hannay, Margaret 27
Harrison, William 8
Harvey, Gabriel 8
Havelok the Dane 74 n.116, 89 n.174
Hayward, John 9
Heng, Geraldine 15
Herberay, Nicolas de 4
Hippocrates 63 n.55
Holinshed, Raphael 8
Hollyband, Claudius 5
Honoria and Mammon 4
The Honour of Chivalrie 4
Howard, Margaret Audley, *see* Norfolk, Margaret Howard (née Audley), Duchess of (1540–1564)
Howard, Theophilus, *see* Suffolk, Theophilus Howard, Earl of (1584–1640)
Howard, Thomas (1536–1572), *see* Norfolk, Thomas Howard, Duke of (1536–1572)
Howard, Thomas (1561–1626), *see* Suffolk, Thomas Howard, Earl of (1561–1626)
Hudibras 4
humoural theory 63 n.55
Hundred Years' War 15
Huntington Library 39, 40
Huth, Henry 39, 40, 41, 42
Hutson, Lorna 16, 26, 31

Islam 12–14
Italianate novella 1, 2 n.4

J. H.'s Work for Chimny-sweepers: Or A warning for Tabacconists 9
Jonson, Ben 4

Ker, George 9
King James His Entertainment at Theobalds 9
The Knight of the Burning Pestle 4
Krontiris, Tina 6, 7, 15–16, 30–31

Lamb, Mary Ellen 1
Lawrence, Leonard 5
The Little French Lawyer 4
Luján, Pedro de 97 n.209
Lyly, John 4, 9

The Malcontent 4
Manuscripts and early prints:
    Biblioteca Nacional de España MSS/13137: 3
    British Library C.56.d.15: 38
    British Library C. 70.b.27: 39
    British Library C.71.b.34: 41
    Bodleian Douce O 113 (1): 41
    Cambridge University Library Syn. 7.57.22: 41
    Folger Shakespeare Library STC 18860: 39
    Harvard Houghton Library ST 18861: 41
    Henry E. Huntington Library 60627: 39–40
    Henry E. Huntington Library 62809: 38–39
    Henry E. Huntington Library 62814: 41
Marshall, Ralph 7
Martin, Randall 6, 7
Martínez, Marcos 3
Mary, Queen of Scots 6
Massinger, Philip 5
McGrath, Lynette 26
Melusine 82 n.146
Meres, Francis 5
Mirror of Princely Deeds and Knighthood:
    anglicizing elements 19, 22–24, 25, 73 n.104, 133 n.351
    classical allusions in 16–17
    contemporary allusions to 4–5
    place names in 24–25
    publication history 8–9
    romance sub-genre 1, 32–36
    theme of friendship in 22
    title 32
    title page 28, 47 n.2
Montalvo, Rodríguez de 3
Montgomery, Earl of, *see* Pembroke, Philip Herbert, Earl of (1584–1650)
Moors 12–13

Moraes, Francisco de 4
Morte d'Arthur 9, 35
Munday, Anthony:
   authorities' suspicion of texts by 8
   Catholicism 13
   dedications 7
   translation of *Amadís* cycle 4
   treatment of the marvellous 10
   use of *speculum* nomenclature 32

Narcissus 80 n.136
Newcomb, Lori Humphrey 26
Norfolk, Margaret Howard (née Audley), Duchess of (1540–1564) 6
Norfolk, Thomas Howard, Duke of (1536–1572) 6, 7, 48 n.4
Norman Conquest 15

Odyssey 53 n.26
Oliver of Castile 9
Orientalism 12
Orlando Furioso 82 n.146
Ortúñez de Calahorra, Diego 2, 16, 25, 32, 34
Overbury, Thomas 5
Oxford, Edward de Vere, Earl of (1550–1604) 7
Oxford, Henry de Vere, Earl of (1593–1625) 7

A Paire of Turtle Doves, or the Tragicall History of Bellora and Fidelio 5
Palladine of England 4, 7
Palmendos 4
Palmerin d'Oliva 4, 7, 32
Palmerin of England 4
Parke, Robert 3
Parry, Robert 3
patronage 30
Pembroke, Philip Herbert, Earl of (1584–1650) 7
Penelope's Web 32
Perott, Joseph de 3 n.11
Petrarch 42 n.101, 153 n.422
Philaster 4
El poema de mío Cid 14
Pratt, Mary Louise 1
Primaleon 4
Primaleon of Greece 4, 7
Protestant poetics 6, 9–10, 12, 15

Quaritch, Bernard 39, 40

Ralph the Collier 11
Ram Alley 5
Reed, Isaac 42
Reloj de príncipes 94 n.195

Riviere and Sons 40
Rogel de Grecia 3, 97 n.209
romance:
   chivalric 1, 2, 3–4, 5, 13
   chronicle and 32–35, 49 n.7
   exemplary value 49 n.9
   gender and 5, 12, 25–26, 27, 30
   history and 31, 32
   humanist 1, 2 n.4
   the marvellous in 6, 7, 9–12
   metafictional tendencies 31
   Middle English 15, 31
   popularity 1, 3
   Protestant responses to 9–10
   religious alterity in 12–15
   romancero morisco 13
   sentimental 1, 2 n.4, 31
   Spanish 2–4, 5, 13
Roncesvalles 96 n.201

Said, Edward 12
San Pedro, Diego de 5
Saracens 12–15
Satiromastix 4
Savile, John 9
Schleiner, Louise 6, 7, 8
The Scornful Lady 4
Second Book of Songs (Dowland) 9
Shakespeare, William 9
Shelton, Thomas 7
Shirley, John 4
Sidney, Philip 6, 9
Sieber, Harry 3 n.10, 28
Sierra Infanzón, Pedro de la 2–3
Silva, Feliciano de 97 n.209
Silves de la Selva 97 n.209
Sir Lamwell 1
Smith, Jeremy L. 8
Snodham, Thomas 9
Spain:
   Maurophilia in 12–13, 14
   romance genre in 2–4, 5, 13
   Siglo de Oro 13
   tense relations with England 7
speculum texts 32, 47 n.1
Spenser, Edmund 6, 9
Stafford, Simon 3
Stationers' Register 8, 9
Steward, Charles 4
Suffolk, Theophilus Howard, Earl of (1584–1640) 7
Suffolk, Thomas Howard, Earl of (1561–1626) 6, 8, 48 n.4
Surrey, Henry Howard, Earl of (1516/17–1547) 153 n.422

INDEX TO INTRODUCTION AND NOTES

Swetnam, The Woman-Hater 5
Sydserf, Thomas 5

translation:
  compared to prostitution 30
  as contact zone 1
  gender and 1–2, 25–26, 27
  genre and 2 n.3
  as remedy for idleness 50 n.16
  Tyler's method 18–25
  use of direct speech 20–21
The Treasurie of Amadis of Fraunce 4
Tyler, John 6, 8
Tyler, Margaret:
  biographical details 6
  education 15–18
  employment by Thomas Howard 6–7, 48 n.6
  knowledge of Spanish 6, 7, 16
  proto-feminism 29–31
  references to own age 6
  religion 6–15
  theory of authorship 29–30
  translation methodology 1–2, 12, 18–25
  treatment of Saracens 12, 13
  treatment of the marvellous 7, 9, 10–12, 15, 53 n.27

  use of modesty *topos* 25, 27–28, 49 n.8
  will 8
Tyrrell, Margaret 6 n.27

Uman, Deborah 6, 18, 30

Vaughan, William 5
Vives, Juan Luis 25, 28, 32

Werth, Tiffany 9, 11
Wit in a Constable 4
women:
  authorship and 2, 27, 29, 36, 49 n.10
  depictions of sexuality of 12, 17, 28–29
  leadership and 24
  romance genre and 5, 12, 25–26, 27, 30
  spiritual writings and 27, 50 nn.14 & 18
  translation and 1–2, 25, 27
Women Pleased 5
Woodhouse, Anne Bacon 7
Wroth, Mary, Lady 6, 9, 26
Wyatt, Thomas 153 n.421

Ywain and Gawain 82 n.146

Zelauto 7, 13, 14